PSYCHOLOGICAL CAPITAL AND BEYOND

Fred Luthans
Carolyn M. Youssef-Morgan
and
Bruce J. Avolio

OXFORD
UNIVERSITY PRESS

OXFORD
UNIVERSITY PRESS

Oxford University Press is a department of the University of
Oxford. It furthers the University's objective of excellence in research,
scholarship, and education by publishing worldwide.

Oxford   New York
Auckland   Cape Town   Dar es Salaam   Hong Kong   Karachi
Kuala Lumpur   Madrid   Melbourne   Mexico City   Nairobi
New Delhi   Shanghai   Taipei   Toronto

With offices in
Argentina   Austria   Brazil   Chile   Czech Republic   France   Greece
Guatemala   Hungary   Italy   Japan   Poland   Portugal   Singapore
South Korea   Switzerland   Thailand   Turkey   Ukraine   Vietnam

Oxford is a registered trademark of Oxford University Press
in the UK and certain other countries.

Published in the United States of America by
Oxford University Press
198 Madison Avenue, New York, NY 10016

Library of Congress Cataloging-in-Publication Data
Luthans, Fred.
Psychological capital and beyond / Fred Luthans, Carolyn M. Youssef-Morgan, and Bruce J. Avolio.
pages cm
Includes bibliographical references and index.
ISBN 978-0-19-931647-2 (alk. paper)—ISBN 978-0-19-931648-9—
ISBN 978-0-19-931649-6
1. Organizational behavior.   2. Human capital—Psychological aspects.   3. Employee
motivation.   4. Psychology, Industrial.   I. Youssef, Carolyn M.   II. Avolio, Bruce J.   III. Title.
HD58.7.L894 2015
302.3'5—dc23
2014035861

9 8 7 6 5
Printed in the United States of America
on acid-free paper

CONTENTS

PSYCHOLOGICAL CAPITAL AND BEYOND

PREFACE

The major purpose of our first book, *Psychological Capital*, was to bring the perspective, theories, research, and application of the then-emerging positive psychology field to the workplace. For the first time, we comprehensively defined psychological capital, or simply PsyCap, and provided a theoretical and research foundation, a valid self-report measure, and application suggestions for gaining competitive advantage for individuals, teams, and organizations. The response to our formulation of PsyCap has been overwhelming in terms of the number of academic publications across the broad spectrum of management and psychological journals, and exploding interest in the practice community to apply PsyCap in developing leaders and employees and improving their performance. Literally, there are thousands of research and application projects throughout the globe on PsyCap and its implications for individual, group, and organizational effectiveness.

Our original book came out in 2007 around the same time the global markets were beginning to experience one of the most significant economic downturns and escalations in geopolitical turmoil of the last 100 years. This resulted in rapidly increasing rates of unemployment; job insecurity; too-big-to-fail organizations failing; meltdowns in century-old banks, insurance companies, and automobile manufacturers; and bursting bubbles in the housing and financial markets. The human toll was evidenced by major concerns for decreased well-being, feelings of alienation and helplessness among the chronically unemployed, and a decreasing middle class to varying degrees in all parts of the world.

The aftermath of this "Great Recession" and the accompanying flood of negative news have resulted in many organizational leaders and employees losing hope and confidence and becoming pessimistic in their abilities to remain competitive in their own positions, as well as questioning the sustainable competitiveness for their organizations in the turbulent global environment. And when there seems to be signs that economic fortunes are beginning to turn around, unemployment problems remain, one more indictment is made against a political or industrial leader, and yet another government teeters on defaulting on its loans.

We realize that starting this book on the importance of a positive approach with such a bleak, negative outlook seems heretical. However, we feel that by painting this portrait of negativity, we can best get your agreement that the time seems right to go back to the underlying premise of positive psychology and positive organizational behavior. We felt compelled at this time to update and go beyond the original book and reinforce the agenda of research and practice for exploring a more proactive, evidence-based approach to understanding what drives and sustains needed individual, group, and organizational levels of positivity in general and psychological capital in particular.

Although the world certainly has many negative hurdles to overcome, we also realize that we are entering one of the most interesting and dynamic periods of human history in terms of advances in technology and medicine, and in the uplifting of entire societies, such as throughout Africa, a continent frequently neglected in the move toward global development. Just consider the potential positive force of a billion people connected through one company called Facebook, which recently acquired another social media company called Whatsapp, which has nearly 500 million users and is currently adding about a million a day. Breakthroughs appear to be happening at a rapid pace across a broad spectrum of fields from human genomics and stem cell research to electric cars and 3D printers. How will leaders, governments, organizations, communities, and individuals use the amazing tools that are being created and apply them to some of the most intractable problems of the last several hundred years, such as malnutrition, homelessness, and diseases that have long disappeared from first-world countries.

The current global environment certainly conveys plenty of reasons to be stressed out and negative, or hopeful and optimistic. However, now after over a decade of PsyCap research and practice, we feel confident about the best way to proceed, at least when it comes to contributing to advancing human potential and a positive mindset. Instead of dwelling on what we cannot control, what we cannot stay caught up with, or what is wrong with today's employees, managers, and organizations and how to "fix" them, we need to go back to the premise of positive psychology and positive organizational behavior. We need to take a positive perspective and approach. We need to make further inquiry (not advocacy) into understanding the drivers behind, and continue to understand how to optimize, one's hope, efficacy, resilience, and optimism, or what for many years we have called the "HERO within."

Unlike much of the popular positivity literature, our PsyCap takes a "rigor and relevance" approach to understanding how positive psychological resources and their use, beyond more traditional forms of capital (e.g., economic, human, and social), can be leveraged to attain and sustain competitive advantage (for the seminal articles see Luthans, 2002a, 2002b; Luthans & Avolio, 2003; Luthans, Luthans, & Luthans, 2004; Luthans & Youssef, 2004). By rigor, we mean evidence-based support for assessing and developing PsyCap, and by relevance, we mean promoting its applicability to enhancing the individual and collective human condition in all facets of life, especially at work.

The solid theory building and research in positive psychology by scholars such as Ed Diener on happiness and subjective well-being and Barb Fredrickson and her "broaden and build" model provided the necessary background and foundation for what we originally created and termed "positive organizational behavior" (POB), and then more specifically psychological capital (PsyCap). Our scientific criteria for the psychological resources that we specifically used for inclusion in PsyCap were (1) being based on theory and research; (2) having valid measurement; (3) being state-like (as opposed to dispositional, trait-like) and thus open to change and development; and (4) having a positive impact on desired attitudes, behaviors and, especially, performance. The well-known psychological resources from positive psychology of hope, efficacy, resilience, and optimism (or the HERO acronym, see Luthans, 2012) best meet these criteria, even though we suggest others may remain to be added to the collection of PsyCap constructs, such as gratitude, mindfulness, or courage (see Chapters 7 and 8).

In the first book and in this one, we dedicate a separate chapter to summarizing and integrating the literature and research to date on each of the four criteria-meeting components of psychological capital. We also assess the fit of other positive constructs with our scientifically rigorous inclusion criteria. We end the book with Chapter 9 on the measurement, development, and return on investment from psychological capital and Chapter 10 on directions for PsyCap into the future. Most important, the original book offered a blueprint and scientific model for those who wanted to study, research, and apply evidence-based positivity in the workplace, as opposed to the avalanche of popular press books that lack scientific rigor and therefore sustainability and effective evidence-based practice. Our aim for this book is to have a sustainable impact. This means taking a theoretical and research-based approach to PsyCap but also keeping a continuing inquiry, as opposed to an advocacy, perspective. (Although there is obviously carryover, we treat and present this follow-up book as more than a typical new edition since, as you will see, it truly goes well "beyond" the original book of several years ago with new research, perspectives, insights, and suggestions for a broad range of applications.)

What Is New to This Book?

Since the publication of the original book in 2007, there has been an exponential increase in the theory, research, and practice of positive constructs in general and

PsyCap in particular. There is a substantial amount of evidence across industries and global cultures that PsyCap can be validly measured and is a higher order core construct. This means that PsyCap better predicts desired outcomes than each of its four individual components (see Luthans, Avolio, Avey, & Norman, 2007 for the basic research and the 51 studies using and verifying PsyCap as a core construct in the quantitative meta analysis by Avey, Reichard, Luthans, & Mhatre, 2011, and the 66 PsyCap articles identified in a recent comprehensive literature review by Newman, Ucbasaran, Zhu, & Hirst, 2014). In addition, PsyCap has been empirically demonstrated to add value over and above demographics and other established positive traits such as self-evaluations, personality, and person-organization and person-job fit in predicting desired behaviors and relates negatively with undesired behaviors (Avey, Luthans, & Youssef, 2010; also see Choi & Lee, 2014 who controlled for Big Five personality traits). Through experimental (Luthans, Luthans, & Avey, 2014; Luthans, Avey, Avolio, & Peterson, 2010; Luthans, Avey, & Patera, 2008) and longitudinal (Peterson, Luthans, Avolio, Walumbwa, & Zhang, 2011) studies, PsyCap has been empirically demonstrated to be open to development and cause performance improvement.

This evidence-based PsyCap has been supported, not only in the United States but across the globe. Representative of this global research are PsyCap studies conducted in China (Luthans, Avey, Clapp-Smith, & Li, 2008; Wang, Sui, Luthans, Wang, & Wu, 2014; Wang, Liu, Wang, & Wang, 2014), Korea (Choi & Lee, 2014), Australia (Avey, Nimnicht, & Pigeon, 2010), New Zealand (Roche, Haar, & Luthans, 2014), Romania (Karatepe & Karadas, 2014), South Africa (Cascio & Luthans, 2014; Reichard, Dollwet, & Louw-Potgieter, 2014), Vietnam (Nguyen & Nguyen, 2012), Pakistan (Abbas, Raja, Darr, & Bouckenooghe, 2014), Portugal (Rego, Marques, Leal, Sousa, & Pina e Cunha, 2010), and Egypt and the Middle East (Badran & Youssef, 2014; Youssef, 2011). In addition, PsyCap has been conceptually and empirically shown to play an important role in the development of a global mindset (Clapp-Smith, Luthans, & Avolio, 2007; Story, Barbuto, Luthans, & Bovaird, 2014) and in positive global leadership (Youssef & Luthans, 2012).

The Avey, Reichard et al. (2011) meta-analysis quantitatively aggregated prior PsyCap research and found that PsyCap was indeed strongly related to desired employee attitudes, behaviors, and performance. The Newman et al. (2014) review noted that PsyCap was also related to employee creativity (Huang & Luthans, 2014; Rego, Sousa, Marques, & Pina e Cunha, 2012; Sweetman, Luthans, Avey, & Luthans, 2011), problem solving and innovation (Luthans, Youssef, & Rawski, 2011), job search (Chen & Lim, 2012), and well-being (Avey, Luthans, Smith, & Palmer, 2010; Baron, Franklin, & Hmieleski, 2013;

Culbertson, Fullagar, & Mills, 2010; Luthans, Youssef, Sweetman & Harms, 2013; Roche et al., 2014). Even more recent studies have found that PsyCap also has a positive impact on work-family conflict (Karatepe & Karadas, 2014; Wang, Liu et al., 2014) and, at the collective level, on service quality, customer satisfaction and unit revenues (Mathe-Soulek, Scott-Halsell, Kim, & Krawczyk, 2014).

Those interested and passionate about researching and promoting positivity in general and psychological capital in particular have also expanded to include dozens of companies, universities, and research centers around the world. Translations of the original book into Chinese and Korean are best sellers. On the practice side, numerous managers and corporate consultants have found evidence-based PsyCap to be a high-quality substitute or complement to their current models for human resource development and performance management. Many are now incorporating PsyCap interventions as an integral component of their consulting and leadership practices. Conferences and workshops on PsyCap have been held not only in the United States but also China (several times), Korea, Indonesia, Malaysia, Australia, England, Spain, Norway, Finland, Germany, Italy, France, and South Africa. Many more are scheduled in the near future.

In addition, interest in PsyCap has gone beyond the corporate arena. For example, the US Army's Comprehensive Soldier Fitness, the US Air Force's Comprehensive Airman Fitness, and NASA programs are using PsyCap directly or indirectly. Child advocacy centers, mental health programs, school systems, animal rescue centers, and healthcare organizations (especially for staff) are implementing PsyCap-based initiatives. Additional work is ongoing with police service and public and volunteer workers across a broad spectrum of occupations, and one would be hard pressed not to see some discussion of PsyCap included in college and university undergraduate and graduate business and organizational psychology courses around the globe.

Given this exponential increase in interest, research, and practice of positivity in general and psychological capital in particular, the specific objectives of this book are as follows:

• Demonstrating the broad body of evidence that has now accumulated that supports PsyCap as one of the core, pivotal constructs in the area of positive organizational behavior and psychology.
• Making the case for positivity and psychological capital as being critical for the selection, development, and management of talent within a dramatically different, posteconomic recession environment where negative attitudes, downsizing, and slashing training budgets have become the norm.

- Expanding the scope of psychological capital to other national and organizational cultures, as described earlier.
- Providing a more targeted and updated review of the positivity and PsyCap literature in general and especially the "HERO within" components of hope, efficacy, resilience, and optimism. We will also update the other psychological resources we originally reviewed for inclusion, as well as others that have recently emerged or received added emphasis in the positivity literature.
- Offering a wider range of valid and reliable measures of psychological capital; a broader spectrum of newer developmental interventions with demonstrated efficacy over the last few years; and more comprehensive models for assessing the financial benefits of and return on investment in positivity, psychological capital, and their development in the workplace.
- Incorporating new and interesting real case studies and realistic examples of positive workplace applications to address the needs of the growing body of scholar-practitioners, practitioner-scholars, and students at all levels now interested in PsyCap.
- Providing researchers with a broad range of ideas for future research that examines the antecedents and outcomes of PsyCap, the mechanisms through which PsyCap impacts performance and other outcomes, and how to escalate the PsyCap construct to team, unit, organizational, community, and country levels of analysis and application.
- Linking PsyCap to other organizational "intangible" resources such as teamwork, climate, culture, and leadership.
- Offering lessons learned and ways to leverage PsyCap to enhance the well-being of individuals, teams, units, organizations, communities, and countries.

In other words, the breadth and depth of this book reflect the expansion in ongoing work on positivity and PsyCap research and practice. Its orientation reflects the new realities of the current environment and represents our inquiry versus advocacy approach as we continue to make progress on our never-ending PsyCap journey, which is reflected in the "and Beyond" portion of our title.

References

Abbas, M., Raja, U., Darr, W., & Bouckenooghe, D. (2014). Combined effects of perceived politics and psychological capital on job satisfaction, turnover intentions, and performance. *Journal of Management, 40*, 1813–1830.

Avey, J. B., Luthans, F., Smith, R. M., & Palmer, N. F. (2010). Impact of positive psychological capital on employee well-being over time. *Journal of Occupational Health Psychology, 15*, 17–28.

Avey, J. B., Luthans, F., & Youssef, C. M. (2010). The additive value of positive psychological capital in predicting work attitudes and behaviors. *Journal of Management*, *36*, 430–452.

Avey, J. B., Nimnicht, J. L., & Pigeon, N. G. (2010). Two field studies examing the association between positive psychological capital and employee performance. *Leadership and Organizational Development Journal*, *31*, 384–401.

Avey, J. B., Reichard, R. J., Luthans, F., & Mhatre, K. H. (2011). Meta-analysis of the impact of positive psychological capital on employee attitudes, behaviors, and performance. *Human Resource Development Quarterly*, *22*, 127–152.

Badran, M. A., & Youssef-Morgan, C. M. (2014). Psychological capital and job satisfaction in Egypt. *Journal of Managerial Psychology*, in press.

Baron, R. A., Franklin, R. J., & Hmieleski, K. M. (2013). Why entrepreneurs often experience *low*, not high, levels of stress: The joint effects of selection and psychological capital. *Journal of Management*. doi:10.1177/0149206313495411.

Cascio, W., & Luthans, F. (2014). Reflections on the metamorphosis at Robben Island: The role of institutional work and positive psychological capital. *Journal of Management Inquiry*, *23*, 51–67.

Chen, D. J. Q., & Lim, V. K. G. (2012). Strength in adversity: The influence of psychological capital on job search. *Journal of Organizational Behavior*, *33*, 811–839.

Clapp-Smith, R., Luthans, F., & Avolio, B. J. (2007). The role of psychological capital in global mindset development. In M. Hitt, M. Javidan, & R. Steers (Eds.), *Advances in international management* (pp. 105–130). Oxford, UK: Elsevier.

Choi, Y., & Lee, D. (2014). Psychological capital, Big Five traits, and employee outcomes. *Journal of Managerial Psychology*, *29*, 122–140.

Culbertson, S. S., Fullagar, C. J., & Mills, M. F. (2010). Feeling good and doing great: The relationship between psychological capital and well-being. *Journal of Occupational Health Psychology*, *15*, 421–433.

Huang, L., & Luthans, F. (2014). Toward better understanding of the learning goal orientation-creativity relationship: The role of psychological capital. *Applied Psychology: An International Review*. doi:10.111/apps.12028.

Karatepe, O. M., & Karadas, G. (2014). The effect of psychological capital on conflicts in the work-family interface, turnover and absence intentions. *International Journal of Hospitality Management*, *43*, 132–143.

Luthans, B., Luthans, K., & Avey, J.B. (2014). Building the leaders of tomorrow: The development of academic psychological capital. *Journal of Leadership and Organizational Studies*, *21*, 191–199.

Luthans, F. (2002a). The need for and meaning of positive organizational behavior. *Journal of Organizational Behavior*, *23*, 695–706.

Luthans, F. (2002b). Positive organizational behavior: Developing and managing psychological strengths. *Academy of Management Executive*, *16*(1), 57–72.

Luthans, F. (2012). Psychological capital: Implications for HRD, retrospective analysis, and future directions. *Human Resource Development Quarterly*, *23*, 1–8.

Luthans, F., Avey, J. B., Avolio, B. J., & Peterson, S. (2010). The development and resulting performance impact of positive psychological capital. *Human Resource Development Quarterly, 21*, 41–66.

Luthans, F., Avey, J. B., Clapp-Smith, R., & Li, W. (2008). More evidence on the value of Chinese workers' psychological capital: A potentially unlimited competitive resource? *International Journal of Human Resource Management, 19*, 818–827.

Luthans, F., Avey, J. B., & Patera, J. L. (2008). Experimental analysis of a web-based training intervention to develop positive psychological capital. *Academy of Management Learning and Education, 7*, 209–221.

Luthans, F., & Avolio, B. J. (2003). Authentic leadership: A positive development approach. In K. S. Cameron, J. E. Dutton, & R. E. Quinn (Eds.), *Positive organizational scholarship* (pp. 241–258). San Francisco, CA: Berrett-Koehler.

Luthans, F., Avolio, B. J., Avey, J. B., & Norman, S. M. (2007). Positive psychological capital: Measurement and relationship with performance and satisfaction. *Personnel Psychology, 60*, 541–572.

Luthans, F., Luthans, K., & Luthans, B. (2004). Positive psychological capital: Beyond human and social capital. *Business Horizons, 47*, 45–50.

Luthans, F., & Youssef, C. M. (2004). Human, social, and now positive psychological capital management: Investing in people for competitive advantage. *Organizational Dynamics, 33*(2), 143–160.

Luthans, F., Youssef, C. M., & Rawski, S. L. (2011). A tale of two paradigms: The impact of psychological capital and reinforcing feedback on problem solving and innovation. *Journal of Organizational Behavior Management, 31*, 333–350.

Luthans, F., Youssef, C. M., Sweetman, D. S., & Harms, P. D. (2013). Meeting the leadership challenge of employee well-being through relationship PsyCap and health PsyCap. *Journal of Leadership and Organizational Studies, 20*, 118–133.

Mathe-Soulek, K., Scott-Halsell, S., Kim, S., & Krawczyk, M. (2014). Psychological capital in the quick service restaurant industry: A study of unit-level performance. *Journal of Hospitality & Tourism Research*. doi:10.1177/1096348014550923.

Newman, A., Ucbasaran, D., Zhu, F., & Hirst, G. (2014). Psychological capital: A review and synthesis. *Journal of Organizational Behavior, 35*, S120–S138.

Nguyen, T. D., & Nguyen, T. T. M. (2012). Psychological capital, quality of work life, and quality of life of marketers: Evidence from Vietnam. *Journal of Macromarketing, 32*, 87–95.

Peterson, S. J., Luthans, F., Avolio, B. J., Walumbwa, F. O., & Zhang, Z. (2011). Psychological capital and employee performance: A latent growth modeling approach. *Personnel Psychology, 64*, 427–450.

Rego, A., Marques, C., Leal, S., Sousa, F., & Pina e Cunha, M. (2010). Psychological capital and performance of Portuguese civil servants. *International Journal of Human Resource Management, 21*, 1531–1552.

Rego, A., Sousa, F., Marques, C., & Pina e Cunha, M. (2012). Authentic leadership promoting employees' psychological capital and creativity. *Journal of Business Research*, *65*, 429–437.

Reichard, R. J., Dollwet, M., & Louw-Potgieter, J. (2014). Development of cross-cultural psychological capital and its relationship with cultural intelligence and ethnocentrism. *Journal of Leadership and Organizational Studies*, *21*, 150–164.

Roche, M. A., Haar, J. M., & Luthans, F. (2014). The role of mindfulness and psychological capital on the well-being of organizational leaders. *Journal of Occupational Health Psychology*, *19*, 476–489.

Story, J. S., Barbuto, J. E., Luthans, F., & Bovaird, J. (2014). Meeting the challenges of effective international HRM: Analysis of the antecedents of global mindset. *Human Resource Management*, *53*, 131–155.

Sweetman, D., Luthans, F., Avey, J. B., & Luthans, B. (2011). Relationship between positive psychological capital and creative performance. *Canadian Journal of Administrative Sciences*, *28*, 4–13.

Wang, H., Sui, Y., Luthans, F., Wang, D., & Wu, Y. (2014). Impact of authentic leadership on performance: Role of followers' positive psychological capital and relational processes. *Journal of Organizational Behavior*, *35*, 5–21.

Wang, Y., Liu, L., Wang, J., & Wang, L. (2012). Work-family conflict and burnout among Chinese doctors: The role of psychological capital. *Journal of Occupational Health*, *54*, 232–240.

Youssef, C. M. (2011). Recent events in Egypt and the Middle East: Background, direct observations and a positive analysis. *Organizational Dynamics*, *40*, 222–234.

Youssef, C. M., & Luthans, F. (2012). Positive global leadership. *Journal of World Business*, *47*, 539–547.

1

INTRODUCTION TO THE MEANING OF AND NEED FOR PSYCHOLOGICAL CAPITAL

Each chapter of this book will start with one or more video links featuring thought leaders or examples on the chapter's topics. To maintain objectivity and to provide diverse perspectives, the authors have chosen videos that feature independent views that are not directly influenced by the authors of this book or any of their research colleagues. We hope you find this feature helpful in formulating thoughts, research, and applications.

Opening Video: Tal Ben-Shahar on "Edutaining" the World

Video link: http://www.youtube.com/watch?v=cSREpjLyvUA [Note: Remember because of the dynamic nature of the Internet, the link for this and all other videos throughout the book may change or cease to function. If this occurs, do a search by the title in order to find and view the video.]

Tal Ben-Shahar graduated from Harvard University in 2004 and then joined the faculty there, where he taught a popular course on happiness and positivity. Ben-Shahar consults with executives around the globe, linking leadership and happiness in his presentations and training workshops.

Questions for reflection and/or discussion:

1. As you watch this video, why is it important to shift the focus to happiness in one's life, as well as how we examine the roles we assume in organizations?
2. Are Ben-Shahar's views similar to the way you think about the importance you place on positivity and happiness in your own life and how you think of your future?

3. How do you think we should treat the topic of happiness in terms of what we focus on in our theory, research, and practice?
4. Are you currently at a point in your life where you are very happy? How did you get there, and how might you leverage the components of PsyCap to sustain your happiness in life and at work?

What do individuals, teams, units, organizations, communities, and even countries that defy conventional wisdom, "beat the odds," and thrive despite limited prospects have in common? How did once-devastated countries such as Japan; emerging economies such as Indonesia; struggling communities such as Kalamazoo, Michigan; and aspiring entrepreneurs such as Facebook's Mark Zuckerberg achieve distinct competitive advantages? There is no question that meeting and exceeding expectations in today's hypercompetitive environment is becoming increasingly difficult and requires considerable talent, motivation, and perseverance.

The major intent of this book is to serve as a guide to a promising, evidence-based answer to gaining competitive advantage through people. We call for the investment in and development of what we have termed well over a decade ago as "psychological capital." We define this psychological capital, or what we will refer to throughout the book simply as "PsyCap," as follows: *An individual's positive psychological state of development that is characterized by (1) having confidence (efficacy) to take on and put in the necessary effort to succeed at challenging tasks; (2) making a positive attribution (optimism) about succeeding now and in the future; (3) persevering toward goals and, when necessary, redirecting paths to goals (hope) in order to succeed; and (4) when beset by problems and adversity, sustaining and bouncing back and even beyond (resiliency) to attain success.*

Before we discuss in detail exactly what we mean by PsyCap and how it works, we invite you to complete the following brief self-assessment that will provide you with some initial feedback on how you view yourself in terms of your inner HERO. We will keep referring to this self-assessment throughout the book, so it is best if you complete it now.

Self-Assessment: The Psychological Capital Questionnaire

Instructions

On a card inserted in the front of your book, you will find a unique identifier (formatted as an e-mail address). This will enable you to take the Psychological

Capital Questionnaire (PCQ) and generate a personal report that will describe—and help you develop—your level of psychological capital. (Note: The free online access is only available to individuals who have purchased a personal copy of this book. Other readers can purchase self-assessments at http://www. mindgarden.com/products/pcqconsult.htm#webself.)

Type this link—http://transform.mindgarden.com/rsvp/15368—into your browser address bar (not the search box) and press "Enter." This will take you to a login page, where you will be prompted to enter an e-mail address. Instead of your e-mail, type in the unique identifier and press "Find invitation." On the next page you will create a password of any length. When you click "Create," you will go directly to the questionnaire.

After you take the PCQ, close your window/tab. Type the following address into your browser address bar: http://www.mindgarden.com/login.

To login, you will use the same unique identifier and password. Once you click "Login" you will see a page that shows a report title. Click on the report title and read, download, and/or print the report. (Note: After login you may change your account/profile to your own e-mail address.)

As shown by the widely recognized comprehensive definition of PsyCap stated earlier, and now supported by over a decade of extensive research (see Avey, Reichard, Luthans, & Mhatre, 2011, for a comprehensive review and meta-analysis, and Dawkins, Martin, Scott, & Sanderson, 2013, for a psychometric or measurement review and overall critical analysis), PsyCap is what is called in the research literature a higher order positive construct composed of the four first-order constructs of *h*ope, *e*fficacy, *r*esilience, and *o*ptimism (or the HERO acronym; see Luthans, 2012). An analogy would be the higher order construct intelligence, made up of lower order facets such as verbal, quantitative, reasoning, logic, and so forth.

We use the "HERO within" to summarize and serve as a reminder of the four facets that make up the core construct of PsyCap (see Luthans, 2012). We propose that this PsyCap can augment other tangible (e.g., economic, financial) and intangible (e.g., human, social) forms of capital in contributing to our understanding of how to best create sustainable and human-based competitive advantage. We posit that PsyCap can help overcome many of today's and tomorrow's most pressing challenges, while also moving individuals, teams, and organizations to take advantage of the opportunities being created. As you will learn, PsyCap is open to development and has tangible performance impact, making it highly relevant as an evidence-based, manageable competitive resource for individuals, teams, units, organizations, communities, and countries.

The Need for a Different Approach

Simply concentrating on and accumulating more of the traditional resources once considered vital for organizational success has proven insufficient for attaining sustainable competitive advantage. Examples of such traditional resources include economic and financial capital, advanced technology, and proprietary information, or what has now been elegantly repackaged but vaguely defined and inconsistently operationalized as "structural capital" or "intellectual capital" (see unpublished to date Youssef-Morgan, Poppler, Stark, Ashley, & Moss-Breen for a comprehensive review and critical analysis). The well-recognized resource-based view (RBV; Barney, 1991) attributes competitive advantage to the possession of valuable, rare, inimitable, and nonsubstitutable resources. However, these competitive resource strategies rely on raising entry barriers in order to be out ahead of one's competitors.

In today's dynamic, complex markets, this traditional approach no longer suffices in creating sustainable sources of distinct advantage (Kraaijenbrink, Spender, & Groen, 2010). Increasingly, practitioners across a broad spectrum of organizations from healthcare to financial, to retail, to manufacturing, to nongovernmental organizations (NGOs) realize that positivity is a powerful factor in enhancing human and organizational performance. Instead of just focusing on the more traditional resources, dynamic capabilities, which are primarily human based, enable organizations to reconfigure, integrate, and leverage their resources on an ongoing basis in order to remain competitive in rapidly changing environments. Thus, the dynamism in creation, acquisition, deployment, and reconfiguration of resources in unique, idiosyncratic patterns in response to environmental change is what may best lead to sustainable competitive advantage (Barreto, 2010; Helfat & Peteraf, 2003; Teece, 2011). And what we are learning is that the conversion rate to dynamic resources in an environment rife with cynicism and negativity, versus one characterized by positivity and high PsyCap, will take much longer to achieve. Importantly, this slower conversion rate can have an appreciable impact on the "tangible" assets of an organization. For example, a large majority of change efforts fail in organizations, and we are increasingly learning that a high percentage of these failures can be directly attributable to employees feeling negative or unsure prior to and during the attempts to change.

Human resource management has been significantly influenced by the resource-based view (e.g., the "War for Talent" perspective that gained momentum several years ago is a good example; see Pfeffer, 2001). Because of that influence, organizations seem to have become adept at luring away their competitors' best employees, or in a self-destructive manner increasing their own employees' levels of dissatisfaction to force them to explore greener pastures elsewhere. Potential employees are often sought for their human capital, that is, "what they know," which includes their explicit and implicit knowledge, skills, and abilities, often objectively measured by their education and experience. Potential employees may also be pursued for their social capital, that is, "who they know," their relationships, the density of and their strategic position in their personal and professional networks (now readily measured through social network analysis techniques, e.g., see Wasserman & Faust, 1994), and the potential connections they will bring in (Adler & Kwon, 2002; Coleman, 1988; Hitt & Ireland, 2002; Luthans & Youssef, 2004; Youssef-Morgan et al., 2014). After being hired, new organizational members may be "invested in" through training and development initiatives that target the enrichment of their human and/or social capital.

We see two potential problems with this widely advocated approach. First, hiring and developing human or social capital provides no guarantees that these forms of "capital" will in fact be wisely invested or converted in order to yield the desired returns. Even the early seminal work on human capital clearly recognized that employees themselves are not "capital" owned by the organization. They are "capitalists," or "investors," with free will of thought and action. They can therefore choose how much of their capital to invest in their jobs based on the risks, returns, and opportunity costs (e.g., see Becker, 1964; Davenport, 1999; Schultz, 1961). For example, a manufacturing employee told us that before his current plant manager came to lead his workplace, he would come to work and place his brain (metaphorically) on a hook, go in, and mindlessly do his job. He was drawing little, if any, of the "HERO within" him (our addition), and then going home at night and taking his brain along with him!

Although it is certainly important to hire the right people and develop their human and social capital, these organizational expenditures can only be turned into "investments" by employees themselves and with help from their leaders, both of whom are the agents in control of this "capital." This is why the intangible "capital" literature has often been heavily criticized for being circular, its definitions tautological, and its claims ex-post and defiant of ex-ante predictive validity (Bechtel, 2007; Dean & Kretschmer, 2007).

Second, the human and social capital an employee possesses today may or may not be valuable tomorrow. The rate of knowledge development and acquisition accelerates in many fields such that what one knows at the time is obsolete less than 5 years later. Organizational needs for human and social capital are a moving target, which requires continuous adjustment, and in some cases might mean even daily adjustment by the organization and the employee to stay relevant and competitive. The type of employees needed to provide the necessary "dynamic capabilities" cannot and should not depend solely upon "what they know" (human capital) or "who they know" (social capital). This is where psychological capital enters (not substitutes) in the "capital equation" for sustainable competitive advantage. PsyCap enters not only as an augmentation to these other capitals but also in how it can interact with them to foster the optimization of all capital resources.

Although linked, PsyCap goes beyond human and social capital. Specifically, PsyCap is concerned with "who you are" now and, in the developmental sense, "who you are capable of becoming" in the future (Avolio & Luthans, 2006; Luthans, Luthans, & Luthans, 2004; Luthans & Youssef, 2004). PsyCap does influence and therefore include knowledge, skills, technical abilities, education, and experience because these are also "who you are." The same is true of social capital. PsyCap influences and therefore includes group-level metaconstructs such as social support and the network of relationships that are part of "who you are," particularly in times of psychological stress (Sarason, Sarason, Shearin, & Pierce, 1987). For example, a young CEO who just took his firm through an initial public offering (IPO) talked to MBA students about the importance of maintaining the positive mindset of his workforce after many employees became rich overnight, while others next to them, who came in a week after the stock options program ended, saw no bump in their net wealth. How does one maintain a high level of HERO among such a workforce going into, going through, and following an IPO to sustain the growth and development of one's firm? We suggest that a critical resource resides in leaders who understand the power of one's own psychological capital and how best to sustain and deploy it through others in what seemingly is a positive time, yet stressful in terms of organizational growth and change.

We argue throughout this book that PsyCap "goes beyond" the other more well-known capitals, and that these positive psychological resources have generally been ignored in human and social capital, especially the developmental dimension of PsyCap of "what you and others are becoming." That is, PsyCap recognizes moving (developing) from the actual self (human, social, and psychological capital) to the possible self, or in an organizational sense, collective selves (see Avolio & Luthans, 2006).

Instead of just introducing yet another set of "competencies" or "best practices" for organizational behavior researchers and human resources practitioners to use, either individually or in combination, we propose that PsyCap offers a more comprehensive, higher order conceptual framework for understanding and capitalizing upon human positive psychological resources in today's organizations and those just being formed for tomorrow (Avolio & Luthans, 2006; Luthans et al., 2004; Luthans & Youssef, 2004; Luthans, Youssef, & Avolio, 2007). We believe that synergistically integrating human, social, and psychological capital is central to actualizing human potential (i.e., attaining "the best possible self or selves," not to be directly equated with the intervention exercise commonly used in positive psychology). For example, many of the assets necessary for building and maintaining resilience in the face of problems and adversity are in fact integral elements of human capital (knowledge, skills, abilities, education, and experiences). Assets that are supportive and contribute to one's resiliency also include vital elements of social capital (e.g., relationships and social networks). Similarly, integral to efficacy development is the presence of effective role models and sources of socially persuading positive feedback (i.e., social capital). However, when considered in terms of their dynamic interaction, we propose that PsyCap has a greater desired impact than human or social capital alone, and the whole of all three "capitals" is greater than the sum of its parts, as we have shown with the PsyCap higher order construct itself.

The Need for a Positive Approach

Decades of relentless research on negatively oriented perspectives and problems in foundational behavioral science disciplines to organizational behavior and human resources management (HRM) such as psychology and sociology provided little understanding of human strengths, flourishing, and optimal functioning. Unfortunately, although certainly not as pronounced in terms of theory and practice, the emphasis on negativity has also penetrated the organizational behavior and HRM fields. Positive psychologist Barb Fredrickson's (2001, 2009) broaden-and-build model can be used to help explain why this "deficit-oriented," negative approach has resulted in an incomplete understanding of how to leverage human resources and organizational leadership for sustainable competitive advantage. Fredrickson's research clearly indicates that positivity yields broadened thought-action repertoires and builds physical, social, and psychological resources. It allows individuals and organizations to be more open to dynamically exploring new possibilities.

Negativity, on the other hand, exposes individuals and organizations to the danger of shifting to a fight-or-flight mode, where scarce time, energy, and resources are only invested in a much narrower set of tried-and-true survival mechanisms. A negative approach also focuses on minimizing what is wrong or a deficit reduction model of human resource, leadership, and organizational development, which of course has its limits—you can only eliminate your problems to none, where the upside is essentially infinite in terms of positive growth. Richer, more positive alternatives with potentially higher returns are shunned as too risky, too soft, or too time consuming, considering the criticalness of the situation at hand. As a result, impending threats can be mitigated in the short term, but the individual or organization is left depleted of critical resources that can only be replenished through subsequent episodes of positivity, broadening, and building out individual and collective human potential.

Tracing the history of psychology can be used to demonstrate this. Prior to World War II, psychologists were charged with a three-pronged mission: healing mental illness, helping healthy people become happier and more productive, and actualizing human potential. However, as the supposed war to end all wars concluded, tremendous needs existed for reparative psychological treatment, and substantial resources were allocated to damage-control and weakness-fixing mechanisms, at the expense of psychology's other two missions. We saw some of this again as US forces and other coalition forces came back from deployments in Iraq and Afghanistan with very high incidents of posttraumatic stress disorder (PTSD), whereby posttraumatic growth (PTG) was largely ignored. Overall, until the turn of this century, very little attention in psychology was devoted to investigating or leveraging human strengths. Even the prevention of psychological problems, beyond philosophical discourses and scattered extrapolations from research findings based on proactive applications of the same disease-oriented paradigm, were largely absent from the field of psychology (Keyes & Haidt, 2002; Seligman & Csikszentmihalyi, 2000).

Similar to what happened in psychology, we propose that the short-term-oriented, crisis management model that characterizes today's management literature (both popular and academic) has also too often resulted in a negative perspective. For example, considerable attention has been given to negatively oriented constructs such as stress, burnout, work-life conflict, abusive supervision, and unethical behavior, or what many of our colleagues refer to as the "dark side" constructs. Most recently, the attention has shifted to unemployment, escalating healthcare costs, cyber-bullying, and workplace incivility. We certainly do not intend to diminish the importance of these topics. The harmful effects of these negative constructs are widely recognized by scholars and practitioners alike. However, there are two problems with a predominantly negative perspective.

The first problem with a disproportionate negative approach is that it tends to absorb great amounts of time, energy, and resources, leaving high-performing individuals and groups largely ignored, understudied, and underappreciated. For instance, instead of investing in identifying, celebrating, and rewarding exceptional performance, many organizations spend enormous resources on dealing with the poor performance of a few dysfunctional employees, or using the infamous Jack Welch at GE "rank and yank" approach, whereby management continually focuses on the bottom 10%. Fortunately, such negatively focused evaluation systems are being abandoned; for example, the leaders at Microsoft saw this system lead to incredibly destructive infighting, one-upmanship, and dysfunctional, territorial cultures and have now dropped it.

Organizations have instituted elaborate systems, policies, and procedures that indiscriminately complicate everyone's life and make them feel micromanaged and untrusted, essentially punishing such things as collaboration or even co-optition, while ignoring placing increasingly greater attention on the higher end best employees in the process. Classic examples include time clocks, online monitoring systems, check-ins with the manager on most everything, impersonal formal performance reviews, standardized training requirements, and so on. These processes and procedures reliably drain positivity and PsyCap from organizations.

The second problem is not characteristic of negative perspectives per se, but of scholars' and practitioners' tendency to extrapolate their understanding and applications of positivity from what is known about negatively oriented constructs and perspectives. Unfortunately, the logic of this approach is flawed. For example, organizational behavior pioneer Frederick Herzberg pointed out that reducing job dissatisfaction is not necessarily conducive to increased job satisfaction, as those two attitudes may be influenced by different factors (Herzberg, Muesner, & Snyderman, 1993). Negatively oriented research and practice are limited in their ability to yield a better understanding of strengths, optimal functioning, and actualizing human potential.

Positive Versus Negative: Not Opposite Ends of the Continuum

In positive psychology, it is widely recognized that freedom from mental illness is not equivalent to flourishing and leading a fulfilled life. There is substantial support in the literature that positive and negative constructs often represent distinct continuums, rather than opposite ends of the same continuum. Numerous positive and negative constructs were once thought to be polar opposites but are now recognized to be distinct, with unique antecedents, outcomes, and underlying mechanisms. Examples include burnout and engagement (Schaufeli & Bakker, 2004); organizational citizenship behaviors and counterproductive work behaviors (Dunlop & Lee, 2004; Sackett, Berry, Wiemann, & Laczo, 2006); positive and negative attitudes and evaluative processes (Cacioppo & Berntson, 1994; Pittinsky, Rosenthal, & Montoya, 2011); optimism and pessimism (Chang, Maydeu-Olivares, & D'Zurilla, 1997; Kubzansky, Kubzansky, & Maselko, 2004); and positive and negative affect (PANA; Watson, Clark, & Tellegen, 1988). Thus, positivity should be independently studied and applied, not extrapolated from negatively oriented perspectives.

By nature, humans tend to be attracted to what is positive, pleasant, and life enhancing, in the same way that plants lean toward light. Despite these "heliotropic," "hedonic," and "eudemonic" tendencies (see Huta, 2013, for a comparison and in-depth discussion), Cameron (2008) highlights several mechanisms that can help explain the prevalent bias toward negativity:

- *Intensity*: Negative stimuli are experienced more intensely than positive stimuli because they are perceived as threats that need to be addressed more immediately and resolutely, which we might attribute to human evolution.
- *Novelty*: The base rate of normal positive events is more commonplace, so they tend to go unnoticed. Negative events tend to be more unusual or unexpected aberrations to our everyday functioning, so they stand out and capture our attention. This might explain why many employees say, "If it ain't broke, don't try to fix it." Positive events that are experienced more frequently pale in relation to negative incidents that are relatively scarce.
- *Adaptation*: Negative stimuli signal maladaptation and a need for change. Contrarily, positive stimuli provide affirmative feedback that "everything is OK." They provide limited motivation for change.
- *Singularity*: In any system, a single negative or defective component can cause the whole system to malfunction. On the other hand, a single positive or properly functioning component cannot guarantee optimal system functioning.

For these reasons, negativity tends to have a stronger effect on our information processing, memory, self-concept, and relationships (Baumeister, Bratslavsky, Finkenauer, & Vohs, 2001). The outcomes of positivity often seem evasive because they are distal, vague, uncertain, and underspecified (Wright & Quick, 2009), at least in the short term. As a result, positivity is usually put on hold until negative events can be dealt with. To resolve this negative bias, balance can be restored by intensifying the frequency of positive experiences and interactions. For example, it has been found that marriages need about five or six positive interactions to balance each negative interaction in order to begin to thrive and to be sustained over extended periods of time (Gottman, 1994).

We emphasize again that we are not against investigating or even practicing negativity, whereby something gets challenged in a more critical way. Some questioning and negativity may be necessary to maintain realism. In this regard, the research literature supports that too much positivity is not necessarily optimal (Diener, Ng, & Tov, 2009; Oishi, Diener, & Lucas, 2007), as is the case with overconfidence (Vancouver, Thompson, Tischner, & Putka, 2002; Vancouver, Thompson, & Williams, 2001), false hope (Snyder, 2000), and unrealistic optimism (Davidson & Prkachin, 1997; Peterson & Chang, 2002; Schneider, 2001). Fredrickson (2009) uses two interesting metaphors to highlight the tension between positivity and negativity, and the need for balance. First, she compares positivity and negativity to levity and gravity. Everyone needs a "lift" in order to soar, but we also need gravity to remain grounded and real. The second metaphor is that of a sailboat, with an enormous mast, representing positivity, and a smaller keel, representing negativity. Hidden underwater, the keel is vital in keeping the boat from wandering aimlessly or tipping over.

The Contribution of Positive Psychology

Psychologists led by Martin Seligman, a well-known researcher in the traditional negative approach (e.g., learned helplessness), toward the turn of the 21st century, took inventory of their achievements under the disease model for over 50 years in the post–World War II era. Despite definite accomplishments in finding effective treatments for mental illness and dysfunctional behavior, psychology as a whole had paid relatively very little attention to psychologically healthy individuals in terms of growth, development, self-actualization, and well-being.

The call was made by Seligman and a few others (e.g., Mike Csikszentmihalyi, Ed Diener) for redirecting psychological research toward psychology's two forgotten missions of helping psychologically healthy people become happier and more productive and actualizing their human potential. This charge to restore more of a balance resulted in not only a surge of interest in the value of positivity but also theory-building and empirical research, and it became what is now known as positive psychology.

What started out in 1999 as a Summit Conference in Lincoln, Nebraska, sponsored by Gallup and the first author as an interested participant, soon followed by a few articles, debates at other conferences, and special issues in academic journals (e.g., see the January 2000 and March 2001 special issues of the *American Psychologist* and the 2003 second issue of *Psychological Inquiry*), is now widely recognized in the psychological field and even has its own *Journal of Positive Psychology*. There is also an increasing number of edited handbooks and books devoted to positive psychology (e.g., Aspinwall & Staudinger, 2003; Carr, 2011; Compton & Hoffman, 2012; David, Boniwell, & Conley Ayers, 2013; Keyes & Haidt, 2002; Linley, Harrington, & Garcea, 2010; Linley & Joseph, 2004; Lopez & Snyder, 2003, 2009; Peterson, 2006; Peterson & Seligman, 2004; Sheldon, Kashdan, & Steger, 2011; Snyder, Lopez, & Pedrotti, 2011) and an exploding number of practitioner-oriented best sellers written by leading positive psychology scholars (e.g., Achor, 2010, 2013; Ben-Shahar, 2007; Diener & Biswas-Diener, 2008; Fredrickson, 2009, 2013; Gilbert, 2005; Lopez, 2013; Lyubomirsky, 2007, 2013; Seligman, 2002, 2011).

Importantly, positive psychology bases its conclusions on rigorous scientific methods rather than philosophy, rhetoric, anecdotes, conventional wisdom, gurus, or personal experience and opinion. It is noteworthy that the theory and research requirement of positive psychology was intended and indeed has differentiated it from the plethora of popular literature on the power of positive thinking over the years and much of positively oriented humanistic psychology, personal development, and the human potential movement. This scientific basis also deliberately serves as an important precedent and perspective and has become an absolute prerequisite for our application of evidence-based positivity to the workplace in the form of PsyCap. The scientific perspective and approach is something we continually reinforce in all of our work. It is our brand differentiator, and there is certainly a lot of "brand blur" out there, where even the top organizations and their leaders will buy into the next best-selling pop-psychology book without ever questioning the scientific underpinnings of the text.

The Contribution of Positive Organizational Scholarship

Besides positive psychology, organization theory and behavior scholars have recognized the untapped potential of a science-based positively oriented approach that has resulted in two major parallel, and complementary, movements. These are commonly referred to as positive organizational scholarship (POS; see Cameron, Dutton, & Quinn, 2003; Cameron & Spreitzer, 2012) and our positive organizational behavior (POB; Luthans, 2002a; 2002b; Luthans & Youssef, 2007), which serves as the foundational perspective for psychological capital or PsyCap.

POS is a "movement in organizational science that focuses on the dynamics leading to exceptional individual and organizational performance such as developing human strength, producing resilience and restoration, and fostering vitality" (Cameron & Caza, 2004, p. 731). Similar to positive psychology, POS is viewed as an "umbrella concept" that integrates a variety of positive approaches, including positive traits, states, processes, dynamics, perspectives, and outcomes. An example of POS as an umbrella construct is that our chapter on psychological capital (Youssef & Luthans, 2012) leads off 77 other chapters on various positive topics in the organizational sciences in the recently published *Handbook of Positive Organizational Scholarship* (Cameron & Spreitzer, 2012). However, unique to POS relative to POB is its primary focus on positive phenomena that occur in organizational contexts. These phenomena can occur at various levels of analysis, including our more individual-level, and to a lesser extent team-level, PsyCap construct (see Cameron & Spreitzer, 2012).

One of the most important contributions of POS has been the unique perspectives it offers for defining and mapping the domain of organizational positivity. For example, Cameron and Spreitzer (2012) provide four perspectives on the uniqueness of positivity. First, a positive approach adopts a unique or alternative lens, altering the interpretation of phenomena that may or may not be positive. For example, problems, obstacles, and adversities are not ignored, but rather interpreted as opportunities for learning, development, and generative growth. Second, positivity focuses on spectacular results and extraordinary outcomes, which go beyond ordinary success. Third, there is an affirmative bias that places a higher weight on positive attributes, dynamics, and outcomes that can perpetuate growth in resources and capabilities, more so than on negative constructs. Finally, positivity is concerned with understanding the best of the human condition, such as flourishing, thriving, optimal functioning, excellence, virtuousness, forgiveness, compassion, goodness, and other life-giving dynamics for their own sake, rather than just as means toward other ends.

As we elaborate next and throughout this book, POB and PsyCap draw extensively from the contributions of POS (e.g., see Paterson, Luthans, & Jeung, 2014). However, while POS is a general "umbrella concept," POB and PsyCap tend to be more specific in their conceptualization, measurement, and outcomes, and they primarily focus on the individual level of analysis but also are moving toward team, unit, organizational, community, and country levels.

Case Study: The Zappos Company
Focus on Happiness and Values

Video link: http://www.youtube.com/watch?v=5CcLIPaUz3E

In this video, the employees of famous online shoe company Zappos discuss the importance of their company culture and the core values that support it to explain their company's growth and success. The primary focus of this company is on its employees and then, in turn, on its customers. The core values include the "Daily Wow," "Being Humble," and "Delivering Happiness."

Questions for reflection and/or discussion:

1. What is the sense that you get about the authenticity of these values that were expressed in this video?
2. How do you see the core values becoming an institutionalized part of the organization?
3. Why would focusing on delivering happiness to employees and customers help a company to be more competitive?
4. Do you think the value of happiness can apply across organizations other than Zappos and, if so, how?

References

Achor, S. (2010). *The happiness advantage: The seven principles of positive psychology that fuel success and performance at work.* New York, NY: Crown.

Achor, S. (2013). *Before happiness.* New York, NY: Crown.

Adler, P. S., & Kwon, S. (2002). Social capital: Prospects for a new concept. *Academy of Management Review, 27,* 17–40.

Aspinwall, L., & Staudinger, U. (Eds.). (2003). *A psychology of human strengths: Fundamental questions and future directions for a positive psychology.* Washington, DC: American Psychological Association.

Avey, J. B., Reichard, R. J., Luthans, F., & Mhatre, K. H. (2011). Meta-analysis of the impact of positive psychological capital on employee attitudes, behaviors, and performance. *Human Resource Development Quarterly, 22,* 127–152.

Avolio, B. J., & Luthans, F. (2006). *The high impact leader: Moments matter in accelerating authentic leadership development.* New York, NY: McGraw-Hill.

Barney, J. (1991). Firm resources and sustained competitive advantage. *Journal of Management, 17,* 99–120.

Barreto, I. (2010). Dynamic capabilities: A review of past research and an agenda for the future. *Journal of Management, 36,* 256–280.

Baumeister, R. F., Bratslavsky, E., Finkenauer, C., & Vohs, K. D. (2001). Bad is stronger than good. *Review of General Psychology, 5,* 323–370.

Bechtel, R. (2007). Calculating human capital: The market based valuation of the human resource. *German Journal of Human Resource Research, 21,* 206–231.

Becker, G. S. (1964). *Human capital.* New York, NY: Columbia University.

Ben-Shahar, T. (2007). *Happier.* New York, NY: McGraw-Hill.

Cacioppo, J. T., & Berntson, G. G. (1994). Relationship between attitudes and evaluative space: A critical review, with emphasis on the separability of positive and negative substrates. *Psychological Bulletin, 115,* 401–423.

Cameron, K. S. (2008). Paradox in positive organizational change. *Journal of Applied Behavioral Science, 44,* 7–24.

Cameron, K. S., & Caza, A. (2004). Contributions to the discipline of positive organizational scholarship. *American Behavioral Scientist, 47,* 731–739.

Cameron, K., Dutton, J., & Quinn, R. (Eds.). (2003). *Positive organizational scholarship.* San Francisco, CA: Berrett-Koehler.

Cameron K., & Spreitzer, G. M. (Eds.). (2012). *Oxford handbook of positive organizational scholarship.* New York, NY: Oxford University Press.

Carr, A. (2011). *Positive psychology: The science of happiness and human strengths* (2nd ed.). New York, NY: Brunner-Routledge.

Chang, E. C., Maydeu-Olivares, A., & D'Zurilla, T. J. (1997). Optimism and pessimism as partially independent constructs: Relations to positive and negative affectivity and psychological well-being. *Personality and Individual Differences, 23,* 433–440.

Coleman, J. S. (1988). Social capital in the creation of human capital. *American Journal of Sociology, 94,* S95–S120.

Compton, W. C., & Hoffman, E. (2012). *Positive psychology: The science of happiness and flourishing* (2nd ed.). Belmont, CA: Wadsworth.

Davenport, T. O. (1999). *Human capital.* San Francisco, CA: Jossey-Bass.

David, S., Boniwell, I., & Conley Ayers, A. (Eds.). (2013). *Oxford handbook of happiness.* New York, NY: Oxford University Press.

Davidson, K., & Prkachin, K. (1997). Optimism and unrealistic optimism have an interacting impact on health-promoting behavior and knowledge changes. *Personality and Social Psychology Bulletin, 23,* 617–625.

Dawkins, S., Martin, A., Scott, J., & Sanderson, K. (2013). Building on the positives: A psychometric review and critical analysis of the construct of Psychological Capital. *Journal of Occupational and Organizational Psychology, 86,* 348–370.

Dean, A., & Kretschmer, M. (2007). Can ideas be capital? Factors of production in the postindustrial economy: A review and critique. *Academy of Management Review, 32,* 573–594.

Diener, E., & Biswas-Diener, R. (2008). *Happiness: Unlocking the mysteries of psychological wealth.* Malden, MA: Blackwell.

Diener, E., Ng, W., & Tov, W. (2009). Balance in life and declining marginal utility of diverse resources. *Applied Research in Quality of Life, 3,* 277–291.

Dunlop, P. D., & Lee, K. (2004). Workplace deviance, organizational citizenship behavior, and business unit performance: the bad apples do spoil the whole barrel. *Journal of Organizational Behavior, 25,* 67–80.

Fredrickson, B. L. (2001). The role of positive emotions in positive psychology: The broaden-and-build theory of positive emotions. *American Psychologist, 56,* 218–226.

Fredrickson, B. L. (2009). *Positivity.* New York, NY: Crown.

Fredrickson, B. L. (2013) *Love 2.0.* New York, NY: Hudson.

Gilbert, D. (2005). *Stumbling on happiness.* New York, NY: Vintage.

Gottman, J. M. (1994). *What predicts divorce?* Hillsdale, NJ: Erlbaum.

Helfat, C. E., & Peteraf, M. A. (2003). The dynamic resource based view: Capability lifecycles. *Strategic Management Journal, 24,* 997–1010.

Herzberg, F., Mausner, B., & Snyderman, B. (1993). *The motivation to work.* Somerset, NJ: Transaction.

Hitt, M. A., & Ireland D. (2002). The essence of strategic management: Managing human and social capital. *Journal of Leadership and Organizational Studies, 9,* 3–14.

Huta, V. (2013). Eudaimonia. In S. A. David, I. Boniwell, & A. C. Ayers (Eds.), *The Oxford handbook of happiness* (pp. 201–213). Oxford, UK: Oxford University Press.

Keyes, C., & Haidt, J. (Eds.). (2002). *Flourishing: Positive psychology and the life well-lived.* Washington, DC: APA.

Kraaijenbrink, J., Spender, J. C., & Groen, A. J. (2010). The resource-based view: A review and assessment of its critiques. *Journal of Management, 36,* 349–372.

Kubzansky, L. D., Kubzansky, P. E., & Maselko, J. (2004). Optimism and pessimism in the context of health: Bipolar opposites or separate constructs? *Personality and Social Psychology Bulletin, 30,* 943–956.

Linley, P. A., Harrington, S., & Garcea, N. (Eds.). (2010). *Oxford handbook of positive psychology and work.* Oxford, UK: Oxford University Press.

Linley, P. A., & Joseph, S. (Eds.). (2004). *Positive psychology in practice.* Hoboken, NJ: Wiley.

Lopez, S. (2013). *Making hope happen: Create the future you want for yourself and others.* New York, NY: Atria.

Lopez, S., & Snyder, C. R. (Eds.). (2003). *Positive psychological assessment: A handbook of models and measures.* Washington, DC: American Psychological Association.

Lopez, S., & Snyder, C. R. (Eds.). (2009). *Oxford Handbook of positive psychology* (2nd ed.). New York, NY: Oxford University Press.

Luthans, F. (2002a). The need for and meaning of positive organizational behavior. *Journal of Organizational Behavior, 23,* 695–706.

Luthans, F. (2002b). Positive organizational behavior: Developing and managing psychological strengths. *Academy of Management Executive, 16*(1), 57–72.

Luthans, F. (2012). Psychological capital: Implications for HRD, retrospective analysis, and future directions. *Human Resource Development Quarterly, 23,* 1–8.

Luthans, F., Luthans, K., & Luthans, B. (2004). Positive psychological capital: Going beyond human and social capital. *Business Horizons, 47*(1), 45–50.

Luthans, F., & Youssef, C. M. (2004). Human, social, and now positive psychological capital management: Investing in people for competitive advantage. *Organizational Dynamics, 33*(2), 143–160.

Luthans, F., & Youssef, C. M. (2007). Emerging positive organizational behavior. *Journal of Management, 33,* 321–349.

Luthans, F., Youssef, C. M., & Avolio, B. J. (2007). Psychological capital: Investing and developing positive organizational behavior. In D. Nelson & C. L. Cooper (Eds.), *Positive organizational behavior* (pp. 9–24). Thousand Oaks, CA: Sage.

Lyubomirsky, S. (2007). *The how of happiness.* New York, NY: Penguin.

Lyubomirsky, S. (2013). *The myths of happiness.* New York, NY: Penguin.

Oishi, S., Diener, E., & Lucas, R. (2007). The optimum level of well-being: Can people be too happy? *Perspectives on Psychological Science, 2,* 346–360.

Paterson, T. A., Luthans, F., & Jeung, W. (2014). Thriving at work: Impact of psychological capital and supervisor support. *Journal of Organizational Behavior, 35,* 434–446.

Peterson, C. (2006). *A primer in positive psychology.* Oxford, UK: Oxford University Press.

Peterson, C., & Chang, E. (2002). Optimism and flourishing. In C. Keyes & J. Haidt (Eds.), *Flourishing: Positive psychology and the life well-lived* (pp. 55–79). Washington, DC: American Psychological Association.

Peterson, C., & Seligman, M. (2004). *Character strengths and virtues: A handbook and classification.* New York, NY: Oxford University Press.

Pfeffer, J. (2001). Fighting the war for talent is hazardous to your organization's health. *Organizational Dynamics, 29,* 248–259.

Pittinsky, T. L., Rosenthal, S., & Montoya, R. M. (2011). Liking is not the opposite of disliking: The functional separability of positive and negative attitudes toward minority groups. *Cultural Diversity and Ethnic Minority Psychology, 17,* 134–143.

Sackett, P. R., Berry, C. M., Wiemann, S. A., & Laczo, R. M. (2006). Citizenship and counterproductive behavior: Clarifying relations between the two domains. *Human Performance, 19,* 441–464.

Sarason, I., Sarason, B., Shearin, E., & Pierce, G. (1987). A brief measure of social support: Practical and theoretical implications. *Journal of Social and Personal Relationships, 4,* 497–510.

Schaufeli, W. B., & Bakker, A. B. (2004). Job demands, job resources, and their relationship with burnout and engagement: A multi-sample study. *Journal of Organizational Behavior, 25,* 293–315.

Schneider, S. L. (2001). In search of realistic optimism. *American Psychologist, 56,* 250–263.

Schultz, T. W. (1961). Investment in human capital. *American Economic Review, 1,* 1–17.

Seligman, M. E. P. (2002). *Authentic happiness.* New York, NY: Free Press.

Seligman, M. E. P. (2011). *Flourish.* New York, NY: Atria.

Seligman, M. E. P., & Csikszentmihalyi, M. (2000). Positive psychology. *American Psychologist, 55,* 5–14.

Sheldon, K. M., Kashdan, T. B., & Steger, M. F. (Eds.). (2011). *Designing positive psychology: Taking stock and moving forward.* Oxford, UK: Oxford University Press.

Snyder, C. R. (2000). *Handbook of hope.* San Diego, CA: Academic Press.

Snyder, C. R., Lopez, S. J., & Pedrotti, J. T. (2011). *Positive psychology: The scientific and practical explorations of human strengths* (2nd ed.). Oxford, UK: Sage.

Teece, D. J. (2011). *Dynamic capabilities and strategic management: Organizing for innovation and growth.* New York, NY: Oxford University Press.

Vancouver, J., Thompson, C., Tischner, E., & Putka, D. (2002). Two studies examining the negative effect of self-efficacy on performance. *Journal of Applied Psychology, 87,* 506–516.

Vancouver, J., Thompson, C., & Williams, A. (2001). The changing signs in the relationship between self-efficacy, personal goals, and performance. *Journal of Applied Psychology, 86,* 605–620.

Wasserman, S., & Faust, K. (1994). *Social network analysis.* New York, NY: Cambridge University Press.

Watson, D., Clark, L. A., & Tellegen, A. (1988). Development and validation of brief measures of positive and negative affect: The PANAS scales. *Journal of Personality and Social Psychology, 54*, 1063–1070.

Wright, T. A., & Quick, J. C. (2009). Special issue: The emerging positive agenda. *Journal of Organizational Behavior, 30*, 147–336.

Youssef, C. M., & Luthans, F. (2012). Psychological capital: Meaning, findings, and future directions. In D. C. Cameron & G. M. Spreitzer (Eds.), *The Oxford handbook of positive organizational scholarship* (pp.17–27). New York, NY: Oxford University Press.

2 POSITIVE ORGANIZATIONAL BEHAVIOR

FRAMEWORK FOR PSYCHOLOGICAL CAPITAL

Opening Video: Shawn Achor on Positivity

Video link: http://www.youtube.com/watch?v=CNsZM94vrP0 (or search for "Shawn Achor at the UP")

In this video, Shawn Achor, a former Harvard fellow and now consultant, speaker, and author, shares experiences and research findings from positive psychology about happiness and success with many organizations and conferences around the world.

Questions for reflection and/or discussion:

1. After watching this video, what have you learned about positivity, happiness, and success?
2. How are Shawn Achor's views similar to or different from your own? What could be some of the causes of those similarities and/or differences?
3. Based on this video presentation, what are some questions that you would like to find answers for through reading this book and/or your additional research?
4. How do Shawn Achor's thoughts and comments coincide with the body of research and practice in positive psychology?

Positive organizational behavior (POB) was first defined as "the study and application of positively oriented human resource strengths and psychological capacities that can be measured, developed, and effectively managed for performance improvement in today's workplace" (Luthans, 2002b, p. 59). Thus, for a psychological strength or resource to be included in our conception of POB, it must be positive, measurable, state-like, or open development and related to desired attitudinal, behavioral, and especially performance outcomes. Most important, it must meet the scientific criteria of being both theory and research based. The approach we have taken in formulating POB is very much in line with a growing trend in both medicine and in the organizational sciences for evidenced-based practices (Pfeffer & Sutton, 2006).

The aforementioned set of POB criteria serves vital purposes that go beyond mere branding and marketing of a new research stream or human resource management and leadership buzzword or fad. Similar to positive psychology and POS, which was covered in Chapter 1, we recognize the continued importance of studying negatively oriented constructs and approaches, but we also propose that POB can represent a paradigm shift that over the past decade has demonstrated the potential to stimulate and transform organizational behavior, leadership, and human resource management research and practice. Thus, we begin this chapter with a more detailed discussion and rationale behind each of the POB inclusion criteria.

The Positivity Criterion of Positive Organizational Behavior

The deficits and disease perspective commonly guiding work in clinical psychology fails to adequately recognize and enhance our understanding and appreciation of the full range of optimal functioning. Analogously, but admittedly not to the same degree, negatively oriented organizational theories and practices have emphasized ineffective and abusive leaders, unethical managers and employees, stress, burnout and conflict, dysfunctional attitudes and behaviors, and counterproductive organizational structures, strategies, and cultures.

We argue that such a negative orientation has detracted from giving at least balanced attention to truly superior performance, continuous learning and development, and proactive, strategic change and adaptation. These positive organizational phenomena have generally been ignored and certainly undervalued (Cameron & Spreitzer, 2012). Too often, the management approach has been to only equip organizations and their members with some basic survival skills that may help them sustain "average" performance for a reasonable period of time by reducing what is wrong versus enhancing and building on what is right. However, such "average" performance, or "just getting by," is no longer adequate for sustainability in today's highly competitive environment. A new, proactive positive approach seemed needed to complement and build on existing approaches (Avolio & Luthans, 2006; Sutcliffe & Vogus, 2003).

So, what is *positivity* when applied to the study and application in the field of organizational behavior? Positive organizational scholars define it as "elevating processes and outcomes" (Cameron & Caza, 2004, p. 731), "intentional behaviors that depart from the norm of a reference group in honorable ways" (Spreitzer & Sonenshein, 2003, p. 209), and outcomes that "dramatically exceed common or expected performance . . . spectacular results, surprising outcomes, extraordinary achievements . . . exceptional performance" (Cameron, 2008, p. 8). In other words, understanding positivity requires deeper investigation of the explanatory mechanisms that can account for exceptional positively deviant behaviors and outcomes.

Based on these characteristics, we define positivity as "an integrated system of antecedents, processes, practices and outcomes that can be readily identified and agreed upon by diverse observers and stakeholders as uniquely surpassing standards of adequate functioning and adding sustainable value to both the individual and the context" (Youssef-Morgan & Luthans, 2013, p. 149). This comprehensive definition implies that positivity needs to be understood from a whole-system perspective, including context, rather than the singular perspective that characterizes negativity. It should also be manifested in the form of objectively verifiable or evidence-based outcomes that are observable to others and impactful on the environmental context within which it occurs.

Theory- and Research-Based Criterion of Positive Organizational Behavior

In response to the apparent inadequacy of a predominantly negative approach to understanding human functioning and potential, the intuitive appeal of positivity has led to a proliferation of positively oriented popular self-help books through the years such as Norman Vincent Peale's *The Power of Positive Thinking*, Dale Carnegie's *How to Win Friends and Influence People*, Kenneth Blanchard's *One Minute Manager*, Steven Covey's *Seven Habits of Highly Effective People*, and Spencer Johnson's *Who Moved My Cheese?* Although filling a significant void and promoting positivity, these easy-to-read, engaging best sellers provide very limited, if any, scientific theory or research to support their claims and thus do not qualify as being evidence based. Even when anecdotal, descriptive findings are reported, they lack the minimal criteria of scientific rigor and meaningful, sustainable knowledge to know what has caused what to occur. Therefore, anyone using the prescriptions in these books for practice may be risking unintended consequences and sustainable impact.

Also, when these books offer self-assessment questionnaires, they may have face validity, and be creative and fun to complete, but they lack any empirically derived construct validity and/or evidence for cause and effect. When applications to the workplace are provided, serious internal and external validity threats exist and the "important findings" are often extrapolated out of context.

For example, oftentimes practitioners who are touting a particular approach or application technique that may have legitimately worked fail to realize that what works in one setting may not generalize to another, which is a high bar standard used in science to determine whether a "practice" is both reliable and valid. More important, the fact that the approach or technique was used does not necessarily mean it caused the changes observed. This can only be ascertained by conducting highly controlled experimental research. As noted by Pfeffer and Sutton (2006), managers are often quite ignorant about which prescriptions work and do not work and have little motivation to find out. Many managers yearn for remedies without sufficient evidence to warrant their continued use in organizations. Can you imagine an engineer being satisfied with the same level of evidence for building a new bridge, airplane, or anything?

Using positive psychology instead of these popular books as the foundation standard, POB is committed to pursuing a scientific approach for inclusion and accumulating a sustainable, impactful body of knowledge for leadership and human resource development and performance management. By using a scientific approach, we can be best assured we are working with the right positive constructs that contribute to sustainable growth and performance improvement.

Valid Measurement Criterion of Positive Organizational Behavior

Measurement has always been at the core of scientific research and application. Most scholars follow the dictum "Without valid measurement, you have nothing." The existence of reliable and valid instruments for measuring work-related constructs has raised organizational behavior in general and POB in particular (see the favorable critical review by Dawkins, Martin, Scott, & Sanderson, 2013) into the realm of science. With valid measurement, systematic analysis, prediction, and control become possible. Again, following the lead of positive psychology (e.g., see Lopez & Snyder, 2003, for a comprehensive summary of a number of positive psychological assessments), POB requires that for a construct to be included, there must be reliable and valid measures. This criterion excludes many interesting, but highly philosophical metaconstructs that do not lend themselves to operationalization and assessment. In addition, the "soft" qualities and positive characteristics supported by anecdotal accounts and limited personal experience used by the popular best sellers for credibility and success are also ruled out.

At the beginning of Chapter 1, you were asked to complete some assessments of your PsyCap. These assessments are our scientifically validated measures of PsyCap, published in the scholarly literature (Avey, Avolio, & Luthans, 2011; Harms & Luthans, 2012; Luthans, Avolio, Avey, & Norman, 2007; Luthans, Youssef, Sweetman, & Harms, 2013; Wernsing, 2014) and used by positive organizational behavioral scholars across the world. As of this writing, the number of formal requests for using our PsyCap measures was approaching 2,000. We will revisit these PsyCap assessments in subsequent chapters and in Chapter 9, where we discuss the psychometrics of these PsyCap scales as well as their similarities and differences.

The State-Like, Open to Development Criterion of Positive Organizational Behavior

There is a wide variety of research-based predictive traits used for selection in human resource management. For example, there are a large number of personality traits with demonstrated relationships with performance and attitudinal work outcomes. These are legally defensible for use as human resources selection tools. Examples include the Big Five personality traits (Barrick & Mount, 1991), core self-evaluations (Judge & Bono, 2001), and cognitive mental abilities (Schmidt, 2009).

Similarly, positive psychology offers many trait-like character strengths and virtues that tend to exhibit considerable stability over time (Lopez & Snyder, 2009; Peterson & Seligman, 2004). Unlike genetically determined factors, positive psychological traits show some malleability and thus may be able to experience some growth and development over one's life span, given optimal situational factors, certain trigger moments, jolts, or extensive counseling (Avolio & Luthans, 2006; Linley & Joseph, 2004). However, little change is likely in the short term, and thus these positive traits are difficult to develop and change in human resource development and performance management.

In today's environment, which is characterized by high turnover rates and emphasis on continuous improvement and required steep learning curves, most long-term initiatives for creating or nurturing job-related talents, character strengths, positive virtues, and relatively stable personality traits are not cost-effective or, in most instances, even possible. The importance of coming to the workplace prepared with such enduring talents, strengths, and especially personality traits, as well as the relatively early age they are developed, has led such initiatives to be mostly transferred to educational institutions at all levels. Thus, within the domain of the workplace, human resources traits have been the focus for effective recruitment, selection, and placement "fit" initiatives, but not human resource development and performance management.

We certainly believe that selecting the right people and placing them in the right roles (i.e., the right fit) is necessary for effective human resource management, but once again, that in and of itself is far from being sufficient. We believe human development/potential is much more elastic and developable than has been previously assumed. By the same token, just focusing on developing knowledge, skills, and technical abilities (i.e., human capital) is also necessary but not sufficient. In our proposed POB, although there may be evidence of a given construct being both trait-like *and* state-like, we only include positive psychological resources that have been clearly demonstrated to be state-like and malleable. Being state-like, these positive resources are open to development and improvement using relatively brief training programs, on-the-job activities, and short, highly focused "micro-interventions" (Luthans, Luthans, & Avey, 2014; Luthans, Avey, Avolio, Norman, & Combs, 2006; Luthans, Avey, Avolio, & Peterson, 2010; Luthans, Avey, & Patera, 2008). The model for our PsyCap interventions is shown at the end of Chapter 9.

The state-like criterion of POB is perhaps the biggest differentiator from positive psychology and POS, which tend to be more dominated by dispositional, trait-like constructs. To further shape this trait-state distinction, we (Luthans, Avolio, et al., 2007; Luthans & Youssef, 2007) present traits and states on a continuum that ranges from "pure traits" (genetically determined and nearly impossible to alter such as intelligence, height, or eye color) to "pure states" (volatile and momentarily changing such as moods and fleeting emotions). Relatively stable or "trait-like" personality characteristics can be positioned near the trait end on the continuum, while more malleable, but not highly volatile characteristics, such as PsyCap, fit closer to the state end of the continuum. Figure 2.1 depicts this trait-state continuum.

Importantly, we use a continuum because most positive psychologists note that even states and state-like characteristics still have a trait baseline or the so-called set point. Based on nature (i.e., biological input and heredity) and nurture (i.e., cultural input and learning/development), this set point explains about half of the variance in one's level of positivity (Lyubomirsky, 2007). On the other hand, up to 40% of one's level of positivity is open to intentional development and self-control. We believe that PsyCap can be placed within this 40%. Only 10% is left to uncontrollable circumstances, which influence the more momentary and hard-to-manage "pure states." And perhaps even more important,

Positive STATES	"State-Like"	"Trait-Like"	Positive TRAITS
Our momentary moods & feelings	Our PsyCap	Our personalities & strengths	Our "hard-wiring"
(Very difficult to get sustained change and development)	(Open to change and development)	(Difficult to change & develop in adults. Need to select and/or fit the situation)	(Extremely difficult to change & develop)

FIGURE 2.1   An evidenced-based continuum of PsyCap change and development.

nature and nurture interact over time, so even the 40% estimate is likely to be low (Avolio, 2011).

Conventional wisdom gives circumstances (e.g., age, income, location, and even appearance) much credit for determining one's happiness and positivity. On the other hand, one cannot do much about the set point. So that leaves the still huge 40% intentional input that is under one's control in determining happiness and positivity. In other words, drawing from Bandura's mantra: We are both products (i.e., the 50% set point and 10% circumstances) *and* producers (i.e., the 40% intentional input) of our positivity. It is this intentional, agentic (Bandura, 2001, 2008) portion of one's positivity that helps explain the developmental, changeable nature of PsyCap. Empirical evidence from experimental (Luthans et al., 2008, 2010, 2014) and longitudinal (Peterson, Luthans, Avolio, Walumbwa, & Zhang, 2011) studies supports changes in participants' PsyCap and its outcomes.

Besides the roles that nature, nurture, circumstances, and intentions/agency play in positivity, recently increased attention is being given to the brain. Specifically, evidence from neuroscience is showing that positivity and negativity are much more than primitive evolutionary emotional reactions. They are being traced to the prefrontal cortex, the same part of the brain that processes higher order rational thinking. This area of the brain shows notable plasticity toward higher positivity, optimism, and resilience (Davidson, 2012). Thus, human potential for increased positivity may go well beyond the 40% that is believed to be open to intentional development. In other words, even the 50% set point that has been traditionally thought to be largely predetermined through genetics or "hard wiring" may be able to be adapted and changed, as we suggested earlier with respect to the interaction between nature and nurture. Indeed, biogeneticists argue today that evolution may be occurring in a single life span, not across multiple life spans, arguing further for human plasticity in terms of development.

Neuroscience research supports (a) "differential susceptibility," a notion that implies variations in plasticity across individuals; (b) "vantage sensitivity," a heightened sensitivity to positive influences; and (c) "diatheses-stress," a heightened sensitivity to negative events (Pluess & Belsky, 2013). These findings may go against the notions of a fixed trait-state mix across individuals. Beginning analysis indicates that there are neuroscientific implications for PsyCap (Peterson, Balthazard, Waldman, & Thatcher, 2008). Thus, future PsyCap research needs to go beyond positioning PsyCap just within the trait-state continuum to also investigate the mechanisms through which PsyCap can alter existing traits and help people reach their full potential.

In addition to the fit of developmental states within the context of the workplace, it is also important to note that POB can expand the domain of positive psychological resources beyond just the prediction of work performance and into domains such as relationships, health, and overall well-being (Avey, Luthans, Smith, & Palmer, 2010; Luthans et al., 2013). As indicated with regard to evidence-based management, only through the manipulation of POB factors in an experimental intervention study can causal conclusions be firmly established with these other important domains. The measurement of the state before and after a micro-intervention to develop it (especially when compared to a randomly assigned matched control group that either did not receive the developmental intervention or better yet received the next best alternative) can demonstrate that the state can be developed and cause improvement in one's relationships, health, and well-being. Chapter 9 will report that such development of PsyCap has indeed been demonstrated through our micro-intervention studies and future studies need to determine whether this development causes these outcomes to improve.

As work performance measures are taken pre- and post-PsyCap intervention in both the experimental and control groups, and since the performance increased with the PsyCap treatment group but not the control group, we have a strong case that the increased PsyCap in the treatment group caused their performance to improve (Luthans et al., 2010). By contrast, the stability of personality traits limits their explanatory power in the workplace. Although identifying relatively stable traits such as conscientiousness is desirable for various reasons, including being related to performance (see Barrick & Mount, 1991) and thus effective (and valid) for selection and career planning, the value of developable states such as found in PsyCap has traditionally been overlooked.

By emphasizing states rather than traits, POB creates new opportunities and dimensions for human resource development and performance management, and in the future building better relationships, health, and well-being both in and outside the organization.

The Performance Impact Criterion of Positive Organizational Behavior

Quantifying the dollar return on human resources in general and human resources training and development investments in particular has become of vital concern to organizational decision makers (e.g., Cascio & Boudreau, 2011; Fitz-Enz, 2009; Hubbard, 2010; Kravetz, 2004). As various attractive investments compete for the scarce resources in an organization, an adequate return becomes one of the most critical factors in determining the extent to which human resource development initiatives receive organizational support. It is generally acknowledged that many human resource investments may have a high potential for yielding above-average returns. However, the questionable assumptions and difficulties associated with quantifying these returns may channel resources away from such worthwhile investments toward the accumulation of more traditional assets such as physical, financial, and technological capital.

In selecting only positive psychological capacities that meet the criterion of being related to performance, POB can have a significant impact on work outcomes. As indicated, the meta-analysis of 51 studies supports significant relationships between employees' PsyCap and a wide range of work outcomes (Avey, Reichard, Luthans, & Mhatre, 2011). There was a positive relationship with performance (measured multiple ways), job satisfaction, organizational commitment, psychological well-being, organizational citizenship behaviors, and a negative relationship with cynicism, turnover intentions, stress, anxiety, and counterproductive work behaviors. The Newman, Ucbasaran, Zhu, and Hirst (2014) more recent PsyCap literature review also found strong support for these and other behaviors such as job search of the unemployed and outcomes such as creative performance and safety climate. More and more research continues to show the positive impact PsyCap has on performance (e.g., Mathe-Soulek, Scott-Halsell, Kim, & Krawczyk, 2014; Choi & Lee, 2014). We believe that this demonstrated performance-orientation and bottom-line relevance as outlined in detail in Chapter 9 distinguishes PsyCap in an important way that warrants the attention and buy-in of today's and tomorrow's organizations.

Positive Psychological Resources That Meet Positive Organizational Behavior Criteria

After the aforementioned criteria were established for POB, several positive psychological resources found in positive psychology were considered for inclusion. Those that were determined to best meet the POB inclusion criteria were hope, efficacy, resilience, and optimism and, when combined, become psychological capital (Luthans, 2002a; also see Luthans & Avolio, 2003; Luthans, Luthans, & Luthans, 2004; Luthans & Youssef, 2004; Luthans, Youssef, & Avolio, 2007). As indicated in our introductory comments, the four components are now sometimes referred to as the HERO within for ease of recall. We will only briefly introduce each of these four capacities since an in-depth discussion of each is presented in the following four chapters.

Founded on the extensive work of Albert Bandura (1997) and specifically his social cognitive theory, *efficacy*, or simply confidence (e.g., see Kanter, 2004), can be defined as "one's belief about his or her ability to mobilize the motivation, cognitive resources, and courses of action necessary to execute a specific action within a given context" (Stajkovic & Luthans, 1998b, p. 66). Meta-analytical findings support a highly significant positive relationship between efficacy and work-related performance (Stajkovic & Luthans, 1998a).

Of the four capacities we determined meet our POB inclusion criteria, efficacy has the most established theoretical foundation and empirical research base, particularly in the workplace. Efficacy development approaches have also been well established in the research literature. These include mastery experiences, vicarious learning/modeling, social persuasion, and physiological and psychological arousal (Bandura, 1997). We have devoted the next chapter of this book to this powerful positive psychological resource that plays such an important role in psychological capital.

Based on the late, well-known positive psychologist Rick Snyder's (2000) extensive theory-building and research, *hope* is defined as "a positive motivational state that is based on an interactively derived sense of successful (1) agency (goal-directed energy) and (2) pathways (planning to meet goals)" (Snyder, Irving, & Anderson, 1991, p. 287). The agency (or willpower) and pathways (or waypower) components of hope make it particularly relevant to the emphasis in today's workplace on self-motivation, autonomy, and contingency actions. Hope has been recently shown to relate conceptually and empirically to performance in various domains, including the workplace (e.g., see Adams et al., 2003; Jensen & Luthans, 2002; Luthans, Avolio, et al., 2007; Luthans & Jensen, 2002; Luthans, Van Wyk, & Walumbwa, 2004; Luthans & Youssef, 2004; Peterson &

Byron, 2008; Peterson & Luthans, 2003; Snyder, 1995; Youssef & Luthans, 2005b, 2006, 2007).

Although hope can be conceived and measured as trait-like (Snyder et al., 1991; Tong, Fredrickson, Chang, & Lim, 2010), importantly, hope is also recognized as a developmental state (Snyder et al., 1996). Practical approaches for developing hope include setting challenging "stretch" goals, contingency planning, and regoaling when necessary to avoid false hope. Hope is fully discussed in Chapter 4.

A third positive psychological resource that meets our POB inclusion criteria is *optimism*, which is commonly portrayed as a generalized positive outlook or expectancy (Carver, Scheier, Miller, & Fulford, 2009). However, under the influence of Martin Seligman, optimism is also defined as an attributional style that explains positive events in terms of personal, permanent, and pervasive causes, and negative events as external, temporary, and situation specific (Seligman, 1998). In other words, like hope, although optimism is sometimes portrayed as dispositional (Kluemper, Little, & DeGroot, 2009; Scheier & Carver, 1987), as an optimistic explanatory style it can be learned and developed (Seligman, 1998). In addition, its potential contributions to work performance have been empirically demonstrated (Luthans, Avolio, et al., 2005, 2007; Seligman, 1998; Youssef & Luthans, 2007). Particularly relevant to the workplace is that optimism be realistic (Schneider, 2001) and flexible (Peterson, 2000). Organizational leaders and employees must be flexible when discerning when to use optimistic versus pessimistic explanatory styles, as well as the capacity to adapt these styles realistically to the situation at hand. Chapter 5 presents a detailed discussion of such flexible, realistic optimism.

Fourth is the positive psychological resource of *resilience*, which we define as "the developable capacity to rebound or bounce back from adversity, conflict, and failure or even positive events, progress, and increased responsibility" (Luthans, 2002a, p. 702). Factors drawn from clinical and positive psychology that have been found to contribute or hinder resilience include one's inventory of physiological, cognitive, affective, and social assets; the nature, intensity, and frequency of risks encountered; adaptational processes utilized to balance the use of assets in facing risks; and underlying value systems (Coutu, 2002; Masten, 2001; Masten, Cutuli, Herbers, & Reed, 2009). We have also drawn from this growing resiliency literature and from developmental psychology to make the case for resiliency as relevant and necessary in today's workplace (Luthans, Vogelgesang, & Lester, 2006) and have shown empirically that it relates to performance outcomes (Luthans et al., 2005, 2007; Youssef & Luthans, 2005a, 2007). Resilience is given detailed attention in Chapter 7.

It is important to note that both positive psychology and POS have a growing body of research on a number of positive constructs besides the four we have delineated. Some of these other capacities meet some of our inclusion criteria to varying degrees. As they develop and others emerge, we do not rule out their inclusion in PsyCap in the future. We devote Chapters 7 and 8 to the careful assessment of such potential positive psychological resources that to varying degrees may meet POB criteria. Specifically, we recognize the potential of creativity, flow, mindfulness, gratitude, forgiveness, emotional intelligence, spirituality, authenticity, and courage as candidates for the future, and they are discussed in detail in Chapters 7 and 8.

PsyCap as a Higher Order Core Construct

As indicated, we formulated psychological capital by integrating the four positive psychological resources that meet POB criteria not only additively, but upon empirical analysis they turned out to be synergistic, a higher order core construct (Luthans, Avolio, et al., 2007). Thus, the resulting impact of investing in, developing, and managing overall PsyCap on attitudinal, behavioral, and performance outcomes is expected to be larger than the individual positive psychological capacities that make it up (see Avey, Reichard, et al., 2011; Luthans, Avolio, et al., 2007). In other words, the whole (PsyCap) is greater than the sum of its parts (hope, efficacy, resilience, and optimism). Specifically, the basic underlying theoretical mechanism connecting hope, efficacy, resilience, and optimism is a "positive appraisal of circumstances and probability for success based on motivated effort and perseverance" (Luthans, Avolio, et al., 2007, p. 550).

Drawing from social cognitive and agency theory (Bandura, 2001, 2008), hope, efficacy, resilience, and optimism share a first-order internalized sense of agency, control, and intentionality. This agentic and "conative" mechanism (Youssef & Luthans, 2013, Youssef-Morgan & Luthans, 2013) promotes a positive outlook, selection of challenging goals, and investment of energy and resources in pursuit of those goals despite potential problems, obstacles, and setbacks. This is because circumstances and chances of success are consistently, but realistically, appraised in a positive light. These positive expectancies become powerful driving forces, yielding motivation for resource investment and perseverance toward goal attainment with accompanying desirable attitudes, behaviors, and performance.

The factors of PsyCap interact synergistically. For example, hopeful individuals who possess the agency and pathways to achieve their goals will be more motivated to and capable of overcoming adversities, and thus be more resilient. Efficacious people will be able to transfer and apply their hope, optimism, and resilience to the specific tasks within specific domains of their life. Resilient individuals will be adept in utilizing the adaptational mechanisms necessary for realistic and flexible optimism. PsyCap efficacy, hope, and resilience can in turn contribute to an optimistic explanatory style through internalized perceptions of being in control. These are just representative of the countless positive synergies that result from the interaction among the four factors that effect overall PsyCap.

In more analytical terms, it is through the discriminant validity across the four individual PsyCap capacities (e.g., see Alarcon, Bowling, & Khazon, 2013; Bryant & Cvengros, 2004; Gallaghar & Lopez, 2009; Magaletta & Oliver, 1999; Rand, Martin, & Shea, 2011) that each adds unique variance and becomes additive to overall PsyCap (Luthans, Avolio, et al., 2007). Furthermore, both conceptual developments (e.g., see Avolio & Luthans, 2006; Bandura & Locke, 2003; Gillham, 2000; Hannah & Luthans, 2008; Luthans & Youssef, 2004, 2007; Snyder, 2000; Youssef & Luthans, 2013; Youssef-Morgan & Luthans, 2013) and empirical evidence (Avey, Reichard et al., 2011; Luthans, Avolio, et al., 2007) support the convergent validity of the four capacities of hope, efficacy, resilience, and optimism that meet POB criteria. This theory and research supports an underlying latent PsyCap core construct to which the individual resources synergistically contribute. Importantly, following the recent person-centered (as opposed to variable-centered), latent profile analysis (LPA) of the multi-dimensional construct of organizational commitment (Meyer, Stanley & Vandenberg, 2013), we are also conducting such analysis to refine and determine if and how the different combinations or profiles of the underlying components of PsyCap may differentially effect outcomes (see unpublished to date research by Bouckenooghe, DeClercq, Raja & Luthans).

The Contribution of Resource Theory

To provide further support by "theory borrowing" (see Whetten, Felin, & King, 2009) for PsyCap as a higher order construct, we can also draw from psychological resource theories (e.g., see Hobfoll, 2002, for a review). These widely recognized theories emphasize the necessity to treat individuals' psychological resources (in this case the four positive resources) as manifestations of an underlying central construct or an integrated resource set (in this case PsyCap), rather than in isolation. For example, key resource theories (e.g., Thoits, 1994) have identified individual-level resources such as self-efficacy, optimism, resilience, and degree of goal pursuit (an integral component of hope) as essential foundational resources for managing and adapting other resources to achieve favorable outcomes. Such key resources have been empirically supported as interactive and synergistic (Cozzarelli, 1993; Rini, Dunkel-Schetter, Wadhwa, & Sandman, 1999).

Similarly, multiple-component resource theories support resource synergies, in which the whole is greater than the sum of the constituent parts. Examples of such theories include the theory of sense of coherence (Antonovsky, 1979), which is conceptually similar to PsyCap optimism, as well as the well-known construct of hardiness (Kobasa, 1979), which in many ways parallels PsyCap resilience (see Hobfoll, 2002). In other words, resource theory could be used for theoretical understanding and support our own theory building and research that synergies may exist both within the components of individual PsyCap capacities, as well as between the capacities that constitute PsyCap as a higher order construct.

The Contribution of Measurement and Development

Still another contribution to PsyCap as a higher order construct worth highlighting is its unique measurement. For our research on PsyCap, we systematically constructed a self-report measure. Specifically, we determined and then adapted six of the most relevant items for each of the four PsyCap components from widely recognized standardized measures of self-efficacy (Parker, 1998), state hope (Snyder et al., 1996), optimism (Scheier & Carver, 1987), and resilience (Wagnild & Young, 1993). We called this the Psychological Capital Questionnaire or PCQ-24 and provided supporting psychometric analysis and validation (Luthans, Avolio, et al., 2007). The majority of PsyCap studies to date have used this PCQ-24 measure (Newman et al., 2014). In addition, however, we have statistically determined and validated a reduced version, PCQ-12, by psychometrically selecting from the PCQ-24 three items for efficacy, four items for hope (two for agency and two for pathways), three items for resilience, and two items for optimism (see Avey, Avolio et al., 2011).

Over the years, this PCQ measure has repeatedly demonstrated its reliability and validity and has been used to statistically determine the higher order nature of PsyCap and its added value over the individual components in predicting outcomes (see Avey, Reichard, et al., 2011; Dawkins et al., 2013; Luthans, Avolio, et al., 2007). Also, in recent years to help combat the problem of social desirability and faking with self-report measures in general and especially the "I should be positive" mindset associated with measures such as the PCQ, we have developed and validated an easy-to-administer Implicit Psychological Capital Questionnaire or I-PCQ (Harms & Luthans, 2012). To measure our expansion beyond Work PsyCap into Relationship PsyCap, Health PsyCap, and overall Well-Being PsyCap, we have also recently adapted and validated our PCQ for these domains as well (Luthans et al., 2013). In Chapter 9 we discuss these measures in more detail.

Finally, using our developing PsyCap theoretical framework as presented in this book, we have been able to introduce micro-interventions (2-hour to day-long, face-to-face workshops, and also online offerings) for PsyCap development in the workplace (see Luthans, Avey, et al., 2006, and Chapter 9). As indicated, through experimental research designs we have been able to show that these micro-interventions can cause the level of participants' PsyCap to increase significantly (Luthans et al., 2008, 2010, 2014) and also cause performance to improve (Luthans et al., 2010); furthermore, using utility analysis demonstrates that such development can yield a very high (over 200%) return on investment (Luthans, Avey, et al., 2006, and Chapter 9). We present these micro-interventions and offer practical techniques for calculating the potential return on PsyCap investment, or what we prefer to call PsyCap return on development (ROD, see Avolio, Avey, & Quisenberry, 2010), under various conditions and applications in Chapter 9.

PsyCap and Authentic Leadership

From the outset, we have positioned PsyCap as being a major input into authentic leadership development (ALD) (Avolio & Luthans, 2006; Luthans & Avolio, 2003). Specifically, when PsyCap development efforts are introduced within a positive organizational context in which planned and unplanned trigger events are integrated, developing leaders can enhance their self-awareness, self-regulation, and self-development. The result is not only leaders with higher PsyCap but also more authentic leaders. And if the leaders are both higher in PsyCap and also more authentic, we expect the same will be true in terms of the development of followers (Avey, Avolio, et al., 2011; Avolio, Gardner, Walumbwa, Luthans, & May, 2004; Gardner, Avolio, Luthans, May, & Walumbwa, 2005; Wang, Sui, Luthans, Wang, & Wu, 2014).

In addition to self-development, one of the primary characteristics of authentic leaders is that they are capable of and motivated to develop their followers. The integrity, balance in terms of justice/fairness, trust, and transparency of the authentic leader can encourage reciprocity from followers and an organizational culture in which openness, sharing, and ongoing PsyCap development become the norm. Indeed, the possibility that positivity may exhibit both downward and upward spirals and contagion effects has been consistently utilized as a backdrop in POS and positive psychological research (Cameron, Dutton, & Quinn, 2003; Fredrickson, 2001). We integrate such notions in our recent work, both conceptually (Luthans, Norman, & Hughes, 2006; Youssef & Luthans, 2005a; Youssef-Morgan & Luthans, 2013) and empirically (Avey, Avolio, et al., 2011; Haar, Roche, & Luthans, 2014; Story, Youssef, Luthans, Barbuto, & Bovaird, 2013).

Extending PsyCap Levels of Analysis in the United States and Internationally

Taking PsyCap from the individual to the leader and follower is just the first step in recognizing the need to extend PsyCap's level of analysis. For example, the possibility of multiple levels of analysis is needed for PsyCap in the future. Of particular recent interest is how PsyCap can be elevated higher to team, unit, organizational, community, or country levels of analysis. Already an increasing number of studies have begun to analyze PsyCap at the team, collective level (e.g., Haar et al., 2014; Mathe-Soulek et al., 2014), and a recent study has taken PsyCap to the organizational level of analysis (Memili, Welsh, & Kaciak, 2014; Memili, Welsh, & Luthans, 2013). However, the extent of "conceptual isomorphism" (whether the operationalization and nomological network of the construct vary across levels of analysis) and "functional isomorphism" (whether the higher level construct predicts the same outcomes as its lower level counterpart) is yet to be thoroughly examined (McKenny, Short, & Payne, 2013). Standing in contrast to the upward spirals and positive downward contagion effects, resource theories such as conservation of resources (COR) (Hobfoll, 1989) and the selective optimization with compensation (SOC) (Baltes, 1997) have primarily focused on the dynamics through which people deal with losses and deterioration of resources. Thus, a valid question for extending PsyCap becomes whether previously built PsyCap can deteriorate over time.

Since PsyCap capacities are states rather than enduring traits, we would expect them to fluctuate over time, increasing or decreasing depending on the existing conditions at the time of their assessment. For example, since efficacy is a domain-specific capacity, an employee who has been recently promoted to a more demanding job with unfamiliar and/or uncertain responsibilities will likely exhibit at least a temporary drop in efficacy. Thus, ongoing efficacy development efforts may be necessary to maintain a high level of efficacy in today's constantly changing work environment. Similarly, a manager who may have been very effective when operating locally may appear to "lose" his resilience when sent as an expatriate on an international assignment. This loss of resilience may result because significant sources of social support have been withdrawn. On the other hand, through ongoing mentoring and support by the home office, as well as the manager's involvement establishing new relationships and connections in the new locale, resilience can be rebuilt, perhaps at an accelerated rate to the extent the interventions are focused and evidence based.

Despite these potential problems and limitations, we contend that, unlike traditional human and social capital, or even the individual positive psychological resources, our proposed synergistic PsyCap offers a dynamic resource potential that can grow and be sustainable over time. For example, expatriates whose resilience may become threatened by losses of social assets can capitalize on their PsyCap hope pathways to find new ways to overcome and bounce back from the obstacles they may face. Expats may draw upon and enhance their personal relationships with an accompanying spouse and children and new coworkers, which may result in long-term resource gains, rather than losses. Also, when they return home prematurely, there is a significant cost to the organization with regard to relocation expenses, disruption in workflows, and PsyCap (e.g., loss of efficacy). They may also establish a new social network through friendships and activities within the new community to bolster their PsyCap. Such socializing will likely reflect on the reputation of the organization, as well as on expats' well-being and their followers' responsiveness and cooperation.

Similarly, expats in this example may capitalize upon their previously built efficacy if they have been successful in other international assignments. They can also capitalize on their optimism by explaining initial negative events using causes that are external (e.g., "It is natural for anyone in my cultural shock situation to feel that way at the beginning"), temporary (e.g., "This is only for a while, but everything will eventually be fine"), and situation specific (e.g., "I must be feeling this way because my first meeting with the staff did not go very well"). Such approaches can help expatriates maintain or even enhance their resilience, bouncing back to an even higher level of performance and well-being.

This example points to how the state-like positive resources that make up PsyCap may differ from other resources in psychological resource theory. Instead of competing for scarce, nonrenewable resources that are subject to obsolescence, depletion, or loss to the competition, we propose that the four PsyCap resources tend to be renewable, complementary, and synergistic. We further posit that high PsyCap individuals or teams can flexibly and adaptively meet the dynamic demands of their jobs, while their PsyCap simultaneously helps them experience higher levels of competence and well-being. This is in contrast to the stress and strain traditionally associated with resource acquisition processes (e.g., hours of technical training to acquire human capital and/or impression management and political maneuvering to build social capital).

This new PsyCap position does not negate the need for some resource sacrifices throughout the PsyCap development process (e.g., time, energy, and even financial resources). However, as we show in Chapter 9, these sacrifices should be viewed as investments with very high potential returns (a balance sheet and "bottom-line" perspective), rather than as gains and losses (a short-term, income statement approach). High-return investments in PsyCap are proactively pursued in self-management and organizational leadership, not only because they are desirable from a financial perspective but also because they are motivating and can have positive impacts on both shorter and longer term performance. By the same token, losses tend to be feared and avoided, or reactively and passively handled as necessary. PsyCap is certainly better aligned with the positive reactions and well-being at all levels (individual employees, leaders, teams, units, and the overall organization), rather than the negativity and downward spiral associated with stagnation, stress, burnout, turnover, downsizing, and financial losses.

Also relevant to extending PsyCap are cross-cultural applications. Since PsyCap is state-like and developmental, it will be influenced by cultural contexts. Cultural differentiation is in line with Hobfoll's (2002, p. 312) notion of "resource caravans" that influence the resource sets that people acquire over their life spans. For example, since efficacy and hope are more self-based, while optimism and resilience are more dependent on others and the external environment, there may be resulting differences between individualistic and collectivistic cultures to the extent to which the development of these PsyCap resources is encouraged.

As indicated, our work to date supports the relevance of PsyCap for diverse cultural backgrounds in general (Wernsing, 2014; Youssef & Luthans, 2003), as well as in specific countries such as China (Huang & Luthans, 2014; Luthans, Avey, Clapp-Smith, & Li, 2008; Luthans et al., 2005), South Africa (Cascio & Luthans, 2014; Reichard, Dollwet, & Louw-Potgieter, 2014), and the Middle East (Youssef, 2011; Youssef & Luthans, 2006). At this stage of development, we believe that PsyCap represents a high-potential construct for both domestic as well as cross-cultural research and applications, one that is generalizable across a diverse range of cultures and contexts.

A Final Word

To conclude the opening two foundational chapters, we strongly encourage maintaining a "big picture," overall PsyCap perspective as each of the succeeding chapters takes a deeper dive into each of the four criteria-meeting positive resources (hope, efficacy, resilience and optimism, a.k.a. the "HERO within" components) and also explore some of the other potential PsyCap resources for the future. It should be remembered that PsyCap as a higher order core construct is greater than the sum of its parts. We hope you will not be satisfied with just learning about one or two of these resources that may be of interest to you for academic or practical purposes. To reiterate, our intent is to take an inquiry perspective by continually exploring new criteria-meeting psychological resources, building theory, conducting research on newly emerging research questions, and improving applications to practice. After reading this book, you should have the confidence that you have learned much about PsyCap as a whole and the dramatic impact it can have on who you are as an individual, but more important, who you (and your people) can become. This book can help in your self-awareness and development, but it can also serve as a new paradigm for developing and managing human resources for performance improvement and competitive advantage.

Case Study: Randy Pausch's Last Lecture

Video link: http://www.cmu.edu/randyslecture/

In this video, Randy Pausch, a Carnegie Mellon professor, inspires his audience with his exceptionally positive presentation, shortly after he was told that he had 3–6 months to live due to his advanced-stage pancreatic cancer. Each chapter of this book will end with one or more of these case studies that apply the chapter's topics.

Questions for reflection and/or discussion:

1. In what ways does Randy Pausch exemplify psychological capital?
2. What are some of the life events and personal attitudes that seem to have contributed to Randy Pausch's efficacy, hope, optimism, and resilience?
3. To what extent is Randy Pausch's positivity an inherent trait? To what extent is it a developmental state? What is the evidence supporting each perspective from his presentation?
4. What are some lessons that you have learned from this case study, and how have they contributed to your own level of positivity and psychological capital?

References

Adams, V. H., Snyder, C. R., Rand, K. L., King, E. A., Sigmon, D. R., & Pulvers, K. M. (2003). Hope in the workplace. In R. Giacolone & C. Jurkiewicz (Eds.), *Handbook of workplace spirituality and organizational performance* (pp. 367–377). New York, NY: Sharpe.

Alarcon, G. M., Bowling, N. A., & Khazon, S. (2013). Great expectations: A meta-analytic examination of optimism and hope. *Personality and Individual Differences, 54,* 821–827.

Antonovsky, A. (1979). *Health, stress, and coping.* San Francisco, CA: Jossey-Bass.

Avey, J. B., Avolio, B. J., & Luthans, F. (2011). Experimentally analyzing the impact of leader positivity on follower positivity and performance. *Leadership Quarterly, 21,* 350–364.

Avey, J. B., Luthans, F., Smith, R. M., & Palmer, N. F. (2010). Impact of positive psychological capital on employee well-being over time. *Journal of Occupational Health Psychology, 15*, 17–28.

Avey, J. B., Reichard, R. J., Luthans, F., & Mhatre, K. H. (2011). Meta-analysis of the impact of positive psychological capital on employee attitudes, behaviors, and performance. *Human Resource Development Quarterly, 22*, 127–152.

Avolio, B. J. (2011). *Full range leadership development.* Thousand Oaks, CA: Sage.

Avolio, B. J., Avey, J. B., & Quisenberry, D. (2010). Estimating return on leadership development investment. *Leadership Quarterly, 21*, 633–644.

Avolio, B. J., Gardner, W. L., Walumbwa, F. O., Luthans, F., & May, D. R. (2004). Unlocking the mask: A look at the process by which authentic leaders impact follower attitudes and behaviors. *Leadership Quarterly, 15*, 801–823.

Avolio, B. J., & Luthans, F. (2006). *The high impact leader: Moments matter in accelerating authentic leadership development.* New York, NY: McGraw-Hill.

Baltes, P. (1997). On the incomplete architecture of human ontogeny: Selection, optimization, and compensation as foundation of development theory. *American Psychologist, 52*, 366–380.

Bandura, A. (1997). *Self-efficacy: The exercise of control.* New York, NY: Freeman.

Bandura, A. (2001). Social cognitive theory: An agentic perspective. *Annual Review of Psychology, 52*, 1–26.

Bandura, A. (2008). An agentic perspective on positive psychology. In S. J. Lopez (Ed.), *Positive psychology: Exploring the best in people* (pp. 167–196). Westport, CT: Greenwood.

Bandura, A., & Locke, E. A. (2003). Negative self-efficacy and goal effects revisited. *Journal of Applied Psychology, 88*, 87–99.

Barrick, M. R., & Mount, M. K. (1991). The big five personality dimensions and job performance: A meta-analysis. *Personnel Psychology, 44*, 1–26.

Bryant, F. B., & Cvengros, J. A. (2004). Distinguishing hope and optimism. *Journal of Social and Clinical Psychology, 23*, 273–302.

Cameron, K., Dutton, J., & Quinn, R. (Eds.). (2003). *Positive organizational scholarship.* San Francisco, CA: Berrett-Koehler.

Cameron K., & Spreitzer, G. M. (Eds.). (2012). *Oxford handbook of positive organizational scholarship.* New York, NY: Oxford University Press.

Cameron, K. S. (2008). Paradox in positive organizational change. *Journal of Applied Behavioral Science, 44*, 7–24.

Cameron, K. S., & Caza, A. (2004). Contributions to the discipline of positive organizational scholarship. *American Behavioral Scientist, 47*, 731–739.

Carver, C., Scheier, M., Miller, C., & Fulford, D. (2009). Optimism. In S. Lopez & C. R. Snyder (Eds.), *Oxford handbook of positive psychology* (2nd ed., pp. 303–312). New York, NY: Oxford University Press.

Cascio, W., & Luthans, F. (2014). Reflections on the metamorphosis at Robben Island: The role of institutional work and positive psychological capital. *Journal of Management Inquiry, 23*, 51–67.

Cascio, W. F., & Boudreau, J. W. (2011). *Investing in people: Financial impact of human resource initiatives* (2nd ed.). Upper Saddle River, NJ: Pearson Education.

Choi, Y., & Lee, D. (2014). Psychological capital, Big Five traits, and employee outcomes. *Journal of Managerial Psychology, 29*, 122–140.

Coutu, D. L. (2002). How resilience works. *Harvard Business Review, 80*(3), 46–55.

Cozzarelli, C. (1993). Personality and self-efficacy as predictors of coping with abortion. *Journal of Personality and Social Psychology, 65*, 1224–1237.

Davidson, R. (2012). *The emotional life of your brain.* New York, NY: Hudson/Penguin.

Dawkins, S., Martin, A., Scott, J., & Sanderson, K. (2013). Building on the positives: A psychometric review and critical analysis of the construct of psychological capital. *Journal of Occupational and Organizational Psychology, 86*, 348–370.

Fitz-Enz, J. (2009). *The ROI of human capital: Measuring the economic value of employee performance.* New York, NY: AMACOM.

Fredrickson, B. L. (2001). The role of positive emotions in positive psychology: The broaden-and-build theory of positive emotions. *American Psychologist, 56*, 218–226.

Gallaghar, M. W., & Lopez, S. J. (2009). Positive expectancies and mental health: Identifying the unique contributions of hope and optimism. *Journal of Positive Psychology, 4*, 548–556.

Gardner, W. L., Avolio, B. J., Luthans, F., May, D. R., & Walumbwa, F. O. (2005). "Can you see the real me?" A self-based model of authentic leader and follower development. *Leadership Quarterly, 16*, 343–372.

Gillham, J. (Ed.). (2000). *The science of optimism and hope.* Radnor, PA: Templeton Foundation.

Haar, J. M., Roche, M. A., & Luthans, F. (August 1–5, 2014). *Do leaders' psychological capital and engagement influence follower teams or vice-versa?* Paper presented at Academy of Management Conference, Philadelphia, PA.

Hannah, S., & Luthans, F. (2008) A cognitive affective processing explanation of positive leadership: Toward a theoretical explanation of the role of psychological capital. In R. Humphrey (Ed.), *Affect and emotion: New directions in management theory and research* (pp. 95–134). Charlotte, NC: Information Age.

Harms, P., & Luthans, F. (2012). Measuring implicit psychological constructs in organizational behavior: An example using psychological capital. *Journal of Organizational Behavior, 33*, 589–594.

Hobfoll, S. (1989). Conservation of resources: A new attempt at conceptualizing stress. *American Psychologist, 44*, 513–524.

Hobfoll, S. (2002). Social and psychological resources and adaptation. *Review of General Psychology, 6*, 307–324.

Huang, L., & Luthans, F. (2014). Toward better understanding of the learning goal orientation-creativity relationship: The role of psychological capital. *Applied Psychology: An International Review*, doi:10.111/apps.12028.

Hubbard, D. W. (2010). *How to measure anything: Finding the value of "intangibles" in business* (2nd ed.). Hoboken, NJ: Wiley.

Jensen, S. M., & Luthans, F. (2002). The impact of hope in the entrepreneurial process: Exploratory research findings. In *Decision Sciences Institute Conference Proceedings*. San Diego, CA; Decision Sciences Institute.

Judge, T. A., & Bono, J. E. (2001). Relationship of core self-evaluations traits—self-esteem, generalized self-efficacy, locus of control, and emotional stability—with job satisfaction and job performance: A meta-analysis. *Journal of Applied Psychology, 86,* 80–92.

Kanter, R. M. (2004). *Confidence.* New York, NY: Crown Business.

Kluemper, D. H., Little, L. M., & DeGroot, T. (2009). State or trait: Effects of state optimism on job-related outcomes. *Journal of Organizational Behavior, 30,* 209–231.

Kobasa, S. (1979). Stressful life events, personality and health: An inquiry into hardiness. *Journal of Personality and Social Psychology, 37,* 1–11.

Kravetz, D. (2004). *Measuring human capital: Converting workplace behavior into dollars.* Mesa, AZ: KAP.

Linley, P. A., & Joseph, S. (Eds.). (2004). *Positive psychology in practice.* Hoboken, NJ: Wiley.

Lopez, S., & Snyder, C. R. (Eds.). (2003). *Positive psychological assessment: A handbook of models and measures.* Washington, DC: American Psychological Association.

Lopez, S., & Snyder, C. R. (Eds.). (2009). *Oxford handbook of positive psychology* (2nd ed.). New York, NY: Oxford University Press.

Luthans, B. C., Luthans, K. W., & Avey, J. B. (2014). Building the leaders of tomorrow: The development of academic psychological capital. *Journal of Leadership and Organizational Studies, 21,* 191–199.

Luthans, F. (2002a). The need for and meaning of positive organizational behavior. *Journal of Organizational Behavior, 23,* 695–706.

Luthans, F. (2002b). Positive organizational behavior: Developing and managing psychological strengths. *Academy of Management Executive, 16*(1), 57–72.

Luthans, F., Avey, J. B., Avolio, B. J., Norman, S. M., & Combs, G. J. (2006). Psychological capital development: Toward a micro-intervention. *Journal of Organizational Behavior, 27,* 387–393.

Luthans, F., Avey, J. B., Avolio, B. J., & Peterson, S. (2010). The development and resulting performance impact of positive psychological capital. *Human Resource Development Quarterly, 21,* 41–66.

Luthans, F., Avey, J. B., Clapp-Smith, R., & Li, W. (2008). More evidence of the value of Chinese workers' psychological capital: A potentially unlimited competitive resource? *International Journal of Human Resource Management, 19,* 818–827.

Luthans, F., Avey, J. B., & Patera, J. L. (2008). Experimental analysis of a web-based training intervention to develop positive psychological capital. *Academy of Management Learning and Education, 7,* 209–221.

Luthans, F., & Avolio, B. (2003). Authentic leadership: A positive development approach. In K. S. Cameron, J. E. Dutton, & R. E. Quinn (Eds.), *Positive organizational scholarship* (pp. 241–258). San Francisco, CA: Berrett-Koehler.

Luthans, F., Avolio, B. J., Avey, J. B., & Norman, S. M. (2007). Positive psychological capital: Measurement and relationship with performance and satisfaction. *Personnel Psychology, 60*, 541–572.

Luthans, F., & Jensen, S. M. (2002). Hope: A new positive strength for human resource development. *Human Resource Development Review, 1*, 304–322.

Luthans, F., Luthans, K., & Luthans, B. (2004). Positive psychological capital: Going beyond human and social capital. *Business Horizons, 47*(1), 45–50.

Luthans, F., Norman, S. M., & Hughes, L. (2006). Authentic leadership. In R. Burke & C. Cooper (Eds.), *Inspiring leaders* (pp. 84–204). London, UK: Routledge, Taylor & Francis.

Luthans, F., Van Wyk, R., & Walumbwa, F. O. (2004). Recognition and development of hope for South African organizational leaders. *Leadership and Organization Development Journal, 25*, 512–527.

Luthans, F., Vogelgesang, G. R., & Lester, P. B. (2006). Developing the psychological capital of resiliency. *Human Resource Development Review, 5*, 25–44.

Luthans, F., & Youssef, C. M. (2004). Human, social, and now positive psychological capital management: Investing in people for competitive advantage. *Organizational Dynamics, 33*(2), 143–160.

Luthans, F., & Youssef, C. M. (2007). Emerging positive organizational behavior. *Journal of Management, 33*, 321–349.

Luthans, F., Youssef, C. M., & Avolio, B. J. (2007). Psychological capital: Investing and developing positive organizational behavior. In D. Nelson & C. L. Cooper (Eds.), *Positive organizational behavior* (pp. 9–24). Thousand Oaks, CA: Sage.

Luthans, F., Youssef, C. M., Sweetman, D., & Harms, P. (2013). Meeting the leadership challenge of employee well-being through relationship PsyCap and health PsyCap. *Journal of Leadership and Organizational Studies, 20*, 114–129.

Lyubomirsky, S. (2007). *The how of happiness*. New York, NY: Penguin.

Magaletta, P. R. & Oliver, J. M. (1999). The hope construct, will and ways: Their relations with self-efficacy, optimism and well-being. *Journal of Clinical Psychology, 55*, 539–551.

Masten, A. S. (2001). Ordinary magic: Resilience processes in development. *American Psychologist, 56*, 227–239.

Masten, A. S., Cutuli, J. J., Herbers, J. E, & Reed, M. G. J. (2009). Resilience in Development. In S. J. Lopez & C. R. Snyder (Eds.), *Oxford handbook of positive psychology* (2nd ed., pp. 117–131). New York, NY: Oxford University Press.

Mathe-Soulek, K., Scott-Halsell, S., Kim, S., & Krawczyk, M. (2014). Psychological capital in the quick serve restaurant industry: A study of unit-level performance. *Journal of Hospitality & Tourism Research*, doi:10.1177/1096348014550923

McKenny, A. F., Short, J. C., & Payne, T. (2013). Using computer-aided text analysis to elevate constructs: An illustration using psychological capital. *Organizational Research Methods, 16,* 152–184.

Memili, E., Welsh, D., & Luthans, F. (2013). Going beyond research on goal setting: A proposed role for organizational psychological capital of family firms. *Entrepreneurhsip Theory and Practice, 37,* 1289–1296.

Memili, E., Welsh, D. H., & Kaciak, E. (2014). Organizational psychological capital of family franchise firms through the lens of the leader-member exchange theory. *Journal of Leadership and Organizational Studies, 21,* 200–209.

Meyer, J. P., Stanley, L. J., & Vandenberg, R. J. (2013). A person-centered approach to the study of commitment. *Human Resource Management Review, 23,* 190–202.

Newman, A., Ucbasaran, D., Zhu, F., & Hirst, G. (2014). Psychological capital: A review and synthesis. *Journal of Organizational Behavior, 35,* S120–S138.

Parker, S. (1998). Enhancing role-breadth self-efficacy: The roles of job enrichment and other organizational interventions. *Journal of Applied Psychology, 83,* 835–852.

Peterson, C. (2000). The future of optimism. *American Psychologist, 55,* 44–55.

Peterson, C., & Seligman, M. (2004). *Character strengths and virtues.* Washington, DC: American Psychological Association.

Peterson, S. J., Balthazard, P. A., Waldman, D. A., & Thatcher, R. W. (2008). Neuroscientific implications of psychological capital. *Organizational Dynamics, 37,* 342–353.

Peterson, S. J., & Byron, K. (2008). Exploring the role of hope in performance: Results from four studies. *Journal of Organizational Behavior, 29,* 785–803.

Peterson, S. J., & Luthans, F. (2003). The positive impact and development of hopeful leaders. *Leadership and Organization Development Journal, 24*(1), 26–31.

Peterson, S. J., Luthans, F., Avolio, B. J., Walumbwa, F. O., & Zhang, Z. (2011). Psychological capital and employee performance: A latent growth modeling approach. *Personnel Psychology, 64,* 427–450.

Pfeffer, J., & Sutton, R. I. (2006). Evidenced-based management. *Harvard Business Review, 84*(1), 63–74.

Pluess, M., & Belsky, J. (2013). Vantage sensitivity: Individual differences in response to positive experiences. *Psychological Bulletin, 139,* 901–916.

Rand, K. L., Martin, A. D., & Shea, A. (2011). Hope, but not optimism, predicts academic performance of law students beyond previous academic achievement. *Journal of Research in Personality, 45,* 683–686.

Rini, C. K., Dunkel-Schetter, C., Wadhwa, P. D., & Sandman, C. A. (1999). Psychological adaptation and birth outcomes: The role of personal resources, stress, and socio-cultural context in pregnancy. *Health Psychology, 18,* 333–345.

Scheier, M. F., & Carver, C. S. (1987). Dispositional optimism and physical well-being: The influence of generalized outcome expectancies on health. *Journal of Personality, 55,* 169–210.

Schmidt, F. (2009). Select on intelligence. In E. Locke (Ed.), *Handbook of principles of organizational behavior* (2nd ed., pp. 3–17). West Sussex, UK: Wiley.

Schneider, S. L. (2001). In search of realistic optimism. *American Psychologist, 56*, 250–263.

Seligman, M. E. P. (1998). *Learned optimism.* New York, NY: Pocket Books.

Snyder, C. R. (1995). Managing for high hope. *R & D Innovator, 4*(6), 6–7.

Snyder, C. R. (2000). *Handbook of hope.* San Diego, CA: Academic Press.

Snyder, C. R., Harris, C., Anderson, J. R., Holleran, S. A., Irving, L. M., Sigmon, S. T., . . . Harney, P. (1991). The will and the ways: Development and validation of an individual differences measure of hope. *Journal of Personality and Social Psychology, 60*, 570–585.

Snyder, C. R., Irving, L., & Anderson, J. (1991). Hope and health: Measuring the will and the ways. In C. R. Snyder & D. R. Forsyth (Eds.), *Handbook of social and clinical psychology* (pp. 285–305). Elmsford, NY: Pergamon.

Snyder, C. R., Sympson, S. C., Ybasco, F. C., Borders, T. F., Babyak, M. A., & Higgins, R. L. (1996). Development and validation of the state hope scale. *Journal of Personality and Social Psychology, 70*, 321–335.

Spreitzer, G., & Sonenshein, S. (2003). Positive deviance and extraordinary organization. In K. Cameron, J. K. Dutton, & R. Quinn (Eds.), *Positive organizational scholarship* (pp. 207–224). San Francisco, CA: Berrett Koehler.

Reichard, R. J., Dollwet, M., & Louw-Potgieter, J. (2014). Development of cross-cultural psychological capital and its relationship with cultural intelligence and ethnocentrism. *Journal of Leadership and Organizational Studies, 21*, 150–164.

Stajkovic, A. D., & Luthans, F. (1998a). Self-efficacy and work-related performance: A meta-analysis. *Psychological Bulletin, 124*, 240–261.

Stajkovic, A. D., & Luthans, F. (1998b). Social cognitive theory and self-efficacy: Going beyond traditional motivational and behavioral approaches. *Organizational Dynamics, 26*, 62–74.

Story, J. S. P., Youssef, C. M., Luthans, F., Barbuto, J. E., & Bovaird, J. (2013). Contagion effect of global leaders' positive psychological capital on followers: Does distance and quality of relationship matter? *International Journal of Human Resource Management, 24*, 2534–2553.

Sutcliffe, K. M., & Vogus, T. (2003). Organizing for resilience. In K. S. Cameron, J. E. Dutton, & R. E. Quinn (Eds.), *Positive organizational scholarship* (pp. 94–110). San Francisco, CA: Berrett-Koehler.

Thoits, P. (1994). Stressors and problem solving: The individual as a psychological activist. *Journal of Health and Social Behavior, 35*, 143–160.

Tong, E., Fredrickson, B. E., Chang, W., & Lim, Z. X. (2010). Re-examining hope: The roles of agency thinking and pathways thinking. *Cognition and Emotion, 24*, 1207–1215.

Wagnild, G. M., & Young, H. M. (1993). *Journal of Nursing Management, 1*(2), 165–178.

Wang, H., Sui, Y., Luthans, F., Wang, D., & Wu, Y. (2014). Impact of authentic leadership on performance: Role of followers' positive psychological capital and relational processes. *Journal of Organizational Behavior, 35,* 5–12.

Wernsing, T. (2014). Psychological capital: A test of measurement invariance across 12 national cultures. *Journal of Leadership and Organization Studies, 21,* 179–190.

Whetten, D., Felin, T., & King, B. (2009). The practice of theory borrowing in organization studies. *Journal of Management, 35,* 537–563.

Youssef, C. M. (2011). Recent events in Egypt and the Middle East: Background, direct observations and a positive analysis. *Organizational Dynamics, 40,* 222–234.

Youssef, C. M., & Luthans, F. (2003). Immigrant psychological capital: Contribution to the war for talent and competitive advantage. *Singapore Nanyang Business Review, 2*(2), 1–14.

Youssef, C. M., & Luthans, F. (2005a). Resiliency development of organizations, leaders and employees: Multi-level theory building for sustained performance. In W. Gardner, B. Avolio, & F. Walumbwa (Eds.), *Authentic leadership theory and practice: Origins, effects and development. Monographs in leadership and management* (Vol. 3, pp. 303–343). Oxford, UK: Elsevier.

Youssef, C. M., & Luthans, F. (2005b). A positive organizational behavior approach to ethical performance. In R. Giacalone, C. Jurkiewicz, & C. Dunn (Eds.), *Positive psychology in business ethics and corporate social responsibility* (pp. 1–22). Greenwich, CT: Information Age.

Youssef, C. M., & Luthans, F. (2006). Positivity in the Middle East: Developing hopeful Egyptian organizational leaders. In W. Mobley & E. Weldon (Eds.), *Advances in global leadership* (Vol. 4, pp. 283–297). Oxford, UK: Elsevier.

Youssef, C. M., & Luthans, F. (2007). Positive organizational behavior in the workplace: The impact of hope, optimism, and resilience. *Journal of Management, 33,* 774–800.

Youssef, C. M., & Luthans, F. (2013). Developing psychological capital in organizations: Cognitive, affective and conative contributions of happiness. In S. A. David, I. Boniwell, & A. C. Ayers (Eds.), *Oxford handbook of happiness* (pp. 751–766). New York, NY: Oxford University Press.

Youssef-Morgan, C. M., & Luthans, F. (2013). Psychological capital theory: Toward a positive holistic model. In A. Bakker (Ed.), *Advances in positive organizational psychology.* Bingley, UK: Emerald.

PSYCAP EFFICACY

CONFIDENCE

Opening Video: Albert Bandura on Social Cognitive Theory and Self-Efficacy

Video link: http://www.youtube.com/watch?v=OMBlwjEoy j4&list=TLkARooMHClsk (or search for "Bandura's Social Cognitive Theory: An Introduction")

Albert Bandura is a longtime professor at Stanford University and is widely recognized as one of the most influential scholars in the history of psychology. He is considered the father of social cognitive theory and is best known for his work in self-efficacy and most recently agency theory. Bandura's theories and research have significantly influenced our work in general, particularly psychological capital.

Questions for reflection and/or discussion:

1. How does efficacy influence success in various areas of life?
2. How can efficacy be developed?
3. Does success equal efficacy?
4. Is there a downside to efficacy?
5. How much is efficacy shaped by others' contribution to one's development?

In answering each of these questions, use the content of the video, then reflect on your personal experiences and/or observations of others' experiences.

Do you believe in yourself? Do you know that you have what it takes to be successful? These questions could also be lead-ins for our other PsyCap chapters on hope and optimism, but they are especially relevant to this chapter on PsyCap efficacy.

Underlying our capacity to engage in various activities is our motivation, which is often based on our beliefs and perceptions of the probability that we will be successful in our endeavors. Albert Bandura (1997) referred to the probability that people as "agents" estimate that they can take on a particular task as an estimate of their efficacy. For example, we can observe leaders to see whether they are able to inspire others to work or to get others to think about problems and issues in new ways. The probability level to which leaders are able to do just that reflects their level of efficacy.

Although commonly conceptualized as applying to a very specific set of tasks in a specific context, there is increasing recognition that individuals can also have a "generalized" level of efficacy across a common domain of challenges, tasks, and contexts such as is found in the workplace (Parker, 1998). For example, skilled employees may believe they are good problem-solvers whether working on an engineering task or a pricing issue. This broader, domain-level sense of efficacy is a more realistic approach for conceptualizing, measuring, and developing efficacy, and it is a more effective perspective to realize the full scope of its potential benefits (Bandura, 2012).

There is increasing evidence that the answers to the questions posed earlier are not just found in your knowledge, skills, or abilities, not just in your IQ (or EQ, emotional intelligence) or your personality traits, although these can all help. We have argued in the introductory chapter that your PsyCap has a large input into who you are, what you believe you can do, what you do, and who you can become. In particular, perhaps the strength and psychological capacity that best meets the PsyCap criteria outlined in Chapter 1 of being theory and research based, state-like and open to development, and related to performance impact is PsyCap efficacy or simply PsyCap confidence. So a good answer to the opening questions is your level of self-efficacy. It motivates you to choose and welcome challenges, and to use your strengths and your skills to meet and, in many cases, excel in meeting those challenges. It encourages and energizes you to pursue your goals and invest the time and hard work that may be necessary to accomplish them. It helps you to persevere when you are faced with obstacles that may otherwise lead you to give up, and thus it also relates to your hope, optimism, and resilience, which we explained earlier as being part of the synergy associated with PsyCap. It is something you have learned about yourself and developed over time. It is an aspect of yourself and your awareness about who you are that can be positively changed or further developed to spur you on to what you can become.

You may think of yourself as a very confident person, or otherwise. However, in order to accurately assess your level of PsyCap efficacy, you need to analyze what it is that you are confident about and how that confidence may vary over time and situations. People tend to have comfort zones, areas that they have mastered and thus feel very confident about. Most people also have new domains that they are interested in venturing into some day, which if related to domains they have been successful in the past, will likely boost their efficacy for a new challenge in a related domain. However, this only happens if they can overcome their fears and resistance to change, raise their confidence level beyond a certain threshold, and take and welcome that important first step.

As a way to get you as the reader more personally engaged in the understanding of each of the four major components of PsyCap, we will start off this and the subsequent three chapters on hope, optimism, and resilience with an exercise and case example. We feel this will not only get you more actively involved in the learning process but will also cause you to reflect on your own PsyCap development and give more meaning to the academically based discussion of the PsyCap constructs in the balance of the chapters.

So, after the following brief reflection exercise, this chapter will present an in-depth discussion of the meaning, process, and development of the important efficacy or confidence component of PsyCap.

Personal Reflections Exercise on PsyCap Efficacy

As part of this opening reflection exercise for PsyCap efficacy, we ask you to choose a specific domain of your life you feel very confident about. It can be your job, your education, your family, your friendships, a favorite sport, a leadership role, or a hobby. Then, carefully note the various tasks that you need to perform in this domain in order to achieve success. For example, at work, you may need to utilize your analytical skills to solve problems or make decisions, especially if you are in a leadership role. Most managers and employees also need to use their communication skills in interacting with others and with customers to convince them to pursue the solutions that the leader has come up with. For example, those in marketing or sales often capitalize on their presentation or closure skills. Your job may also involve some written communication, in which your writing skills can become vital. If you are in an administrative role, organization and coordination skills are important. Other positions may require negotiation skills, creativity, or use of social media. The list can become quite lengthy when you break it down into the specific tasks within the larger domain of inquiry.

Next, prioritize your list: focus on the most critical three or four tasks, those that have the biggest impact on overall success. Then, on a scale of 0% to 100%, how confident are you that you can:

- At least get by on these tasks?
- Meet your own and others' expectations in performing these tasks?
- Excel in accomplishing these tasks?

Next, we ask you to leave your comfort zone and areas of mastery and to start focusing on your dreams and aspirations. Choose any domain of life that you have always wanted to try or to be better at. Using similar analysis, try to break it down into its critical tasks or components. Then, use the three questions again as guidelines for assessing your level of confidence regarding each of your identified tasks or components. Can you generalize what you are good at in one domain to some of these new, yet unexplored domains?

What were some of your key discoveries with the exercise? How far from the mastery set of domains did you choose to focus your energies on? In other words, did you step outside your "comfort zone"? Was the challenge you identified related to your strengths, or was it an area that had no previous linkages to what you felt confident in being able to do? Did you think about what you couldn't do before what you can do now, thus focusing on the negative side? What would boost your efficacy for addressing these new challenges in terms of support, guidance, and/or resources?

Five Key Discoveries of PsyCap Efficacy

As you go through the reflection exercise, you are likely to experience at least five important discoveries about PsyCap efficacy. These illuminating discoveries should help you understand the nature of your own PsyCap efficacy, and they will hopefully not only guide your journey of further developing and nurturing your own confidence level in various life domains but also serve as a platform and point of departure for better understanding the more academic-based discussion of PsyCap confidence and efficacy that follows.

Discovery 1: PsyCap Efficacy Is Domain Specific

Based on your reflective analysis, you should begin to realize that no matter how confident you are in some areas of your life, you may be very unsure about other areas. In other words, your PsyCap efficacy is generally more specific to the domain being analyzed. Thus, previously built confidence in one domain may not be readily transferable to other domains that you are either familiar with or not familiar with until you uncover some of the common elements across domains that contribute to success. For example, as a leader, you may be highly confident in being a great one-on-one developer. However, being an inspirational platform speaker may be way outside your comfort zone and have only a small overlap with your ability to read and develop others one at a time. However, you may see that there are elements like focusing on individuals that may be generalized to how you convey your views for handling followers in a different setting, thus using your strength from one domain in another related domain.

Discovery 2: PsyCap Efficacy Comes From Practice or Mastery

It is likely that the tasks that you are most confident about are the ones that you have repeatedly practiced and mastered. Tasks that you are not confident about are likely to be ones that you tend to avoid or in which you have little experience. Efficacy is based on your estimate of your future probability of success, and therefore it requires that you have some experience to come up with a positive estimate of your efficacy. However, as we said earlier, some people can generalize positive experiences from one task to another in judging their efficacy, leading to a more positive sense of generalized efficacy. For example, someone who has great balance riding a horse may do very well on a snow board, once he or she realizes that balance matters in both domains!

Discovery 3: There Is Always Room for Improvement in PsyCap Efficacy

Even in the domains that you thought you are very confident about, there are still tasks with which you are not really comfortable. For example, you may be a great technical person but not a people person. You may have wonderful social skills but worry that you cannot think analytically as well as you should.

Discovery 4: Your PsyCap Efficacy Is Influenced by Others

What other people tell you about yourself affects your own self-evaluation. If others believe that you can succeed, many times they can persuade you to think the same way; thus, in that way, other people can be a "means" to boosting one's own efficacy. At the extreme, we refer to this as a self-fulfilling prophecy or Pygmalion effect, where someone believes in you and that alone causes you to believe in yourself. More important, when you watch others who may be similar to you in many respects accomplish certain tasks and achieve certain goals that are of interest to you, you start developing confidence that you can do that also. This sort of vicarious learning or modeling is a very powerful form of increasing your efficacy, oftentimes without a lot of forethought on your part. The key is your ability to identify with the role model being observed, and that the model is relevant to you, so that you can realistically relate this individual's success to what you can do.

Discovery 5: Your PsyCap Efficacy Is Variable

Your confidence level depends on many factors. Some of those factors are within your control, such as gaining the knowledge, skills, and abilities that can help you accomplish a certain goal. Other factors may exist in the context within which you need to execute the steps necessary for a goal to be accomplished. For example, you may have a wonderful idea for an innovative product, but your organization may lack the financial resources to help you make your dream come true. Even your physical and psychological well-being can contribute to your PsyCap efficacy. For example, when you lead a healthy lifestyle and are content in your relationships, you tend to be more confident than when you have insomnia and get little sleep or are in constant conflict with your spouse. In fact, having the proper resources can be viewed as another form of efficacy known as "means efficacy" (Eden, Ganzach, Flumin-Granat, & Zignman, 2010). You can judge whether you have the means to be successful, and this can contribute to or detract from your efficacy.

Hopefully, upon reflection you actually experienced most of these five discoveries about PsyCap efficacy from your exercise, or at least have insight into them. Now, as in the next three chapters, we will turn to a more in-depth discussion of the nature and ways to develop PsyCap efficacy.

What Is PsyCap Efficacy?

Drawing from Bandura's (1986, 1997) extensive theory and research, PsyCap efficacy, or simply confidence, can be defined as "one's belief about his or her ability to mobilize the motivation, cognitive resources, and courses of action necessary to execute a specific action within a given context" (Stajkovic & Luthans, 1998b, p. 66). Although Bandura (1997) sparingly uses the term "confidence" and most efficacy theorists tend to treat confidence as conceptually subordinate to efficacy, especially in positive psychology the two terms are used more interchangeably (e.g., see Maddux, 2009). Moreover, when used in the more applied domain of sports or business performance, "confidence" is the preferred term (e.g., see Kanter, 2004).

In PsyCap we have chosen to use the two terms interchangeably to reflect the rich theoretical and research base of efficacy (e.g., Bandura, 1997) and the more applied orientation associated with confidence (e.g., Kanter, 2004). Whether we use "efficacy" or "confidence" in the earlier definition, it is important to emphasize the link to one's belief. Self-efficacious people are distinguished by five important characteristics:

1. They set high goals for themselves and self-select into difficult tasks.
2. They welcome and thrive on challenge.
3. They are highly self-motivated.
4. They invest the necessary effort to accomplish their goals.
5. When faced with obstacles, they persevere.

These five characteristics equip high-efficacy individuals with the capacity to independently develop and effectively perform, even with little external input for extended periods of time. High PsyCap efficacy people do not wait for challenging goals to be set for them, which is often referred to as "discrepancy reduction." On the contrary, they create their own discrepancies, by continuously challenging themselves with higher and higher self-set goals and by seeking and voluntarily opting for difficult tasks. Self-doubt, skepticism, negative feedback, social criticism, obstacles and setbacks, and even repeated failure, which can be devastating for people with low efficacy, have little impact on highly efficacious individuals (Bandura & Locke, 2003).

The Supporting Cognitive Processes

Deeply based in Bandura's (1986, 1997, 2001) social cognitive theory, PsyCap efficacy is built on his five identified cognitive processes that are vital constituents of the efficacy equation: symbolizing, forethought, observation, self-regulation, and self-reflection. For example, Jerome is confident that he can help the firm he works for in winning an important contract. In *symbolizing*, or creating a mental image/model in his mind, he may study the potential client's decision-making process and develop a mental model of the players involved, their capacities and relative power, and the nature of their interactions. This symbolizing can then serve as a guide for future actions, such as contacting the right people at the right times and catering to the needs of the various stakeholders involved based on their relative weight in the process.

In the process of *forethought*, Jerome plans his actions based on the level of performance he is targeting (i.e., the performance impact point), and the consequences he expects in large part based on past experiences and successes. For example, if Jerome's research supports that the client is looking for the cheapest possible product, he will make sure that his proposal portrays an efficient, cost-effective, no-frills solution. On the other hand, if he knows that the client emphasizes quality and professionalism, then he is likely to offer a range of competitive but upscale quality alternatives, focus on the uniqueness and sophistication of his products, return all of the client's representatives' phone calls very promptly, and be fully prepared with information that he expects may be requested.

Jerome is also likely to utilize his *observational* (or modeling) cognitive processing in which he would learn from relevant others, such as his manager and his more experienced colleagues. He feels he can learn from their advice and feedback, but more important, he learns what tends to work and what does not by watching them in action, their winning performance behaviors, and especially the reinforcing consequences that their actions tend to accomplish. The observational component in this process highlights the importance of one's manager displaying certain behaviors and actions that will "teach" followers how to be able to achieve positive results themselves. Oftentimes, managers are not cognizant of the fact that by their actions they are teaching followers across many levels to become more efficacious and, of course, in the case of ineffective managers, less efficacious.

Jerome will need to utilize his *self-regulatory* processing in which he agentically sets specific goals and standards for his own performance and constantly assesses where he stands in relation to these self-set standards. This will help him better focus on the energies needed in order to develop, improve, and eventually reach his goals. For example, as Jerome prepares to win the contract (the goal), he may realize that he needs to further study his client or adapt his products in order to create a winning proposal. Without a sufficient level of agency to start, Jerome would not even consider pursuing these alternative pathways.

Oftentimes, when we are trying to change the behavior of individuals, we are in effect trying to stimulate self-awareness to lead to a change in self-regulation. The self-regulation part is where thinking and behavior actually change, and it is probably highly impacted by the receptivity of the context to the change. For example, if the organizational values and culture encourage risk-taking and change and there is considerable social and financial support for it, then one's self-regulated change in thinking and behavior will be reinforced and will tend to occur again in the future. In this case, we highlight that the context matters to translating self-awareness to changes in self-regulation.

Finally, and perhaps most directly relevant to Jerome's efficacy, he uses his *self-reflective* processing. Specifically, he reflects back on his past actions, successes, and failures. Extracting some learning from these previous experiences,

Jerome reaches a specific level of efficacy for his current challenge, namely winning the contract for himself and the company. If Jerome embraces and channels his cognitive processing of symbolizing, forethought, observation, self-regulation, and self-reflection in the right direction, he is likely not only to win the contract but also to build his future PsyCap efficacy and subsequent success in similar challenge domains. In other words, efficacy breeds success, and success breeds efficacy, but importantly, as will be explained later, success does not just equal efficacy, in that we must also include how success is interpreted by someone like Jerome.

Somewhat paradoxically, by looking back, the individual is actually moving forward in terms of development of efficacy. It is why we oftentimes argue that one needs to take the time to debrief both successes and failures in order to advance in terms of self-awareness, self-regulation, and self-development. By "debriefing," we mean taking time to reflect, learn, and then to utilize that self-knowledge to improve and move forward effectively; that is, this process allows you to figure out missteps and avoid them in the future.

Other Factors Influencing PsyCap Efficacy

The earlier example provides two key points about the nature of PsyCap efficacy. First, although success has an important, in fact, the most important, input into one's confidence or efficacy, success does not equal efficacy. Instead, as demonstrated by the example of Jerome, it is not just his previous success but also his cognitive processing (i.e., symbolizing, forethought, observation, self-regulation, and self-reflection) that determines the input into his confidence and efficacy. For example, if the success came too easily to Jerome or was not the result of his efforts and abilities, he will probably not have enhanced subsequent efficacy—"Anyone could have done this." A good example would be those who build a very successful business from scratch. They would tend to have high efficacy based on this type of success, as they know full well how they have circumnavigated through a myriad of challenges. However, if their sons or daughters take over the business and it continues to be successful, this would not necessarily contribute to their efficacy because they did not do it themselves and it was relatively easy for them to simply maintain an established, successful business. This lack of opportunity for efficacy building is a major problem for succession in family firms.

Besides the nature of success in contributing to efficacy, a second point is that one's PsyCap efficacy tends to be specific to the domain at hand, in the example of Jerome winning a customer contract. Jerome's PsyCap efficacy does not necessarily carry over to other domains of his work or life. For example, if he is transferred to a technical job or decides to change his career, his previously built efficacy beliefs in his ability to win customer contracts may not be as relevant. He will need to experience success in his new domain and reinitiate his cognitive processing to interpret the relevance of that success to his agency in order to rebuild his efficacy. Using a sports analogy, an athletic young man may have high efficacy for playing basketball where he has experienced success, but not football where he has been unsuccessful. Carrying this even further, he may have high efficacy rebounding the basketball where he leads the team, but not shooting the ball where he has the lowest percentage on the team. Like Jerome, if this athlete switched sports or roles on the basketball team, he would need to practice to attain mastery and then reinitiate his cognitive processing to build efficacy in his new sport or role on the basketball team. Indeed, Michael Jordan, arguably the best basketball player to ever play the game, was just a mediocre minor league baseball player who could not hit a curve ball!

Another point to make about understanding PsyCap efficacy is its magnitude and strength. The magnitude dimension refers to the level of difficulty a person expects to successfully master. The strength dimension, on the other hand, is one's degree of certainty about the ability to achieve each level of difficulty (Bandura, 1997; Locke, Frederick, Lee, & Bobko, 1984; Stajkovic & Luthans, 1998b). For example, in the opening reflective exercise, you were given the opportunity to assess the magnitude and strength of your own PsyCap efficacy. We encourage you to reflect back on these earlier responses to the rating from 0% to 100% of how confident you were on your selected critical tasks and to spend some time in utilizing your cognitive capacities of symbolizing, forethought, observation, self-regulation, and self-reflection, in regard to what you selected for the exercise and for your various roles and life domains. This reflection exercise can put more personal meaning and understanding into the points just discussed about the nature of efficacy.

PsyCap Efficacy and Work Performance

Unlike PsyCap hope and resilience where workplace applications are relatively recent and still emerging, the relationship between PsyCap efficacy and work-related performance has been well established in the research literature. For example, a meta-analytical investigation of 114 studies showed a strong positive correlation (.38) between efficacy and work-related performance at the individual level (Stajkovic & Luthans, 1998a). Similar meta-analyses at the group level also support the relationship between collective efficacy and performance (Gully, Incalcaterra, Joshi, & Beaubien, 2002; Stajkovic, Lee, & Nyberg, 2009).

Indeed, this relationship between individual efficacy and performance is higher than meta-analyses of other widely recognized performance impact organizational behavior concepts and techniques such as goal setting (Kleingeld, van Mierlo, & Arends 2011; Wood, Mento, & Locke, 1987); feedback (Kluger & DeNisi, 1996); job satisfaction (Judge, Thoresen, Bono, & Patton, 2001); the Big Five personality traits, including conscientiousness (Barrick & Mount, 1991); transformational leadership (Avolio, 1999; Wang, Oh, Courtright, & Colbert, 2011); and organizational behavior modification or O.B. Mod. (Stajkovic & Luthans, 1997, 2003). In addition to the Stajkovic and Luthans's (1998a) study, there are several other large-scale studies, meta-analyses, and comprehensive reviews consistently demonstrating the strong relationship between individual efficacy and the level of motivation and performance (Bandura, 2012; Bandura & Locke, 2003).

Although PsyCap efficacy is domain specific, there are numerous studies showing its positive impact in various workplace applications. The long list includes leadership efficacy (Chemers, Watson, & May, 2000; Hannah, Avolio, Luthans, & Harms, 2008; Luthans, Luthans, Hodgetts, & Luthans, 2001; Youssef & Luthans, 2012; Youssef-Morgan & Luthans, 2013), moral/ethical efficacy (May, Chan, Hodges, & Avolio, 2003; Palmer, 2013; Youssef & Luthans, 2005), creative efficacy (Abbott, 2010; Richter, Hirst, van Knippenberg, & Baer, 2012; Tierney & Farmer, 2002), test-taking efficacy of job applicants (Truxillo, Bauer, Campion, & Paronto, 2002), computer efficacy (Thatcher & Perrewe, 2002), job change efficacy (Cunningham et al., 2002), participation efficacy (Lam, Chen, & Schaubroeck, 2002), career decision-making efficacy (Nilsson, Schmidt, & Meek, 2002), learning efficacy (Ramakrishna, 2002), and entrepreneurial efficacy (Boyd & Vozikis, 1994; Chandler & Jansen, 1997; Chen, Greene, & Crick, 1998; Drnovšek, Wincent, & Cardon, 2010; Hayward, Forster, Sarasvathy, & Fredrickson, 2009; Luthans & Ibrayeva, 2006; Neck, Neck, Manz, & Godwin, 1999; Wilson, Kickul, & Marlino, 2007; Zhao, Seibert, & Hills, 2005).

Besides performance outcomes, efficacy has also been shown to relate to work attitudes across cultures (Badran & Youssef-Morgan, 2014; Luthans, Zhu, & Avolio, 2006) and enhanced health and psychosocial capacities (Holden, 1991; Holden, Moncher, Schinke, & Barker, 1990; Luthans, Youssef, Sweetman, & Harms, 2013). Moreover, efficacy has often been supported as a significant contributor to effective functioning under stress, fear, and challenge, primarily due to one's perceptions of personal control (Bandura & Locke, 2003). Again, the depth and breadth of research findings support PsyCap confidence or efficacy as best meeting the PsyCap criterion of having an impact on performance outcomes and, as we will see next, also being open to development.

As we learn more about the transfer of efficacy from one domain to another, we may be able to also accelerate the development of self-efficacy in a new, challenging domain. For example, future training efforts to develop PsyCap efficacy may focus on helping the individual to identify points of transferability from success in one domain to another. Specifically, what are the criteria in one domain that apply to another, for example, technical skills, that can be leveraged to enhance efficacy across seemingly different performance domains? Such transferability is likely associated with the previously noted concept of generalized efficacy.

Developing PsyCap Confidence and Efficacy in Organizational Leaders and Employees

As pointed out in Chapter 2, PsyCap hope, optimism, and resilience have theoretical and research support for being state-like. However, we will recognize in the more in-depth discussion of these constructs that they can perhaps be better presented along a conceptual continuum of being both trait-like *and*, as components of PsyCap, state-like and open to development. This conceptual continuum does not apply as much to efficacy. Following Bandura's (1997) widely recognized theory that we briefly summarized earlier, efficacy is clearly more state-like and thus readily open to development.

The strong theoretical foundation and considerable research supports that PsyCap confidence and efficacy can be developed and enhanced in today's organizational leaders and employees. However, this efficacy development will likely vary in difficulty depending on the challenge within the domain. In particular, Bandura (1997) and others have demonstrated that efficacy can be developed through the opportunities to experience mastery/success, vicarious learning/ modeling, social persuasion and positive feedback, and psychological and physiological arousal and well-being (Bandura, 1997, 2000; Hannah et al., 2008; Luthans et al., 2001; Luthans, Luthans, & Luthans, 2004; Luthans & Youssef, 2004; Maddux, 2009; Stajkovic & Luthans, 1998a, 1998b). These efficacy-building experiences can occur through highly focused workplace micro-interventions (Luthans, Avey, Avolio, Norman, & Combs, 2006; Luthans, Avey, Avolio, & Peterson, 2010; Luthans, Avey, & Patera, 2008), as well as through simple, less formal initiatives, and even through spontaneous life events (Avolio & Luthans, 2006; Luthans & Avolio, 2003). The following sections provide details of the four major identified sources of efficacy and how they can be developed.

Mastery Experiences and Success to Develop PsyCap Efficacy

While "practice makes perfect," success builds confidence. As we noted, the most tried-and-true approach to developing PsyCap confidence or efficacy is repeatedly experiencing success in accomplishing the tasks in which efficacy is to be built. As we emphasized, however, success does not equate with efficacy because of the cognitive processing of the success, or how it is ultimately interpreted by the person. Yet success definitely contributes to confidence, which in turn leads to even higher performance and success, and thus there can be a continual upward spiral. However, this does not mean that low performers, or those who have never had any experience with a certain task, are destined to be failures.

There are many approaches that allow managers and employees to build their mastery experiences and thus their PsyCap confidence over time. For example, a trainer or coach can break down a complex task into subcomponents and teach the trainee each of the simple subskills, one at a time. This allows the trainee to experience "small wins" more frequently, which in turn helps in building PsyCap efficacy. These simpler tasks and skills can then be gradually integrated into a broader, more complex whole, with opportunities for practice and mastery at each step of the way.

Another way to provide managers and employees with mastery experiences is to intentionally place them in situations where the probability of success is relatively high, where they have a good chance to experience success. This is why selection, orientation, placement, mentoring, and career planning are so important. People need to be set up for success as much as possible, rather than put into uncertain environments that turn out to not be a good fit for them, which results in poor performance or failure. Thus, it is important to provide people with environments where they can experience a sufficient level of success to continue to work toward mastery.

In the training arena, stretch goals should be established and the training should be conducted in a risk- and distraction-free environment. Such training goals and conditions lead to a higher probability of correctly assimilating and applying the new knowledge, skills, and abilities. These training procedures minimize the transfer of training problems and have better chances of mastery and success, which in turn can enhance PsyCap efficacy. Simulations, case studies, what-if analyses, and other hands-on but off-the-job development techniques that are commonly utilized in professional workshops and executive retreats also tend to promote PsyCap efficacy in a safe, focused, and positive environment. These environments allow individuals to systematically break down how they performed in a task, and then to go back and try again, without a great deal of costs associated with failure. The higher the "fidelity" of the simulations or exercises for the real work to be done, the more likely the individual's efficacy will generalize from the training to the real-world context.

Vicarious Learning/Modeling to Develop PsyCap Efficacy

In many situations, opportunities for mastery and successful experiences are unavailable or just do not happen due to circumstances beyond the control of the individual, the group, or even the organization (e.g., budget constraints or not technically possible). However, fortunately, the trial-and-error process or direct experience, often associated with mastery and success, is not the only way to build PsyCap efficacy. Using cognitive processes such as the vicarious learning/modeling presented earlier, people can also build their own confidence by observing relevant others' mastery experiences and successes, as well as their mistakes and failures.

Although directly experienced mastery and success are usually more effective than vicarious learning and modeling opportunities in building PsyCap efficacy, observational experiences allow individuals to process and learn from the success and mistakes of others and selectively imitate their successful actions. This learning enhances the observer's own chances for future personal mastery experiences and success. However, in order for modeling experiences to be effective in enhancing PsyCap efficacy, there must be both model and situational similarity, and time allocated by the learner for some degree of reflection and practice.

The more similar the role model is to the developing manager or employee, the more likely the observer's PsyCap efficacy will be affected by that role model's success and desired, reinforcing consequences. This implies that peer-mentors, self-managed teams, and even informally being "shown the ropes" by respected colleagues at the same level may be more effective for building PsyCap efficacy than formal training by an extremely knowledgeable but far-removed executive, professional trainer, or renowned external consultant. Peers tend to be perceived as more similar in terms of background, motivation, abilities, and career goals. Thus, observing respected peers perform and be reinforced can instill in the developing manager or employee the belief that "if they can do it, I can do it, too," and their efficacy is enhanced. By picking the right role models that trainees can identify with, they are more likely to positively accelerate their levels of efficacy. Also by picking peers in context, the challenges associated with transferring what was learned are minimized.

In addition to relating to the model, the more similar the situation being observed is to the real task such as noted earlier in terms of "fidelity," the more likely the observational experience will enhance PsyCap efficacy. This is in line with PsyCap efficacy being domain specific. From the analysis of traditional training experiences, it is clear that most of these interventions suffer from lack of subsequent transferability back to the real job. This is because, in the hopes of building the trainees' confidence, traditional training tends to present oversimplified, idealized versions of the job's realities and exclude many of the complexities, interactions, and uncertainties involved back on the job. Efficacy-building interventions need to present realistically challenging expectations (e.g., a realistic job preview), rather than act as unrealistic, "incubator" training and development environments that rarely exist in today's typically turbulent workplace. The use of real cases the participants can identify with is critical to enhancing the transferability of what was learned into efficacious practice. The same is true of holding the training sessions in the actual environment as much as possible with its typical sights and sounds instead of an unrealistic sterile classroom-type environment.

Particularly in managerial decision-making, highly technical situations and other complex cognitive endeavors, observing the final decisions and behavioral patterns of a role model may not be sufficient for efficacy building. The developing individual needs to also be able to follow the often unobservable logic of the model and understand the reasoning process, criteria, and underlying assumptions that led to the selected course of action and/or pattern of behavior. In such complex situations, the model can facilitate building the PsyCap efficacy of the observer by "thinking aloud" and encouraging the vicarious learner to do the same, as they cognitively contemplate situational complexities and weigh potential alternatives.

What if relevant role models and comparable situations are not available? In today's environment dominated by tumultuous change and paradigm shifts, leaders, and even front-line employees are often expected to swiftly act upon scarce information and uncertain probabilities. In such situations, imagining oneself succeeding in a certain situation, and mentally rehearsing one's potential actions in various contingencies of the situation, can also enhance PsyCap efficacy. In other words, actual mastery and vicarious learning can be substituted with "imaginal" experiences, in which the imagined successful self becomes the role model in imagined challenging situations. This involves what we have referred to as bringing the future back to the present and moving from the actual self to the possible self in authentic leadership development (Avolio & Luthans, 2006). Specifically, as we emphasized in Chapter 1, we are proposing that individuals should think about their possible self engaging in a new challenge. It is this imagined self that motivates a change in the current self, or what the individual feels capable of doing in a particular role or challenge. Of course, if the imagination is so unrealistic as to be applicable to the real context, additional support will need to be in place such as through coaching to move the individual's level of efficacy upward.

In many developmental contexts, including leadership and efficacy building, we are proposing that individuals need to be encouraged to see themselves in a role in which they have not served before. This can be done by providing them with successful role models to observe, by providing positive feedback, and by encouraging them to use reflection to learn from their experiences. All of these components make up what Bandura (2001) discussed as being the social learning theory process and being an agentic "producer" of one's behavior, and not just a "product."

Social Persuasion/Positive Feedback to Develop PsyCap Efficacy

Simply hearing others urge you on (i.e., have confidence in you) and provide positive feedback on your progress can transform your self-doubting beliefs into efficacy expectancies. In other words, as you listen to others' encouraging "you can do it" and "you are doing so well in accomplishing the first step of_____," your internal thoughts and beliefs begin to shift to a confident "I can do it" perspective and belief. In fact, over two decades of empirical research strongly support the impact that contingently applied positive feedback and social recognition has on enhancing employees' performance, even beyond monetary rewards and other motivational techniques (see Stajkovic & Luthans, 1997, 2003, for comprehensive meta-analyses).

The impact that these nonfinancial positive reinforcers such as attention, recognition, and positive feedback have on performance has been interpreted in terms of cognitive processes such as self-efficacy (Peterson & Luthans, 2006; Stajkovic & Luthans, 2001, 2003). In reality, most of today's organizations invest heavily in technical training and very costly financial reward systems. Yet most organizations and managers still tend to ignore a significant resource they possess in unlimited amounts and at no cost. This resource involves the powerful performance impact of acknowledging, genuinely appreciating, and providing positive feedback and recognition to employees that not only has a reinforcing effect on desired employee behaviors with performance impact but is also building their PsyCap efficacy.

Psychological and Physiological Arousal/Well-Being

Although less directly related to efficacy beliefs than success, modeling, and persuasion/feedback, people's emotional state or arousal and their psychological and physiological well-being can also contribute to their PsyCap efficacy. For instance, a positive psychological state can stimulate and energize people's cognitive processes of symbolizing, inquiry, forethought, observation, self-regulation, and self-reflection. This processing will tend to invigorate their perceptions and beliefs of confidence and personal control. On the other hand, an individual with a negative psychological state and outlook (e.g., someone who is burned out or stressed to the limit and falls into a downward spiral of ruminating) will tend to experience hopelessness, helplessness, pessimism, and a downward spiral of self-doubt and deteriorating efficacy.

For example, working with employees in an Animal Rescue center, we found that over time due to poor leadership, employees began to ruminate about their ability to save animals from being euthanized. Even where they could be successful, oftentimes they lacked the confidence to step up and show they could perform more effectively. Discussions with these staff members showed extensive ruminating about what did not work, what was not successful, and why things around here will never change. Thus, positive psychological states can boost individuals to support and sustain change in their perspective about what they can accomplish and in the aforementioned example a lot of that boost could have come from the leadership.

The same is true of physical health and fitness. Feeling good and being in good physical condition can have a positive impact on one's cognitive and emotional states, including efficacy beliefs and expectancies of success. Athletic and military training recognize this benefit of physical fitness. On the other hand, being ill, fatigued, and out of shape can have a negative impact. We know that when people are highly stressed, their physiological responses are degraded. This, in turn, can negatively impact their psychological processes, such as their confidence, information processing, and decision making.

Importantly, as we indicated, this mental and physical arousal and wellness do not have as big an impact as the other more focused sources of efficacy, but, if negative, it can be a major blow to one's level of efficacy. If one has "had it" emotionally or psychologically, or even worse is very physically ill, then efficacy rapidly deteriorates or goes to zero. The person really suffering psychologically or physically has little or no confidence left and may just give up, not only on a specific task, but also it may generalize to other domains.

Although certainly more difficult to control because of its often extraorganizational nature, organizations can still intervene and manage some dimensions of their employees' emotional, psychological, and physiological well-being, as noted with the Animal Rescue example. And we are seeing more and more in highly stressful healthcare settings, proper attention by leaders to the stress associated with healthcare delivery can have a profound impact on not only employee efficacy but also patient engagement and patient outcomes.

There are numerous things that organizations can do to boost efficacy, ranging from onsite exercise wellness programs, to family-friendly benefits such as childcare facilities, to comprehensive employee assistance programs, and even informal social activities and gatherings. These various programs can help today's organizational participants in managing the psychological and physical toll of an increasingly stressful work environment, with a documented, quantifiable bottom-line impact (Cascio & Boudreau, 2011).

The list of "Best Places to Work" (e.g., the renowned culture and benefits of Google, Zappos or software firm SAS) is proof that employee well-being can be accomplished with not only successful outcomes such as higher retention rates, but we would also argue higher levels of PsyCap efficacy leading to higher performance. Key to building these organizational contexts is the nature of leadership exhibited by the top management team and CEO, and how such leadership is cascaded across levels, which can determine the boundaries of the climate in the organization at subsequent levels (see Hannah et al., 2013).

By creating a more positive forward-seeking climate and culture that is supportive of well-being, it is likely that such leadership can reduce injury rates, stress, burnout, turnover, absenteeism, and disengagement. Positivity and authenticity from top leadership can have a contagion effect throughout the organization to not only improve performance and reduce stress and conflict but also build PsyCap efficacy (Avolio & Luthans, 2006; Clapp-Smith, Vogelgesang, & Avey, 2009; Luthans, Norman & Hughes, 2006; Rego, Sousa, Marques, & Pina e Cunha, 2012; Story, Youssef, Luthans, Barbuto & Bovaird, 2013).

The Confident Group or Organization: Collective Efficacy

Today's organizations are consistently discovering that they are often at the intersection of and can experience the synergies between various technological, economic, global, and social/cultural changes. The combinatory nature of coping with and exploiting these changes can be called organizational learning. It can result in value creation as organizational members balance the exploration of new information and mental models. The learning organization can leverage existing knowledge and approaches in new, exciting, and effective ways (e.g., Barkema & Vermeulen, 1998; Fiol, 1995; Katila & Ahuja, 2002; Vermeulen & Barkema, 2001). Such organizational learning also now plays out in the increased dependence on cross-functional teams and their impact on performance (Hackman & Katz, 2010). In addition, emphasis is being given to providing all participants from top to bottom, and outside stakeholders, exposure to the "big picture." This big picture includes the interdisciplinary nature of organizational training and developmental initiatives, as well as the importance of diversity-promotion efforts.

In this new "flat-world" environment where everything and everybody is linked across the planet and the playing field is becoming more level (see Friedman, 2005), while at the same time more challenging, it is evident that individual mastery is necessary but no longer sufficient. Domain-specific personal efficacy can be more effectively utilized when integrated with others' PsyCap efficacy regarding their respective domains. The integrated group or team becomes the referent for such efficacy, which we now label "collective efficacy." Bandura (1997, p. 477) precisely defines this collective efficacy as "a group's shared belief in its conjoint capabilities to organize and execute the courses of action required to produce given levels of attainments." For example, recent research shows that groups are more confident than individuals and outperform them in decision making (Bonner & Bolinger, 2013).

The more interdependent the members' and units' roles are in an organization, the more the synergies and complementary relationships of collective efficacy can be capitalized upon (Bandura, 1997). In other words, collective efficacy is a realistic admission by organizational members that no matter how efficacious they are about their own independent capabilities, their individual confidence does not mean much in the organizational context until they are tightly jigsawed side by side with those of others, including those who interact mostly virtually today in the global marketplace. Put simply, shared goals and collaborative decision making are the channels through which collective efficacy can be exercised in an organization (Maddux, 2009), and "collective" can at certain points really mean "the organizational collective."

Although research on collective efficacy is not as extensive as on personal efficacy, there is compelling empirical evidence that collective efficacy is related to group attainment of performance outcomes (Bandura, 1993); team effectiveness and motivation (Prussia & Kinicki, 1996); transformational leadership, potency, and high unit performance (Bass, Avolio, Jung, & Berson, 2002); and problem-solving vigilance (Tasa & Whyte, 2005). To-date, two meta-analyses also support a positive relationship between team efficacy and performance. The relationship was even stronger at the team level than at the individual level, especially among teams with higher task interdependence (Gully et al., 2002; Stajkovic et al., 2009). Collective efficacy has also been shown to be positively related to group members' organizational commitment and job satisfaction, and negatively related to job and work withdrawal (Walumbwa, Wang, Lawler, & Shi, 2004).

Cases of Collective Efficacy in Action

In the first PsyCap book that we authored, we presented a case by Professor Mohga Badran, of the American University in Cairo, Egypt, in which collective efficacy was exhibited in the organizational change at a well-known Egyptian public-sector hotel. At the time, as a developing country under heavy international debt and economic reform, major privatization efforts were sweeping the nation. This hotel was one of the very best in the old days, but then the organizational culture became replete with apathy and disengagement. The following brief facts communicate the situation at the time the hotel was to be offered for sale to private sector investors, including well known global chains.

- Only 25% of the rooms were occupiable, and out of those, only 10% were actually occupied.
- To avoid responsibility, managers and supervisors tended to "keep everything." This did not only include accurate records and inventory controls but also broken plates, torn chairs and sofas, leaking toilets, and many other "collectors' items." Of course, conference rooms were perfect for storage space (and very little beyond that).
- Many employees also worked for a private-sector hotel close by, as their wages at the public-sector hotel were dismally low. And, giving new meaning to moonlighting, they did their work at the private hotel during their working hours at the public-sector hotel. As long as they clocked in at the hotel in the morning and clocked out by the end of the day, their "disappearance" throughout the day went unnoticed (or probably more accurately ignored by their managers, who were doing the same thing). Interestingly, and importantly to this discussion, these employees were seen as high performers in their alternate jobs, which is indicative of high personal efficacy.

A new managing director was hired to get the old, badly rundown hotel in shape for sale. This ambitious leader knew he had a lot of work cut out for him. He also knew that his primary focus had to be on changing the organizational culture. Pragmatically, he decided that he could keep no more than 20% of the existing staff. To select the managers and employees who were to stay, he interviewed every one of them, but he asked only one telling question in each of his interviews: "Do you believe that there is any hope for this hotel to go back to being the best in the country?" If they said yes, they were retained. If they said no, they were let go.

Interestingly, many of those who said yes and were kept were among those with the longest tenure. They had actually witnessed the "glory days" of this grand old hotel, so it was possible for them to imagine it at its best again. To make a long story short, the survivors formed a dedicated and motivated, hard-working staff. With an incentive program in place, the employees became very engaged and committed to making their hotel into what it once was—successful. It was completely revamped, bought by a big international hotel chain, and by recent accounts, returned to its glory days.

The new leader realized that the hotel staff did not lack the knowledge or the skills to be high performers (they had proven that in their "other" job). These people also did not lack personal efficacy to perform well on the necessary tasks. However, what they were truly missing was a sense of collective belief that as a team, they could achieve a shared goal, with their workplace being the reference point for their shared aspirations and engaged efforts. These employees may have been very individually confident about their abilities to accomplish the tasks and goals of their respective roles at the old hotel, but without collective efficacy, the outcome was a collective disaster, also fueled of course by the pursuit of self-interest and incentives. On the other hand, when personal efficacy was properly channeled and assimilated in a high-engagement culture of collective efficacy, with the necessary rewards/incentives in place for self-interests, positive outcomes were realized. This occurred at both at the organizational and personal levels. In other words, the collective PsyCap efficacy of the personnel at the Egyptian hotel was invested in and leveraged for a successful outcome.

Now fast-forward several years to the so-called Arab Spring when a series of semiorganized revolutions swept the Middle East, toppling decades of oppressive leadership regimes. Egypt was one of those countries. Professor Badran again provided input for an article written by the second author of this book, which described the ensuing events and applied psychological capital to them (Youssef, 2011). Highly efficacious activists such as Egyptian former Google executive Wael Ghonim and many others collectively developed a vision for a new Egypt. Gradually, the goals of different groups of protesters became aligned and integrated through collaboration and teamwork. Through a growing level of collective efficacy that a nation could be transformed, and very little more beyond it in the way of tangible resources, formal leadership, preplanning, or organization, a 30-year regime was toppled in 18 days.

Although no one individual or group could have accomplished this grand accomplishment alone, the collectively shared belief in the nation's ability to spontaneously organize and execute the necessary actions became the *collective leadership* of that revolution (Youssef, 2011). Not only that, but when a new leader was subsequently elected but did not meet the people's expectations, within a year the people revolted again despite negative international publicity and threats to withhold foreign aid. Again, collective efficacy replaced apathy, fear, uncertainty avoidance, and reliance on others. Vicariously, several other countries in the region followed the same example, mobilizing collective efficacy to fight for their freedom from political, social, and economic oppression. Only time will tell what the final outcome will be, but the power of collective efficacy was certainly demonstrated in these events, even though we fully recognize there are many other factors that will sustain such enormous change, including external support during the most fragile periods of change.

In a very different context, Bass, Avolio, Jung, and Berson (2003) examined the transformational leadership of US Army platoon leaders in Garrison prior to going off to participate in high-fidelity, complex war simulations. They also measured the platoon's perception of its collective efficacy. Approximately 2–3 months later, these platoons went off to the Joint Readiness Training Centers (JRTCs) to participate in the simulations. What the researchers found was that those platoon leaders seen by their members as more transformational had units that were more efficacious and they performed significantly better in a variety of near-combat simulations. Where the relationship between say the lieutenant and the sergeant was not efficacious, the platoon was nearly broken and incapable of performing successfully in these challenging 2-week simulations. In this case, as in the Egyptian example, both leadership and collective efficacy mattered to the ultimate performance gains.

Potential Pitfalls of PsyCap Efficacy

As we have seen, mastery and success experiences, vicarious learning/modeling opportunities, social persuasion/positive feedback, and emotional, psychological, and physiological arousal/wellness can all influence PsyCap confidence or efficacy. However, in order for these factors to enhance PsyCap efficacy, as Bandura (1997) pointed out, it is necessary for this information to be selected, cognitively processed, and acted upon through symbolizing, forethought, observation, self-regulation, and self-reflection. In other words, an individual's perceptions and interpretations of events, not just success or failure, models, social persuasion, and wellness, can boost or dull the impact on PsyCap efficacy or confidence.

In the military example mentioned earlier, instructors focus the learning on what they call After Action Reviews (AARs). In those reviews, they get the leaders and unit members to visualize what happened, what could be improved, and how they could reengage the task more successfully. By using this AAR process, the instructors are employing a type of social learning process by enhancing the involved individuals' efficacy and the unit's collective efficacy.

Drawing from Bandura (2000) once again, he presents some key perceptual and attributional biases that can act as potential inhibitors of PsyCap efficacy development. For example, as mentioned earlier, success can lose some of its value if the developing individual perceives the task to have been too easy, attributes much of the success to others' help, focuses on how slow the rate of improvement was, or emphasizes memories of the failures that led up to the success. Again, in terms of the impact of modeling, it can be dampened by the perceived degree of dissimilarity or relevancy of the model or situation. Social persuasion/positive feedback can also be interpreted in a biased manner if the credibility, expertise, or genuineness of the source can be challenged, or if there is lack of consensus across various sources of the feedback and appraisal. Even psychological and physiological states can interact with other sources of PsyCap efficacy, causing difficult-to-change but possibly inaccurate assumptions, decision-making heuristics, and inclinations.

It is also important to discuss the potential problems of PsyCap efficacy beliefs that result in unrealistic overconfidence, that is, false efficacy. Although this issue started out in a limited scope, there have been some research findings that even when based on high past performance (mastery), unrealistic overconfidence can cause imprudence and thus may reduce subsequent performance (Vancouver & Kendall, 2006; Vancouver, Thompson, Tischner, & Putka, 2002; Vancouver, Thompson, & Williams, 2001). One of the potential explanatory mechanisms for overconfidence is that it serves a status-enhancement purpose where others attribute higher ability and social status to those who are overconfident, regardless of their actual abilities. Even when actual abilities are revealed, overconfident individuals do not lose their credibility but continue to maintain their enhanced status, which reinforces their unwarranted confidence (Kennedy, Anderson, & Moore, 2013). Also, in another study, group decision making and collective efficacy were shown to have a curvilinear relationship with vigilant problem solving, indicating a similar overconfidence effect at the group level as well (Tasa & Whyte, 2005).

Although Bandura and Locke (2003) challenged the validity of the studies that showed negative efficacy effects early on, evidence continues to emerge that these negative effects are possible. Specifically, while a positive relationship between efficacy and performance is often supported at the between-persons level of analysis, at the within-person level, this relationship may be negative or insignificant (Yeo & Neal, 2006). Moreover, recent research evidence supports an opposite causal direction, where past performance (which leads to mastery experiences) possibly drives subsequent efficacy beliefs, rather than efficacy driving future performance (Sitzmann & Yeo, 2013), which may simply mean that these processes are reciprocal in terms of causation.

Proponents of the null or negative efficacy effects or reverse causal direction primarily cite resource allocation theories and their predecessors such as the mechanical cybernetic model and Powers's (1991) perceptual control theory. The idea here is that within-person confidence reduces perceived discrepancies between goals and achievements. This leads to promoting a feedback loop of resource reallocation away from high-efficacy tasks, which in turn compromises subsequent performance effects (Powers, 1991; Yeo & Neal, 2013). On the other hand, Bandura and proponents of the social cognitive theory emphasize self-motivation, approach-goals, and agentic pursuit of challenges, rather than discrepancy reduction, as the primary mechanisms. In other words, even when goals are met and discrepancies are closed, efficacious individuals choose to pursue higher goals and mobilize the effort and personal resources to achieve those goals, rather than just become complacent and redirect their energy and resources to other areas (Bandura, 2012).

Despite these recent contrary study results, the vast body of extensive research over the years supports the positive relationship between PsyCap efficacy and performance in a wide range of work (Stajkovic & Luthans, 1998a) and life domains (Bandura, 2012; Bandura & Locke, 2003). For example, according to Bandura's (2012) recent comprehensive review, the negative efficacy effects were found in only 5.5% of individual-level studies and 6.8% of collective-level studies. This overwhelming positive evidence indicates that most individuals and organizations are not far enough along the confidence curve to worry about a potential overconfidence effect.

In today's workplace, where adversities and setbacks are commonplace, PsyCap efficacy is challenged on an almost daily basis. Developing PsyCap efficacy becomes critical to sustaining effective leadership and high performance over time (Avolio & Luthans, 2006). The need for and importance of PsyCap efficacy is so vital that in situations where organizations and their members may be drowning in a downward spiral of doubt and uncertainty, even minor distortions of reality to communicate a slightly inaccurate illusion of control should be encouraged. This is because this perception can result in self-fulfilling prophecies of efficacy beliefs and expectancies (Maddux, 2009). Whether front-line employees, organizational leaders, or collectively in a group, from a hotel in Egypt to a major global corporation, investment in and development of PsyCap confidence or efficacy is a key contributor to competitive advantage now and certainly in the future.

Looking back over this chapter, our intent was to highlight what comprises one of the more critical components of individual development and performance, as well as to place that component in the context of social learning theory and particularly PsyCap. We believe that if organizational leaders and human resource managers were to focus on just this single area of employee development, then minimally they could significantly improve the performance output of their organization. The evidence for this statement is based on the efficacy–performance relationship reported in the large individual-level meta-analysis conducted by Stajkovic and Luthans (1998a) and the two group-level meta-analyses conducted by Gully and colleagues (2002) and Stajkovic and colleagues (2009).

In practice, the results could be considerably more due to the broader impact on employee attitudes, health and well-being, organizational citizenship behaviors, turnover, and other desirable outcomes with documented effects on tangible, bottom-line results. What we must now focus on is challenging managers/leaders to have the discipline to focus on enhancing each follower's level of efficacy and in turn being cognizant of the importance of also focusing on developing and nurturing collective efficacy. This PsyCap efficacy has evidence of being a very powerful force for performance impact and success at the individual and group/team levels and potentially for organizational, community, and country levels as well.

Future Implications and Directions for PsyCap Efficacy Research and Practice

As we indicated in the introductory comments, among the various PsyCap positive resources that we have determined for best fit, efficacy is the most extensively studied, and its workplace implications have been established and supported with a number of years of research and practice. However, we also assert that today's environment presents researchers and practitioners alike with unprecedented opportunities to capitalize upon the still untapped potential of PsyCap efficacy. We end this chapter with a few of the many challenging opportunities and future directions that lie ahead:

- Although self-efficacy is domain specific, the blurring boundaries across domains, roles, and organizational levels as organizations flatten their hierarchies and increasingly utilize cross-functional teams necessitates further understanding of the mechanisms through which individuals and groups perceive themselves and their roles as concurrently unique and integrated within a larger system or network (e.g., Rouse, Cannon-Bowers, & Salas, 1992). As organizational participants experience evolving roles, the potential for flexibly defining one's domain becomes vital, as does the adaptive ability to transfer previously built efficacy to related, though different domains. Bandura (2012) blames some of the conflicting findings in recent efficacy research on the choice of tasks that are too narrow. It is important to remember that efficacy is still conceived as relatively domain specific, but as we move forward it does not have to be confined to a narrow slice of work, which may be both invalid for research purposes and impractical in application in today's organizational context.
- Also related to this direction, both researchers and practicing managers need to be aware of the implications of levels-of-analysis issues for studying PsyCap efficacy. Bandura (1997) warns that in addition to the methodological challenges associated with the currently available tools for aggregating group beliefs and performance, there are conceptual challenges as "beliefs of personal

efficacy are not detached from the larger social system in which the members function. In appraising their personal efficacies, individuals inevitably consider group processes that enhance or hinder their efforts . . . [Therefore], judgments of personal efficacy are heavily infused with the unique dynamics of the group" (pp. 478–479). More recent efficacy research shows conflicting findings at the between-persons and within-person levels of analysis (Sitzmann & Yeo, 2013; Yeo & Neal, 2006, 2013). Future research needs to embrace the challenge of incorporating these cross-level synergies for better understanding of PsyCap efficacy at both the individual and collective level. What this clearly suggests is that context at multiple levels matters. Moreover, future research needs to examine the mechanisms through which self-efficacy among members of a group morphs into collective efficacy and how that can best be supported.

• We have also proposed that PsyCap efficacy can lead to an upward spiral of confidence contributing to authentic leadership and veritable performance (Avolio & Luthans, 2006; Luthans & Avolio, 2003; Luthans, Norman, & Hughes, 2006). The potential for upward spirals and contagion effects of PsyCap self-efficacy provides considerable development implications, for both leaders and followers. In Chapter 9 we present various approaches for calculating the return on investment in PsyCap development and human resource management. However, if leaders' PsyCap efficacy can trickle down to their followers, then investments in authentic leadership development (ALD), which incorporates the development of leaders' PsyCap efficacy, as well as the leaders' development of their own followers, are likely to yield exponential returns that may far exceed conservative estimates (Avolio & Luthans, 2006). The unwarranted assumptions of bottom-line-oriented decision makers that human resource investments are not worth their while are being consistently challenged in today's business environment (Cascio & Boudreau, 2011; Pfeffer, 1998). PsyCap efficacy presents researchers and practitioners with yet another contribution to the increasing evidence supporting the vital role of human resources in creating sustainable competitive advantage.

• Moreover, as confidence is likely to enhance employees' ability to perform independently, various leadership style contingencies are also likely to surface. For example, it is possible that PsyCap efficacy may act as a leadership substitute (e.g., Kerr & Jermier, 1978), which may discourage leaders from developing their followers' PsyCap efficacy. This was brought out in a recent study which found the relationship between perceived authentic leadership, leader-member exchange (LMX), and performance was actually stronger among low-PsyCap employees (Wang, Sui, Luthans, Wang, & Wu, 2014). Mediating and moderating factors (e.g., task complexity, degree of diversity) in the organizational structure and culture should also be considered in order to more fully account for the salient role of organizational leaders in nurturing versus inhibiting the development of PsyCap efficacy in their followers.

- In a global context, we also encourage future research to explore what constitutes PsyCap efficacy in working across time, distance, and cultures. What is the base point of efficacy for a leader leading virtually across time, distance, and culture (e.g., see Story et al., 2013)? As yet, there is little available evidence on the level of efficacy of most leaders and, more important, on developing such efficacy (Avolio, Kahai, & Dodge, 2001; Avolio, Sosik, Kahai, & Baker, 2014; Vogelgesang, Clapp-Smith, & Osland, 2014; Youssef & Luthans, 2012; Youssef-Morgan & Luthans, 2013).

- Finally, there is a tremendous potential for enhancing the external validity of PsyCap efficacy research through applications to new work contexts, particularly across different work environments and cross-cultural settings (e.g., Reichard, Dollwet, & Louw-Potgieter, 2014; Wernsing, 2014).

Case Study: Confidence-Building Through Extreme Experiences

Video link: http://www.youtube.com/watch?v=NsuSR1Fo9Pk (or search: Chinese boy, 5, becomes youngest person to fly plane)

In this video, Duoduo, a very young Chinese boy, sets a new record for flying a plane, at age 5! This latest accomplishment is one of many extreme adventures that his father has exposed him to, some of which verge of being considered abusive. Duoduo's father believes that these risky endeavors are necessary for building confidence and character.

Questions for reflection and/or discussion:

1. Do you consider Duoduo to be a confident child? Why? Why not?
2. To what extent are extreme experiences necessary or effective for building confidence? Reflect on Duoduo's case as an example, then reflect on some personal examples.
3. In what ways can extreme experiences backfire despite their potential benefits in terms of boosting confidence? Use Duoduo's case as an example, then reflect on some personal examples.
4. What are some examples of extreme (but still reasonably safe and legal) experiences that can be applied in the workplace to build confidence? If you are in a position of authority, how would you go about implementing them, and how would you select the right employees for them?

References

Abbott, D. H. (2010). *Constructing a creative self-efficacy inventory: A mixed methods inquiry.* Unpublished Ph.D. dissertation, University of Nebraska, Lincoln.

Avolio, B. J. (1999). *Full leadership development: Building the vital forces in organizations.* Thousand Oaks, CA: Sage.

Avolio, B. J., Kahai, S., & Dodge, G. E. (2001). E-leadership: Implications for theory, research, and practice. *Leadership Quarterly, 11,* 615–668.

Avolio, B. J., & Luthans, F. (2006). *The high impact leader.* New York, NY: McGraw-Hill.

Avolio, B. J., Sosik, J. J., Kahai, S. S., & Baker, B. (2014). E-leadership: Re-examining transformations in leadership source and transmission. *Leadership Quarterly, 25*(1), 105–131.

Badran, M. A., & Youssef-Morgan, C. M. (2014). Psychological capital and job satisfaction in Egypt. *Journal of Managerial Psychology,* in press.

Bandura, A. (1986). *Social foundations of thought and action: A social cognitive theory.* Englewood Cliffs, NJ: Prentice-Hall.

Bandura, A. (1993). Perceived self-efficacy in cognitive development and functioning. *Educational Psychologist, 28,* 117–148.

Bandura, A. (1997). *Self-efficacy: The exercise of control.* New York, NY: Freeman.

Bandura, A. (2000). Cultivate self-efficacy for personal and organizational effectiveness. In E. Locke (Ed.), *Handbook of principles of organizational behavior* (pp. 120–136). Oxford, UK: Blackwell.

Bandura, A. (2001). Social cognitive theory: An agentic perspective. *Annual Review of Psychology, 52,* 1–26.

Bandura, A. (2012). On the functional properties of perceived self-efficacy revisited. *Journal of Management, 38,* 9–44.

Bandura, A., & Locke, E. (2003). Negative self-efficacy and goal effects revisited. *Journal of Applied Psychology, 88,* 87–99.

Barkema, H., & Vermeulen, F. (1998). International expansion through start-up or acquisition: A learning perspective. *Academy of Management Journal, 31,* 7–26.

Barrick, M. R., & Mount, M. K. (1991). The big five personality dimensions and job performance: A meta-analysis. *Personnel Psychology, 44,* 1–26.

Bass, B. M., Avolio, B. J., Jung, D. I., & Berson, Y. (2003). Predicting unit performance by transformational and transactional leadership. *Journal of Applied Psychology, 88,* 207–218.

Bonner, B. L., & Bolinger, A. R. (2013). Separating the confident from the correct: Leveraging member knowledge in groups to improve decision making and performance. *Organizational Behavior and Human Decision Processes, 122,* 214–221.

Boyd, N. G., & Vozikis, G. S. (1994). The influence of self-efficacy on the development of entrepreneurial intentions and actions. *Entrepreneurship Theory and Practice, Summer,* 63–77.

Cascio, W., & Boudreau, J. (2011). *Investing in people: Financial impact of human resource initiatives* (2nd ed.). Upper Saddle River, NJ: Pearson/FT Press.

Chandler, G. N., & Jansen, E. (1997). Founder self-efficacy and venture performance: A longitudinal study. *Academy of Management Proceedings*, 98–102.

Chemers, M. M., Watson, C. B., & May, S. T. (2000). Dispositional affect and leadership effectiveness: A comparison of self-esteem, optimism, and efficacy. *Personality and Social Psychology Bulletin, 26*, 267–277.

Chen, C. C., Greene, P. G., & Crick, A. (1998). Does entrepreneurial self-efficacy distinguish entrepreneurs from managers? *Journal of Business Venturing, 13*, 295–316.

Clapp-Smith, R., Vogelgesang, G. R., & Avey, J. B. (2009). Authentic leadership and positive psychological capital: The mediating role of trust at the group level of analysis. *Organizational Studies, 15*, 227–240.

Cunningham, C., Woodward, C., Shannon, H., Macintosh, J., Lendrum, B., Rosenbloom, D., & Brown, J. (2002). Readiness for organizational change: A longitudinal study of workplace, psychological and behavioral correlates. *Journal of Occupational and Organizational Psychology, 75*, 377–352.

Drnovšek, M., Wincent, J., & Cardon, M. S. (2010). Entrepreneurial self-efficacy and business start-up: Developing a multi-dimensional definition. *International Journal of Entrepreneurial Behaviour and Research, 16*, 329–348.

Eden, D., Ganzach, Y., Flumin-Granat, R., & Zignman, T. (2010). Augmenting means efficacy to boost performance: Two field experiments. *Journal of Management, 36*, 687–713.

Fiol, M. (1995). Thought worlds colliding: The role of contradiction in corporate innovation processes. *Entrepreneurship Theory and Practice, 19*(3), 71–90.

Friedman, T. L. (2005). *The world is flat.* New York, NY: Farrar, Straus and Giroux.

Gully, S. M., Incalcaterra, K. A., Joshi, A., & Beaubien, J. M. (2002). A meta-analysis of team-efficacy, potency, and performance: Interdependence and level of analysis as moderators of observed relationships. *Journal of Applied Psychology, 87*, 819–832.

Hackman, J. R., & Katz, N. (2010). Group behavior and performance. In S. T. Fiske, D. T. Gilbert, & G. Lindzey (Eds.), *Handbook of social psychology* (pp. 1208–1251). New York, NY: Wiley.

Hannah, S. T., Avolio, B. J., Luthans, F., & Harms, P. D. (2008). Leadership efficacy: Review and future directions. *Leadership Quarterly, 19*, 669–692.

Hannah, S. T., Schaubroeck, J., Peng, A. C., Lord, R. L., Trevino, L. K., Kozlowski, S. W. J., . . . Doty, J. (2013). Joint influences of individual and work unit abusive supervision on ethical intentions and behaviors: A moderated mediation model. *Journal of Applied Psychology, 98*, 579–592.

Hayward, M. L. A., Forster, W. R., Sarasvathy, S. D., & Fredrickson, B. L. (2009). Beyond hubris: How highly confident entrepreneurs rebound to venture again. *Journal of Business Venturing, 25*, 569–578.

Holden, G. (1991). The relationship of self-efficacy appraisals to subsequent health-related outcomes: A meta-analysis. *Social Work in Health Care, 16*, 53–93.

Holden, G., Moncher, M., Schinke, S., & Barker, K. (1990). Self-efficacy in children and adolescents. A meta-analysis. *Psychological Reports, 66,* 1044–1046.

Judge, T. A., Thoresen, C. J., Bono, J. E., & Patton, G. K. (2001). The job satisfaction-job performance relationship: A qualitative and quantitative review. *Psychological Bulletin, 127,* 376–407

Kanter, R. M. (2004). *Confidence.* New York, NY: Crown Business.

Katila, R., & Ahuja, G. (2002). Something old, something new: A longitudinal study of search behavior and new product introduction. *Academy of Management Journal, 45,* 1183–1194.

Kennedy, J. A., Anderson, C., & Moore, D. A. (2013). When overconfidence is revealed to others: Testing the status-enhancement theory of overconfidence. *Organizational Behavior and Human Decision Processes, 112,* 266–279.

Kerr, S., & Jermier, J. (1978). Substitutes for leadership: Their meaning and measurement. *Organizational behavior and human performance, 22,* 375–403.

Kleingeld, A., van Mierlo, H., & Arends, L. (2011). The effect of goal setting on group performance: A meta-analysis. *Journal of Applied Psychology, 96,* 1289–1304.

Kluger, A. N., & DeNisi, A. (1996). The effects of feedback intervention on performance: A historical review, a meta-analysis, and a preliminary feedback intervention theory. *Psychological Bulletin, 119,* 254–284.

Lam, S., Chen, X., & Schaubroeck, J. (2002). Participative decision making and employee performance in different cultures: The moderating effects of allocentrism/idiocentrism and efficacy. *Academy of Management Journal, 45,* 905–914.

Locke, E., Frederick, E., Lee, C., & Bobko, P. (1984). Effects of self-efficacy, goals and task strategies on task performance. *Journal of Applied Psychology, 69,* 241–251.

Luthans, F., Avey, J. B., Avolio, B. J., Norman, S. M., & Combs, G. M. (2006). Psychological capital development: Toward a micro-intervention. *Journal of Organizational Behavior, 27,* 387–393.

Luthans, F., Avey, J. B., Avolio, B. J., & Peterson, S. (2010). The development and resulting performance impact of positive psychological capital. *Human Resource Development Quarterly, 21,* 41–66.

Luthans, F., Avey, J. B., & Patera, J. L. (2008). Experimental analysis of a web-based training intervention to develop positive psychological capital. *Academy of Management Learning and Education, 7,* 209–221.

Luthans, F., & Avolio, B. (2003). Authentic leadership: A positive development approach. In K. S. Cameron, J. E. Dutton, & R. E. Quinn (Eds.), *Positive organizational scholarship* (pp. 241–258). San Francisco, CA: Berrett-Koehler.

Luthans, F., & Ibrayeva, E. S. (2006). Entrepreneurial self-efficacy in Central Asian economies: Quantitative and qualitative analyses. *Journal of International Business Studies, 37,* 92–110.

Luthans, F., Luthans, K., Hodgetts, R., & Luthans, B. (2001). Positive approach to leadership (PAL): Implications for today's organizations. *Journal of Leadership Studies, 8*(2), 3–20.

Luthans, F., Luthans, K., & Luthans, B. (2004). Positive psychological capital: Going beyond human and social capital. *Business Horizons, 47*(1), 45–50.

Luthans, F., Norman, S. M., & Hughes, L. (2006). Authentic leadership: A new approach for a new time. In R. Burke & C. Cooper (Eds.), *Inspiring leaders* (pp. 84–104). London, UK: Routledge, Taylor & Francis.

Luthans, F., & Youssef, C. M. (2004). Human, social and now positive psychological capital management: Investing in people for competitive advantage. *Organizational Dynamics, 33*, 143–160.

Luthans, F., Youssef, C. M., Sweetman, D., & Harms, P. (2013). Meeting the leadership challenge of employee well-being through relationship PsyCap and health PsyCap. *Journal of Leadership and Organizational Studies, 20*, 114–129.

Luthans, F., Zhu, W., & Avolio, B. J. (2006). The impact of efficacy on work attitudes across cultures. *Journal of World Business, 41*, 121–132.

Maddux, J. E. (2009). Self-efficacy: The power of believing you can. In S. Lopez & C. R. Snyder (Eds.), *Oxford handbook of positive psychology* (2nd ed., pp. 335–343). New York, NY: Oxford University Press.

May, D., Chan, A., Hodges, T., & Avolio, B. (2003). Developing the moral component of authentic leadership. *Organizational Dynamics, 32*, 247–260.

Neck, C. P., Neck, H. M., Manz, C. C., & Godwin, J. (1999). "I think I can; I think I can": A self leadership perspective toward enhancing entrepreneurial thought patterns, self-efficacy, and performance. *Journal of Management Psychology, 14*, 477–501.

Nilsson, J., Schmidt, C., & Meek, W. (2002). Reliability generalization: An examination of the career decision-making self-efficacy scale. *Educational and Psychological Measurement, 62*, 647–658.

Palmer, N. F. (2013). *The effects of leader behavior on follower ethical behavior: Examining the mediating roles of ethical efficacy and moral disengagement.* Unpublished Ph.D. dissertation, University of Nebraska, Lincoln.

Parker, S. (1998). Enhancing role-breadth self-efficacy. *Journal of Applied Psychology, 83*, 835–852.

Pfeffer, J. (1998). *The human equation.* Boston, MA: Harvard Business School Press.

Peterson, S. J., & Luthans, F. (2006). The impact of financial and non-financial incentives on business unit outcomes over time. *Journal of Applied Psychology, 91*, 156–165.

Powers, W. T. (1991). Comment on Bandura's "human agency". *American Psychologist, 46*, 151–153.

Prussia, G., & Kinicki, A. (1996). A motivational investigation of group effectiveness using social cognitive theory. *Journal of Applied Psychology, 81*, 187–198.

Ramakrishna, H. (2002). The moderating role of updating climate perceptions in the relationship between goal orientation, self-efficacy, and job performance. *Human Performance, 15*, 275–297.

Rego, A., Sousa, F., Marques, C., & Pina e Cunha, M. (2012). Authentic leadership promoting employees' psychological capital and creativity. *Journal of Business Research, 65*, 429–437.

Reichard, R. J., Dollwet, M., & Louw-Potgieter, J. (2014). Development of cross-cultural psychological capital and its relationship with cultural intelligence and ethnocentrism. *Journal of Leadership and Organizational Studies, 21*(2), 150–164.

Richter, A. W., Hirst, G., van Knippenberg, D., & Baer, M. (2012). Creative self-efficacy and individual creativity in team contexts: Cross-level interactions with team informational resources. *Journal of Applied Psychology, 97*, 1282–1290.

Rouse, W. B., Cannon-Bowers, J. A., & Salas, E. (1992). The role of mental models in team performance in complex systems. *IEEE Transactions on Systems, Man, and Cybernetics, 22*, 1296–1308.

Sitzmann, T., & Yeo, G. (2013). a meta-analytic investigation of the within-person self-efficacy domain: Is self-efficacy a product of past performance or a driver of future performance? *Personnel Psychology, 66*, 531–568.

Stajkovic, A. D., Lee, D., & Nyberg, A. (2009). Collective efficacy, group potency, and group performance: Meta-analysis of their relationships, and test of a mediation model. *Journal of Applied Psychology, 94*, 814–828.

Stajkovic, A. D., & Luthans, F. (1997). A meta-analysis of the effects of organizational behavior modification on task performance: 1975-95. *Academy of Management Journal, 40*, 1122–1149.

Stajkovic, A. D., & Luthans, F. (1998a). Self-efficacy and work-related performance: A meta-analysis. *Psychological Bulletin, 124*, 240–261.

Stajkovic, A. D., & Luthans, F. (1998b). Social cognitive theory and self-efficacy: Going beyond traditional motivational and behavioral approaches. *Organizational Dynamics, 26*, 62–74.

Stajkovic, A. D., & Luthans, F. (2001). Differential effects of incentive motivators on work performance. *Academy of Management Journal, 44*, 580–590.

Stajkovic, A., & Luthans F. (2003) Behavioral management and task performance in organizations: Conceptual background, meta-analysis, and test of alternative models. *Personnel Psychology, 56*, 155–194.

Story, J., Youssef, C. M., Luthans, F., Bartbuto, J., & Bovaird, J. (2013). The contagion effect of global leaders' positive psychological capital on followers. *International Journal of Human Resource Mnaagement, 24*, 2534–2553.

Tasa, K., & Whyte, G. (2005). Collective efficacy and vigilant problem solving in group decision making: A non-linear model. *Organizational Behavior and Human Decision Processes, 96*(2), 119–129.

Thatcher, J., & Perrewe, P. (2002). An empirical examination of individual traits as antecedents to computer anxiety and computer self-efficacy. *MIS Quarterly, 26*, 381–396.

Tierney, P., & Farmer, S. (2002). Creative self-efficacy: Its potential antecedents and relationship to creative performance. *Academy of Management Journal, 45*, 1137–1148.

Truxillo, D., Bauer, T., Campion, M., & Paronto, M. (2002). Selection fairness information and applicant reactions: A longitudinal field study. *Journal of Applied Psychology, 87*, 1020–1031.

Vancouver, J. B., & Kendall, L. N. (2006). When self-efficacy negatively relates to motivation and performance in a learning context. *Journal of Applied Psychology, 91*, 1146–1153.

Vancouver, J. B., Thompson, C., Tischner, E., & Putka, D. (2002). Two studies examining the negative effect of self-efficacy on performance. *Journal of Applied Psychology, 87*, 506–516.

Vancouver, J. B., Thompson, C., & Williams, A. (2001). The changing signs in the relationship between self-efficacy, personal goals, and performance. *Journal of Applied Psychology, 86*, 605–620.

Vermeulen, F., & Barkema, H. (2001). Learning through acquisitions. *Academy of Management Journal, 44*, 457–476.

Vogelgesang, G., Clapp-Smith, R., & Osland, J. (2014). The relationship between positive psychological capital and global mindset in the context of global leadership. *Journal of Leadership and Organizational Studies, 21*(2), 165–178.

Walumbwa, F., Wang, P., Lawler, J., & Shi, K. (2004). The role of collective efficacy in the relations between transformational leadership and work outcomes. *Journal of Occupational and Organizational Psychology, 77*, 515–530.

Wang, G., Oh, I. S., Courtright, S. H., & Colbert, A. E. (2011). Transformational leadership and performance across criteria and levels: A meta-analytic review of 25 years of research. *Group and Organization Management, 36*, 223–270.

Wang, H., Sui, Y., Luthans, F., Wang, D., & Wu, Y. (2014). Impact of authentic leadership on performance: Role of followers' positive psychological capital and relational processes. *Journal of Organizational Behavior, 35*, 5–21.

Wernsing, T. (2014). Psychological capital: A test of measurement instrument invariance across twelve national cultures. *Journal of Leadership and Organizational Studies*, in press.

Wilson, F., Kickul, J., & Marlino, D. (2007). Gender, entrepreneurial self efficacy, and entrepreneurial career intentions: Implications for entrepreneurship education. *Entrepreneurship Theory and Practice, 31*, 387–406.

Wood, R. E., Mento, A. J., & Locke, E. A. (1987). Task complexity as a moderator of goal effects: A meta analysis. *Journal of Applied Psychology, 72*, 416–425.

Yeo, G. B., & Neal, A. (2006). An examination of the dynamic relationship between self-efficacy and performance across levels of analysis and levels of specificity. *Journal of Applied Psychology, 91*, 1088–1101.

Yeo, G. B., & Neal, A. (2013). Revisiting the functional properties of self-efficacy: A dynamic perspective. *Journal of Management, 39*, 1385–1396.

Youssef, C. M. (2011). Recent events in Egypt and the Middle East: Background, direct observations and a positive analysis. *Organizational Dynamics, 40*, 222–234.

Youssef, C. M., & Luthans, F. (2005). A positive organizational behavior approach to ethical performance. In R. A. Giacalone, C. Jurkiewicz, & C. Dunn (Eds.), *Positive psychology in business ethics and corporate social responsibility* (pp. 1–22). Greenwich, CT: Information Age.

Youssef, C. M., & Luthans, F. (2012). Positive global leadership. *Journal of World Business, 47*, 539–547.

Youssef-Morgan, C. M., & Luthans, F. (2013). Positive leadership: Meaning and application across cultures. *Organizational Dynamics, 42*, 198–208.

Zhao, H., Seibert, S. E., & Hills, G. E. (2005). The mediating role of self-efficacy in the development of entrepreneurial intentions. *Journal of Applied Psychology, 91*, 1265–1272.

4 PSYCAP HOPE

THE WILL AND THE WAY

Opening Video: Shane Lopez on Hope

Video link: http://www.youtube.com/watch?v=Bka3sI5_WZ4
(or search for "Interview with Dr. Shane Lopez")

Video link: http://www.youtube.com/watch?v=UN3ZvG-Z0vg
(or search for "Making Hope Happen with Shane Lopez")

Shane Lopez is a professor at the University of Kansas and is currently a Gallup Senior Scientist and Research Director for the Clifton Strengths Institute. He is also author of *Making Hope Happen* and coauthor of the *Handbook of Positive Psychology*. He collaborated extensively with the late C. Rick Snyder, who is well known for over two decades of extensive research on hope.

Questions for reflection and/or discussion:

1. How do hopeful people differ from less hopeful people in their thoughts and actions?
2. How do hopeful employees think and behave differently from their less hopeful counterparts?
3. How can hope help mitigate life's challenges?
4. How can you differentiate between hopeful and wishful thinking in yourself and in others (e.g., friends, family members, coworkers)?
5. How can you develop hope in yourself and in others who are important to you?

Are you strong willed? Are you determined to achieve your goals? Do you feel you are in control of your own destiny? Can you go relentlessly for hours, days, even months until you have accomplished what you have set your mind to do? Is it difficult to distract you away from your targeted endeavors? When there are no set goals for you, do you tend to set your own? Are the goals you set for yourself extremely challenging? Do you enjoy engaging in such goals?

If your answers are mostly "yes" to these types of questions, then you are indicating the willpower component of hope. However, having such will is necessary but not sufficient for PsyCap hope. To have PsyCap hope to carry out your willpower, you must also know the pathways to your goals and have determined proactively alternative pathways when the way is blocked. In other words, you have to have both the willpower and the pathways (i.e., the "will" and the "way") to have a high level of hope to accomplish your goals successfully. To have the pathways component of a high level of PsyCap hope, you must also answer affirmatively to questions such as the following: Do you proactively determine the way to accomplish your goals? Do you tend to figure out, evaluate, and know how to implement alternative paths to the same destination? When you are severely challenged, or when your efforts are frustrated with obstacles, do you have alternatives already determined that can circumvent the obstacles? Do you have strengths to draw from to manage around your areas of weakness and vulnerability?

As shown in the example in the last chapter with animal rescue workers, these individuals enter the field, in which they are frequently poorly paid, with a passion for saving animals. Yet, having worked with some of the worst leaders, they start to lose touch with the ways that these animals can be saved, and that begins to erode their willpower, thus reducing levels of their PsyCap hope.

The opposite of this deteriorating condition is where leaders create a context, climate, and culture in which employees continually seek alternative ways to overcome an existing obstacle. In one organization, the leader had a saying, "If it's dumb, don't do it." He was signaling to what had become a very cynical and disenfranchised work group that they should continually question the way they do things and find new pathways to achieve the mission. He would frequently give examples of dumb ways of doing things and then put a stop to them by empowering his employees to do the same.

Personal Reflections Exercise on PsyCap Hope

As an exercise to get you personally involved in hope, think about the last very difficult situation you confronted at work. Use the following questions as your guide. What happened once you were alerted to this situation in terms of the way you thought about it and the way you addressed it? Did you find yourself ruminating at some point, which is that downward spiral? Were you able to realize you were ruminating and turn your attention to exploring different pathways of possibilities? Specifically, were you able to reframe the challenge to keep moving forward to new pathways?

Besides the will and the way, there are many possible circumstances that may affect your level of PsyCap hope. For example, how would you react if the following types of things happened in your life? What would your immediate, short-term response be? What course(s) of action would you take over the long run?

- You work for a toxic manager.
- You manage totally disengaged employees.
- You are passed over for a promotion a second time.
- You are transferred to a less desired position, location, or both.
- You are given a poor performance rating after completing your most successful project.
- Your business or personal situation goes through a total financial meltdown.
- A best friend at work is laid off.
- A trusted colleague betrays you.
- A valued coworker gets severely injured on the job or has a serious illness.
- A major initiative you are working on gets its funding pulled.

A Story of Hope

A realistic story of hope can also serve as an illustration and backdrop for this chapter as we present the theory and practice of PsyCap hope and its development in the workplace. Jeremy and Kayla are happily married. Jeremy is a claims adjuster in a small insurance company, and Kayla is a part-time customer service representative at a large retailer. Both have gone through difficulties before they met. Kayla was divorced and was raising her son from the previous marriage. Jeremy came from a dysfunctional family, had dropped out of college, and had many low-paying jobs before this one. However, they had one thing in common: They were both determined to have a successful marriage and life. They were both willing to invest the necessary time and energy and do whatever it takes to reach their goal of a good life and family.

After a few years, they thought their dreams were coming true when they had their first child together. They had both accumulated some seniority and grown in their jobs to make a decent living between them. However, their lives became suddenly shattered when Jeremy was struck by a disabling illness. He was no longer able to work at his present job. Three surgeries later, Jeremy and Kayla knew that life would never be the same. They knew their troubles were there for the long haul.

How did Jeremy and Kayla handle this crisis in their lives? Definitely despair and giving up was not an option they considered. Kayla went from working part-time to full-time. She also started her own home-based business in order to bring in a little extra income. Jeremy was able to take over most of the child care and housework duties, and went back to community college in the evenings when medications allowed him to cope with his illness. Presently, Jeremy is scheduled to receive his associate's degree, and he plans to continue through to his bachelor's and possibly master's degrees. His dreams are not unrealistic. So far, he has earned excellent grades throughout his coursework. He has already looked into gaining entrance into the local state university, which is willing to transfer most of his credits into their social work program. He has also been able to establish some contacts through which he is likely to land an internship. This experience should help him find a good-paying job he is capable of performing. In other words, drawing from their high levels of PsyCap hope (i.e., the will and the way), Kayla and Jeremy are on a new pathway to accomplishing their life goals. They defined an alternative future that was possible, not the one defined for them when Jeremy first discovered his illness.

Although this life's story is perhaps not as glamorous as famous historical leaders noted for their strong will and pathways such as Winston Churchill, Franklin Roosevelt, Margaret Thatcher, Victor Frankl, or Nelson Mandela, it demonstrates the role hope can play in accomplishing one's goals and values. Such hope is well established as having a positive impact on life in general, as in this story, and has also been shown to be important for attaining academic and athletic success. We are bringing such hope to the workplace as a key component of PsyCap. After first defining precisely what we mean by PsyCap hope, this chapter then examines in turn the relationship hope has with performance; specific guidelines for its development; profiles of the hopeful manager, employee, and organization; and some potential pitfalls that need to be avoided for sustainable impact.

What Is PsyCap Hope?

Hope is commonly used in everyday language. However, as a positive psychological resource, there are many misperceptions about what constitutes hope and what are the characteristics of hopeful individuals, teams, organizations, communities, and countries. Many confuse hope with wishful thinking (Lopez, 2013), an unsubstantiated positive attitude, an emotional high, or even an illusion.

According to the late C. Rick Snyder, who was a professor of clinical psychology at the University of Kansas and the most widely recognized theory-builder and researcher on hope in positive psychology, it can be defined as "a positive motivational state that is based on an interactively derived sense of successful (1) agency (goal-directed energy) and (2) pathways (planning to meet goals)" (Snyder, Irving, & Anderson, 1991, p. 287). You can see the word *agency* used here, which should signal that hope is linked synergistically to what we discussed in the last chapter as being associated with the agency that comes from efficacy.

Snyder's research supports that hope is more of a cognitive or "thinking" state in which an individual is capable of setting realistic but challenging goals and expectations, and then reaching out for those aims through a self-directed determination, energy, and perception of internalized control. This is what Snyder and colleagues refer to as "agency" or "willpower." However, as indicated in the opening comments, often overlooked in common usage of the term, but as defined by Snyder and colleagues, another equally necessary and integral component of hope is what is referred to as the "pathways" or "waypower." In this component of hope, people are capable of proactively generating alternative paths to their desired destinations should the original ones become blocked (Snyder, 1994a, 1995a, 2000; Snyder, Ilardi, Michael, & Cheavens, 2000; Snyder, Rand, & Sigmon, 2002).

The pathways component is what mainly separates PsyCap hope from the everyday usage of the term and from the other PsyCap states such as resilience, efficacy, and optimism (e.g., see Bryant & Cvengros, 2004; Luthans & Jensen, 2002, pp. 309–312; Magaletta & Oliver, 1999; Snyder, 2002, pp. 256–258 for conceptual and empirical summaries of the distinctions, i.e., the discriminative validity of hope). Finally, there is a continuous reiteration between agency and pathways. Specifically, one's willpower and determination motivate the search for new pathways, while the creativity, innovation, and resourcefulness involved in developing pathways in turn ignite one's energy and sense of control, which when taken together result in an upward spiral of hope (Lopez, 2013; Snyder, 1993, 2000, 2002). If one has the potential to control engaging with, when necessary, predetermined alternative pathways that "just might work," then hope is sustainable and can even grow.

Reflecting back on the Jeremy and Kayla example at the beginning of the chapter, their embodiment of high levels of hope is clear in several ways. First, both had clear goals: to maintain and grow their marriage, children, and quality of life. Second, they were both determined to achieve their goals, as exhibited in the strength of their willpower, the amount of energy they invested, and their clear sense of agency and control over their destiny. Third, even when obstacles and setbacks were about to put a halt to attaining their goals, they were able to shift to alternative, creative pathways around their problems and continue to pursue their goals without disruption. When people get stuck on only one pathway (or worse yet, see none), and their way is blocked and they have no predetermined alternative, in the extreme we could describe them as not only frustrated but being at an early stage of what Seligman (1972) termed in the disease model as "learned helplessness." In the original experiments using dogs, it was found that when they were forced to endure shock with no way to escape, they eventually would just continue to take the shock even when they could easily escape it. In other words, they learned to be helpless, or they learned they could not control this situation even when it became clear that they could. By contrast, in Jeremy and Kayla's case, their positive hope orientation was "learned hopefulness" (rather than helplessness) and it helped redirect them to some alternative pathways around the adversities for goal attainment.

Finally, as some of this couple's new pathways proved effective, this further sparked their enthusiasm, which in turn enhanced their chances of success and had an upward spiral effect on their hope. As long as there is some possibility for forward momentum down an alternative pathway, there is the potential for a positive contagion effect, where one advance leads to another and another. This is the beauty of positivity in general and PsyCap hope in particular.

The Relationship Between Hope and Performance

Despite the relatively recent emergence of positive psychological research, the relationship between hope and performance in various life domains has been clearly demonstrated. This hope research includes areas such as the following: academic and athletic achievement, physical and mental health, survival and coping beliefs and skills, and other desirable positive life and well-being outcomes (Curry, Snyder, Cook, Ruby, & Rehm, 1997; Kwon, 2000; Onwuegbuzie & Snyder, 2000; Range & Pentin, 1994; Scioli et al., 1997; Snyder, 2000; also see Lopez, 2013, and Rand & Cheavens, 2009, for comprehensive reviews of a wide range of hope outcomes).

Although research on hope is most closely associated with clinical psychology, its relevancy to the workplace has been clearly argued (Luthans, 2002a, 2002b; Luthans et al., 2005; Luthans & Jensen, 2002; Luthans & Youssef, 2004; Snyder, 1995b; Youssef & Luthans, 2003, 2005a, 2005b, 2006). In addition, there are empirical studies such as Peterson and Luthans's (2003) study that have found a positive relationship between organizational leaders' level of hope and the profitability of their units and the satisfaction and retention of their employees. Youssef and Luthans (2007) showed that the hope level of over 1,000 managers and employees was positively related to their performance, job satisfaction, work happiness, and organizational commitment. In four studies, Peterson and Byron (2008) found that service workers, mortgage brokers, and telecommunications management executives with high hope had higher performance, and that higher hope executives from a financial services company generated more and higher quality solutions to work-related problems. Ouweneel, Le Blanc, Shaufeli, and van Wijhe (2012) found that variations in hope over time had lagged effects on work engagement (vigor, dedication, and absorption). Hope has been found to be positively related to organizational profitability (Adams et al., 2002) and entrepreneurs' hope levels have been found to predict their expressed satisfaction with business ownership (Jensen & Luthans, 2002).

Hope has also been applied conceptually or empirically in several cross-cultural settings (Wernsing, 2014) and in specific countries such as Egypt (Badran & Youssef-Morgan, 2014; Youssef & Luthans, 2006; Youssef, 2011), China (Huimei & Xuan, 2011; Luthans, Avey, Clapp-Smith, & Li, 2008;), Australia (Avey, Nimnicht, & Pigeon, 2010), Iran (Mehrabi, Babri, Frohar, Khabazuan, & Salili, 2013), Hungary (Lehoczky, 2013), Taiwan (Huang & Lin, 2013), New Zealand (Roche, Haar, & Luthans, 2014), and South Africa (Luthans, Van Wyk, & Walumbwa, 2004; Reichard, Dollwet, & Louw-Potgieter, 2014). In other words, to date the relationship between PsyCap hope and work-related outcomes has received considerable conceptual and empirical support (Avey, Reichard, Luthans, & Mhatre, 2011; Reichard, Avey, Lopez, & Dowlett, 2013; Youssef-Morgan, 2014).

Developing Hope in Today's Managers and Employees

Modern challenges around the world unfortunately leave many people hopeless and rob them, even at an early age, of the ability to hope. Consider the following: outdated school curricula with little life relevance; substandard teaching methods that emphasize assessment over learning and application; uncaring parents, teachers, and role models who are at best distant and minimally involved and at worst have damaging psychological effects; unsafe neighborhoods that impose unnecessary obstacles and distractions; and poorly designed jobs and ineffective leaders that place more obstacles than pathways for success and achievement. These examples of some of the problems are increasingly affecting children and youth, and they are detrimental to their hope and future prospects.

Pete Carroll, the 2014 winning Super Bowl coach of the Seattle Seahawks, has spent the last decade quietly going into some of the worst neighborhoods in Los Angeles, both when he was coaching in the collegiate ranks at USC and now since working in the NFL in Seattle. His attitude is very positive and hopeful, to such an extent that it has become infectious with players, staff, and some might also say even the fans and the surrounding community. Pete goes into these inner-city neighborhoods oftentimes with a player or two who came from a similar, very difficult neighborhood. They talk with these kids about different pathways available to them other than entering gangs, which frequently seems to them like the only viable option for survival. Pete provides pathways to disadvantaged, at-risk youth that were long ago abandoned. In other words, he is creating hope.

One could argue that the current generation is facing a hope crisis. This is because they lack three essential ingredients of hope: (a) at least one exciting future goal, (b) the belief that they have the power (agency) and resources (pathways) to achieve their goals, and (c) at least one caring other person to cheer them on (Lopez, 2013). Hope is tightly intertwined with the individual's ability to imagine a better future or indeed futures, as well as the enabling relational and collective processes that facilitate open-ended thinking and ideation to develop new goals, pathways, and possibilities in general (Carlsen, Hagen, & Mortensen, 2012).

Hope has been portrayed as a dispositional trait and thus not readily adaptable to change (Snyder et al., 1991). However, consistent with our PsyCap inclusion criteria outlined in Chapter 1 (Luthans, 2002a, 2002b), hope has also been demonstrated to be a developmental state (e.g., Snyder, 1995a, 1995b; Snyder et al., 1996; Snyder, Tran, et al., 2000; Veninga, 2000) and can change over the course of hours and days (Ouweneel et al., 2012). Hope development can be facilitated in organizational settings by capitalizing on and nurturing its essential ingredients, the goals, agency, and pathways, as well their underlying relational and collective processes. Several specific approaches have been successful in developing and nurturing hope. These include the following:

1. *Goal Setting.* Goals have a way of motivating us, getting us out of bed in the morning, and pushing us through life, or what Lopez (2013) literally and metaphorically labels as "showing up." While physical presence does not guarantee success, it is an important prerequisite. When we know where we are (point A) and where we want to go (point B), we are motivated to find ways to get from here to there (Snyder, 1994b), which is the essence of hope. When we lose sight of point B (the goal), we lose hope.

Substantial research support exists for the relationship between effective goal setting and performance (e.g., Locke & Latham, 1990, 2002, 2006). In line with the theory of hope, performance gains are achieved when goals are internalized and committed to, and when goal achievement is self-regulated. Moreover, consistent with the agency component of hope, goals that are self-set, participatory, or even assigned, but explained using a logical rationale that one can buy into will tend to yield higher performance than dictated, unexplained goals (Latham, Erez, & Locke, 1988; Latham, Winters, & Locke, 1994). Finally, appropriate goal setting not only influences one's level of motivation, choices made, effort extended, and persistence but also the willingness and ability to design creative ways to achieve one's goals, that is, hope pathways (Latham, 2000).

2. *Stretch Goals.* Goals that are conducive to developing and nurturing hopeful thinking, and consequently performance enhancement, need to be specific, measurable, and challenging, yet achievable. Stretch goals are those that are difficult enough to stimulate excitement and exploration, yet still perceived to be within reach. They warrant trial and reasonable expectations of accomplishment given extra effort. They typically tap into the "reserve potential" that flies below the radar screen but is almost always there, ready to be tapped into to address some daunting, yet doable, challenge.

3. *Approach Goals.* Many people frame their goals in terms of what they should *not* do or where they do *not* want to end up. These types of goals are referred to as "avoidance goals." While sometimes necessary, avoidance goals do not provide us with the same motivation and are not as exciting or sustainable as "approach goals" (Coats, Janoff-Bulman, & Alpert, 1996; Elliot, 2006). Avoidance goals and negative framing in general promote narrow fight-or-flight mechanisms. A good example is the frequently made New Year's resolution "I will not eat any (sweets, fast food, junk food, red meat, carbs, and so on)." Of course, as time goes by, deprivation promotes even more thinking about the forbidden foods, which can cause many people to give up on their goals. This is because self-regulation and delayed gratification, although important, exist in limited quantities. Over time, when our physical, mental, and emotional resources wear out, we give in. Once the resolution is broken, we feel defeated and may stop trying, in large part because we considered just one pathway and now that pathway is blocked.

On the other hand, "approach goals" such as "I will eat more fruits and vegetables" and "I will exercise every day," accompanied by a clear plan to meet these goals (e.g., I will add vegetables and fruits to every meal, I will go to the gym for 1 hour every day after work), tend to work better. Every day that the goal is achieved, there is a tangible accomplishment, a milestone to celebrate, and a rewarding sense of agency and control that promote another cycle of goal pursuit. Even when we fall off the bandwagon for a while, we continue to remember this sense of accomplishment, which motivates us to get back on track with renewed energy. Sometimes the plan may need to be adapted (e.g., change the time of daily exercise or substitute a walk or a bike ride with the family on a beautiful spring evening). However, the sense of accomplishment and reinforcement associated with approach goals helps sustain those goals and our willpower and waypower to achieve them. Consequently, one has to think of the goal as scaffolding, and that there are different ways to ascend the scaffolding depending the goals created and pathways that unfold.

4. *Stepping.* Stepping is an integral component of hopeful goal achievement. In the stepping process, difficult, long-term, and possibly even overwhelming goals are broken down into smaller, proximate, and thus more manageable milestones. As gradual progress is made toward distant goals, agency and pathways are enriched, building a more sustainable base for pursuing one's extreme challenges successfully (Latham, 2000; Luthans, 2000a, 2000b; Luthans et al., 2004: Luthans & Jensen, 2002; Luthans & Youssef, 2004; Snyder, 1995a, 1995b; Youssef & Luthans, 2006).

5. *Mental Rehearsals.* One of the most effective approaches to pathways thinking is rehearsing the steps toward achieving our goals. Mental rehearsals provide us with opportunities to think about and prepare for the future, as opposed to ruminating on limited options presented to us in the past. They allow us to practice our thoughts and actions that will lead to goal accomplishment, including facing and overcoming obstacles and switching to alternate pathways. When actual obstacles appear, we are better prepared to face them after they have been mentally rehearsed. For example, a meta-analysis showed that when people spell out in advance when, where, and how they will pursue their goals, they have a significantly higher chance of achieving them compared to having only the intentions to achieve the same goals (Gollwitzer & Sheeran, 2006). Even people with low hope levels fare better when they utilize mental rehearsal strategies (Berg, Snyder, & Hamilton, 2008).

6. *Rituals.* Even with goals, agency, and pathways fully mobilized it can still be difficult to persist in our goal pursuit due to limited time and physical, mental, or emotional resources (although we said earlier that hope is largely cognitive, we know that emotions also matter), or social support. One of the most effective strategies to sustain goal pursuit when our energy runs low is when we set up rituals that will keep us on track without having to think too much about them or exert a lot of energy in building up willpower and/ or waypower. They involve specific behaviors at specific times; for example, brushing one's teeth is a common ritual. Similar to mental rehearsals, rituals allow us to put our brains on autopilot while still pursuing our goals.

In some of the stories about famous leaders, you see that they would set up certain rituals or routines to keep them moving through the day, taking one day at a time. In Mandela's case, it was his exercise regimen, and time for reflection, learning a new language to speak with his captors and creating a "university-like" environment to turn the prison guards and fellow political prisoners in his favor. Through this approach, he was able to change the "hell hole" that was Robben Island Prison, where he and his fellow political prisoners were brutally incarcerated, into Robben Island "University" where conditions were still difficult but learning and a purposeful life were also attained (Cascio & Luthans, 2014). Regardless of who you are, you have to have purpose and something left to focus on in order to avoid learned helplessness. After all, this was the captors' initial goal: to have Mandela and his fellow prisoners give up hope!

For everyone, a good example is exercising at a particular time of the day. Getting into the habit of exercising at that particular time every day prevents us from committing to other activities at the same time, and it protects us from procrastination. It also signals to others around us that this activity is important to us and conditions them not to distract us with other demands at that time because they know we are not available. The same applies to other important repetitive goals such as studying or staying up to date on one's professional field, meditation and other spiritual activities, and investing in relationships through regular time with family and friends.

For example, when the first author's four kids were growing up, every Sunday afternoon was formally designated as family "Fun Day." After getting out of Sunday School, the kids would rush into the car and breathlessly ask, "What are we going to do on Fun Day?" Needless to say, this put a lot of pressure on the parents to come up with interesting things to do every week, and of course Dad had to put his golf game on hold during those wonderful times. In other words, good intentions and willpower alone may not be enough to maintain important goals, especially when more urgent and pressing issues often seem to vie for our time, attention, and energy. Ritualistically keeping a set schedule for what we believe is important helps us stay committed while conserving our limited mental energy and resources.

7. *Involvement.* Emphasis on bottom-up decision making and communication, opportunities for participation, employee empowerment, engagement, delegation, and increased autonomy have documented desirable workplace outcomes. For example, studies have found such involvement works in terms of increased performance and in increasing employee satisfaction, commitment, and other desirable attitudinal outcomes such as psychological engagement and identification (e.g., see Conger & Kanungo, 1988; Hackman & Oldham, 1980; Harter, Schmidt, & Hayes, 2002; Spreitzer, 1995; Srivastva, 1986).

In analyzing the role of involvement techniques in terms of building hope, it is clear that these approaches provide today's workforce with the power, freedom, and authority to make decisions and choices, that is, agency. They also encourage the initiation and implementation of self-designed courses of action, that is, pathways. In line with our conceptualization of PsyCap hope, the role of participation in enhancing performance is not just emotional or motivational but also involves cognitive processing in that it gets individuals to analyze and consider what seemed impossible to become possible (Wagner, Leana, Locke, & Schweiger, 1997).

8. *Reward Systems.* The rich body of knowledge on behavioral performance management demonstrates beyond a doubt that you get what you reinforce (see meta-analyses by Stajkovic & Luthans, 1997, 2003). Reinforcing PsyCap hope thinking can be accomplished by rewarding, through genuine recognition and positive feedback, those who contribute to the appropriate goals, take effective goal-setting initiatives, exhibit internalized control and self-regulating behaviors (agency), and creatively and relentlessly pursue multiple alternative pathways toward goal achievement. Integral to the success of such a process is the understanding that well-designed reward systems in essence align organizational goals with personal intrinsic and extrinsic rewards. In most organizational situations, reward systems typically do not make the type of connection that will result in sustainable motivation and performance. Many individuals do not see a connection between what they do and the recognition they receive at work because most rewards are not specifically tied to the daily actions of an individual or a team (Luthans, 2000). This disconnect can drain one's motivation and lower performance. Showing people how their actions are directly instrumental to specific rewards has been shown over time to be highly motivating (Peterson & Luthans, 2006; Stajkovic & Luthans, 1997, 2001, 2003).

9. *Resources.* Becoming frustrated by blockages in trying to attain goals is inevitable in today's ever-changing, hypercompetitive environment. Thus, alternate pathways for maintaining and enhancing hope become critically important. The title of one popular business magazine exhorted, "Change or Die." With respect to PsyCap hope, change involves alternating one's pathways to find the route that will work best to achieve one's goals. However, with highly disengaged employees, situational constraints, such as the lack of access to necessary resources, can encourage an externalized, victimized perspective and quickly exhaust the available pathways, resulting in hopelessness, apathy, and disengagement. Needless to say, clearly set priorities and effective allocation of resources are vital to sustaining hope and resulting goal attainment. Support from the leader and organization to explore alternative pathways also helps.

In addition to obvious material resources, managerial support and commitment are also indispensable resources. For example, without top management support, very few important goals can be attained, regardless of the amount of willpower and waypower that middle managers and front-line employees may possess. In fact, the more hopeful organizational members are, the more frustrated they are likely to be in an environment that lacks top-down and organizational support.

In an interview with Jeff Immelt, the CEO of General Electric, he talked about how his father would behave at the family's dinner table depending upon who was his supervisor at the time. Jeff's father also worked for G.E. and in some periods of his career when he had a bad boss, "he came home in a bad mood, uncertain about the future. And when he had a good boss, he was pumped" (Byrne, 2005, p. 62). Notice the words he used to describe his motivation: "uncertain about the future" versus "pumped." This exemplifies what supervisor/manager support can do to provide hopelessness about the future or enthusiasm and hope for the future.

10. *Strategic Alignment*. Contemporary strategic management perspectives tend to overlook the salience of human resources as a primary resource for competitive advantage in the current global work environment (Pfeffer, 1998). Yet we are increasingly seeing more attention being given to strategic leadership and the need to provide employees with a clearer line of sight regarding the possibilities for the future. One can clearly see this in companies that are growing at exponential rates such as Google. Senior managers are energized by focusing their own motivation and that of their employees on "why" they do what they do that is propelling them into a broad range of new businesses and pathways for achieving success.

We also know, based on research from behavioral economics, that analysts valuing firms judge the value of leadership and the firm based on leaders' positivity in the comments they make to the "street." Recent research shown that how senior leaders in publicly traded firms shared their views on the state of their organizations had a significant impact on financial analysts' valuation of the firm (Avolio & Dunn, 2013). For example, Mayew and Venkatachalam (2012) reported positive and negative affect exhibited by strategic leaders during earnings calls predicting stock returns and future unexpected earnings in the direction consistent with the leader's expressed affect.

How senior leaders express hope both internally and externally matters in terms of workforce motivation and in terms of tangible financial returns. In the same way that effective strategic management emphasizes the proper allocation of financial and material resources to where they yield the highest return, developing the agency and pathways of hope necessitates the careful alignment of the placement and development of human resources with each employee's talents and strengths. From hope's focus on pathways, it follows that getting people aligned provides them with a broader set of pathway choices in which to be successful at work. The opposite extreme is getting people totally mismatched with their job responsibilities to the extent they have little chance for success. Such misalignment limits the pathway possibilities, along with the employees' hope.

11. *Training.* Even organizations that act upon the belief their human resources are their most important asset, and invest in their people through training, still need to be careful in adopting underlying training philosophies and in implementing training programs. Why? Prescriptive training approaches can promote passivity and limit pathways thinking. One-way, noninteractive training delivery techniques can diminish participants' sense of agency. Skill-oriented programs that solely disseminate standard technical knowledge and task-specific information, though sometimes necessary, can be limiting. On the other hand, hope-promoting types of training are hands-on, interactive, and participative. They are oriented toward enhancing general competencies and developing talents into strengths, which can subsequently be adapted to various situations. Hope-related training coupled with learned skills can be equipping and enabling but also leaves room for a corresponding focus on self-awareness, self-regulation, self-evaluation, and self-development.

There needs to be room for those being trained to develop goals that they own and are passionate about. Hope cannot grow on "borrowed" agency and assigned pathways. Using this underlying perspective in highly focused micro-interventions, we have been able to demonstrate positive impact on developing hope (as well as the other three positive resources and overall PsyCap; see Chapter 8 for details). These micro-intervention studies have significantly developed the hope (and overall PsyCap) of management students, managers, engineers, and employees of all types (Luthans, Avey, Avolio, Norman, & Combs, 2006; Luthans, Avey, Avolio, & Peterson, 2010; Luthans, Avey, & Patera, 2008; Luthans, Luthans, & Avey, 2014).

The Hopeful Organizational Leader or Manager

In light of the present turmoil in today's global environment, hopeful organizational leaders and managers become crucial to the growth, if not the very survival, of any organization. Leaders and managers need to keep the organization moving ahead, and underlying such growth is hope. Hopeful managers are not just "good managers," who effectively perform the classic managerial functions of planning, organizing, and controlling. Nor are they individuals with just the three recognized skills that managers need: conceptual, technical, and human (Katz, 1974).

Although such traditional approaches are still necessary for effective management, they are no longer sufficient in today's new paradigm, "flat-world" (Friedman, 2005) competitive environment, and neither is the classic, methodical manner of implementation. Our current times require that organizations take full advantage of growing the hope of their workforce in order to remain on the top end of the innovation and productivity curve. The advantage of building hope is that it is difficult to replicate by competitors without considerable effort and discipline on the part of leaders and managers. This makes it an enduring competitive advantage, which is typically anchored in one of the most difficult things for leaders to replicate: a hopeful culture.

The hopeful manager and leader needed for today's workplace is one who possesses goals that excite others, goal-directed willpower and waypower. Hopeful managers possess energy and determination that can trickle down to their followers, motivating them to have high performance impact. (We also know that abusive leadership can also trickle down in the same manner.) They are effective planners who can set specific, challenging goals and align those goals to the organization's most important objectives. They stimulate and set the context for their followers to determine their own goals, establish higher standards, and stretch their limits. They accept and respect their followers as individuals, supporting their self-set goals, and rewarding their creative pathways, even if nontraditional and unusual. Studies show that followers need leaders who are compassionate, stable, trustworthy, and hopeful. Hopeful managers are mentors, coaches, and developers of their associates. They produce the reaction: "I'm pumped."

Connecting this discussion to the emerging leadership literature, we see the hopeful manager as being one very critical component of an authentic leader (Avolio & Luthans, 2006; Luthans & Avolio, 2003; Luthans, Norman, & Hughes, 2006). Hopeful managers who are self-aware and know their capabilities, identities, vulnerabilities, values, emotions, and goals are by definition more authentic. Such individuals are capable of self-regulating their cognitions, emotions, and actions in themselves and others. Their consistent desire for self-verification and self-improvement motivates them to seek their followers' feedback and involvement (Avolio, 2004; Avolio & Luthans, 2006), which over time grows both the leader and follower, in what we would call a more authentic relationship. Indeed, being hopeful provides the energy to explore oneself to a greater extent, thus supporting leader self-awareness. Where there is no hope, there is neither a rationale to explore oneself to improve nor the motivation or energy to do so.

Even when decisions need to be made quickly and with little participation, hopeful managers explain the rationale for their actions in a genuine, transparent, trust-building manner. This authentic process encourages buy-in and maintains followers' dignity, as well as their sense of agency and pathways thinking. It also helps grow them into leaders as they are demonstrating the type of leadership one would "hope" current followers would exhibit with their future followers. Moreover, by being transparent and consistent, we know such leaders are then seen as displaying higher levels of integrity. In the authentic leadership literature, a higher level of displayed transparency builds followers' views of higher integrity and trust in the leader (Simons, 2002, 2008; Simons, Friedman, Liu, & McLean Parks, 2007).

The Hopeful Employee

Besides hopeful managers and leaders, it is also beneficial and necessary to portray a snapshot of the characteristics of hopeful employees. Although hope is a malleable state and thus variable, managers who are capable of identifying hopeful tendencies (or signs of hopelessness) can be better equipped to diagnose the state of hope among their employees. Effective managers are proactively prepared to nurture and reinforce hope in their associates.

More hopeful employees tend to display greater levels of independence in their thinking. They also possess what in the personality literature has been called an internal locus of control (i.e., they tend to make internal attributions such as their effort in interpreting their success on a task). Thus, they need and will seek a high degree of autonomy in order to express and utilize their agency. They may easily get offended and discouraged if micromanaged and will likely try to search for alternative pathways to regain control, which may be seen by the manager as being noncompliant. They have very strong needs for growth and achievement, and are intrinsically motivated by enriched jobs such as those described by Oldham and Hackman (1980) as having high levels of experienced meaningfulness and responsibility and that provide substantial feedback. Hopeful employees tend to be creative and resourceful, even with tight budgets, but they may also portray an impression of chaos and disorganization as they pursue nontraditional, out-of-the-box pathways. In other words, on the surface high hopers may appear to be nonconforming troublemakers, challenging the status quo or even high risk-takers. Many times we refer to those with such characteristics as "successful entrepreneurs."

On the other side of the coin, employees who lack hope may come off as conforming to organizational rules and having mindless obedience to their managers. Low hopers may be perceived by managers and coworkers as coopera-tive and "good soldiers." Unfortunately, most organizational reward systems are informally, if not formally, geared toward such benign attitudes and behaviors. However, if these are symptomatic of low agency and limited or no pathways, then, especially in today's environment, there are problems ahead for the man-ager and the organization. Such employees oftentimes become disengaged and just spend their hours at work looking busy. Worse yet, they may become actively disengaged and spend their time thinking of pathways to obstruct what the management and leadership is trying to accomplish.

Effective managers and leaders need to deal proactively with associates exhib-iting signs of hopelessness. Low hopers often exhibit an unwillingness or inabil-ity to assume additional responsibilities, make independent decisions, or solve challenging problems. Too many managers fall into the power trap of setting all the goals, making all the decisions, and carefully detailing every step to take for their associates. Although their intentions may be to enhance their units' perfor-mance through what they perceive to be hands-on leadership and tight controls, this micro-management approach may breed hopelessness and complacency among their people. It certainly will not contribute to developing an adapt-able or agile employee workforce that at least entertains the idea of change, as opposed to being immune to change. Fortunately, hopeful leaders and managers do the opposite and develop effective, hopeful employees, who not only are ener-gized to perform their own work but also find ways to support each other's work.

The Hopeful Organization: Nurturing a Culture of Hope and High Performance

Hopeful leaders, managers, and employees are an important asset for today's organization, as has been reflected in the vast literature on transformational leaders (Bass, 2008). However, there might be some challenges in attaining a hopeful organization. For example, managers and employees who are high on hope may become more readily frustrated with dead-end jobs, vaguely defined goals and promotion criteria, petty politics and policies, micromanagement, and centralized decision making. As a result, their attitudes and performance may suffer. That is why a supportive organizational climate has been found to be an important antecedent to the PsyCap–performance relationship (Luthans, Norman, Avolio, & Avey, 2008).

Apparently, high-hope managers and employees who possess the agency and pathways for their jobs have a lot more to offer than they are allowed to give in some organizations. In a restrictive, nonsupportive work environment, hopeful managers and employees become frustrated in that they have a level of energy they are not able to allocate in positive directions. Although these high hopers may continue to perform well in spite of their poor organizational situation, over time their deteriorating job satisfaction (e.g., Judge, Thoresen, Bono, & Patton, 2001), happiness (e.g., Fordyce, 1988), and organizational commitment (Allen & Meyer, 1990) may negatively impact their performance.

A specific example we are familiar with points to this problem. In this organization, telemarketers and telephone customer service representatives were hired with the implication that this entry-level position would lead to a career path in marketing or sales. It seemed that the organization-wide knowledge of this expectation had a positive impact on retention of these telemarketers, which in the United States (not India) is perceived as a dead-end or at best transitional job. Informally understood promotion criteria in this firm included job tenure and pursuing and attaining a college degree. The more hopeful employees in the telemarketing jobs patiently waited for their "turn to be promoted" into sales and marketing as they put in their time and pursued their degrees. In other words, they took it upon themselves (agency) to move up (be promoted into sales/marketing), and they found the means (pathways through seniority and higher education) to do so, even when the organization did not offer any tuition reimbursement programs or even time release for attending classes.

As the "big day" came and an opening was posted in sales, those who perceived themselves to be qualified according to the "criteria" (tenure and education) applied for the sales position. However, upon interviewing these hopeful internal candidates and a few outsiders, an external candidate was selected. The chosen candidate was a fresh college graduate and had no experience in this industry and thus did not meet the existing employees' perceived "criteria." Internal candidates were not informed about the criteria that were used to select this outside candidate's qualifications over theirs. Disappointment and frustration caused several of these high-hope telemarketers to quit, while many others updated their resumes and began job hunting.

In terms of hope in this example, the internalized determination and motivation to move up into a better job, which the hopeful employees possessed, was shot down by the organization. These hopeful employees now perceived they were faced with an unbalanced or inequitable situation and lost trust in management. However, their strongly desired goals for growth and advancement, as well as the resourcefulness and waypower to reach these goals, stimulated them to rechannel their agency into another pathway that reduced their commitment to their present organization and eventually their job performance. They pursued alternative employment opportunities. As we noted earlier, if desirable alternatives are limited within the current organization and the hopeful employee is forced into undesirable pathways, he or she may become actively disengaged and delight in derailing management's agenda. On the other hand, less hopeful employees simply accepted the fact that their careers are determined by the organization and not through their own efforts (low agency). These low hopers did not pursue alternative undesirable possibilities (pathways), and they remained in the organization, but they also were low performers.

Several factors can promote the organizational culture needed for hope development and sustainability. Strategic initiatives emphasizing long-term goal setting, coordination, integration, and contingency planning can create an organizational environment where agency and pathways thinking can thrive. Clearly, we are speaking here of an organizational climate and culture that stimulates and reinforces such thinking and behavior. Organizations such as the well-known "Best Place to Work For" North Carolina software firm SAS present their members with a well-developed "master plan" with which to align their personal/professional goals with the organizational goals. Such a plan effectively facilitates and capitalizes on their participants' PsyCap hope. The organization can also provide the appropriate boundaries and open unexplored territories for PsyCap hope to be channeled and to flourish.

Hopeful organizations are proactive in seeking and creating opportunities for members and in controlling the environment to facilitate achieving their goals. When organizations explicitly verbalize their philosophies into an inspiring, value-based vision, a clear mission statement, and a practical, realistic set of objectives, they are in essence creating a realistic organizational preview for existing and potential participants. Hopeful new hires that identify with the organization's strategic direction are likely to self-select, buy into, and build upon the organization's course of action. The same is true of existing hopeful managers and employees. Even those less hopeful can be socialized into the hopeful organization's culture as their agency and pathways thinking are developed over time and then are maintained.

Open and transparent flows of communication through flat, organic structures, participative decision making, empowerment, and other flexible, high-engagement techniques can provide a culture of hope that encourages its members to take initiatives, seek responsibility, accept accountability, and expect to be treated fairly and rewarded when doing so. These are some of the ways hopeful organizations can stimulate, maintain, and enhance the willpower and waypower of participants. In such a hopeful organizational culture, transparency and authenticity allow resources, including traditional economic, but also human, social, and psychological capital, to be readily shared and swiftly allocated to their best uses (Avolio & Luthans, 2006; Luthans & Youssef, 2004; Youssef & Luthans, 2006).

On the dark side, in a nontransparent or unethical organization, people figure out pathways to avoid giving up the resources they have and in the extreme create what is referred to in war as an "insurgency." This phenomenon oftentimes coincides with silos being created in organizations where one function won't help another. For example, a colleague of one of the authors said she would never lend a helping hand to that other department because it would detract from "our" work, and more important management may see us as having too many employees, if we have time to help others. So this individual struggled with her desire to reach out and help others, and the mandate from her supervisor to "stay in her lane" or else!

Moreover, organizations that thrive on policies and procedures that cover every intricate detail of their operations tend to stifle hope. The false sense of security and control of highly structured operations and heavily bureaucratic top-down decision making may appear efficient, but, because of the negative impact on hope, can be detrimental over time. Individuals need to have the context to grow in over time, and having no options to deviate from strict rules and procedures is a recipe for stifling growth and creating hopelessness.

We recently heard a nuclear facility plant manager saying, "We are very creative in our plant to help continuously grow our employees." He then added, "now don't worry we are not being 'creative' in how we run our plant, even though in our simulations I must say we strive for absolute creativity." What this manager was saying is that even though the job had very set rules stemming from necessary strict regulatory and safety regulations for dealing with nuclear power generation, there is always a way to grow one's employees, and they did so in this organization through elaborate learning simulations.

The organizational inertia caused by mechanistic structures and centralized decision making stands in stark contrast to the agency and pathways thinking of hopeful managers and employees that is needed in today's rapidly changing, new paradigm landscape. Indeed, in the nuclear facility, as in any high-reliability organizational context, it is possible to have creativity *and* pay attention to the routine, and these do not necessarily have to be in conflict. Indeed, the creativity culture of the organization may eventually unleash the power of hopeful participants to improve upon that which is currently routine operations.

Potential Pitfalls

Once again, hopeful managers, leaders, employees, and organizations are very goal directed, agentic, and resourceful. They are capable of setting and accomplishing challenging goals through their determined willpower and creative waypower. The iterative nature of hope allows goal achievement to further nurture agency and pathways into even higher levels of hope. However, as with the other dimensions of PsyCap, realism is required for hope to be effective. "False hope" is certainly a potential threat, so likely we have an inverted U-shaped relationship between hope and success. At some point, where hope becomes unrealistic, performance may precipitously decline along with success.

Polivy and Herman (2002) offer an elaborate model of this "false hope syndrome." In the context of dieting and weight loss, they argue that false hope is primarily caused by the unrealistic expectations regarding the likely speed, amount, ease, and consequences of weight loss. These unrealistic expectations are often promoted by the ingenious marketing of commercial weight loss products and programs (e.g., lose 10 pounds in 10 days without dieting or exercise). People are often led to overestimate how much weight they will lose, how fast they will lose it, and how easy the process will be. Most important, they adopt unrealistic expectations regarding the benefits they will gain from losing weight, such as looking and feeling good, or being more successful romantically or professionally. Even with repeated failure or rebound, instead of adjusting unrealistic goals, they may attribute their less-than-desirable results to insufficient effort or blame it on the particular diet they followed and jump on the next marketing fad that the diet industry wants them to believe.

Because of this vicious cycle, Polivy and Herman (2002) marvel at people's ability to sustain false hope, even casting doubt on the efficacy of many important self-change efforts such as giving up smoking, excessive drinking, and drug abuse. It is not that aiming too high is always wrong. Dreaming is necessary for achieving revolutionary change, and some goals are worth pursuing no matter how challenging. Challenging goals give life meaning and purpose, and the risk of failure is what boosts our determination to beat the odds, conquer our fears, and succeed (Lopez, 2013). However, repeated failure should prompt adjustment of goals, pathways, or both. This process of continuous tweaking is what eventually leads to success and goal achievement. Low-hope people may fall victim to false hope because they often fail to revise their expectations. High-hope people know the difference. They know when, how, and how often to adjust their expectations and pathways to stay on track (Snyder & Rand, 2003).

Unrealistically hopeful organizations or individuals may commit their energy and resources to goals that are beyond their reach. They may also fall into the trap of escalation of commitment and continue to enthusiastically pursue goals that may be challenging but that are no longer strategically significant or realistically attainable. Snyder (1995a) advises that along with hope development, the skill of "regoaling" is necessary to continuously redirect the energies and creativity of hopeful individuals to the right goals, and away from obsolete goals or those that have proven over time to be unreachable.

Another potential pitfall for high-hope organizations and their members is to avoid "the end justifies the means" type of mentality. In their relentless pursuit of valuable personal or organizational goals, some hopeful individuals may be tempted to seek pathways that compromise their own and their organization's ethical values or social responsibility in relation to internal or external stakeholders. For example, some personal goals, agency, and pathways may be self-serving. Other goals may benefit one group of stakeholders at the expense of others, as is the case in situations such as union–management negotiations, interdepartmental competition, or shareholder wealth maximization.

On the other hand, a clearly communicated and emphasized set of organizational values, along with the proper alignment of individual, group, and organizational goals and objectives, may help guide and channel hope's willpower and waypower toward appropriate and ethically sound goals. Coupled with an equitable transactional contingent reward system and authentic leadership, the resulting agreed-upon goals and means are likely to balance and support the needs and rights of various stakeholders. The reward system and authentic leadership can contribute to maintaining the organization's vision and enhancing its reputation and long-term veritable, sustained performance (Avolio & Luthans, 2006; Youssef & Luthans, 2004).

Finally, as the PsyCap hope development process takes place, let's not allow the nobleness of the cause to obscure the joy of the journey. Pragmatically, goal attainment is extremely important. However, if we view hope to be just about setting and achieving goals, no matter how important or noble the goals are, this perspective might be too narrow. Hope is much more than that. It is about opening ourselves up to new possibilities and experiences beyond what we thought possible. It is about reinterpreting the past, resisting the closedness and limitations of the present, and willingly accepting the uncertainties of the future. This type of hope is facilitated when pursued in a relational context such as a team, an organization, or a community (Carlsen et al., 2012).

In practical terms, organizations, managers, and employees are well advised to not only admire hope's agency and pathways as terminal outcomes but also to enjoy the hope-building process in which the components of hope are developed and maintained. Goal setting, stretch goals, stepping, and regoaling should be perceived as invaluable to learning, growth, and self-actualization experiences. Participation, delegation, and other agency-development techniques should be designed to be perceived as opportunities for gradually increasing autonomy and responsibility, rather than useless time-wasting management fads or ways for blame shifting. Building pathways should enhance managers' and employees' creative decision-making and problem-solving repertoire, and allow these hopeful organizational participants to continuously overcome frustrating obstacles and blocked routes. This PsyCap hope building is beneficial for lifelong learning and adaptation, both personally and professionally. For those with PsyCap hope, blockages in goal achievement can be viewed as challenges and opportunities for development, rather than dead ends and excuses for disengagement, apathy, and stagnation.

Future Implications and Directions for PsyCap Hope Research and Practice

As a criteria-meeting PsyCap capacity, hope represents an invaluable, but still overlooked, positive resource for human resource development and performance management. We conclude this chapter on PsyCap hope with some of the most promising areas for future research and practice:

- Although much is now known about what hope is, the theoretical and practical mechanisms through which hope operates still need further investigation. For example, hope is a combination of prospection and introspection. The cognitive and affective mechanisms through which the past is used to bring the future to the present for effective goal setting, planning, and elaboration deserve further investigation. Neuroscience is beginning to scratch the surface on some of these mechanisms (Addis, Wong, & Schacter, 2007), and business applications are also emerging (Peterson, Balthazard, Waldman, & Thatcher, 2008). Moreover, although hope is believed to be contagious, its contagion mechanisms are still largely unknown. Some of those mechanisms may be social in nature, but emerging neurophysiological research is also discovering more tangible mechanisms in the form of what has been called "mirror neurons" that prime mimicry (Cattaneo & Rizzolatti, 2009; Rizzolatti & Craighero, 2004). Such neurological mechanisms represent exciting new opportunities for the cross-disciplinary study and application of hope.
- Particularly with PsyCap hope (and optimism, as we discuss in the next chapter), the possibility for its development leading to "too much of a good thing" needs to be more fully recognized and explored (e.g., see Held, 2004). Conceptually, Snyder (1995a) recommends that the development of hope should also constitute enhancing the skill of regoaling to avoid "false hope," or the inverted-U relationship between hope and performance that we suggested in our discussion. Empirically examining such a relationship, as well as the situational contingencies that may influence its shape and threshold point(s), may be challenging but necessary for effective application. Empirical research across diverse organizational populations can contribute to such a broader spectrum of hope and performance levels. Moreover, studying and

understanding "outliers" who researchers or practicing managers may ordinarily dismiss as "too hopeful" or "too hopeless" may be of key importance.

- Relevant to the first two points is the need for using more diversified tools for assessing PsyCap hope in order to triangulate findings. Embedding researchers in organizations to examine qualitatively how hope is developed and how it manifests in communications, for example, would be a very useful avenue to pursue in future research. The same is true for employing both qualitative and quantitative in a mixed method design (Creswell & Plano Clark, 2011). Studying the more tangible biological evidence is still another.

- As more empirical research emerges, more meta-analytical studies of PsyCap hope to extend existing work (e.g., Reichard et al., 2013) and can also more accurately and comprehensively depict the breadth of these complex and possibly nonlinear relationships, while also exploring potential mediating and/or moderating factors.

- In his conceptualization of hope, Snyder (1993) contends that there is a continuous reiteration between the analysis of agency and pathways related to a goal in one's cognitive activity, with hope reflecting the cumulative level of perceived agency and pathways. However, the current instruments available to assess PsyCap hope (Snyder, 2000; Snyder et al., 1996) give hope's willpower and waypower equal additive weights. Further development in this area could account for the potential interactions between the agency and pathways components of hope, as well as any potential situational factors that may influence the relative weights that these two components bear on one's hopefulness and performance.

- Similarly, hope has been primarily viewed as a cognitive capacity, with positive emotions emerging as a by-product of successful goal achievement (Snyder, 2000, 2002). However, more recently, positive emotions have assumed a more integral role in hope. They can act as "cognitive guides" that direct our thinking toward the right goals and pathways and steer us away from unproductive thoughts (Lopez, 2013). Recent studies show that positive emotions may be antecedents to hope when investigated both experimentally (Fredrickson, Cohn, Coffey, Pek, & Finkel, 2008) and over time (Ouweneel et al., 2012). The relationships are likely reciprocal, but further investigation of the causal direction, intensity, and, most important, the cognitive and affective mechanisms of hope remain unexplored.

- We suspect that it is not only what the leader does and says but also the attributes of the leader that may give him or her a better starting point for building PsyCap hope. We need to learn more about how the characteristics of the leader as well as the nature of the context contribute to PsyCap hope development. Also, one area that needs to be examined more closely is how the impression management strategies used by the leader contribute to PsyCap hope.

- Short interventions to boost PsyCap hope need to be explored to determine ways that both the leader and followers willpower and waypower can be enhanced. As with the other PsyCap components, we know relatively little about the type of interventions that will build and sustain the highest levels of PsyCap hope. Today, we can reach out to employees through social media, smartphones, and even "fit" devices that can signal them to recall a time when they seemed to be at their last pathway, but then another emerged, or simply to prime the individual to think that there may be one more way to approach this problem he or she hasn't thought of yet. These technologies now in use for exercising could be invaluable for promoting greater positivity and hope in the workplace.

- Finally, the implications of potential cross-level issues, upward and downward spirals, contagion effects, and cross-cultural differences that we presented for PsyCap efficacy in the last chapter are also relevant to future PsyCap hope research and practice.

Case Study: I Am Malala

Video link: http://www.youtube.com/results?search_query=malala+yousafz ai+daily+show&oq=malala&gs_l=youtube.1.0.0i3l3j0l7.3086.5037.0.9605. 6.4.0.0.0.0.352.629.2j1j0j1.4.0...0.0...1ac.1.11.youtube.hFlOfRJA28c

Malala Yousafzai is a young Pakistani who became a worldwide advocate of female education; she suffered greatly for it, both physically and psychologically. She is the all-time youngest nominee for a Nobel Prize for Peace. As she tells her story in this video and in her book *I Am Malala*, her hope is demonstrated through an exceptional ability to set clear goals, determination to achieve her goals, pathways thinking, and mental rehearsals of her goals and pathways.

Questions for reflection and/or discussion:

1. What could have been potential excuses for Malala to live a life of hopelessness and despair?
2. In what ways do goals, agency, and pathways play a role in Malala's hope?
3. Does Malala's hope seem to be justified and potentially conducive to positive change, or is it more accurate to describe it as "false hope"?
4. What aspects of her context, support from family, friends, or other role models, helped to foster greater hope in this remarkable young woman?

Case Study: Good Job = High Hope; No Job = No Hope

Video link: http://www.youtube.com/watch?v=TTLy7I3PWGY

Video link: http://www.youtube.com/watch?v=bKH0a9DdB54

In these two videos, the importance of having a good job for instilling hope is demonstrated. In one case, Cody Preston, profiled by the *Wall Street Journal* in two stories about high unemployment among young men, finds new hope. His life is transformed through a new, steady job. In another case, Tim Quay, a Chinese worker, considers his limited options as he faces a seemingly hopeless situation when he and some of his family members face unemployment.

Questions for reflection and/or discussion:

1. In what ways did goals, agency, and pathways play a role in Cody Preston's hope?

2. Apply the hope components of goals, agency, and pathways to Tim Quay's situation. Do Tim Quay and his family appear to have lost hope? Why? Why not? If lost, how might it be triggered in order to be regained?

3. Why is a good job an important source of hope? How does work, especially a good job, contribute to one's goals, agency, and pathways? Reflect on the these two stories, then apply to your own experiences.

4. When can one's job become a cause of hopelessness? Make sure you apply the hope components of goals, agency, and pathways when answering this question.

5. What are alternative approaches for maintaining hope during an economic downturn, an extended period of unemployment, or an unfavorable present job situation?

References

Adams, V. H., Snyder, C. R., Rand, K. L., King, E. A., Sigman, D. R., & Pulvers, K, M. (2002). Hope in the workplace. In R. Giacolone & C. Jurkiewicz (Eds.), *Workplace spirituality and organizational performance* (pp. 367–377). New York, NY: Sharpe.

Addis, D. R., Wong, A. T., & Schacter, D. L. (2007). Remembering the past and imagining the future: Common and distinct neural substrates during event construction and elaboration. *Neuropsychologica, 45,* 1363–1377.

Allen, N. J., & Meyer, J. P. (1990). The measurement and antecedents of affective, continuance and normative commitment to the organization. *Journal of Occupational Psychology*, *63*, 1–18.

Avey, J. B., Nimnicht J. L., & Pigeon, N. G. (2010). Two field studies examining the association between positive psychological capital and employee performance. *Leadership and organization Development Journal*, *31*, 384–401.

Avey, J. B., Reichard, R. J., Luthans, F., & Mhatre, K. H. (2011). Meta-analysis of the impact of positive psychological capital on employee attitudes, behaviors, and performance. *Human Resource Development Quarterly*, *22*, 127–152.

Avolio, B. J. (2004). Examining the full range model of leadership: Looking back to transform forward. In D. Day & S. Zaccarro (Eds.), *Leadership development for transforming organizations* (pp. 71–98). Mahwab, NJ: Erlbaum.

Avolio, B. J., & Dunn, S. (2013). Monetizing leadership quality. *Chief Executive, Mar/Apr 2013*, 12.

Avolio, B. J., & Luthans, F. (2006). *The high impact leader*. New York, NY: McGraw-Hill.

Badran, M. A., & Youssef-Morgan, C. M. (2014). Psychological capital and job satisfaction in Egypt. *Journal of Managerial Psychology*, in press.

Bass, B. M. (2008). *Bass and Stogdill's Handbook of Leadership* (3rd Edition). NY: Free Press.

Berg, C. J., Snyder, C. R., & Hamilton, N. (2008). The effectiveness of a hope intervention in coping with cold pressor pain. *Journal of Health Psychology*, *13*, 804–809.

Bryant, F. B., & Cvengros, J. A. (2004). Distinguishing hope and optimism. *Journal of Social and Clinical Psychology*, *23*, 273–302.

Byrne, J. (2005). The Fast Company interview: Jeff Immelt. *Fast Company*, *96*, 60–65.

Carlsen, A., Hagen, A. L., & Mortensen, T. F. (2012). Imagining hope in organizations: From individual goal-attainment to horizons of relational possibility. In K. S. Cameron & G. M. Spreitzer (Eds.), *The Oxford handbook of positive organizational scholarship* (pp. 288–303). New York, NY: Oxford University Press.

Cascio, W. F., & Luthans, F. (2014). Reflections on the metamorphosis at Robben Island: The role of institutional work and positive psychological capital. *Journal of Management Inquiry*, *23*, 51–67.

Cattaneo, L., & Rizzolatti, G. (2009). The mirror neuron system. *Archives of Neurology*, *66*, 557–560.

Coats, E. J., Janoff-Bulman, R., & Alpert, N. (1996). Approach versus avoidance goals: Differences in self-evaluation and well-being. *Personality and Social Psychology Bulletin*, *22*, 1057–1067.

Conger, J., & Kanungo, R. (1988). The empowerment process: Integrating theory and practice. *Academy of Management Review*, *31*, 471–482.

Creswell, J. W., & Plano Clark, V. L. (2011). *Designing and conducting mixed methods research*. Thousand Oaks, CA: Sage.

Curry, L. A., Snyder, C. R., Cook, D. I., Ruby, B. C., & Rehm, M. (1997). The role of hope in student-athlete academic and sport achievement. *Journal of Personality and Social Psychology, 73*, 1257–1267.

Elliot, A. (2006). The hierarchical model of approach-avoidance motivation. *Motivation and Emotion, 30*(2), 111–116.

Fordyce, M. W. (1988). A review of research on the happiness measures: A sixty second index of happiness and health. *Social Indicators Research, 20*, 355–381.

Fredrickson, B. L., Cohn, M. A., Coffey, K. A., Pek, J., & Finkel, S. M. (2008). Open hearts build lives: Positive emotions, induced through loving-kindness meditation, build consequential personal resources. *Journal of Personality and Social Psychology, 95*, 1045–1062.

Friedman, T. L. (2005). *The world is flat.* New York, NY: Farror, Straus and Giroux.

Gollwitzer, P. M., & Sheeran, P. (2006). Implementation intentions and goal achievement: A meta-analysis of effects and processes. *Advances in Experimental Social Psychology, 38*, 69–119.

Hackman, J., & Oldham, G. (1980). *Work redesign.* Reading, MA: Addison-Wesley.

Harter, J., Schmidt, F., & Hayes, T. (2002). Business-unit-level relationship between employee satisfaction, employee engagement, and business outcomes: A meta-analysis. *Journal of Applied Psychology, 87*, 268–279.

Held, B. S. (2004). The negative side of positive psychology. *Journal of Humanistic Psychology, 44*, 9–46.

Huang, P. H., & Lin, Y. C. (2013, June). Moderating effect of psychological capital on the relationship between career capital and career success. In *Proceedings of the 16 the Conference on Interdisciplinary and Multifunctional Business Management & High Education Forum on Business Management, Soochow University, Department of Business Administration, Taiwan University* (pp. 1–15).

Huimei, W., & Xuan, L. (2011, Nov. 3–Dec. 2). Study on psychological capital and organizational identity. In *Proceedings of the 8th International Conference on Innovation and Management, Kitakyushu, Japan* (pp. 662–665).

Judge, T. A., Thoresen, C. J., Bono, J. E., & Patton, G. K. (2001). The job satisfaction-job performance relationship: A qualitative and quantitative review. *Psychological Bulletin, 127*, 376–407.

Jensen, S. M., & Luthans, F. (2002). *The impact of hope in the entrepreneurial process: Exploratory research findings.* Paper presented at the Decision Sciences Institute Conference, San Diego, CA.

Katz, R. (1974). Skills of an effective administrator. *Harvard Business Review, 52*, 90–102.

Kwon, P. (2000). Hope and dysphoria: The moderating role of defense mechanisms. *Journal of Personality, 68*(2), 199–223.

Latham, G. (2000). Motivate employee performance through goal-setting. In E. Locke (Ed.), *Handbook of principles of organizational behavior* (pp. 107–119). Oxford, UK: Blackwell.

Latham, G., Erez, M., & Locke, E. (1988). Resolving scientific disputes by the joint design of crucial experiments by the antagonists: Application to the Erez-Latham dispute regarding participation in goal setting. *Journal of Applied Psychology, 73,* 753–772.

Latham, G., Winters, D., & Locke, E. (1994). Cognitive and motivational effects of participation: A mediator study. *Journal of Organizational Behavior, 15,* 49–63.

Lehoczky, M. H. (2013). The socio-democratic correlations of psychological capital. *European Scientific Journal, 9*(29), 26–42.

Locke, E. A., & Latham, G. (1990). *A theory of goal setting and task performance.* Englewood Cliffs, NJ: Prentice Hall.

Locke, E. A., & Latham, G. P. (2002). Building a practically useful theory of goal setting and task motivation: A 35-year odyssey. *American Psychologist, 57,* 705–717.

Locke, E. A., & Latham, G.P. (2006). New directions in goal-setting theory. *Current Directions in Psychological Science, 15,* 265–268.

Lopez, S. (2013). *Making hope happen.* New York, NY: Atria.

Luthans, B., Luthans, K., & Avey, J. B. (2014). Building the leaders of tomorrow: The development of academic psychological capital. *Journal of Leadership and Organizational Studies, 21*(2), 191–199.

Luthans, F. (2002a). The need for and meaning of positive organizational behavior. *Journal of Organizational Behavior, 23,* 695–706

Luthans, F. (2002b). Positive organizational behavior: Developing and managing psychological strengths. *Academy of Management Executive, 16,* 57–72.

Luthans, F., Avey, J. B., Avolio, B. J., Norman, S. M., & Combs, G. J. (2006). Psychological capital development: Toward a micro-intervention. *Journal of Organizational Behavior, 27,* 387–393.

Luthans, F., Avey, J. B., Avolio, B. J., & Peterson, S. (2010). The development and resulting performance impact of positive psychological capital. *Human Resource Development Quarterly, 21,* 41–66.

Luthans, F., Avey, J. B., Clapp-Smith, R., & Li, W. (2008). More evidence on the value of Chinese workers' psychological capital: A potentially unlimited competitive resource. *International Journal of Human Resource Management, 19,* 818–827.

Luthans, F., Avey, J. B., & Patera, J. L. (2008). Experimental analysis of a web-based training intervention to develop positive psychological capital. *Academy of Management Learning and Education, 7,* 209–221.

Luthans, F., & Avolio, B. J. (2003). Authentic leadership: A positive development approach. In K. S. Cameron, J. E. Dutton, & R. E. Quinn (Eds.), *Positive organizational scholarship* (pp. 241–258). San Francisco, CA: Berrett-Koehler.

Luthans, F., & Jensen, S. M. (2002). Hope: A new positive strength for human resource development. *Human Resource Development Review, 1,* 304–322.

Luthans, F., Norman, S. M., Avolio, B. J., & Avey, J. B. (2008). The mediating role of psychological capital in the supportive organizational climate-employee performance relationship. *Journal of Organizational Behavior, 29,* 219–238.

Luthans, F., Norman, S., & Hughes, L. (2006). Authentic leadership: A new approach for a new time. In R. Burke & C. Cooper (Eds.), *Inspiring leaders* (pp. 84–104). London, UK: Routledge, Taylor & Francis.

Luthans, F., Van Wyk, R., & Walumbwa, F.O. (2004). Recognition and development of hope for South African organizational leaders. *Leadership and Organization Development Journal, 25,* 512–527.

Luthans, F., & Youssef, C. M. (2004). Human, social and now positive psychological capital management: Investing in people for competitive advantage. *Organizational Dynamics, 33,* 143–160.

Luthans, K. W. (2000). Recognition: A powerful, but often overlooked leadership tool to improve employee performance. *Journal of Leadership Studies, 7,* 31–39.

Magaletta, P. R., & Oliver, J. M. (1999). The hope construct, will and ways: Their relations with self-efficacy, optimism, and well being. *Journal of Clinical Psychology, 55,* 539–551.

Mayew, W. J., & Venkatachalam, M. (2012). The power of voice: Managerial affective states and future firm performance. *The Journal of Finance, 67*(1), 1–43.

Mehrabi, S., Babri, H., Frohar, M., Khabazuan, B., & Salili, S. (2013). Investigating the relationship between organizational psychological capital and meaning in the employees' work (Shahid Beheshti University as a case study). *International Journal of Human Resource Studies, 3*(2), 42–50.

Oldham, G., & Hackman, J. (1980). Work design in the organizational context. *Research in Organizational Behavior, 2,* 247–278.

Onwuegbuzie, A. J., & Snyder, C. R. (2000). Relations between hope and graduate students' coping strategies for studying and examination taking. *Psychological Reports, 86,* 803–806.

Ouweneel, E., Le Blanc, P. M., Shaufeli, W. B., & van Wijhe, C. I. (2012). Good morning, good day: A diary study on positive emotions, hope, and work engagement. *Human Relations, 65,* 1129–1154.

Peterson, S. J., Balthazard, P. A., Waldman, D. A., & Thatcher, R. W. (2008). Neuroscientific implications of psychological capital: Are the brains of optimistic, hopeful, confident, and resilient leaders different? *Organizational Dynamics, 37,* 342–353.

Peterson, S. J., & Byron, K. (2008). Exploring the role of hope in job performance: Results from four studies. *Journal of Organizational Behavior, 29,* 785–803.

Peterson, S. J., & Luthans, F. (2006). The impact of financial and nonfinancial incentives on business-unit outcomes over time. *Journal of Applied Psychology, 91,* 156–165.

Peterson, S. J., & Luthans, F. (2003). The positive impact and development of hopeful leaders. *Leadership and Organization Development Journal, 24*(1), 26–31.

Pfeffer, J. (1998). *The human equation.* Boston, MA: Harvard Business School Press.

Polivy, J., & Herman, C. P. (2002). If at first you don't succeed: False hopes of self-change. *American Psychologist, 57,* 677–689.

Rand, K. L., & Cheavens, J. S. (2009). Hope theory. In S. J. Lopez & C. R. Snyder (Eds.), *Handbook of positive psychology* (2nd ed., pp. 323–333). New York, NY: Oxford University Press.

Range, L., & Pentin, S. (1994). Hope, hopelessness and suicidality in college students. *Psychological Reports, 75*, 456–458.

Reichard, R. J., Avey, J. B., Lopez, S. J., & Dowlett, M. (2013). Having the will and finding the way: A review and meta-analysis of hope at work. *Journal of Positive Psychology, 8*, 292–304.

Reichard, R. J., Dollwet, M., & Louw-Potgieter, J. (2014). Development of cross-cultural psychological capital and its relationship with cultural intelligence and ethnocentrism. *Journal of Leadership and Organizational Studies, 21*, 150–164.

Rizzolatti, G., & Craighero, L. (2004). The mirror-neuron system. *Annual Review of Neuroscience, 27*, 169–192.

Roche, M. A., Haar, J. M., & Luthans, F. (2014). The role of mindfulness and psychological capital on the well-being of organizational leaders. *Journal of Occupational Health Psychology, 19*, 476–489.

Scioli, A., Chamberlin, C., Samor, C. M., LaPointe, A. B., Campbell, T. L., MacLeod, A. R., & McLenon, J. A. (1997). A prospective study of hope, optimism, and health. *Psychological Reports, 81*, 723–733.

Seligman, M. E. P. (1972). Learned helplessness. *Annual Review of Medicine, 23*, 407–412.

Simons, T. (2002). Behavioral integrity: The perceived alignment between managers' words and deeds as a research focus. *Organization Science, 13*(1), 18–35.

Simons, T. (2008). *The integrity dividend: Leading by the power of your word.* San Francisco, CA: Jossey-Bass.

Simons, T., Friedman, R., Liu, L. A., & McLean Parks, J. (2007). Racial differences in sensitivity to behavioral integrity: Attitudinal consequences, in-group effects, and "trickle down" among Black and non-Black employees. *Journal of Applied Psychology, 92*(3), 650.

Snyder, C. R. (1993). Hope for the journey. In A. P. Turnbull, J. M. Patterson, S. K. Behr, D. L. Murphy, J. G. Marquis, & M. J. Blue-Banning (Eds.), *Cognitive coping, families, and disability* (pp. 271–286). Baltimore, MD: Paul H. Brooks.

Snyder, C. R. (1994a). Hope and optimism. In S. Ramachandran (Ed.), *Encyclopedia of human behavior* (Vol. 2, pp. 535–542). San Diego, CA: Academic Press.

Snyder, C. R. (1994b). *The psychology of hope: You can get here from there.* New York, NY: Free Press.

Snyder, C. R. (1995a). Conceptualizing, measuring, and nurturing hope. *Journal of Counseling and Development, 73*, 355–360.

Snyder, C. R. (1995b). Managing for high hope. *R and D Innovator, 4*(6), 6–7.

Snyder, C. R. (2000). *Handbook of hope.* San Diego, CA: Academic Press.

Snyder, C. R. (2002). Hope theory: Rainbows in the mind. *Psychological Inquiry, 13*, 249–275.

Snyder, C. R., Harris, C., Anderson, J. R., Holleran, S. A., Irving, L. M., Sigmon, S. T., . . . Harney, P. (1991). The will and the ways. Development and validation of an individual-differences measure of hope. *Journal of Personality and Social Psychology, 60,* 570–585.

Snyder, C. R., Ilardi, S., Michael, S. T., & Cheavens, J. (2000). Hope theory: Updating a common process for psychological change. In C. R. Snyder & R. E. Ingram (Eds.), *Handbook of psychological change: Psychotherapy processes and practices for the 21st century* (pp. 128–153). New York, NY: Wiley.

Snyder, C. R., Irving, L., & Anderson, J. (1991). Hope and health: Measuring the will and the ways. In C. R. Snyder & D. R. Forsyth (Eds.), *Handbook of social and clinical psychology* (pp. 285–305). Elmsford, NY: Pergamon.

Snyder, C. R., & Rand, L. L. (2003). The case against false hope. *American Psychologist, 58,* 820–822.

Snyder, C. R., Rand, K. L., & Sigmon, D. R. (2002). Hope theory. In C. R. Snyder & S. Lopez (Eds.), *Handbook of positive psychology* (pp. 257–276). Oxford, UK: Oxford University Press.

Snyder, C. R., Sympson, S. C., Ybasco, F. C., Borders, T. F., Babyak, M. A., & Higgins, R. L. (1996). Development and validation of the state hope scale. *Journal of Personality and Social Psychology, 70,* 321–335.

Snyder, C. R., Tran, T., Schroeder, L. L., Pulvers, K. M., Adam, V., III, & Laub, L. (2000). Teaching the hope recipe: Setting goals, finding pathways to those goals, and getting motivated. *National Educational Service, Summer,* 46–50.

Spreitzer, G. (1995). Individual empowerment in the workplace: Dimensions, measurement, and validation. *Academy of Management Journal, 38,* 1442–1465.

Srivastra, S. (1986). *Executive power.* San Francisco, CA: Jossey-Bass.

Stajkovic, A. D., & Luthans, F. (1997). A meta-analysis of the effects of organizational behavior modification on task performance: 1975–95. *Academy of Management Journal, 40,* 1122–1149.

Stajkovic, A., & Luthans F. (2003) Behavioral management and task performance in organizations: Conceptual background, meta-analysis, and test of alternative models. *Personnel Psychology, 56,* 155–194.

Stajkovic, A. D., & Luthans, F. (2001). The differential effects of incentive motivators on work performance. *Academy of Management Journal, 44,* 580–590.

Veninga, R. L. (2000). Managing hope in the workplace: Five simple strategies can help transform organizations. *Health Progress, 81,* 22–24.

Wagner, J., III, Leana, C., Locke, E., & Schweiger, D. (1997). Cognitive and motivational frameworks in research on participation: A meta-analysis of effects. *Journal of Organizational Behavior, 18,* 49–65.

Wernsing, T. (2014). Psychological capital: A test of measurement instrument invariance across twelve national cultures. *Journal of Leadership and Organizational Studies, 21,* 179–190.

Youssef, C. M. (2011). Recent events in Egypt and the Middle East: Background, direct observations and a positive analysis. *Organizational Dynamics, 40,* 222–234.

Youssef, C. M., & Luthans, F. (2003). Immigrant psychological capital: Contribution to the war for talent and competitive advantage. *Singapore Nanyang Business Review, 2(2),* 1–14.

Youssef, C. M., & Luthans, F. (2005a). A positive organizational behavior approach to ethical performance. In R. Giacalone, C. Jurkiewicz, & C. Dunn (Eds.), *Positive psychology in business ethics and corporate social responsibility* (pp. 1–22). Greenwich, CT: Information Age.

Youssef, C. M., & Luthans, F. (2005b). Resiliency development of organizations, leaders and employees: Multi-level theory building for sustained performance. In W. Gardner, B. Avolio, & F. Walumbwa (Eds.), *Authentic leadership theory and practice: Origins, effects and development. Monographs in leadership and management* (Vol. 3, pp. 303–343). Oxford, UK: Elsevier.

Youssef, C. M., & Luthans, F. (2006). Positivity in the Middle East: Developing hopeful Egyptian organizational leaders. In W. Mobley & E. Weldon (Eds.), *Advances in global leadership* (Vol. 4, pp. 283–297). Oxford, UK: Elsevier Science/JAI.

Youssef, C. M., & Luthans, F. (2007). Positive organizational behavior in the workplace: The impact of hope, optimism, and resilience. *Journal of Management, 33,* 774–800.

Youssef-Morgan, C. M. (2014). Advancing OB research: An illustration using psychological capital. *Journal of Leadership and Organizational Studies, 21,* 130–140.

5 PSYCAP OPTIMISM

REALISTIC AND FLEXIBLE

Opening Video: Martin Seligman on Optimism

Video link: http://www.youtube.com/watch?v=8-rMuJW-UKg

Video link: http://www.youtube.com/watch?v=T6loWc55YTM

Martin Seligman is a professor of psychology at the University of Pennsylvania. As former president of the American Psychological Association, he became recognized as the founding father of positive psychology for calling on psychologists to redirect their energy from focusing exclusively on pathology and suffering to also discovering and understanding health, happiness, and flourishing. In the first video, Seligman briefly explains his definition of optimism. The second video is a humorous account of a fictitious intervention contrasting Seligman's views with those of Sigmund Freud, the historically important founding father of psychoanalysis.

Questions for reflection and/or discussion:

1. How do optimistic people differ from pessimistic people in their explanatory styles?
2. When you reflect on your own explanatory style, is it generally optimistic or pessimistic? Think about specific situations, positive and negative, and apply Seligman's description of optimistic and pessimistic explanatory styles.
3. What are the advantages and disadvantages of your current explanatory style? How would you go about balancing your optimism and pessimism? Apply Seligman's ABCDE technique.

4. Reflect on the explanatory styles of others that are close to you (immediate family, close friends, manager, coworkers, or associates). Which ones of them exhibit a more optimistic explanatory style? Which ones exhibit a more pessimistic style? Which ones are happier? Which ones are more successful?

5. How can you teach optimism to an excessively pessimistic person?

6. How did watching these two videos change your view and understanding of the concept of optimism as it is being used in everyday language?

Optimism is one of the most talked about but least understood positive psychological resources. In everyday language, an optimist is one who expects positive and desirable events in the future, while a pessimist is one who constantly has negative thoughts and is convinced that undesirable events will happen. Some have even viewed optimism as emotional, shallow, irrational, unrealistic, and even as a misleading illusion (e.g., Taylor, 1989; Tiger, 1979). Moreover, a number of researchers present optimism as a dispositional personality trait (e.g., Scheier & Carver, 1987).

As an important criteria-meeting component of PsyCap, optimism may have some of these surface meanings, but it is much more. PsyCap optimism is not just about a dispositional tendency to expect good things to happen in the future. PsyCap optimism includes global positive expectations (Carver, Scheier, Miller, & Fulford, 2009), but these expectations also depend on the reasons and attributions one uses to explain why specific events, positive and negative, occur in the past, present, and future (Seligman, 1998). For instance, you may spend a lot of time and energy focusing on positive events, but if you do not interpret each specific one of them using an optimistic explanatory style, you may still be on the pessimistic side. As with the previous two chapters on PsyCap efficacy and hope, the following reflection exercise on optimism can help you dig deeper and go beyond what your future forecasts look like. These detailed questions can help shape the impact that various past, present, and future life events have on your own PsyCap optimism, and they will be used to help better understand the rest of this chapter's more in-depth discussion of PsyCap optimism.

Personal Reflections Exercise on PsyCap Optimism

We first ask you to identify a highly memorable positive event that recently occurred in your life. It can be a work accomplishment, a pleasant family event, an exciting surprise, a new relationship, a revival of an old friendship, a successful purchase, or a philanthropic act. Any event that you consider favorable will qualify for this reflection exercise.

Once you can vividly recall the details of this event, answer as best you can the following questions. Remember, the more honest and thorough you are in your responses, the more insights you can gain as you delve into understanding PsyCap optimism in the rest of the chapter.

- Describe your selected positive event in detail by including your thoughts, feelings, and behaviors before, during, and after the event occurred, as well as those of anyone else involved. (Spending a little more time and attention on this should make the rest of the questions easier and faster to answer.)
- What are the possible reasons and circumstances that led to the occurrence of this favorable event?
- Which of these reasons would you give yourself credit for? In other words, which of the factors that led to the event were controlled by you?
- In what ways was this control expressed and utilized to cause the positive event to occur?
- Which of the factors would you consider to be beyond your control (e.g., luck, other people, external circumstances, and so on)?
- To what extent do you believe each of the external factors contributed to the occurrence of the positive event?
- Of the external factors you identified, are there any that you could have had control over? If so, how?
- Why do you think you did not need to, or choose to, exhibit control over the factors that you did have power over?

Now that you have reflected on the circumstances, causes, and consequences of the selected positive event, we ask you to shift your thinking to a more future-oriented perspective and answer the following questions:

- Do you believe that in the future this type of positive event can happen again?
- Of the factors that you believe to have contributed to the positive event, both the ones that are in your control and the ones that are not, which one(s) can you safely count on to almost always exist should you need it (them) in the future? Which one(s) do you consider to be temporary, one-time happenstances?
- Of the factors that you believe to have contributed to the positive event, both the ones that are in your control and the ones that are not, which one(s) do you believe can also be useful in other situations and events that may in the future occur in your life? Which ones do you consider to be specific to only this situation or to substantially similar ones?
- What would you do differently should you be in this same situation in the future?

Next, spend some time identifying a highly memorable negative event that you recently encountered. Again, it can be in any of your life domains, as long as you consider it unfavorable and significant enough to warrant your analysis. Once you can bring the details of this negative event to memory, we ask you to go through a similar set of questions as for the just completed positive event analysis.

- Start off by describing in detail the negative event. Remember to address your thoughts, feelings, and behaviors before, during, and after the selected negative event.
- What are the possible causes that you believe to have led to the occurrence of this unfavorable event?
- Which of these causal factors would you consider to be beyond your control (e.g., bad luck, other people's fault, external circumstances)?
- To what extent do you believe each of the external factors contributed to the occurrence of this negative event?
- Which of the reasons that caused this unfortunate event would you blame on yourself?
- What decisions and actions did you make in trying to prevent and/or handle the situation?
- Which of your decisions and actions do you think were especially effective in managing the situation?
- What mistakes do you believe you personally committed, either in causing or in handling this situation?
- How could you have prevented or managed the situation to avoid or better deal with it?
- Overall, could you have exerted any more control than you did over any of the factors you believe to have caused this negative event? If so, how?

Now, at this point switch your thinking to the future and answer the following questions:

- Do you believe that this negative event can happen again in your lifetime?
- Of the factors that you believe to have contributed to the negative event, both the ones that are in your control and the ones that are not, which one(s) are you worried will continue into the future? Which one(s) do you consider to be temporary, one-time setbacks?
- Of the factors that you believe to have contributed to the negative event, both the ones that are in your control and the ones that are not, which one(s) do you feel threatened by in other future situations that you may encounter? Which one(s) do you consider to be specific only to this or very similar situations?
- What would you do differently should you be in this situation in the future?

These questions and your answers have hopefully immersed you in thinking about your general positive and negative expectations, as well as the causes and your explanations of positive and negative situations and events that you have personally encountered. This self-reflection should serve as a good point of departure for better understanding the process of PsyCap optimism.

PsyCap Optimism as Global Positive Expectations

As we mentioned at the beginning of the chapter, one of the recognized views of optimism is that it is a global, cross-situational tendency to form positive expectations about life in general. In that view, optimism can be a more general form of confidence, which, as discussed in Chapter 2, tends to be more task or situation specific. Also in this view, optimism and pessimism are opposite ends of the same continuum, a view that as we discuss later is not shared by many positive psychologists, who view optimism and pessimism as independent constructs.

One of the important contributions of this global view of optimism is a better understanding of the different mechanisms through which optimism and pessimism operate to produce favorable or unfavorable outcomes such as health and well-being, which have been supported across hundreds of studies and in at least three meta-analyses (Alarcon, Bowling, & Khazon, 2013; Andersson, 1996; Rasmussen, Scheier, & Greenhouse, 2009). This research demonstrates optimists do not fare better simply because they are more cheerful and maintain a positive outlook. They exhibit fundamentally different coping mechanisms from pessimists.

When optimists face adversities, they keep trying, which as we repeatedly have noted, is in part related to the other PsyCap components such as hope's waypower. They adopt problem-focused coping, especially when the situation is within their control. They frame the situation more positively, but they tend to accept the realities of the situation that they cannot control. Similar to the approach goals in Chapter 3, optimists can be considered "approach copers." They focus less on the negative aspects of the situation and more on making plans to prepare themselves for the future. They even try to relieve the negativity of their situation with humor. In contrast, despite pessimists' negative expectations, when adversities do occur, they tend to confront them with more passive reactions such as denial, escape, fatalism, or cognitive avoidance, distracting or distancing themselves from the problem. They may sometimes engage in self-blame or wishful thinking, which causes them to disengage, give up, or stop trying (Carver et al., 2009).

Where do you stand? Think back to your answers to the introductory reflection questions. Do you tend to have a positive or a negative outlook with respect to the balance as they are not likely either or? How do you cope with problems and does your coping vary if the problem is a work-related problem, a relationship problem, a family problem, and so on? If you tend to escape to a fantasy world, put off dealing with the problem as long as possible, or feel sorry for yourself, you may be a pessimist, or perhaps a procrastinator on the slippery slope toward pessimism. If you face the problem head on, accept it for what it is, and actively work your way through it, you are likely an optimist.

PsyCap Optimism as an Explanatory or Attributional Style

As presented by Martin Seligman, optimism is an explanatory style that attributes positive events to personal, permanent, and pervasive causes, and interprets negative events in terms of external, temporary, and situation-specific factors. On the other hand, a pessimistic explanatory style would interpret positive events with external, temporary, and situation-specific attributes, and explain negative events in terms of personal, permanent, and pervasive causes (Seligman, 1998).

The primary mechanism underlying optimistic and pessimistic explanatory styles is the individual's assessment of "response-outcome independence." When we feel in control, and that our future depends on our actions, we are motivated to try and fight for a better future. It is as if we are "immunized" against helplessness. On the other hand, when we perceive events to be uncontrollable, with no connection between our actions and the outcomes they yield, we stop trying and learn to become helpless (i.e., like Seligman's [1972] dogs in his famous study on learned helplessness covered in the previous chapter). Even when the situation presents evidence that we may have some control to change our futures, we passively let these opportunities pass (Peterson & Steen, 2009).

Based on this widely recognized definitional framework, optimists take credit for the positive happenstances in their lives. They view the causes of these desirable events as being within their power and control. Optimists would expect these causes to continue to exist into the future, and to be useful in handling other situations across life domains. Thus, their optimistic explanatory style allows them to positively view and internalize the good aspects of their lives, not only in the past and the present but also into the future. For example, optimistic employees who received some positive feedback and recognition from their supervisor will attribute this positive event to their work ethic and will assure themselves that they will always be able to work hard and be successful, not only in this job but in any endeavor they choose.

By the same token, when experiencing negative events or faced with undesirable situations, optimistic people attribute the causes to be external, temporary, and situation specific. Thus, they continue to remain positive and confident about their future. For example, if optimistic employees receive negative feedback regarding say a report they presented, they will probably use rationalizations such as they were not themselves when they worked on or presented the report, that their colleagues did not provide the necessary information to enhance the quality of the report, or that the boss was simply in a bad mood when giving the negative feedback. The report was really not that bad after all and certainly will not be in the future.

In contrast to this optimistic explanatory style, pessimists do not give themselves credit for the positive events that occur in their lives. For example, a pessimistic person who has just received a promotion might explain it in terms of external reasons, such as good luck, other candidates lacking the needed experience, the new job being undesirable, and so on. In addition, the attributional causes pessimists use tend to be temporary and situation specific, and thus they believe positive events hold little chance of happening again in the future.

Moreover, pessimists tend to blame themselves for the negative things that happen in their lives. They internalize the causes of unfortunate situations and negative events. They assume bad things will continue to exist for them into the future and threaten their success and well-being, not only in similar situations but across all domains of their life. For example, pessimists who just got passed over for a promotion may attribute this to say a lack of their intelligence or not coming from the right educational background, school, and so on. They will tend to dwell on the assumption that their lack of intelligence or background will continue to haunt them in the future. They assume that it will not only affect their career but may also ruin their relationships and destroy any chances they might have for higher education, training, or even an alternative career path. As a result, they feel helpless, defeated, and unmotivated to try again.

So, how did you come out? Go back to your answers to the questions you reflected on in the beginning exercise. Think back on the causes you used to explain the positive event that you experienced. If most of those causes are factors that you believe to be in your control and thus are able to take the credit, then you are making personal attributions that are in line with an optimistic explanatory style. Moreover, if you expect those factors to always be there over time and across situations, then you are making permanent and pervasive attributions, which are also consistent with an optimistic explanatory style. On the other hand, if most of the reasons you came up with for your identified positive event were not in your power to control, were temporary, and/or were situation specific, then you were using a pessimistic explanatory style. This pessimism comes through even though you were reflecting on a positive event or situation.

Next, examine the causes you used to explain your selected negative event. If you attributed mostly causes to being external, temporary, and situation-specific one-time occurrences, then you are using an optimistic explanatory style. You are revealing an optimistic tendency in how you handle negative events. On the other hand, if you mostly blamed yourself and dwelled on the permanence and pervasiveness of the causes of this negative event, then you are exhibiting more of a pessimistic explanatory style.

Within the view of optimism as an explanatory style, the unidimensionality of optimism and pessimism has been challenged (Chang, Maydeu-Olivares, & D'Zurilla, 1997; Kubzansky, Kubzansky, & Maselko, 2004; Lai, 1994; Peterson & Steen, 2009; also see Peterson & Chang, 2002 for a comprehensive review). Although optimism and pessimism are usually negatively correlated, the way these constructs have been studied precludes definitive answers regarding their independence. Researchers often only focus on specific outcomes of interest. Some focus exclusively on positive outcomes as they relate to optimism, including physical and mental health or well-being (Peterson, 1999; Peterson & Bossio, 1991; Scheier & Carver, 1987, 1992; Seeman, 1989), effective coping with difficult life situations (Lazarus & Folkman, 1984; Scheier & Carver, 1985), recovery from illness (Scheier et al., 1989) and addiction (Strack, Carver, & Blaney, 1987), and life satisfaction and "authentic happiness" (Seligman, 2002). Indeed, optimism has been shown to positively relate to many desirable outcomes, including workplace performance (Avey, Reichard, Luthans, & Mhatre, 2011; Seligman, 1998), as well as performance in various other life domains, such as health, well-being, education, sports, and politics (Peterson & Barrett, 1987; Peterson & Seligman, 2004; Peterson & Steen, 2009; Prola & Stern, 1984; Seligman, 2002).

On the other hand, clinical psychology researchers have focused on negative outcomes, such as depression (Abrahamson, Metalsky, & Alloy, 1989; Peterson & Seligman, 1984), physical illness (Peterson, Seligman, & Vaillant, 1988), and poor performance in general. However, there is very limited research, if any, on optimism and pessimism, as well as their positive and negative outcomes, in a parallel, comprehensive manner. Studying the broad perspective of optimism and pessimism seems necessary in order to fully understand the broad spectrum of implications, possible extrapolations, and potential discontinuities.

As an example, in the reflective questions we asked you to answer in the opening exercise, we could have only asked you to analyze a positive event. You would have then probably concluded that you have an optimistic explanatory style because most of your explanations of the positive event were personal, permanent, and pervasive (i.e., you probably would employ the well-known self-serving bias of positive events). On the other hand, if you had used external, temporary, and situation-specific causes, the opposite conclusion of being a pessimist would have been made. By asking you to analyze both a positive and a negative event, we have increased the probability of more accurately uncovering the various explanatory styles that you use perhaps in balance or, for some, out of balance.

For instance, if you used personal, permanent, and pervasive explanations in both positive and negative situations, you now have a better understanding that your explanatory style is optimistic with respect to your positive event but pessimistic with respect to your negative event. In other words, you can be both an optimist and a pessimist, depending on the nature of the event. Even further in-depth understanding can be accomplished by analyzing more than one event in each category. We will return to this important situational contingency issue of optimism and pessimism toward the end of the chapter.

Value of Being Overly Optimistic

Contrary to the gloom and doom world that the media tends to portray, most people tend to be optimistically biased. They believe that negative events are less likely to happen to them than to others, especially when they perceive themselves to have a reasonable amount of control over a situation, regardless of whether that perception of control is accurate (Klein & Helweg-Larsen, 2002). Does this mean that optimism is simply an illusion, a form of judgment bias, or a detour from rational thinking? This question has perplexed philosophers, scholars, practitioners, and people in general. Is it better to be positive and optimistic or to be accurate and realistic in our predictions? Recently, more attention is being given to these questions that shed light on the value of optimism.

First of all, the value of optimism seems to go beyond the accuracy of its predictions. In most occasions, accurate predictions of the future are nearly impossible. In those cases, the motivating effects of optimism are far more beneficial than the calculative accuracy of pessimism. In other words, optimism serves other critical cognitive, affective, and even social functions that go beyond predictions and may be more valuable than mere accuracy, which makes erring on the side of optimism more rational and beneficial (Armor, Massey, & Sackett, 2008).

Haselton and Nettle (2006) expand on this idea from an evolutionary perspective. Drawing from error management theory, they show that under conditions of uncertainty, overoptimism is selected when it is perceived to lead to the least costly errors, such as minimizing missed opportunities. Of course, occasionally overpessimism may also be selected if it is perceived to lead to less costly errors. However, people tend to overestimate the costs of misses (false negatives) and underestimate the costs of false alarms (false positives), because the goal is not necessarily to minimize error rates but to minimize overall costs. In many cases, overoptimism tends to optimize this equation. For example, an optimistic bias may be one of the few driving forces for people to pursue their dreams that otherwise, objectively speaking, have slim chances of success. The value of these perceptual biases has been foundational for the development of behavioral economics, which challenged the underlying assumptions of traditional theories in economics, political science, and many other fields (Kahneman, 2011).

Overoptimism serves another important function: preparedness. Since optimism is state-like and thus open to change over time, people tend to start out optimistic, which motivates them to approach challenging goals, take advantage of opportunities, and deal with impending setbacks. In the process of pursuing their goals, as they gather more information, receive feedback, place higher value on the outcomes of their decisions, or perceive the outcomes to be less controllable, they may adjust their levels of optimism accordingly. Thus, the numerous motivational and health benefits of optimism are realized, limiting periods of distress and fear to those closer to the relatively sparse "moments of truth." This combination tends to lead to optimal levels of preparedness through balancing the many benefits of optimism with the occasional benefits of pessimism such as adjusting expectations to avoid disappointment (Sweeny, Carroll, & Shepperd, 2006).

Another explanatory mechanism for overoptimism is outcome desirability. Our desires influence our future expectations in many ways. Krizan and Windschitl (2007) offer several mechanisms for this linkage. For example, outcome desirability can promote optimism through valence priming (rating the importance of the desired outcome), repeated simulation (imagination of the desired outcome and its availability in memory), confirmation bias (searching for evidence to support one's hypotheses), focalism (focusing on the desired outcome and neglecting the alternatives), differential scrutiny (more readily accepting confirmatory evidence and heavily scrutinizing or seeking to falsify contradictory evidence), and strategic optimism (optimism about perceivably controllable situations to gain energy and motivation). In some cases, outcome desirability can promote pessimism through the negativity bias, enhanced accuracy, or strategic pessimism, because the more desirable the outcome, the more it is perceived to be at stake, which can lead to more search behaviors, distress, or "bracing for loss" to avoid disappointment.

Based on these arguments, optimism is more prevalent and, for the most part, more beneficial than pessimism, even if at times unfounded or exaggerated. However, there are also risks associated with overoptimism that are particularly dangerous in the workplace. In the next section, we discuss some of these risks and make the case for realistic and flexible optimism.

Realistic and Flexible Qualifiers for PsyCap Optimism

Optimism, like hope, has considerable intuitive appeal and is often associated with many positive and desirable outcomes, as discussed earlier. However, a nonscrutinizing optimistic explanatory style may have some undesirable side effects or even dangerous implications. In particular, nondiscriminatory, blatantly optimistic people may expose themselves to higher risks. For example, there is some evidence that optimists may underestimate the potential dangers of risks (Davidson & Prkachin, 1997; Kok, Ho, Heng, & Ong, 1990; Peterson & Chang, 2002; Weinstein, 1989). For example, generally healthy people may decide to eat an unhealthy and imbalanced diet, exercise less, and expose themselves to tremendous amounts of stress at work. They reason that because they have had no problems to date, they optimistically assume they can handle such risk factors. However, it is also important to note that there is counterevidence that optimists do take proactive steps toward health promotion and preventive care, and that pessimists may engage in more health-defeating behaviors (see Carver et al., 2009). However, the potential risks of overoptimism still warrant attention, particularly in the workplace.

For example, if optimists expose themselves, their organization, units, coworkers, friends, and family to increased risks, and negative consequences result, they are less likely to learn from their mistakes. This is because they will externalize the risk factors or perhaps fail to take steps to mitigate risks they have control over. Unrealistic optimists fail to take charge and properly analyze the situation to understand which causes could have been personal, permanent, or pervasive, and which can be safely externalized or less emphasized as temporary or situation specific. For example, it would be very irresponsible and potentially dangerous for a safety engineer to adopt an optimistic explanatory style and proceed to shift the blame to somebody or something else every time an accident takes place, instead of updating and enforcing safety regulations and preventative techniques. However, even if the safety engineer performs all the necessary responsibilities, an accident may still take place at some point in time. In this situation, once the causes have been analyzed and determined to be beyond this engineer's control, she should then be able to accept an optimistic external, temporary, and situation-specific interpretation of this unfortunate event, in order to positively move on and overcome this setback. In other words, we would advocate the engineer use what Peterson (2000) refers to as "flexible optimism." In this flexible PsyCap optimism, the individual tries to correctly appraise the situation and then choose when to utilize optimistic and pessimistic explanatory styles.

Unfortunately, explanatory styles are based on one's subjective perceptions and attributions, which may not always be realistic or allow for flexibility. Optimistic individuals may try to exert too much control over their lives and their destinies, thinking that if they try hard enough, they will always be successful, and they should take credit for their success. Putting such high expectations and pressures on oneself can have undesirable consequences. For example, Peterson and Chang (2002) found that unrealistic optimism exacerbates the negative implications of repeated negative life events on physical health and psychological well-being. In other words, as the unwarranted sense of agency that optimists possess was challenged, they could not repeatedly externalize negative events (as optimists are supposed to do), and they suffered physically and emotionally. This is also in line with the research that supports the relationship between angry, aggressive personalities and susceptibility to physical problems such as hypertension, diabetes, and heart disease (Dolnick, 1995). Seligman (1998) also supports that one of the primary causes of experiencing helplessness is the increased emphasis on the self and the decreased interest in factors beyond oneself (e.g., family, religion, or national commitment). These are reasons why Schneider (2001) advocates the need for "realistic optimism."

For PsyCap, we emphasize the need for the strength of optimism to be realistic and flexible. Effective PsyCap optimism should not take extremes, neither in internalizing success and trying to take control of every aspect of one's work life, nor in externalizing all types of failure and thus shirking responsibility.

Realistic, flexible PsyCap optimism should not be portrayed as just another feel-good, illusive ego boost. PsyCap optimism represents a strong lesson in self-discipline, analysis of past events, contingency planning, and preventive care. PsyCap optimism also comprehensively combines most of the earlier conceptualizations and multiple facets of optimism.

For PsyCap we propose that realistic, flexible optimists can enjoy and learn from various life course and workplace events (or what we call trigger moments) to the fullest extent possible (Avolio & Luthans, 2006). In good times, those with high PsyCap optimism are able to enjoy both the cognitive and emotional implications of being able to take credit for their success and be in control of their destinies, without unknowingly exposing themselves to added risk or to others' disdain of a lack of humility.

Those with high PsyCap optimism are also able to express their thanks and appreciation to relevant others and factors that may have contributed to their success. They are able to capitalize on the opportunities that the situation may present them with, develop their skills and abilities, and thus improve their chances in the future. By the same token, in bad times, they are able to sift through the noise, find the facts, learn from their mistakes, accept what they cannot change, and positively move on. This is where PsyCap resilience of bouncing back and beyond, covered in the next chapter, also comes into play.

Do We Need Employees With PsyCap Optimism?

Before getting into the obvious implications PsyCap optimism has for organizational leaders, what about employees in general? We all realize today's employees are functioning in an environment that is very different from what used to exist not too long ago. Complexity, change, and uncertainty have now become the norm. Not only is the frequency of change increasing but the nature of today's and tomorrow's changes is fundamentally different. This change is cutting through the very core of every employee's job. The boundaries have become blurred across most jobs and professions. Not only media commentators, authors, and professors but employees themselves are observing and experiencing how their jobs are dramatically changing as their organization transforms itself to match the complex environment.

To take an example of one firm we are very familiar with, we have repeatedly witnessed how its ability to stay on top with respect to its value-based strategies and practices has been greatly facilitated by employees who are able to accept, enjoy, and capitalize upon their continuously changing roles. Employees at this firm no longer define themselves using a job title, but refer to their respective roles as "what I am paid to do." They now expect to change as frequently as necessary for their organization to stay on top in an increasingly competitive industry.

This story relates to ownership, another possible addition to the PsyCap group of constructs in the future. Psychological ownership at the higher levels represents individuals who are willing to step up and be responsible for work that may not be directly in their domain but is important to the overall success of the organization (Avey, Avolio, Crossley, & Luthans, 2008). For example, a director of a large healthcare system asked one of the maintenance workers how his day was going in the elevator ride up to his office. The worker optimistically replied, "I am improving patient flow and safety." The director was delighted to hear this and asked the maintenance worker how he affected these important organizational performance metrics. The maintenance worker simply said, "Look, if I don't change the bed sheets, patients stay in emergency, and if they don't have clean bed sheets, well that isn't safe, now is it?"

This particular director had been reinforcing a campaign of taking ownership for the patient's care, and one could visibly see in the way employees were engaged as well as based on hard metrics that things were changing. In 3 years, the facility he directed went from almost being closed because it was one of the worst in the industry to being one of the best, in the same old facility and structure.

Even in professions that were traditionally considered stable and structured, enormous changes are currently taking place. For example, the plethora of accounting scandals culminated in the enactment of the Sarbanes-Oxley Act in 2002, and the face of the accounting profession as we knew it became dramatically changed (e.g., see Gullapalli, 2005), including making board members take ownership for their firm's reporting on performance. The same is true of most jobs. For example, technology workers who thought they were on the cutting edge are finding their knowledge to repeatedly face premature obsolescence as new advances are introduced. And the list goes on.

Optimistic and pessimistic employees react very differently to these turbulent times. Optimists are more likely to embrace the changes, see the opportunities that the future holds, and focus on capitalizing on those opportunities. Optimists will react differently than pessimists to changes that cause adverse consequences. Downsizing is a classic example. A realistically optimistic employee will tend to attribute being laid off to the current economic and technological environment. Optimists interpret the layoff as being due to external, temporary, and situation-specific causal factors, rather than indulging in feelings of inadequacy and self-blame. This optimistic explanatory style will help downsized employees to have positive expectations about the future (e.g., the economy will improve; I can retool my technical know-how) and to act upon these expectations with agency and motivation (e.g., I am going back to school to better prepare myself to ride the next wave).

Thus, an optimistic explanatory style would help employees in taking charge and being in control of their own destiny. Importantly, this optimistic processing of events is likely to cause their positive outlook to actually come true. In other words, PsyCap optimism can lead to a self-fulfilling prophecy (Peterson & Chang, 2002) and can be both motivated and motivating (Peterson, 2000) to achieving long-term success.

This value of employee PsyCap optimism can also draw from what has been identified as "career resiliency" (Waterman, Waterman, & Collard, 1994) discussed in the next chapter on PsyCap resilience. As applied to optimism, today's organizations are in great need of career-resilient employees who realize that they are responsible for their own careers, for reinventing themselves to make their skills marketable (i.e., employable) and useful for their current and future employers. Career resiliency combines flexibility and adaptability with proactive, self-initiated development and continuous learning. Realistic, flexible optimism is a PsyCap capacity that can be of tremendous value for employees to build such career resiliency on more objective self-assessments, while at the same time having optimistic employees welcoming challenges with less fear, resistance, and self-doubt.

Employees' capacity to work independently is increasingly becoming necessary, not only for their career management but also for their effective performance in most jobs. Many organizations today have eliminated middle management levels and flattened their hierarchies in hopes of enhancing their speed, responsiveness, interactive teamwork, and quality of communication (and, of course, to cut costs). However, flattened structures also increase managers' span of control, making it impossible for them to provide close supervision and therefore requiring employees to step up and take greater ownership. Again, optimistic and pessimistic employees will interpret this situation very differently. Optimists will welcome the challenge and enjoy being able to take credit for their accomplishments. Pessimists, on the other hand, will likely dwell on incidences of failure or poor performance and stunt their own growth opportunities as they continue to demand more structure and certainty in their work lives.

Seligman's (1998) work with the huge Metropolitan Life Insurance sales staff demonstrates the performance impact optimistic employees can have. He found that optimistic sales representatives outsold pessimistic ones over time, even among those who had initially failed the traditional industry selection test. Seligman and researchers in the marketing field (e.g., Dixon & Schertzer, 2005; Rich, 1999) conclude that optimism is extremely important in sales positions, maybe even beyond technical knowledge. We augment this argument by proposing that an optimistic explanatory style may also promote further technical self-development that may help correct some of the initial knowledge deficiencies among those who are technically deficient. Pessimism, on the other hand, may thwart similar efforts, even among those who are initially technically competent.

In the old paradigm environment and organizations, a relatively more pessimistic workforce may have even been preferred in order to maintain responsibility, accountability, and control. Now, in the new paradigm, selecting for and developing employees' realistic and flexible PsyCap optimism represents a fresh opportunity for a positive, healthy, and productive workforce that is also independent, change-embracing, and open to new ideas and workplace developments. Without such optimistic workforces, the chances of survival are considerably diminished.

Organizational Leaders With PsyCap Optimism

Would it be too risky for those in charge of today's organizations' strategic directives and implementing decisions to be optimistic? Would shareholders prefer that their investments be managed by conservative, and even somewhat pessimistic, leaders? This "sadder-but-wiser" position has often been studied on the assumption that positivity may be associated with unrealistically favorable expectations or carelessness about the future. The heightened awareness of the needs for contingency planning and redundant systems after the dot-com bubble burst and the 9/11 tragedy exemplify the sadder-but-wiser hypothesis (MacSweeney, 2002). However, research supports that leaders who are positive are also more authentic and effective (Avolio & Luthans, 2006; Jensen & Luthans, 2006; Luthans, Norman, & Hughes, 2006; Walumbwa, Peterson, Avolio, & Hartnell, 2010).

There is also research evidence that leaders who think positively are more effective interpersonally and in terms of the quality of their decisions, including superior ability to collect and use more information, and to identify and act upon situational contingencies (Staw & Barsade, 1993; also see Avey, Avolio, & Luthans, 2011). And as we indicated earlier, those leaders that promote positivity in their language about reporting on a firm's performance tend to have a more positive impact on the value ascribed to those firms by financial analysts. On the other hand, negativity has been shown to be related with various performance-inhibiting mechanisms, such as memory decay (Judge & Ilies, 2004, see also Cameron, 2008 for a comprehensive review).

As to authentic leadership, PsyCap optimism contributes to and is the result of the strong foundation of self-awareness (Avolio & Luthans, 2006; Luthans & Avolio, 2003; Luthans, Norman, & Hughes, 2006). The self-awareness of authentic leaders draws its accuracy and objectivity from multisource feedback, motivated by the authentic leader's genuine desire for sustainable improvement and transparent trust building. Moreover, authentic leaders' capacity of self-regulation is conducive to adaptiveness, responsiveness, and continuous self-development that are highly consistent with PsyCap optimism (Avolio & Luthans, 2006; Luthans & Avolio, 2003; Luthans et al., 2006).

Organizational leaders with a high level of PsyCap optimism are risk takers, but because they are realistic and flexible, they tend to only take calculated and necessary risks. They know that their role is to be change agents, not window dressers. They dare to dream for themselves, their associates, and their organizations. They then enthusiastically pursue their dreams as they inspire, motivate, and involve their associates. In addition, however, leaders with high PsyCap optimism would have a good handle on the realities of their capacities and vulnerabilities, as well as those of their followers, and are self-aware and in control. Their PsyCap optimism motivates them to develop and improve themselves and their followers. They do not resort to blame shifting and shallow impression management techniques in order to take credit for more than what their efforts have warranted; nor do they avoid responsibility or accountability. They are secure in their positive outlook and have realistic, accurate knowledge of their own and their followers' accomplishments.

Leaders with high PsyCap optimism emphasize the development of their followers. They take pride in the success of their followers, rather than envying them and trying to take credit for their accomplishments as if they were their own. Most important, as these effective leaders develop their associates, they help them build their own realistic, flexible optimism. Rather than doing everything and making all the decisions for them, high PsyCap optimistic leaders enable, empower, delegate, and trust their followers to achieve the desired outcomes (e.g., see Norman, Avolio, & Luthans, 2010). They equip their people with the necessary knowledge, skills, abilities, and motivation not only to succeed but also to be able to make personal, permanent, and pervasive attributions of their own.

Developing PsyCap Optimism in Today's Employees

As indicated, optimism has been depicted as both dispositional and trait-like and thus relatively fixed (e.g., Scheier et al., 1989) but also state-like (i.e., "learned optimism," Seligman, 1998; also see Carver et al., 2009). Even though we recognize a conceptual continuum may exist (Luthans & Youssef, 2007; Youssef-Morgan, 2014; also see Figure 1.1), in order to meet the criteria of PsyCap optimism, we emphasize its state-like, developmental properties. Specifically, PsyCap optimism can be developed by creating more positive expectations, altering a pessimistic explanatory style, or enriching the dimensions of an optimistic explanatory style.

Consider Taylor, the production manager of a mid-sized electronic manufacturing plant. The plant has just failed to meet its production quota for the month. Taylor's pessimistic explanatory style would automatically drive her thought processes toward personal causes (e.g., It is my fault) that are permanent (e.g., I will never be able to meet senior management's expectations) and pervasive (e.g., I am a bad manager). Taylor is now prone to considerable stress and burnout. Moreover, if she holds onto her pessimistic explanatory style long enough, she may be a candidate for a multitude of physical and psychological problems. In addition, Taylor is likely to create negative self-fulfilling prophecies that will cause her performance to slip even further, and her attitude may result in contagious dissatisfaction, disengagement, and apathy affecting her associates.

The aforementioned scenario indicating a downward spiral of pessimism can be avoided if this manager can be trained to adopt a more optimistic, yet realistic, explanatory style. Schneider (2001) presents three perspectives that are particularly applicable to developing realistic optimism in the workplace:

1. Leniency for the past
2. Appreciation for the present
3. Opportunity seeking for the future

Leniency for the past does not imply denial or an evasion of responsibility. On the contrary, in line with realistic optimism, it is a positive reframing technique that acknowledges the realities of the situation. It adopts a problem-centered coping approach toward the controllable aspects of the situation, while giving oneself the benefit of the doubt and repositioning the uncontrollable aspects of the situation in the best possible light (Carver et al., 2009). Leniency for the past can help enthusiastic managers like Taylor in managing their Type A personalities and their perfectionist tendencies. It can guide their goal-setting efforts so that they can accurately assess their resources and abilities, and thus set realistic, attainable goals for themselves and their associates. This, in turn, can result in Taylor creating workable plans for better utilizing the human, material, and financial resources that are within her control in order to not only meet but exceed her unit's targeted performance over time.

In the developmental process for PsyCap optimism, external attributions can be created by viewing the situation as one of high consensus, low consistency, and high distinctiveness (Kelley, 1973). If Taylor can receive some helpful feedback that (1) her plant was not the only one that did not meet this month's target (high consensus); (2) this is one of the very few times that her plant did not meet its target (low consistency); and (3) with the exception of production quantity, her plant met other performance expectations such as quality and safety standards (high distinctiveness)—then Taylor may be able to adopt a more optimistic explanatory style. Unfortunately, her regional manager may think that by sharing such positive information, Taylor may not be as motivated to work harder and meet production goals in the future. In fact, many managers fall into the trap of giving only negative feedback in such situations, thinking that this will motivate their employees to perform. Then they find out that over time, their best associates lose their motivation and commitment to high performance.

Following Schneider's (2001) second strategy of developing realistic, flexible optimism, Taylor's explanatory style can also learn to appreciate her present. Any situation, no matter how unfavorable, has its positive aspects that can be reflected upon and enjoyed—finding a "silver lining" in the clouds. This is especially true if these aspects are also internal, permanent, and pervasive. Taylor's flexible optimism can redirect her perspective away from dwelling on the negatives and toward focusing on the positives. For example, she can learn to be thankful for the amount her plant was able to produce despite difficulties. She can still note the quality of the output, the safety of her associates, the positive relationships and teamwork that she maintains among the members of her unit, the understanding and trust of her managers and associates, and even the fact that she still has a good-paying job. Appreciation of the present can protect Taylor from a defeatist attitude that can paralyze her planning efforts and motivation for future improvement.

Finally, if Taylor can realistically accept herself, her unit, and her organization as a "work in progress," she is more likely not only to appreciate the moment but also to look forward to the future, with all the potential opportunities that it presents. In fact, Taylor will be able to proactively seek and act upon future opportunities for herself and her associates, based on her realistic understanding of each of their capabilities and vulnerabilities. Note the similarities between Schneider's three-step strategy for developing optimism and Seligman's ABCDE (Adversity, Belief, Consequences, Disputation, and Energize) model, which you learned about in one of the opening videos at the beginning this chapter. Realistic, flexible PsyCap optimism can be a powerful tool for organizational leaders such as Taylor to inspire and motivate herself and her people to accept, and even choose, challenges to improve performance now and in the future. By reframing adversities and conquering paralyzing and self-defeating beliefs and their debilitating consequences, leaders can move on and get themselves and their associates re-energized about the future.

The Optimistic Organization

Like the overall hopeful organization presented in the last chapter, can the organization also display the positive qualities associated with employees' or leaders' PsyCap optimism? We propose that in light of today's environment, in order for organizations to even survive, let alone thrive, they have to be optimistic. Organizations that can create sustainable competitive advantage need to emphasize an internal, permanent, and pervasive outlook that can lead to positive events now and in the future. Today's organizations cannot simply wait and react, or even passively scan the environment and proactively adapt to the changes they are facing. They have to intentionally create turbulent change themselves and break the rules of the game to their advantage, which can facilitate efficacy, as it is placing greater control in the hands of leaders. They have to create their own future, where they can be in control of their own destinies. Obviously, this is easier said than done, but successful examples speak loudly of these new realities and that it can be done.

At Amazon, which is likely the fastest growing "everything store on earth," the CEO constantly pushes his employees to think really big and be future oriented but at the same time to have a bias for action. He encourages a clash of ideas so that truth will come out and directions can be set appropriately, but it is in the balance of big ideas and the details where Amazon is challenging just about every business in its broad domain of services.

In another 100-year-plus organization, Nordstrom's CEO talks about the inverted pyramid, where he is at the bottom and clients and sales staff are at the top. The whole design of the organization is to create a sense of optimism and energy that supports the employee–customer interface. This structure is in direct contrast to the hierarchical, overly structured, top-down organization where employees are made to feel controlled and not owners of the interface with either each other or clients/customers.

Traditional sources of competitive advantage are being eroded at an accelerating rate. Organizations can no longer depend on traditional inertia-producing entry barriers along material, structural, and technological dimensions. These barriers are coming down because they are now readily available to competitors at decreasing costs; they are easily imitable, even by smaller start-ups (Luthans & Youssef, 2004). An example would be the enormous competition in the software industry from homemade (and at no cost to the user) freeware such as Linux and Firefox. Another example is the explosive emergence of free massive open online courses (MOOCs) in nearly every subject of study, which are now competing with many colleges, technical education, and training venues.

On the other hand, organizations that capitalize on the inimitability of the human, social, and psychological capital of their valuable employees and leaders are likely to enjoy long-term competitive advantage (Luthans & Youssef, 2004; Pfeffer, 1998). For example, Southwest Airlines' long-enduring values of emphasizing people-centered practices, investing in its employees' selection and training, and not treating its employees as if they were disposable, have paid off in terms efficiency, profitability, and customer service (O'Reilly & Pfeffer, 2000). These internal, permanent, and pervasive sources of competitive advantage (i.e., its PsyCap optimism) remained viable and intact, and helped Southwest to remain successful even in the disastrous airline industry post 9/11. Southwest refused to go with the flow of post 9/11 massive layoffs that most of its short-term-oriented competitors felt obliged to undertake. This strategy is certainly in line with our description earlier of the inverted pyramid structure of Nordstrom's.

Another case in point of the value of organizations' recognizing, investing in, and developing their PsyCap optimism can be found in their ethical decision making and socially responsible organizational behavior. In an era where bottom-line considerations rule, organizations that have chosen to operate under morally sound values and to act in a socially responsible manner may have a hard time convincing their short-run-focused shareholders. However, over time and across situations, these organizations have shown to prevail due to their internalized values and strong cultures (Cameron, Bright, & Caza, 2004). On the other hand, the meltdown of Enron, WorldCom, Arthur Anderson, and the others stands witness to the temporary nature of a short-term profitability orientation.

Finally, in the same way that organizational leaders need to be realistic and flexible in their optimism, organizations, too, need to adopt realism and flexibility in optimistically interpreting the events they face, both positive and negative. Leniency for the past is necessary. Regardless of how glamorous (or infamous) an organization's history is, at some point in time, it needs to let go of the past and move on to new territories. If the past and present have been positive, a PsyCap optimistic organization would celebrate its success and extract the lessons to be learned from it. A realistic, flexible optimistic organization would be fully cautious and aware that every success may have been temporary, situation specific, or even an external stroke of good of luck.

A case in point is that many of Jim Collin's (2001) "good-to-great" companies did not sustain their greatness and subsequently struggled or did not survive. This is in part due to Collin's relying on flawed methodology, where he finds successful firms and then explains why they are successful versus a more rigorous approach, which would be to predict not posdict success. For example, in 2004, Fannie Mae came under fire for its accounting practices and subsequently had to restate over 3 years of earnings, leading to billions of dollars in lost earnings and the forced resignation of its CEO and CFO. Circuit City went bankrupt in 2009 after the new CEO, who came over from Best Buy, decided right before the holiday season to fire his best, and of course most highly paid sales people to cut costs. Within 4 months Circuit City was out of business!

Finally, Wells Fargo received a $25 billion bailout from the Troubled Asset Relief Program (TARP) in 2008, which it subsequently repaid. Each of these companies was great at some point in time, but its greatness in the past did not guarantee continued success, and more had to be done in the present to survive the uncertainties of the future.

A PsyCap optimistic organization would not allow success to drive complacency and inertia, but it would continue to reinvent itself and challenge its underlying assumptions. On the other hand, even if the past and present have included failures and undesirable events, the PsyCap optimistic organization would still be able to find what is positive, appreciate it, learn from the controllable aspects of the situation, give itself the benefit of the doubt about that which is truly external and uncontrollable, and seek future opportunities accordingly.

Potential Pitfalls

As we said, some of the commonly recognized potential pitfalls of an optimistic explanatory style include poor physical and psychological preventive care, avoidance of responsibility, accountability and ownership, and learned helplessness as a result of overemphasized agency and individualism (see Peterson & Chang, 2002 for a comprehensive review). However, as also discussed earlier, there are sound conceptual counterarguments and empirical evidence to support the net benefits of optimism, even when accounting for the risks. Realistic, flexible optimism (i.e., PsyCap optimism) we propose also overcomes most of these potential pitfalls.

As we have indicated, optimistic and pessimistic explanatory styles can become self-fulfilling prophecies. Research of the mechanisms through which optimism can lead to positive outcomes is just emerging and primarily conceptual in nature. Empirical testing of these mechanisms is a promising area of future research. However, three general mechanisms particularly warrant our attention due to their applicability to the workplace: cognitive, social, and behavioral. People who adopt an optimistic explanatory style may think, relate to others, and act in ways that actually cause more positive events to occur in their lives (i.e., become self-fulfilling). On the other hand, those with a pessimistic explanatory style are less likely to relate well with others. Often times, pessimists actively dwell on toxic thoughts, intentionally engage in destructive and reckless relationships and behaviors, and in a self-fulfilling manner essentially expose themselves to more and more problems (Peterson & Steen, 2009).

As a hypothetical example, Rosa's optimistic explanatory style leads her to believe that she can perform well in her new job. This in turn facilitates Rosa's motivation to enhance her knowledge, skills, and abilities to set challenging goals for herself and to invest more time and energy in meeting those goals. Rosa quickly finds out that staying away from cynical, disengaged colleagues and associating with motivated high achievers helps her learn faster, enjoy her job more, and create a more positive impression in the eyes of her manager. As she acts upon these beliefs, Rosa builds the right social relationships and utilizes the most effective impression-management techniques. She is putting herself in the right place at the right time, which gives her a better chance of being a high performer and advancing in the organization.

As another example, consider pessimistic Trevor, whose explanatory style drives him to externalize every misfortune that comes his way. Trevor fatalistically believes that nothing he can do can change what he is destined to become. Thus, he accepts the first job that he is offered, even when it is substantially below his skills and abilities. He goes through the motions of the job every day with little enthusiasm, motivation, or desire to grow. He isolates himself from sources of feedback and social support. He even does not follow the organization's safety procedures, endangering himself and others, and jeopardizing his job. Ultimately, Trevor drives himself down a negative spiral of apathy and despair. He definitely increases his chances of facing more negative and undesirable events.

How can such negative spirals be reversed? It is important to capitalize upon a combination of the same cognitive, social, and behavioral mechanisms to change direction upward. Schneider's (2001) previously suggested strategies of leniency for the past, appreciation for the present, and opportunity seeking for the future would be an example of such cognitive mechanisms for effective guidelines in developing optimism. In addition, a social network and support (i.e., social capital) can help in breaking through the vicious cycle of pessimism. Mentoring, coaching, role modeling, peer support groups, teamwork, and even simple workplace friendships and informal social events can be effective techniques to break a pessimist's isolation and facilitate the optimism development process. Moreover, behavioral management techniques that utilize the contingent rewards, particularly positive, constructive feedback and social recognition and attention, can not only motivate positive behaviors but also challenge a pessimist's self-defeating beliefs and attitudes, triggering an upward spiral of positivity and optimism.

Future Implications and Directions for PsyCap Optimism Research and Practice

In light of negative events and developments in the political, economic, and social landscape in general, and the business environment in particular, organizations may launch into a downward spiral of pessimism and apathy. The need for a better understanding of PsyCap optimism is becoming critical. To conclude this chapter, we offer several specific guidelines for the future development of the research and practice of PsyCap optimism.

- To fill the significant void in the optimism literature that we presented earlier (Peterson & Chang, 2002; Peterson & Steen, 2009), comprehensive studies need to investigate the relationship between optimism and pessimism in order to assess their unidimensionality or independence, and the situational factors that may influence the existence and extent of such a relationship. In this broader perspective, a wider range of outcomes should be incorporated. Meta-analytical studies may facilitate the process of integrating current findings, thus significantly contributing to a better understanding of potential relationships, interactions, discontinuities, and moderators and/or mediators. On the other hand, integrating a broader range of findings on specific outcomes of interest may also uncover potential curvilinear relationships, similar to those we suggested for PsyCap hope in the previous chapter.
- In line with our emphasis on flexibility as an integral component of PsyCap optimism, it becomes evident that further understanding of the specific mechanisms and processes involved in flexible optimism becomes necessary. In particular, future research should explore how people actually develop the capacity to switch back and forth between optimistic and at least "less optimistic," if not pessimistic explanatory styles, as well as the selection criteria they employ to decide on which style to use in various situations. Further

theory building in this area would enhance the ability of researchers and practicing managers to create more effective interventions for developing flexible PsyCap optimism.

- Of particular relevance to PsyCap optimism are situational factors that may influence the need for and applicability of optimism. For example, in some industries, a relatively pessimistic outlook may be predominant and even desirable. Examples include accounting, finance, security management, and quality control. Others, such as marketing and sales, may benefit from a more optimistic explanatory style. Furthermore, an optimistic explanatory style may come in stark contrast to some cultural values, as some cultures strongly appreciate, and even consider as virtues, the qualities of humility, deference, and conservatism. In this regard, recent studies point to challenges in PsyCap measurement invariance across cultures, particularly regarding optimism (Wernsing, 2014). Potential spillover effects that the specific characteristics of an industry or a national culture may have on organizational culture, and consequently on its leaders' and employees' optimism, need to be explored.

- As with the other PsyCap components, future research needs to explore ways that we can intervene to boost realistic optimism positively impacting sustainable growth and performance. It will be interesting to determine the types of developmental interventions that can be used to enhance the leader's optimism and the conditions needed to translate that optimism into a contagious optimism among followers.

Case Study: The Greatest Hitter in the World

Video link: http://www.values.com/inspirational-stories-tv-spots/99-The-Greatest

This brief video exemplifies an optimistic outlook in a simplified, humorous, yet powerful way. A lot is left to the imagination and interpretation of the viewer, so after you view the video, ponder the following questions.

Questions for reflection and/or discussion:

1. In what ways does the boy in the video exemplify the positive expectations view of optimism?
2. In what ways does he exemplify an optimistic explanatory style? Elaborate on the internal, permanent, and pervasive dimensions of his optimism?
3. In your opinion, is his optimism an accurate estimation of his capabilities, or is he overly optimistic?

4. What are the benefits of optimism for this boy? What are the benefits of optimism for children in general? What parallels can you draw to yourself and the benefits of optimism to your own life?
5. What are the potential risks of optimism for this boy? Are there any potential risks of optimism for children in general? What parallels can you draw to yourself and the risks of optimism to your own life?
6. Overall, is this boy at an advantage or at a disadvantage based on his capability level and his optimism level combined? Is it more important for children to be positive or to be accurate and realistic about their capabilities? What about adults? What about you?

References

Abrahamson, L., Metalsky, G., & Alloy, L. (1989). Hopelessness depression: A theory-based subtype of depression. *Psychological Review, 96*, 358–372.

Alarcon, G. M., Bowling, N. A., & Khazon, S. (2013). Great expectations: A meta-analytic examination of optimism and hope. *Personality and Individual Differences, 54*, 821–827.

Andersson, G. (1996). The benefits of optimism: A meta-analytic review of the life orientation test. *Personality and Individual Differences, 21*, 719–725.

Armor, D. A., Massey, C., & Sackett, A. M. (2008). Prescribed optimism: Is it right to be wrong about the future? *Psychological Science, 19*, 329–331.

Avey, J. B., Avolio, B. J., & Luthans, F. (2011). Experimentally analyzing the impact of leader positivity on follower positivity and performance. *Leadership Quarterly, 22*, 282–294.

Avey, J. B., Avolio, B. J., Crossley, C. D., & Luthans, F. (2008). Psychological ownership: Theoretical extensions, measurement and relation to work outcomes. *Journal of Organizational Behavior, 29*, 1–19.

Avey, J. B., Reichard, R. J., Luthans, F., & Mhatre, K. H. (2011). Meta-analysis of the impact of positive psychological capital on employee attitudes, behaviors, and performance. *Human Resource Development Quarterly, 22*, 127–152.

Avolio, B. J., & Luthans, F. (2006). *The high impact leader.* New York, NY: McGraw-Hill.

Cameron, K. S. (2008). Paradox in positive organizational change. *Journal of Applied Behavioral Science, 44*, 7–24.

Cameron, K. S., Bright, D., & Caza, A. (2004). Exploring the relationships between organizational virtuousness and performance. *American Behavioral Scientist, 47*, 766–790.

Carver, C., Scheier, M., Miller, C., & Fulford, D. (2009). Optimism. In S. Lopez & C. R. Snyder (Eds.), *Oxford handbook of positive psychology* (2nd ed., pp. 303–312). New York, NY: Oxford University Press.

Chang, E. C., Maydeu-Olivares, A., & D'Zurilla, T. J. (1997). Optimism and pessimism as partially independent constructs: Relations to positive and negative affectivity and psychological well-being. *Personality and Individual Differences, 23,* 433–440.

Collins, J. (2001). *Good to great.* New York, NY: HarperCollins.

Davidson, K., & Prkachin, K. (1997). Optimism and unrealistic optimism have an interacting impact on health-promoting behavior and knowledge changes. *Personality and Social Psychology Bulletin, 23,* 617–625.

Dixon, A. L., & Schertzer, S. M. B. (2005). Bouncing back: How salesperson optimism and self-efficacy influence attributions and behaviors following failure. *Journal of Personal Selling and Sales Management, 25,* 361–369.

Dolnick, E. (1995). Hotheads and heart attacks. *Health, July/August,* 58–64.

Gullapalli, D. (2005, May 4). Take this job and file it: Burdened by extra work created by the Sarbanes-Oxley Act, CPAs leave the big four for better life. *Wall Street Journal,* p. C1.

Haselton, M. G., & Nettle, D. (2006). The paranoid optimist: An integrative evolutionary model of cognitive biases. *Personality and Social Psychology Review, 10,* 47–66.

Jensen, S. M., & Luthans, F. (2006). Relationship between entrepreneurs' psychological capital and their authentic leadership. *Journal of Managerial Issues, 18,* 254–273.

Judge, T., & Ilies, R. (2004). Is positiveness in organizations always desirable? *Academy of Management Executive, 18,* 151–155.

Kahneman, D. (2011). *Thinking fast and slow.* New York, NY: Farrar, Straus and Giroux.

Kelley, H. (1973). The process of causal attribution. *American Psychologist, 29,* 107–128.

Klein, C. T. F., & Helweg-Larsen, M. (2002). Perceived control and the optimistic bias: A meta-analytic review. *Psychology and Health, 17,* 437–446.

Kok, L., Ho, M., Heng, B., & Ong, Y. (1990). A psychological study of high risk subjects for AIDS. *Singapore Medical Journal, 31,* 573–582.

Krizan, Z., & Windschitl, P. D. (2007). The influence of outcome desirability on optimism. *Psychological Bulletin, 133,* 95–121.

Kubzansky, L. D., Kubzansky, P. E., & Maselko, J. (2004). Optimism and pessimism in the context of health: Bipolar opposites or separate constructs? *Personality and Social Psychology Bulletin, 30,* 943–956.

Lai, J. C. (1994). Differential predictive power of the positively versus the negatively worded items of the Life Orientation Test. *Psychological Reports, 75,* 1507–1515.

Lazarus, R., & Folkman, S. (1984). *Stress, appraisal, and coping.* New York, NY: Springer.

Luthans, F., & Avolio, B. (2003). Authentic leadership: A positive development approach. In K. S. Cameron, J. E. Dutton, & R. E. Quinn (Eds.), *Positive organizational scholarship* (pp. 241–258). San Francisco, CA: Berrett-Koehler.

Luthans, F., Norman, S., & Hughes, L. (2006). Authentic leadership: A new approach to a new time. In R. Burke & C. Cooper (Eds.), *Inspiring leaders* (pp. 84–104). London, UK: Routledge, Taylor & Francis.

Luthans, F., & Youssef, C. M. (2004). Human, social and now positive psychological capital management: Investing in people for competitive advantage. *Organizational Dynamics, 33,* 143–160.

Luthans, F., & Youssef, C. M. (2007). Emerging positive organizational behavior. *Journal of Management, 33,* 321–349.

MacSweeney, G. (2002). Disaster recovery planning: Sadder but wiser. *Insurance and Technology, 27*(4), 20–24.

Norman, S. M., Avolio, B. J., & Luthans, F. (2010). The impact of positivity and transparency on trust in leaders and their perceived effectiveness. *Leadership Quarterly, 21,* 350–364.

O'Reilly, C., III, & Pfeffer, J. (2000). *Hidden value: How great companies achieve extraordinary results with ordinary people.* Boston, MA: Harvard Business.

Peterson, C. (1999). Personal control and well-being. In D. Kahneman, E. Diener, & N. Schwarz (Eds.), *Well-being: The foundations of hedonic psychology* (pp. 288–301). New York, NY: Russell Sage.

Peterson, C. (2000). The future of optimism. *American Psychologist, 55,* 44–55.

Peterson, C., & Barrett, L. (1987). Explanatory style and academic performance among university freshmen. *Journal of Personality and Social Psychology, 53,* 603–607.

Peterson, C., & Bossio, L. (1991). *Health and optimism.* New York, NY: Free Press.

Peterson, C., & Chang, E. (2002). Optimism and flourishing. In C. Keyes & J. Haidt (Eds.), *Flourishing: Positive psychology and the life well-lived* (pp. 55–79). Washington, DC: American Psychological Association.

Peterson, C., & Seligman, M. (1984). Causal explanations as a risk factor for depression: Theory and evidence. *Psychological Review, 91,* 347–374.

Peterson, C., & Seligman, M. (2004). *Character strengths and virtues.* Washington, DC: American Psychological Association.

Peterson, C., Seligman, M., & Vaillant, G. (1988). Pessimistic explanatory style is a risk factor for physical illness: A thirty-five year longitudinal study. *Journal of Personality and Social Psychology, 55,* 23–27.

Peterson, C., & Steen, T. (2009). Optimistic explanatory style. In S. Lopez & C.R. Snyder (Eds.), *Oxford handbook of positive psychology* (2nd ed., pp. 313–321). New York, NY: Oxford University Press.

Pfeffer, J. (1998). *The human equation.* Boston, MA: Harvard Business School Press.

Prola, M., & Stern, D. (1984). Optimism about college life and academic performance in college. *Psychological Reports, 55,* 347–350.

Rasmussen, H. N., Scheier, M. F., & Greenhouse, J. B. (2009). Optimism and physical health: A meta-analytic review. *Annals of Behavioral Medicine, 37,* 239–256.

Rich, G. A. (1999). Salesperson optimism. *Journal of Marketing Theory and Practice, 7,* 53–63.

Scheier, M. F., & Carver, C. (1985). Optimism, coping, and health: Assessment and implications of generalized outcome expectancies. *Health Psychology, 4,* 219–247.

Scheier, M. F., & Carver, C. (1987). Dispositional optimism and physical well-being: The influence of generalized outcome expectancies on health. *Journal of Personality, 55,* 169–210.

Scheier, M., & Carver, C. (1992). Effects of optimism on psychological and physical well-being: Theoretical overview and empirical update. *Cognitive Therapy and Research, 16,* 201–228.

Scheier, M., Matthews, K., Owen, J., Magovern, G., Lefebvre, R., Abbott, R. A., & Carver, C. S. (1989). Dispositional optimism and recovery from coronary artery bypass surgery: The beneficial effects of physical and psychological well-being. *Journal of Personality and Social Psychology, 57,* 1024–1040.

Schneider, S. L. (2001). In search of realistic optimism. *American Psychologist, 56,* 250–263.

Seeman, J. (1989). Toward a model of positive health. *American Psychologist, 44,* 1099–1109.

Seligman, M. E. P. (1972). Learned helplessness. *Annual Review of Medicine, 23,* 407–412.

Seligman, M. E. P. (1998). *Learned optimism.* New York, NY: Pocket Books.

Seligman, M. E. P. (2002). *Authentic happiness.* New York, NY: Free Press.

Staw, B., & Barsade, S. (1993). Affect and managerial performance: A test of the sadder-but-wiser vs. happier-and-smarter hypotheses. *Administrative Science Quarterly, 38,* 304–331.

Strack, S., Carver, C., & Blaney, P. (1987). Predicting successful completion of an aftercare program following treatment for alcoholism: The role of dispositional optimism. *Journal of Personality and Social Psychology, 53,* 579–584.

Sweeny, K., Carroll, P. J., & Shepperd, J. A. (2006). Is optimism always best? Future outlooks and preparedness. *Current Directions in Psychological Science, 15,* 302–306.

Taylor, S. (1989). *Positive illusions.* New York, NY: Basic Books.

Tiger, L. (1979). *Optimism: The biology of hope.* New York, NY: Simon and Schuster.

Walumbwa, F. O., Peterson, S. J., Avolio, B. J., & Hartnell, C. A. (2010). An investigation of the relationships among leader and follower psychological capital, service climate, and job performance. *Personnel Psychology, 63,* 937–963.

Waterman, R. H., Waterman, J. A., & Collard, B. A. (1994). Toward a career-resilient workforce. *Harvard Business Review, 72*(4), 87–95.

Weinstein, N. (1989). Optimistic biases about personal risks. *Science, 246*, 1232–1233.

Wernsing, T. (2014). Psychological capital: A test of measurement instrument invariance across twelve national cultures. *Journal of Leadership and Organizational Studies, 21*, 179–190.

Youssef-Morgan, C. M. (2014). Advancing OB research: An illustration using psychological capital. *Journal of Leadership and Organizational Studies, 21*, 130–140.

6

PSYCAP RESILIENCE

BOUNCING BACK AND BEYOND

Opening Video: Ann Masten on Resilience in Children

Video link: http://www.youtube.com/watch?v=ZR9HsVuaUg4 (or search for "Study on Resiliency in Children: Interview with Ann Masten Part 1")

Video link: http://www.youtube.com/watch?v=xAzUjk6DbaU (or search for "Study on Resiliency in Children: Interview with Ann Masten Part 2")

Video link: http://www.youtube.com/watch?v=OJopFhs64Q (or search for "Study on Resiliency in Children: Interview with Ann Masten Part 3")

Ann S. Masten is a psychology professor at the University of Minnesota. She is well-known for her research on resilience in children, which has strongly influenced resilience research in positive psychology in general and its inclusion as a component of PsyCap. Her strategies for developing resilience in children and at-risk youth have been shown to be applicable to many other populations, including managers and employees in the workplace. In these three video segments Dr. Masten speaks about her extensive resilience research that spans the last few decades.

Questions for reflection and/or discussion:

1. What is resilience and how is it measured?
2. What are the key contributing factors to building resilience in children and youth?

3. Which of the resilience contributing factors have been most influential in your own life and personal development?

4. How can these contributing factors be applied in the workplace in order to develop resilience in managers and employees?

5. Which of the resilience contributing factors do you often use in developing resilience in yourself and those around you (family, friends, coworkers, associates)? Explain.

It is rare to pick up a biography of any world-class leader and not be taken aback by the resilience the individual has repeatedly demonstrated. Failure after failure did not deter these leaders from seeking out and achieving the mission they set forth for themselves, their organizations, or even entire societies. The resilience evidenced by such leaders as Nelson Mandela, Mother Teresa, Winston Churchill, Aung San Suu Kyi, and Abraham Lincoln underscores the importance of this "bounce back" capacity in leaders that continues under the most difficult circumstances.

Similar to the predominantly negative focus of the field of psychology prior to the positive psychology movement, for a long time, most of the resilience research and practice (e.g., as in the opening video segments) has been associated with at-risk children, adolescents, and dysfunctional families. Those who were strong enough to lead a "normal" life after facing traumatic experiences were labeled "survivors." They were admired for being "exceptional" (or even "magical," Masten, 2001). Traditionally, research focused on "who" was resilient, for example, anecdotal case studies of exceptional hardiness and the ability to bounce back despite severe problems. Resilience research then moved on to study both who was resilient and what characteristics resilient people possessed.

Positive psychologists such as Ann Masten in the opening videos (2001; Masten, Cutuli, Herbers, & Reed, 2009) through her theory building and research recognize that resilience involves everyday skills and psychological strengths that can be identified, measured, maintained, and nurtured in individuals of all ages and psychological conditions. As Masten (2001, p. 235) notes, resilience comes "from the everyday magic of ordinary, normative human resources" and "has profound implications for promoting competence and human capital in individuals and society."

We have generalized and extended this positive psychology view of resilience to the workplace (e.g., see Avolio & Luthans, 2006; Luthans, 2002; Luthans, Avolio, Avey, & Norman, 2007; Luthans, Luthans, & Luthans, 2004; Luthans & Youssef, 2004; Youssef & Luthans, 2005b, 2007, for our early conceptual and empirical work). As a criteria-meeting component of PsyCap, we defined resilience as "the capacity to rebound or bounce back from adversity, conflict, failure, or even positive events, progress, and increased responsibility" (Luthans, 2002, p. 702). PsyCap resilience also includes not only bouncing back to "normal" but also using adversity as a springboard toward growth and development. For example, instead of an adversity resulting in posttraumatic stress disorder (PTSD), under this perspective the result could be posttraumatic growth (PTG, e.g., see Tedeschi, Park, & Calhoun, 1998).

Similarly, positive organizational scholars B. Caza and Milton (2012) define resilience at work as "a developmental trajectory characterized by demonstrated competence in the face of, and professional growth after, experiences of adversity in the workplace" (p. 896). The two definitions share the following characteristics of resilience: (a) presence of adversity, (b) demonstrated adaptation, and (c) subsequent growth. Thus, the goal of studying resilience in the context of work is to uncover the conditions that help to facilitate such a powerful capacity in employees, leaders, and organizations. This recent work has filled an important void because before its emergence, the body of knowledge that applied resilience to the workplace was characterized as relatively rare, very fragmented, and generally inadequate (Sutcliffe & Vogus, 2003).

Personal Reflections Exercise on PsyCap Resilience

To better understand the more in-depth discussion of resilience, we would like you to once again spend some time reflecting on the following questions:

- When was the last time you encountered what you would consider to be adversity, a conflict, a failure, or even a positive event that you believe to have been overwhelming?
- What was the nature of this event or situation?
- Was it sudden and unexpected, or gradual and emotionally draining?
- What were some of the coping strategies you formulated and tried to implement?
- How effective do you think these strategies were?
- What sort of support was available to you and what did you seek out?
- Do you think you eventually bounced back and fully recovered from this event or situation? Why? Why not?
- What are some of the lessons that you learned from this experience?
- What other ways besides this situation, how you handled it, and the outcome could have taught you these lessons?
- Overall, if you were to assess yourself right now, with the event or situation behind you (or pretty much behind you), do you believe that you have grown and matured, bounced back to your "normal" or even beyond, or have you deteriorated and feel somewhat diminished?

With the same questions, you can also take a look at those you have total respect for as a leader and/or mentor.

- How did these individuals handle the challenges of adversity and what could you learn from their resilience that you can apply to your own development as a leader or committed follower?

We also now invite you to challenge yourself even further by trying to remember a time or times when you voluntarily went out of your way, left your comfort zone for something new and unexpected. For example, ask yourself:

- When was the last time I volunteered for something new and difficult?
- Did something unusual, even though I thought it was risky and unusual for me?
- Traveled abroad?
- Tried a new food that I never tasted before?
- Took a different route to a familiar place, just for a change?
- Chose to listen to a new type of music?
- Read about something purely out of curiosity?
- Accepted someone else's idea over my own because I actually thought it was better?
- Befriended someone despite outward appearance or obvious personality differences?
- Asked someone for help despite status differences?
- Allowed myself to go unprepared and "improvise" on the spot?
- Moved to a new location?
- Took a completely different direction in my career?
- Went back to school to start with a totally new focus and discipline?
- Gave people who work for me total freedom to make a critical decision?

A Resilience Story

Besides reflecting on these questions to gain some insights into your own resilience, consider the following story about Mary, who when she was a teenager lost her mother to cancer and had to live with her verbally abusive father, resentful step-mother, and mentally challenged, much older step-brother. In this situation, she soon started to miss school and then had a few minor scrapes with the law. Court-ordered old-school counseling focused on Mary's at-risk situation, which resulted in her being placed in the foster care system. She moved from one foster home to the next through no fault of her own. For example, her foster families would return her to the system in order to have a child of their own, move to a different city, or even remodel and put the room she was occupying to a different use.

With such tremendous uncertainty and instability in her life after still another placement in a foster home, Mary had a trigger moment with a close friend at school in which the friend verbally challenged her to take charge of her own life. She resolutely decided after this interaction with her friend to hold onto only things that could be in her own control. This she determined to be her mind, her body, and her motivation to succeed. From that moment on, Mary immersed herself and invested her time and energy in education and sports, and worked as hard as she could at whatever she chose to do. She excelled in high school academics and athletics. This earned her a full scholarship to play soccer for one of the top universities in the state.

Besides her hard work that paid off in the classroom and on the soccer field, a less obvious contributor to Mary's success was her ability to surround herself with caring friends and mentors. She established strong relationships not only with her peers but also her coaches, some professors, and community leaders who were supporters of the athletic programs at the university. She would offer to assist in coaching kids in youth leagues and babysit for her mentors' kids. At no additional charge, she would take it upon herself to do household chores while babysitting. As her diligence and conscientiousness were observed and she was repeatedly asked back, she became an important part of the prominent families for whom she worked. She used every opportunity to interact with not only the mentor but also his or her spouse and even the grandparents, from whom she would seek advice on important life decisions. She gained valuable insights and values from observing and interacting with healthy families that she had been denied in her own life course.

Although Mary barely made the soccer team, she was able to maintain her scholarship. She sacrificed an active social life by studying hard and getting above-average grades in her marketing major. However, she also kept in constant contact with the families she babysat for and was often invited to their homes for Sunday dinner or pizza after a game. This network of social contacts paid off for Mary: After her junior year she was offered an attractive summer internship by one of those contacts who was a president of the local bank.

Based on Mary's track record briefly revealed here, the rest of the story should be pretty predictable. However, if we go back to her early teenage years, the prediction would be very bleak. Yet, through a positive trigger moment with a friend, and her conscientious personality, human capital (good college education, playing on a team, internship experience in a bank), social capital (network of friends, mentors), but, especially her psychological capital (confidence, hope, optimism, but mainly, resilience) she not only landed a good entry-level job with the bank upon graduation but in a short number of years became a vice-president in charge of the bank marketing and retail operations. Mary chose a different pathway, which relates to our discussion of hope, but she also demonstrated her capacity to bounce back, once triggered by her friend's comment.

In this story, Mary, the successful bank executive, as a young teen was certainly "at risk" and headed for big problems. This is how many such stories would end. How she moved from "at risk" to "successful exec" could be attributed to her PsyCap resilience. She had a moment that mattered in taking charge of her own life, and through some wise strategies she not only bounced back but went way beyond what would be considered normal or average accomplishments. Was she set back by adverse events in her life course? Definitely. Was she resilient? Definitely. Will she continue to be resilient in her career? Hopefully, but time and understanding of PsyCap resilience may help in finding an answer to this complex question.

What you might derive from reading this story is the idea that if people choose to bounce back, they just might be able to do so. This doesn't mean one won't need support to be successful. It simply means that the support can be condolences or the support can be energizing, so one must choose pathways wisely and be mindful of the choices under one's control.

The Meaning of PsyCap Resilience

From a clinical psychology perspective, Masten et al. (2009, p. 118) define resilience as "patterns of positive adaptation during or following significant adversity or risk." In our PsyCap approach as indicated in our definition of *resilience* in the introductory comments, we broadened the definition to include not only to bounce back from adversity but also very positive challenging events (e.g., record sales performance) and to go beyond the normal or equilibrium point (Avolio & Luthans, 2006; Luthans, 2002; Youssef & Luthans, 2005b).

Besides this recognition of positive as well as negative events, and going beyond the normal or return to equilibrium, various factors from positive psychology have been identified and researched as contributing to or hindering the development of resilience. These factors can be classified into assets, risk factors (Luthans, Vogelgesang, & Lester, 2006; Masten, 2001; Masten et al., 2009; Youssef & Luthans, 2005b), and values (Coutu, 2002; Kobsa, 1982; Richardson, 2002; Youssef & Luthans, 2005a). There is also recognition of adaptational processes that tie these three factors additively, interactively, and synergistically, resulting in resilience (Cowan, Cowan, & Schulz, 1996; Masten et al., 2009).

Resilience Assets

Masten et al. (2009, p. 119) define a resilience asset as "a measurable characteristic in a group of individuals or their situation that predicts positive outcome with respect to a specific outcome criterion . . . across levels of risk." Specifically, they identify cognitive abilities, temperament, positive self-perceptions, faith, a positive outlook on life, emotional stability, self-regulation, a sense of humor, and general appeal or attractiveness as potential assets that can contribute to higher resilience (Masten, 2001). Wolin and Wolin (2005) offer a similar list of assets, including insight, independence, relationships, initiative, creativity, humor, and morality.

Drawing from positive psychology, as was found in the earlier story about Mary, particular emphasis has been given to the importance of relationship-based assets and their contribution to resilience, especially in the context of dealing with adverse or negative events. For example, Masten (2001) discusses the importance of caregiving adults, effective parenting, prosocial and rule-abiding peers, and collective efficacy in the community. Gorman (2005) supports the integral role of both personal and relationship-based assets in enhancing resilience by showing that those who can discover and hone their talents and then find effective mentors who can be their "champions" have higher chances of bouncing back and becoming successful.

Resilience Risk Factors

Masten et al. (2009, p. 119) define resilience risk factors as those that cause an "elevated probability of an undesirable outcome." Also referred to as "vulnerability factors" (Kirby & Fraser, 1997), risk factors may include clearly destructive and dysfunctional experiences such as alcohol and drug abuse (e.g., Johnson et al., 1998; Sandau-Beckler, Devall, & de la Rosa, 2002) and exposure to trauma such as experiencing violence (Qouta, El-Sarraj, & Punamaki, 2001). These risks can also include less obvious, gradual, but eventually detrimental factors such as stress and burnout (e.g., Baron, Eisman, Scuello, Veyzer, & Lieberman, 1996; Smith & Carlson, 1997), poor health, undereducation, and unemployment (e.g., Collins, 2001). For example, recent research shows that recent disasters such as terrorism, war, hurricanes, and school violence have resulted in repeated exposure of today's youth to a different set of contemporary fears that require counselors to design unique prevention and intervention strategies to deal with them (Burnham, 2009).

Risk factors may differentially expose individuals to frequent and intense undesirable events, and thus increase the probability of negative outcomes

(Cowan et al., 1996; Masten, 2001). However, the mere presence of risk factors should not be viewed as automatically conducive to failure and lack of resilience. In today's world, risk factors are inevitable. Therefore, complete risk avoidance and sheltering oneself and others from all sources of risk is, at best, unrealistic. Moreover, the presence of challenges is actually a necessary and invaluable growth and self-actualization opportunity. If properly identified and managed, the process of using assets to overcome risks can help people overcome complacency, explore new domains, and further leverage their existing talents and strengths. In other words, as in the case of Mary, risks can stimulate growth and development and help people to reach their full potential. Just as needs are a requirement in the motivation process, risk factors can be thought of as antecedents for "bouncing back and beyond" in the resilience process. Resilience allows one to take advantage of latent potential that otherwise could go undiscovered.

Cowan and colleagues (1996, p. 9) emphasize this process-focused perspective when they state that "the active ingredients of a risk do not lie in the variable itself, but in the set of processes that flow from the variable, linking risk conditions with specific dysfunctional outcomes." They compare an individual's exposure to and dealing with risk factors to immunization, a process that exposes the person to a small dose of a disease in order to build long-term strength, endurance, and sustainability.

Similarly, Wolin and Wolin (2005) present a positive alternative to the traditional "damage model" of being at risk. The "risk paradigm" that includes the "damage model" presents a self-fulfilling prophecy. That is, those exposed to risk factors (like Mary in the opening story) are too often judged and treated as if they are going to fail. The best developmental efforts under this damage perspective are channeled toward equipping the "at-risk" individual with an inventory of adaptation and coping techniques that may result in "normal" functioning despite adversity. On the other hand, PsyCap resilience would view adversities and setbacks as both risk factors and challenging opportunities for growth and success beyond the normal state. Such a change in perspective taking (or meaning making or mindset) itself could result in a more positive self-fulfilling prophecy. Indeed, Reichard and Avolio (2005) based on a review of the last 100 years of leadership intervention research reported that the greatest impact was attributable to Pygmalion (i.e., self-fulfilling) effects. These effects were created by getting leaders to believe that followers were more or less effective, qualified, and so forth. Such manipulated beliefs resulted in significantly different performance in followers.

The same may be said for the now recognized power of the placebo effect. There is increasing evidence from double-blind experiments in medicine when patients believe they are receiving a medical treatment or pill that will help them but are really not (e.g., receive a sugar pill), they often report improving as much as those who had received the medical treatment/pill. Recent critical reviews of this placebo effect run the whole gamut, but there seems to be psychological implications that cannot be ignored (e.g., for a recent comprehensive review, see Miller, Colloca, Crouch, & Kaptchuk, 2013).

When considering both assets and risk factors in the PsyCap resilience process, it follows that the relationship is not necessarily linear. In other words, resilience should not be assessed as the total resources and capabilities available to an individual (assets), minus the frequency and intensity of exposure to risk factors. Instead, in the PsyCap resilience process, assets and risk factors taken together should be viewed as cumulative and interactive in nature. As Sandau-Beckler and collegues (2002) point out, the specific order or sequence in a "risk chain" can be a fundamental predictor of one's resilience level.

The Role of Values in Resilience

Still another major component of PsyCap resilience is the underlying value system that guides, shapes, and gives consistency and meaning to one's cognitions, emotions, and actions. Values and beliefs help individuals in elevating themselves over difficult and overwhelming present events, linking them to a more pleasant future to which they can look forward. For example, Avolio and Luthans (2006) note that resilient, authentic leaders can look to their future possible selves and bring them back to their present actual selves, even during periods of failure and retain a positive outlook. This bringing the future back to the present can result in motivating themselves and others to higher performance. This perspective also suggests that individuals who are more motivated to develop and learn will likely sustain effort to achieve challenging goals and expectations. And motivation to learn and develop, like resilience, is something that can be developed in individuals and/or diminished, as too often happens with poor leaders and ineffective managers.

Research supports the role of meaning-providing values and beliefs in maintaining resilience through severe psychological (Wong & Mason, 2001) and physical (e.g., Holaday & McPhearson, 1997) challenges. For example, a positive relationship has been found between religiosity and mental health (e.g., Bergin, 1983; Larson, Pattison, Blazer, Omran, & Kaplan, 1986; Ness & Wintrob, 1980), happiness (Paul, 2005), and coping with traumatic experiences (Baron et al., 1996; Gibbs, 1989; Tebbi, Mallon, Richards, & Bigler, 1987). Furthermore, those who act in line with their moral frameworks have been consistently found to experience increased freedom, energy, and resilience (Richardson, 2002). Wolin and Wolin (2005) see morality as enhancing resilience through aligning one's actions to a value system that guides judgment (distinguishing between good and bad), principles (providing a foundation for decisions and behavior), and eventually service (contributing to others' well-being). It suffices to say that a primary contribution of one's values in the process of enhancing resilience lies in the stability of these values as a source of true meaning (Coutu, 2002; Kobsa, 1982).

It is truly amazing to see how persistent some individuals are to a cause if they have a very deep belief in that cause, purpose, or mission. We can label them insurgents, religious zealots, or patriots, but in the end, they all have a deep belief in something that extends their possible selves to a higher purpose, which is another way of saying they have ownership for whatever is being pursued via high levels of identification. At the same time this stronger held belief will likely enhance their resilience level and those they influence. A good example that we also used in our earlier discussion of hope is Nelson Mandela and his fellow Robben Island political prisoners during the apartheid regime in South Africa. They not only endured physical and psychological abuse for over three decades, but in the process they transformed themselves, others (including their initially very brutal guards), and the society at large because of their unwavering beliefs and positive PsyCap (Cascio & Luthans, 2014). As one of the prisoners who was describing the horrendous torture he was subjected to "realized that the guards, his torturers, could do nothing more to hurt him; he felt an inner positive strength knowing that no matter how much his body might hurt, his soul was invincible. In other words, despite facing severe adversity, the prisoners at Robben Island demonstrated remarkable resiliency" (Cascio & Luthans, 2014, p. 57).

The PsyCap Resilience Factors in Action

Besides the historically significant events at Robben Island to demonstrate PsyCap resilience, we can also go back to Mary's story at the beginning of the chapter. She certainly possessed many significant assets, including her obvious intellectual and athletic talents, conscientious personality, and ability to formulate and execute effective life strategies. Importantly, she also had evidence of hope (the will and the way), confidence/efficacy, and also optimism for her future. Covered in the preceding three chapters, confidence, hope, and optimism can also be considered here as assets in the resilience process. Mary's life also contained numerous classic risk factors: the loss of her mother, her dysfunctional family, a failed foster care system, and her nonexistent material and financial resources.

Mary refused to be at the mercy of these classic risks. She challenged them versus accepting them as determining her fate and future. Capitalizing on her assets, she was able to leverage them and further them in terms of her development. She was able to manage her risk factors by formulating and implementing strategies (i.e., adaptational processes) such as building a reliable and diversified network of social support through friends and mentors (i.e., social capital). The strong educational and athletic record indicated she had talent/strengths that also helped mitigate some of her risk factors (e.g., her financial limitations in obtaining a higher education). Also very evident is the role of her strong value system. Mary's strong work ethic and her being able to recognize and seize positive moments such as her friend telling her to take control of her life resulted in enriching her mind through education, her body through sports, and social capital through her social network that eventually led to her first job and eventual career success beyond normal.

If Mary had been born into a wealthy and functionally healthy family (more assets, fewer risk factors), would she have taken the initiative, reached out, and accomplished what she has? The answer is far from certain, but the contribution of adversity, setbacks, and risk factors in building Mary's resilience and subsequent success cannot be ignored or underestimated. Development occurs because we are challenged, not because we have obtained a level of capacity and effort that does not need to be enhanced. Thus, in extreme areas of challenge, resilience may play a critically important role in success.

Mary's early life course is an example of how resilience is typically portrayed in the traditional clinical and even more recent positive psychology discussions. It serves this chapter well to demonstrate the key factors of assets, risk factors, adaptational processes, and values in the resilience process. However, when included as a PsyCap criteria-meeting psychological resource, an understanding and build-out of resilience does not have to be limited to life course risk factors such as death of a loved one, a severe illness, a dysfunctional family, or failed social institutions.

For PsyCap resilience, instead of such negative life course events, attention is given to inevitable adverse factors in today's workplace (e.g., being fired, downsized, or passed over for promotion; failing to reach project goals; or even more subtle ones such as being ignored by teammates or feeling discriminated against). However, as important as the negative is, the role PsyCap resilience may also play in responding to positive events in the workplace cannot be discounted (e.g., a significant increase in responsibility and exposure resulting from a promotion or coming off a record year with heightened expectations).

Perhaps the simplest way of expressing this reaction is that if you are positively or negatively pushed beyond some threshold capacity level, you are at the front end of tapping into resilience. PsyCap resilience is concerned with how it can not just propel leaders and employees back to their normal selves but, like

Mary, reach the capacity that is created by paying attention to their possible selves. The remainder of the chapter uses the definitions and factors discussed so far as a point of departure for examining the performance implications and development of resilience of leaders, employees, and organizations.

Resilience in the Workplace: Performance Implications

As we have discussed so far, both clinical and positive psychological research support the role of resilience in enhancing various aspects of human functioning, especially those related to posttraumatic coping, adaptation, and health (e.g., see Block & Kremen, 1996; Bonanno, 2004; Brunwasser, Gillham, & Kim, 2009; Coutu, 2002; Cowan et al., 1996; Egeland, Carlson, & Sroufe, 1993; Huey & Weisz, 1997; Hunter & Chandler, 1999; Johnson et al., 1998; Kirby & Fraser, 1997; Lee, Sudom, & Zamorski, 2013; Masten, 2001; Masten et al., 2009; Richardson, 2002; Sandau-Beckler et al., 2002; Smith & Carlson, 1997; Stewart, Reid, & Mangham, 1997). A part of PsyCap has also found a positive relationship between resilience and workplace performance outcomes (Avey, Reichard, Luthans, & Mhatre, 2011; Luthans et al., 2005, 2007; Youssef & Luthans, 2007), including unique and extreme working conditions such as military combat (Schaubroeck, Riolli, Peng, & Spain, 2011). Other peripheral resilience applications in the workplace are also emerging at an accelerating rate, among both researchers and practitioners/consultants (e.g., see Conner, 1993, 2003; LaMarch, 1997; Luthans, Vogelgesang, et al., 2006; Vickers & Kouzmin, 2001; Waite & Richardson, 2004; Waterman, Waterman, & Collard, 1994; Zunz, 1998).

The concept of resilience has considerable appeal in today's workplace, which is characterized as increasingly competitive, changing at a dizzying rate, and dominated by shades of gray when it comes to value systems and standards for ethical behavior. Today's organizational participants are uncertain about the underlying assumptions and values they are guided by and their individual psychological contracts, including what they own and don't own in terms of rights and responsibilities. For those who are only capable of passively coping and reactively adapting, this environment is unfriendly, stressful, and can be very dysfunctional for both the individual and the organization. Confining resilience to this passive description that just allows for reactive coping and survival from adversity, as the traditional resilience literature emphasizes, would limit its applications to the current situation most organizational participants now face in the "flat world" global economy.

Today's managers and employees realize that their organizations are looking for top performers who can thrive on chaos, proactively learn and grow through hardships, and excel no matter how many or how intense the inevitable setbacks (Hamel & Välikangas, 2003). Bouncing back to where one initially was before a problem or crisis is necessary but no longer sufficient. Average performance can no longer meet today's rapidly growing expectations. The expectations and commitments have escalated to "better than OK" (Sutcliffe & Vogus, 2003). Today's organizational participants need to not only survive, cope, and recover but also thrive and flourish through the inevitable difficulties and uncertainties they face and to do so faster than their competition (Ryff & Singer, 2003).

PsyCap resilience is not just a minimal coping or neutralizing agent for difficult times (Bonanno, 2004). Viewing resilience as proactive, rather than just reactive, may lead to sustainable positive gains. Reivich and Shatte (2002) support the proactive nature of resilience in describing it as the capacity to overcome, steer through, bounce back, and reach out to pursue new knowledge and experiences, deeper relationships with others, and finding meaning in life. Moreover, drawing from our earlier example of PTG as a positive alternative to PTSD (Tedeschi et al., 1998), it emphasizes that resilient individuals use adversities as a "springboard" to reach higher ground. Ryff and Singer (2003) also assert that resilient people experience enhanced self-reliance, self-efficacy, self-awareness, self-disclosure, relationships, emotional expressiveness, and empathy.

Reflecting on adversities also helps in giving life meaning and value, and in refining one's philosophy of life, goals, and priorities. Richardson's (2002) notion of "resilient reintegration" becomes particularly relevant to this perspective. He suggests that disruptions in one's life routines allow for the exploration and refinement of resilient qualities. These windows of opportunity stemming from adversities and disruptions can result in substantial growth and development, as well as valuable opportunities for reflection and self-assessment. In other words, resilience can be expanded to include personal growth and increased strength through adversities and setbacks. This growth perspective is all-encompassing.

Pragmatically, we expect resilience to be related to improved performance and bottom-line gains, and our research supports such a view. In addition, increased job satisfaction, enhanced organizational commitment, and enriched social capital are also likely to be potential positive outcomes, as well as inputs into a positive spiral of increased resilience.

Developing Resilience in Today's Employees

As we have defined, PsyCap resilience is a dynamic, malleable, developable psychological capacity or strength. It is not a "magical" or "mystical" capacity (Masten, 2001), a "super material" (Sutcliffe & Vogus, 2003), or a "hard-wired," fixed trait. The positive psychology and business consulting fields consider resilience open to development. For example, in positive psychology, George Vaillant (1977, 2000), the director of the Study of Adult Development at Harvard Medical School, has clearly demonstrated that people he studied became markedly more resilient over their lifetimes, and Salvatore R. Maddi, the director of the Hardiness Institute, has effectively used resilience training over the years (Coutu, 2002). Emerging neurological research also supports brain plasticity toward increased resilience. In fact, one of Davidson's (2012) six emotional styles based on this research is called "Resilience" and is objectively measured by how slowly or quickly one recovers from adversity.

As part of their Project Resilience, Wolin and Wolin (2005) offer resilience assessment and training that has been effective in various contexts, including education, treatment, and even prevention. In business consulting, over many years Reivich and Shatte (2002) have conducted resilience development programs for companies. In addition, Conner (1993, 2003) offers resilience development training interventions and solutions specifically tailored to leadership development and change management situations. Waite and Richardson (2004) also empirically supported the effectiveness of training interventions in enhancing resilience in the workplace. Although areas such as sales and marketing have research drawing from efficacy (e.g., Fu, Richards, Hughes, & Jones, 2010), optimism (e.g., Dixon & Schertzer, 2005), and even overall PsyCap (Nguyen & Nguyen, 2012), to date research utilizing resiliency, which would seem particularly relevant given the constant rejection facing sales personnel, has been largely absent from the literature.

As a follow-up to their analysis of the factors in the resilience process, Masten and colleagues (2009) identified three sets of resilience development strategies that can be adapted to the workplace. These can be summarized as follows:

1. *Asset-Focused Strategies*. As the name implies, these strategies focus on enhancing the perceived and actual level of assets and resources that can increase the probability of positive outcomes. In terms of workplace applications, these assets may include human capital (education, experience, knowledge, skills, abilities), social capital (relationships, networking), and even other positive psychological capital components (efficacy, hope, optimism). Human capital, especially its explicit knowledge, skills, and abilities, can be learned and enhanced through traditional training and development programs.

The tacit component of human capital, which is the in-depth understanding of the organization's specific values, culture, structure, strategies, and processes, can be developed through various widely recognized approaches and techniques such as socialization, mentoring, and even job rotation. Social capital can be developed through open communication, trust building, authenticity and transparency, feedback and recognition, teamwork, and work-life balance initiatives (Luthans & Youssef, 2004; Youssef & Luthans, 2005a, 2005b). Such approaches for developing positive psychological capital are recommended throughout the chapters of this book support our point that we are not only building individual PsyCap but over time are positively contributing to collective PsyCap as well.

2. *Risk-Focused Strategies.* Under this strategy, Masten et al. (2009) offer risk factors that can increase the probability of undesired outcomes being prevented. Although heavily emphasized in developmental psychology, in line with our positive perspective on risk factors as challenges and developmental opportunities, our developmental approach emphasizes the management, rather than the avoidance, of most risk factors (Luthans, Vogelgesang et al., 2006). For example, based on our earlier definition of resilience as "the developable capacity to rebound or bounce back from adversity, conflict, and failure or even positive events, progress, and increased responsibility" (Luthans, 2002, p. 702), a promotion can be viewed as a positive event and an opportunity for growth and increased responsibility, but it can also be overwhelming and might be perceived as a high-risk situation. A risk-avoidance strategy would be to turn down such a promotion. On the other hand, an alternative risk-management strategy that would fit this situation may include a developmental approach for enhancing self-efficacy in the new domain. This efficacy development would include coaching and/or mentoring and frequent constructive feedback. Through such risk-management approaches, an inventory of assets that is relevant to the new challenge is built. This asset inventory would help the individual in perceiving the new risk factors as developmental opportunities and would draw from them to bounce back and beyond. This is simply using the time-tested strategy of turning a threat into an opportunity.

Another example of a risk-focused strategy would be entrepreneurial and intrapreneurial initiatives. This would involve out-of-the-box thinking, which tends to motivate calculated but usually high risk taking but has the potential for high returns. In the business environment, such entrepreneurial risk taking is encouraged, commended, and necessary for success in today's competitive environment.

Many individuals, however, with creative capacities and high-potential ideas, forgo their dreams and resort to safer risk-avoidance strategies (e.g., settle for a secure, but often boring job). Again, through equipping individuals with the proper assets, especially social capital (Sanders & Nee, 1996; Teixeira, 2001), even when faced with risk, potential opportunities can be realized through an entrepreneurial, out-of-the-box strategy. Nevertheless, many destructive and unnecessary risk factors still need to be avoided, even by psychologically and physically healthy adults in the context of work. For example, unhealthy eating habits and lack of physical exercise due to the long and increasingly stressful hours that Americans work (Greenhouse, 2001; Koretz, 2001) are a couple of common examples of risk factors that should probably be minimized, if not avoided, by most organizational participants.

3. *Process-Focused Strategies.* Masten et al. (2009) present this third set of strategies as effective adaptational systems and processes. They are mobilized in order to identify, select, develop, employ, and maintain the proper mix of assets in managing pertinent risk factors. This allows overcoming and growing through adversities. For example, in the authentic leadership development model (Avolio & Luthans, 2006; Luthans & Avolio, 2003), the processes of self-awareness and self-regulation become an integral part of the resilience development process. In other words, possessing all the right assets may not be conducive to effective functioning in difficult times, unless the manager has the proper means to accurately assess these assets (self-awareness) and diligently employs and develops them to overcome the risks (self-regulation).

Although process-focused strategies have emphasized various coping mechanisms in the field of child and adolescent psychology, Harland and colleagues' (2005) study of workplace resilience clearly distinguishes between avoidance coping and approach coping. In line with our conceptualization of risk, approach-coping techniques would be more positively associated with resilience that takes the individual back and beyond, while avoidance-coping techniques would tend to be negatively related to the impact of resilience. At the organizational level, Hoffer Gittell (2008) makes the case for relational coordination as a mechanism that is promoted by and that enables resilient responses to external threats and pressures that require organizational change. Similarly, Teixeira and Werther (2013) argue that the way organizations manage their innovation process (not innovation per se, which would be considered an asset) is foundational for its resilience and competitiveness.

Resilient Leaders and Employees

The constant turmoil that is characteristic of our current environment is challenging organizational members' abilities to endure, let alone grow and develop in any targeted, proactive manner. So far, we have emphasized that the impact of these substantial changes on resilience is primarily dependent on the processes through which leaders' and employees' assets, risk factors, and values interact and are managed and integrated. The following examples are by no means exhaustive but simply serve as representative guidelines for analyzing potentially adverse changes that are likely to necessitate the need for PsyCap resilience.

In light of the changing nature of psychological contracts or what employees expect organizations to provide in exchange for what they deliver for that organization (Robinson, Kraatz, & Rousseau, 1994), as we have previously discussed, organizational commitment and mutual trust among managers and their associates has declined. When organizations in recent years can no longer guarantee long-term, secure employment, managers and employees have lost some valuable resilience-enhancing assets. These lost or deteriorating assets include the human and social capital involved in caring leadership, mentoring opportunities, and long-term investments in organization-initiated development and career planning. In addition, the increased risk associated with loss of one's income and job insecurity can result in negative thinking and emotions such as fear of the future, complacency, disengagement, and unwillingness to engage in organizational citizenship behaviors. It can even lead to ethically questionable behaviors out of self-interest and greed, such as embezzlement, sabotage, backstabbing, harassment, and even in rare instances violence.

All of the available evidence suggests that under these difficult conditions, leaders can make a profound difference in how the resulting challenges are perceived. Indeed, the very essence of what originally Burns (1978) and Bass and Avolio (1994) described as transformational leadership was that such leaders helped followers to see looming threats as opportunities for advancement and over time made followers believe they were in charge and owned more of the responsibility for success. In so doing, they were able to transform followers into leaders.

Career Resilience

Fortunately, there may be a positive, "half-full" side to these workplace changes that may seem on the surface to be only dysfunctional and destructive. Today's organizational leaders and employees can learn another type of resilience, "career resilience." According to Waterman, Waterman, and Collard (1994, p. 88), a career-resilient workforce is "a group of employees who not only are dedicated to the idea of continuous learning but also stand ready to reinvent themselves to keep pace with change; who take responsibility for their own career management; and, last but not least, who are committed to the company's success." Leaders can help create the conditions for employees to develop such attitudes toward their future.

With career resilience, the relationship between organizations and their members is shifting away from the traditional views of loyalty and commitment to one career path within one organization and one area of specialization at all costs (elimination of uncertainty and risk). The alternative approach of career resilience is toward a more volatile, flexible relationship between members and the organization that is sustained as long as it is mutually beneficial. Under this perspective, employees become charged with continuously monitoring, benchmarking, and anticipating changes in organizational needs, and then upgrading their skills and abilities (assets) accordingly. In the meantime, this process can contribute to their organizations' goals as well. What is essential to tipping the balance toward positive aspects of resilience is having a sense of trust in the fairness of how one is treated and will be treated. Having to let people go, but helping to maintain their dignity, is resilience enhancing. This approach is something leaders can directly have an impact on in their organizations.

One manager we are aware of indicated that when he had to lay off a group of workers, he went about doing so by treating them as alumni. From both a financial and psychological perspective, he did everything he could to make them feel positive about the organization and his leadership. The net effect of his efforts was that he typically got laid-off employees to come back when the economy was better for business and to make very positive referrals to others about the company.

Under the career resilience approach, organizations are no longer responsible for the traditional employment contract, but rather the "employability" of their members. This employability is accomplished through equipping, rather than prescriptive training, as well as the development and support of lifelong learning that enhances employees' opportunities, both within and outside the organization. In other words, career resilience is not a violation or betrayal of the psychological contract. Instead, it is a new type of psychological contract, with somewhat different but still balanced expectations, including organizations investing in employee development to make them both an internal and external valuable asset (Bagshaw, 1997; Kakabadse & Kakabadse, 2000).

In the career-resilience paradigm, risk factors that may be inherent in organizational strategic decisions, such as downsizing, reengineering, mergers and acquisitions, and outsourcing, may also trigger the development of new assets for resilience. For example, career-resilient managers and employees are likely to invest time and energy in beefing up their resumes, and in networking and building connections beyond their direct units or even their present organization. This newly developed human and social capital is a resource (an asset) to draw upon in times of adversity. When properly managed through well-designed organizational values, policies, and procedures (e.g., those that avoid conflict of interest), these relationships can be aligned and channeled to work for, rather than against, the interests of the organization. Moreover, adaptational mechanisms such as self-awareness, self-regulation, and self-development are expected to mediate the processes through which managers and employees proactively and independently develop their assets, manage their risk factors, refine their values and beliefs, and subsequently build their resilience.

The Impact of Leadership

It is important to note that leadership is an integral contributor to enhanced employee resilience, as evidenced by some of the earlier examples. We have proposed a cascading, trickle-down effect of resilience from managers to their associates (Avolio & Luthans, 2006; Youssef & Luthans, 2005b). Also, in the Harland and colleagues (2005) study it was found that the transformational leadership dimensions of attributed charisma, idealized influence, intellectual stimulation, and individualized consideration were positively related to the employees' resilience. On the other hand, most transactional leadership dimensions were not related to employee resilience. The researchers' assessment of resilience was along a broader spectrum of capacities that included not only coping and bouncing back but also learning, growth, and increased strength.

Clearly, a leadership approach that is consistent with follower development, open communication, trust building, creating more meaning and identification in one's work, and effective mentoring toward increased proactivity and independence is in tune with the recently emerging recognition of the importance of authenticity, integrity, and transparency. In fact, taken in combination, the most powerful leadership approach may involve the authentic, transformational leader. For example, using the examples of a drilling accident, a workplace shooting, and a traumatic retirement experience, Powley and Powley (2012) argued leadership played a critical role in organizational healing and resilience building after organizational crises. Similarly, in a case study of Xerox, Patnaik and Sahoo (2010) showed that CEOs leave a legacy of resilience that can guide future actions and guide turnaround during difficult times.

Authentic leadership is proposed to enhance follower resilience (Avolio & Luthans, 2006; Luthans & Avolio, 2003). Seeking greater self-awareness, authentic leaders transparently open as many communication channels as possible and encourage and reinforce their followers to give them sincere feedback. Such genuine, upward feedback can help authentic leaders understand themselves and their own level of PsyCap and accurately assess their vulnerabilities. This sort of feedback could reduce the risk of unexpected challenges suddenly emerging and reducing one's level of resilience.

Self-awareness helps leaders better target their energies, actions, and resources toward further self-development, and it provides direction for areas where their followers' development, empowerment, and delegation are more likely to be effective. Such a partnership-of-equals encourages continuous development and improvement in a nonthreatening, trusting, transparent environment.

Leaders and followers can bounce back and beyond together while capitalizing on the resources that they can provide each other. They both can also draw from their organizational context, rather than destructively compete for resources and information through destructive power games and political maneuvering. How much energy potential is lost with the type of silo fighting that goes on in many organizations? What are the implications of those losses for building up assets that sustain higher levels of resilience?

The Resilient Organization: Creating a Bounce Back and Beyond Environment

Only recently has the importance of organizational resilience been recognized. It should be clear by now that when it comes to resilience, like overall PsyCap (see Chapter 2), the whole is greater than the sum of its parts. In other words, bringing together a group of resilient managers and employees is not sufficient for the creation of a resilient organization (Coutu, 2002; Horne & Orr, 1998). Synergies occur when the organizational context in which members operate nurtures resilience through catalyzing, augmenting, shielding, and buffering various ingredients of the resilience development process (Youssef & Luthans, 2005b).

Organizational resilience has been defined as the structural and procedural dynamics that equip an organization with the capacity to absorb strain, retain coherence, bounce back, and thus continue to effectively engage in and manage risk (Klarreich, 1998; Worline et al., 2002). Hamel and Välikangas (2003) define organizational resilience as the ability to dynamically reinvent strategies and business models in response to inevitable change.

Like individuals, we have proposed that organizations capitalize on their macro-level assets, risk factors, values, and adaptational processes to develop and maintain their resilience (Youssef & Luthans, 2005b). Organizational assets that can contribute to resilience may include traditional economically oriented capital such as financial, physical, structural, and technological resources. Organizational assets may also include the collective of human capital ingredients discussed earlier, that is, explicit and tacit knowledge. In addition, social capital (interpersonal and interunit relationships, norms, values, trust, and community) may develop in the organization's social context (Luthans & Youssef, 2004). Most important, various components of PsyCap have been shown to be of particular significance even at the organizational level. An example would be collective efficacy or group potency, in which confidence results from the capacities and experiences of the group, rather than the individual (Maddux, 2009), which we earlier referred to as also representing "means efficacy."

As at the individual level, many of the prevalent occurrences and uncertainties in the current business landscape can be considered risk factors that both threaten and present unprecedented opportunities for market leadership and differentiation at the organizational level. Examples include globalization, cut-throat competition, increased consumer power, resource scarcity, litigation, ethical meltdown, shortages in qualified personnel and effective leaders, work-life balance issues, and challenges associated with strategic decisions such as downsizing, outsourcing, and various "right-sizing" initiatives. When handled correctly, such threats can be turned into opportunities for organizational growth and development. For example, Branzei and Abdelnour (2010) even found that enterprise activities in developing countries flourished under the extreme adversities of terrorism conditions (outbreak, escalation, and reduction), yielding higher economic payoffs at higher levels of terrorism, especially for informal enterprises.

Our original presentation of authentic leadership development (Avolio & Luthans, 2006; Luthans & Avolio, 2003) highlights the important role played by developmental trigger events or moments that leaders experience in their development of self-awareness, self-regulation, and ultimately authenticity and resilience. Some trigger events may be unplanned and difficult to predict, thus exposing leaders to risk factors that can best be dealt with through reactive adaptation and coping mechanisms. On the other hand, in our proposed authentic leadership development process, the organization can also proactively expose leaders to planned trigger events that can challenge them and set them on the path to an exciting journey of resilience development (Avolio & Luthans, 2006; Luthans & Avolio, 2003). For example, these can include asking them to rotate into a job for a quarter that they have no experience leading and/or taking on a project well beyond their skill levels. In this resilience development process, organizational and leader strengths are effectively employed, and growth and lifelong learning are monitored, managed, and experienced.

Organizational values are integral to the development of resilience, both at the individual and organizational levels. Coutu (2002, p. 52) articulates this relationship when she states that "strong values infuse an environment with meaning because they offer ways to interpret and shape events." In other words, when well-communicated and thoroughly adopted, organizational values provide direction in times of ambiguity and turbulence. These organizational values give the members stable ground to fall back on and guidelines for programmed and swift but effective ways to respond (Sutcliffe & Vogus, 2003; Weick, 1993). As organizations and their members gradually adapt, stable values allow them to regain balance, gather and organize their energies, and bounce back and even go beyond where they started. Moreover, in line with the importance of values and beliefs being larger than oneself in order to provide a source of meaning (e.g., see Seligman, 1998), strong and stable organizational values that are aligned with the personal goals and aspirations of the managers and employees are likely to enhance resilience at all levels because they also help individuals to make sense of difficult situations that have to be overcome. Such alignment can also be reinforced by the leadership of an organization, contributing further to organizational-level resilience.

As previously noted, organizational resilience requires effective ongoing adaptational processes, buffering mechanisms, and maintenance systems (Worline et al., 2002; Youssef & Luthans, 2005b). These systems continuously acquire, invest in, and accumulate a wealth of structural and procedural resources for the organization in times of ease and stability. They equip the organization for the proper selection, channeling, adaptation, and integration with resources to proactively forecast and effectively deal with adversities; that is, they contribute to organizational resilience. If properly nurtured, such resources can provide the residual capability to sustain the most challenging and stressful events.

Horne and Orr (1998) propose that processes such as strategic planning, organizational alignment, organizational learning, and corporate cultural awareness can significantly enhance organizational resilience. Specifically, strategic planning prepares the organization for difficult times through well-developed goals, objectives, and contingency plans. Alignment of organizational units with overall goals encourages unified action and effective sharing of resources and capabilities, reducing cross silo infighting, which allows the organization collectively to store "more energy." Organizational learning facilitates knowledge acquisition, creation, sharing, and utilization. Corporate cultural awareness allows for the accurate understanding and assessment of the organization's vision and core competencies, as well as areas of weakness and thus potential risk factors.

Worline and colleagues (2002) propose three buffering processes that can contribute to organizational resilience: strengthening, replenishing, and limbering. Strengthening refers to "the dynamic combination of structures and practices that make the unit more vigorous by increasing the unit's resources of various kinds" (Worline et al., 2002, p. 5). For example, quick and timely performance feedback provided when new members first begin working within their expected role can help them avoid wasted efforts, reinforce those behaviors that are most effective, and ultimately increase their confidence levels. On the other hand, at times when performance does decline, consistent and ongoing feedback can help identify and correct for the source of the problem. In this way the feedback is replenishing energy. This refers to "the dynamic combination of practices and structures that restore, regenerate, and renew the unit with resources of various kinds when they have been diminished or weakened in some way" (Worline et al., 2002, p. 5).

Since feedback is an effective way to share best practices, it helps broaden the experience and knowledge base of each member. In this way, shared knowledge expands the list of known strategies and options for the entire unit, which increases its ability to adapt on its own. In this context, feedback is what Worline and colleagues (2002, p. 5) call limbering, which "pertains to the dynamic combination of structures and practices that increase the unit's ability to direct or flex resources to the need at hand, enabling the unit to switch directions or morph resources to meet unexpected needs."

Still another approach to building organizational resilience supports the importance of employee "voice" (Burris, Detert, & Romney, 2013; Morrison, 2011; Van Dyne & LePine, 1998; Vickers & Kouzmin, 2001). This view argues that an organization should create mechanisms that enhance its ability to "hear" its members. By helping followers to "find their voice," leaders are likely connecting them to the larger meaning of what gets done in the organization. At the same time, such leaders are also building a greater sense of ownership in the organization, which likely would positively impact on organizational resilience. These mechanisms include proper, transparent communication channels, openness to nonconforming ideas, and encouragement of creativity, empowerment, and engagement. Other examples of resilience-enhancing organizational systems may include pay-for-performance, equitable and genuine recognition, goal setting, mentoring, teamwork, and other high performance work practices.

Related to helping employees find their voice is the work by Edmonson and colleagues on what they refer to as psychological safety (Edmondson, 1999). In this line of research, it has been shown that some organizational environments are interpreted as being much safer than others to voice one's opinion. This sense of psychological safety is seen as a climate and ultimately a cultural factor that can be influenced by leaders and team members, such that more positive leaders create a higher level of psychological safety among employees (Carmeli & Gittell, 2009).

Organizational resilience is an elaborate, complex, long-term process. Very few organizations, if any, can claim to have achieved their full potential in terms of their resilience. However, drawing from the limited research that describes the characteristics of a resilient organization, Horne and Orr (1998) propose that resilient organizations enjoy what they simply label the seven "C's": community, competence, connections, commitment, communication, coordination, and consideration.

Hamel and Välikangas (2003) describe a resilient organization as one that can effectively overcome four challenges. The first is "cognitive challenge," which refers to the culture of denial and arrogance that success can breed, along with assumptions of immunity and invincibility. The second is "strategic challenge," which refers to "satisficing" (rather than maximizing), and which needs to be substituted with openness to a broader array of strategic possibilities. The third is "political challenge," where risky but high-potential ideas may go untried if the distribution of organizational power and politics prevents the allocation of adequate resources and support to those ideas. The fourth is "ideological challenge," in which optimization and efficiency may substitute for more effective measures of organizational viability such as creativity, innovation, and renewal. As an organization overcomes these four challenges, it is likely to exhibit a greater level of resilience over time. Finally, in a more applied case study, training for resilience was shown to encompass three strategic practices: cultivating foresight, rehearsing nonroutine behaviors and building an experimentation-oriented community (Välikangas & Romme, 2012).

Potential Pitfalls of Resilience

Although resilience can equip today's organizations and their members with tremendous capacities, energies, and protective mechanisms, many organizations and their leaders may be reluctant to intentionally let their employees experience or take part in handling their own or the organization's adversities and setbacks. In the same way that many adults hesitate to accept that allowing a child to face threats or even difficulties is an acceptable, beneficial, and morally sound decision (Wolin & Wolin, 2005), traditional, paternalistic leaders feel responsible for and obliged to handle every problem of their employees. However, such a quick-fix approach to problem solving may not be the most effective in developing strength and endurance, nor will it help the followers to enrich their own repertoires of problem-solving techniques and independence from the leader. Moreover, leaders who carry an unfair burden of crisis management are likely to suffer from higher levels of stress and burnout. In addition to jeopardizing their own well-being, such leaders also hinder their organizations' and their followers' resilience development. Instead, they may be creating dependence, vulnerability, and lack of preparedness in their followers and their units as their stress cascades down throughout the organization.

Decisions made by organizations and their leaders for the perceived "good" of the people may actually result in significant long-term detrimental effects (Vickers & Kouzmin, 2001). When employees appear to have bounced back in the short run when leaders make decisions for them, the leaders mistakenly assume that their employees are resilient. The leaders think the employees' resilience has protected them from the adverse impact of the leaders' unilateral decisions. However, effective short-term coping should not be equated with long-term resilience. If employees are not provided with the proper channels to voice their own concerns, such apparent but unreal and short-lived "resilience" comes at the high cost of future disengagement, passiveness, disloyalty, and distrust of the leaders and the organization.

A case in point is an interview that we had with a leadership-perceived "resilient" employee in an organization that had undergone a significant change, with high repercussions on its employees. Four years ago, the organization automated one of its units, which resulted in a reduction in force (RIF) in this unit from over 500 employees to only five! The communication messages that accompanied the RIF process conveyed to the five survivors that they were retained because they were an "elite" group. They kept the best and the brightest. They were given pay raises, added benefits, and higher levels of responsibility and autonomy.

The five "elite survivors" apparently learned how to cope with the situation, as evidenced by their continued employment and success in the organization. However, very low morale of the elite five was evident not only because of the increased workload and expectations placed on them but also because each of them constantly recalled the lost friendships and needed work relationships, the hardships experienced by laid-off colleagues and their families, and the synergies, teamwork, and tacit knowledge that no longer existed in this unit. It seems that the passive coping attitudes and behaviors these survivors exhibited were incorrectly interpreted and rewarded as a high level of resilience. What is even worse is that such an inaccurate assumption of resilience had led these five to expose themselves to even higher levels of risk and dysfunctional outcomes by accepting to stay with an organization that they resented (actually hated) and in which they had zero trust or commitment.

Another potential pitfall concerns the role of values in enhancing resilience. The impact on resilience is primarily dependent on the stability of those values, rather than just their ethical soundness or their alignment with the organization's values. For example, survival-of-the-fittest mechanisms may have contributed to resilience in many tough situations such as in prisoner-of-war (POW) camps (Coutu, 2002), but when implemented in the workplace, their underlying value system may not prove to be morally acceptable. Thus, the personal beliefs and values that organizational leaders and employees may utilize in order to bounce back from adversities need to be scrutinized and continuously aligned in light of the organization's value system and standards of ethical conduct.

Still another potential pitfall that organizations can fall into is brought out by Rudolph and Repenning's (2002) model of disaster dynamics. The essence of this model is that, over time, some organizational assets can change into risk factors that can have a negative impact on organizational resilience. For example, many currently effective organizational systems are capable of only detecting and dealing with significant changes and discontinuities that are qualitatively different from the status quo. However, these systems may not be sensitive enough to gradually accumulate seemingly harmless events that may erode their viability. These seemingly small but frequent changes can cause the organization to reach a threshold that can lead to an unexpected "quantity-induced" disaster. In other words, an organization may have the appearance of resilience because it is functioning smoothly and has effective self-regulating mechanisms in place, but it may actually be on the verge of collapse, even in some instances failing miserably in its success.

One example of failing miserably in its success was the now defunct Digital Equipment Corporation (DEC). The CEO and founder of this company, Ken Olsen, built the organization's success on its ability to "out-engineer" its competitors. Yet, when the market shifted toward computers that were more of a commodity type, DEC kept plowing along building overengineered computers, which were eventually totally rejected by the market. This singular focus led to catastrophic results for this venerable company.

Hamel and Välikangas (2003) also support that "business-as-usual" and organizational resilience are not necessarily equivalent. In the relatively static business environment of the past, organizations used to "bury their mistakes" and/or create a momentum of entry barriers to maintain profitability. Real crises and discontinuities had to be very significant and hard to miss. They were then dealt with aggressively as one-time events. This is no longer true in the dynamic environment facing today's organizations. Dramatic, paradigmatic changes that are the rule rather than the exception require organizations to be very "nimble," constantly on the lookout for opportunities that warrant the proactive destruction of their own presently successful strategies and business models in anticipation of discontinuities and fast and dramatic strategic shifts. PsyCap resilience is no longer "nice to have" at the individual, leader, and organizational levels; it now has become required in the new "flat world" globalization in which we now live and compete.

Future Implications and Directions for PsyCap Resilience Research and Practice

It can be deduced from this chapter that the current status of the body of knowledge on resilience as it applies to the workplace can be best described as "promising but still emerging." On the one hand, there is a rich body of established research in developmental and clinical psychology that focuses on the negative end of the continuum, and more recent growth in positively oriented applications in psychology (Block & Kremen, 1996; Masten, 2001; Masten et al., 2009) and neuroscience (Davidson, 2012). There has also been increased attention given to work-related resilience research over the past decade as part of PsyCap and POS (e.g., Avey et al., 2011; Caza & Milton, 2012; Luthans, 2002; Luthans et al., 2004, 2005, 2006; 2007; Luthans & Youssef, 2004, 2007; Newman, Ucbasaran, Zhu, & Hirst, 2014; Youssef & Luthans, 2005a, 2005b, 2007, 2012; Youssef-Morgan, 2014; Youssef-Morgan & Luthans, 2013; also see the 2014 special issue [Vol. 21, no. 2] in the *Journal of Leadership and Organizational Studies* on PsyCap).

On the other hand, there is still much more to learn about resilience in today's uncertain workplace. Recent theory-building and empirical research offers a good point of departure, but with the exception of our PsyCap work and a few positive organizational scholarship (POS) scholars (e.g., Caza & Milton, 2012), there seems to be a premature decline in resilience theory development, in favor of empirical research and practical applications. The popular literature reflects an increasing interest from the practice community, which signals the importance and need for resilience in business practice. This is a potential area for scholarly research to make a real impact, particularly in furthering the development of the conceptual frameworks and underlying mechanisms for resilience that can stimulate and then lead to more rigorous empirical research and more effective practical applications. In this regard, we offer the following that would seem to be especially important research needs for the future:

• One of the most serious issues with the construct of resilience is that it tends to be defined in terms of its outcomes, which often leads to circular definitions, tautological arguments, and nonfalsifiable hypotheses. If resilient individuals, groups, organizations, or communities are those who bounce back and grow through adversities, then the only way to detect resilience is retrospectively, which largely precludes ex-ante scientific prediction and explanation. We raised a similar issue in the last chapter with Jim Collins's (2001) "good to great" companies that were selected based on their greatness at the time but several of which subsequently floundered or failed for various reasons. Inductive research is interesting and informative at the exploratory stages of new phenomena, but over time it unfortunately renders the study of the antecedents, mediators, and moderators of resilience speculative at best. Prospective resilience theory building is an area that is ripe for conceptual research. Refined definitions of resilience, and comprehensive models including its antecedents, mediators, moderators, and potential outcomes, particularly in the context of the workplace, can make a huge impact on the quality and rigor of our understanding, measurement, empirical examination, and practical application of resilience at the individual, team, organizational, community, and country levels.

- Similarly, defining resilience in terms of an external antecedent, namely adversity, precludes its prediction or assessment in the absence of adversity. Do individuals who lead relatively stable lives lack resilience? Must they be exposed to adversity to determine their resilience? Perhaps the stability of their lives can be in part attributed to their proactive preventative strategies that may actually characterize them as more, not less, resilient. Thus, in the same way that positive psychology focuses on studying health, well-being, and flourishing, further study and understanding of resilience in the absence of adversity is needed, and it can be beneficial for designing more preemptive strategies for boosting resilience in those who are less fortunate or at risk. Furthermore, what constitutes adversity, and the extent of its severity, might vary across individuals, populations, and situations. This necessitates a more in-depth study of the interactions between "objective" characteristics of adversities, and "subjective" evaluations of those adversities. Importantly, adversities may have nonadditive, cumulative, or sequence-related effects. This requires a better understanding of how the toll of multiple adverse events accumulates over time and across life domains to create unique, nonlinear, or discontinuous forms of resilient or nonresilient reactions (Fletcher & Sarkar, 2013; Seery, Holman, & Silver, 2010).

- Related to the definitions of resilience is the conceptual overlap between resilience and a number of related constructs such as hardiness (Eschleman, Bowling, & Alarcon, 2010), recovery (Sonnentag, Niessen, & Neff, 2012), posttraumatic growth (Calhoun & Tedeschi, 2006; Westphal and Bonanno, 2007), and thriving (Paterson, Luthans, & Jeung, 2014; Spreitzer, Sutcliffe, Dutton, Sonenshein, & Grant, 2005, also see Caza & Milton, 2012 for a comparison). These related constructs of adversity, adaptation, and growth characteristics of resilience are discussed at the beginning of the chapter. They may also share some of the antecedents, mediators, moderators, and outcomes of resilience. Additional research is needed to further delineate the conceptual and empirical convergence and divergence among these overlapping constructs relevant to resilience.

- Although our research supports a relationship between employee resilience and work-related outcomes (Avey et al., 2011; Youssef & Luthans, 2007), unlike PsyCap efficacy, hope, and optimism, which are proactive, resilience is more reactive in nature. Thus, it is difficult to evaluate resilience development because the resilience is not likely to be fully realized until a later point in the future, when the developing organizational participant eventually has to exhibit the capacity to bounce "back and beyond" as unplanned setbacks take place. Thus, it is imperative that a longitudinal approach be employed in order for resilience research to fully capture the resulting performance improvements from resilience development, as well as the sustainability of those enhanced outcomes. To date, two longitudinal studies of PsyCap, in which resilience is a component, did predict work outcomes over time and can serve as a model (Avey, Luthans, Smith, & Palmer, 2010; Peterson, Luthans, Avolio, Walumbwa, & Zhang, 2011). Longitudinal resilience research will not only facilitate the comprehension of the full extent of resilience outcomes but also the understanding of the processes, mechanisms, and strategies involved in the appraisal of risk factors and the employment and adaptation of various assets to mitigate risks and even capitalize upon them for further growth and development.

• Most of the research on resilience either focuses on the individual level (e.g., developmental psychology and PsyCap resilience) or on organizational resilience. However, there are limited attempts at building a multilevel theory of resilience that can help explain the mechanisms through which resilience at the individual level can influence its emergence and growth at higher levels of analysis (for an exception, see Lengnick-Hall, Beck, & Lengnick-Hall, 2011). Such "theory borrowing" (Whetten, Felin, & King, 2009) goes beyond extrapolating constructs and mechanisms from one level of analysis to the next. It examines the "conceptual isomorphism" (establishing that the operationalization and nomological network of the construct is similar across levels of analysis) and "functional isomorphism" (establishing that the higher level construct predicts the same outcomes as its lower level counterpart) of elevated constructs before generalizing them across levels of analysis. Beginning efforts to address this void in the literature are emerging (McKenny, Short, & Payne, 2013). We would particularly advocate investigating the group or team as a target for future research on resilience. We suspect that teams that have worked very successfully together over time might develop a unique "personality" that may better enable such groups to bounce back from difficulties and challenges. These group dynamics may be unique in comparison to those at the individual level or at higher collective levels, and deserve to be studied in their own right.

• Finally, as with the other PsyCap capacities, our initial studies have demonstrated that resilience (and overall PsyCap) can be developed in our short, highly focused micro-interventions (Luthans, Avey, Avolio, Norman, & Combs, 2006; Luthans, Avey, Avolio, & Peterson, 2010; Luthans, Avey, & Patera, 2008). Neurological research also supports the developmental potential of resilience through both short-term and long-term intervention strategies that may currently go beyond what can be offered within the context of the workplace (Davidson, 2012). Experimental studies across more varied settings, levels, populations, and cultures are needed for the future. For example, there has been an increase in interest and investment in understanding, measuring, and building resilience in military personnel and their families. Extensive programs and assessments are under way in this area (Sinclair & Britt, 2013). Such efforts can inform and be informed by interdisciplinary resilience research.

Case Study: Victims of Decades of Kidnapping Show Remarkable Resilience

Video link: http://www.youtube.com/watch?v=ci_22Oqhwtc (or search "Let's get one thing straight! My name is Jaycee Lee Dugard")

Jaycee Lee Dugard was kidnapped at age 11 by Phillip Craig Garrido, a registered sex offender, and his wife Nancy, while walking from her South Lake Tahoe, California, home to a school bus stop. She was kept in a concealed area in the Garridos' backyard, regularly abused sexually and emotionally for more than 18 years, and repeatedly missed by law enforcement officers who visited the home many times as part of Garrido's parole arrangement, until she and her two daughters, born in captivity, were found. Despite the horrific adversities she faced, described in this video and in Dugard's book *A Stolen Life*, this young woman became an icon of resilience and showed remarkable ability to bounce back from a long and terrifying chapter of her life.

Questions for reflection and/or discussion:

1. How did Jaycee show resilience during her years of captivity and after her release? What were her unique approach, resources, and coping mechanisms?

2. Although Jaycee went through an exceptionally horrendous situation, are there some ways that you can identify with her adversities? Have you encountered some particularly difficult life events? What did you do to overcome them? What were some of the resources, opportunities, and challenges that helped or hindered your resilience?

Case Study: Powerball Winner Wants His Old Life Back

Video link: http://usnews.nbcnews.com/_news/2013/09/25/20663854-the-d rama-is-nonstop-powerball-winner-wild-willie-wants-his-old-life-back?l ite&43001 (or search for "Powerball Winner "Wild" Willie wants his old life back—NBC News")

In this video, "Wild" Willie Seeley of Manahawkin, New Jersey, offers insights on how his recent winning of the $450 million Powerball jackpot had changed his life, mostly for the worse! Although most people consider this event to be extremely positive, apparently Willie and his wife, Donna, have a hard time recovering and bouncing back from such a positive, but overwhelming, event.

Questions for reflection and/or discussion:
1. It is common to discuss resilience in the context of adversities and setbacks. Why is resilience necessary in positive situations?
2. In what ways are Willie and Donna showing signs of low resilience?
3. What are some effective ways for bouncing back from extremely positive events? How helpful can these approaches be for Willie and Donna?
4. Reflecting back, what were some positive events in your life or at your work that required resilience, and how did you handle them?
5. Looking forward, how can you handle similar events more resiliently in the future?

References

Avey, J. B., Luthans, F., Smith, R. M., & Palmer, N. F. (2010). Impact of positive psychological capital on employee well-being over time. *Journal of Occupational Health Psychology, 15*, 17–28.

Avey, J. B., Reichard, R. J., Luthans, F., & Mhatre, K. H. (2011). Meta-analysis of the impact of positive psychological capital on employee attitudes, behaviors, and performance. *Human Resource Development Quarterly, 22*, 127–152.

Avolio, B. J., & Luthans, F. (2006). *The high impact leader.* New York, NY: McGraw-Hill.

Bagshaw, M. (1997). Employability: Creating a contract of mutual investment. *Industrial and Commercial Training, 29*(6), 187–189.

Baron, L., Eisman, H., Scuello, M., Veyzer, A., & Lieberman, M. (1996). Stress resilience, locus of control, and religion in children of Holocaust victims. *Journal of Psychology, 130*, 513–525.

Bass, B. M., & Avolio, B. J. (1994). *Improving organizational effectiveness through transformational leadership.* Thousand Oaks, CA: Sage.

Bergin, A. (1983). Religiosity and mental health: A critical re-evaluation and meta-analysis. *Professional Psychology Research and Practice, 14,* 170–184.

Block, J., & Kremen, A. M. (1996). IQ and ego-resiliency: Conceptual and empirical connections and separateness. *Journal of Personality and Social Psychology, 70,* 349–361.

Bonanno, G. A. (2004). Loss, trauma and human resilience. *American Psychologist, 59,* 20–28.

Branzei, O., & Abdelnour, S. (2010). Another day, another dollar: Enterprise resilience under terrorism in developing countries. *Journal of International Business Studies, 41,* 804–825.

Brunwasser, S. M., Gillham, J. E., & Kim, E. S. (2009). A meta-analytic review of the Penn Resiliency Program's effect on depressive symptoms. *Journal of Consulting and Clinical Psychology, 77,* 1042–1054.

Burnham, J. J. (2009). Contemporary fears of children and adolescents: Coping and resiliency in the 21st century. *Journal of Counseling and Development, 87,* 28–35.

Burns, J. M. (1978). *Leadership.* New York, NY: Free Press

Burris, E. R., Detert, J. R., & Romney, A. C. (2013). Speaking up vs. being heard: The disagreement around and outcomes of employee voice. *Organizational Science, 24,* 24–38.

Calhoun, L. G., & Tedeschi, R. G. (Eds.). (2006). *Handbook of posttraumatic growth: Research and practice.* Mahwah, NJ: Erlbaum.

Carmeli, A., & Gittell, J. H. (2009). High-quality relationships, psychological safety, and learning from failures in work organizations. *Journal of Organizational Behavior, 30*(6), 709–729.

Cascio, W. F., & Luthans, F. (2014). Reflections on the metamorphosis at Robben Island: The role of institutional work and positive psychological capital. *Journal of Management Inquiry, 23,* 51–67.

Caza, B. B., & Milton, L. P. (2012). Resilience at work. In K. S. Cameron & G. M. Spreitzer (Eds.), *Oxford handbook of positive organizational scholarship* (pp. 895–908). New York, NY: Oxford University Press.

Collins, J. (2001). *Good to great.* New York, NY: HarperCollins.

Collins, M. E. (2001). Transition to adulthood for vulnerable youths: A review of research and implications for policy. *Social Service Review, 75,* 271–291.

Conner, D. (1993). *Managing at the speed of change: How resilient managers succeed and prosper where others fail.* New York, NY: Villard Books.

Conner, D. (2003, May 12). Training & development—Solutions at Sun Microsystems. Retrieved from http://www.odrinc.com.

Coutu, D. L. (2002). How resilience works. *Harvard Business Review, 80*(5), 46–55.

Cowan, P. A., Cowan, C. P., & Schulz, M. S. (1996). Thinking about risk and resilience in families. In E. M. Hetherington & E. A. Blechman (Eds.), *Stress, coping, and resiliency in children and families* (pp. 1–38). Mahwah, NJ: Erlbaum.

Davidson, R. (2012). *The emotional life of your brain.* New York, NY: Hudson/ Penguin.

Dixon, A. L., & Schertzer, S. M. B. (2005). Bouncing back: How salesperson optimism and self-effcacy influenceattributions and behaviors following failure. *Journal of Personal Selling and Sales Management, 25,* 361–369.

Edmondson, A. (1999). Psychological safety and learning behavior in work teams. *Administrative Science Quarterly, 44,* 350–383.

Egeland, B., Carlson, E., & Sroufe, L. A. (1993). Resilience as a process. *Development and Psychopathology, 5,* 517–528.

Eschleman, K. J., Bowling, N. A., & Alarcon, G. M. (2010). A meta-analytic examination of hardiness. *International Journal of Stress Management, 17,* 277–307.

Fletcher, D., & Sarkar, M. (2013). Psychological resilience: A review and critique of definitions, concepts, and theory. *European Psychologist, 18,* 12–23.

Fu, F. Q., Richards, K. A., Hughes, D. E., & Jones, E. (2010). Motivating sales people to sell new products: The relative influence of attitudes, subjective norms, and self-efficacy. *Journal of Marketing, 74,* 61–76.

Gibbs, M. (1989). Factors in the victim that mediate between disaster and psychotherapy: A review. *Journal of Traumatic Stress, 2*(4), 489–514.

Gorman, C. (2005). The importance of resilience. *Time, 165*(3), A52–A55.

Greenhouse, S. (2001, September 1). Report shows Americans have more labor days. *The New York Times,* p. A6.

Hamel, G., & Välikangas (2003). The quest for resilience. *Harvard Business Review, 81*(9), 52–63.

Harland, L., Harrison, W., Jones, J., & Reiter-Palmon, R. (2005). Leadership behaviors and subordinate resilience. *Journal of Leadership and Organizational Studies, 11,* 2–14.

Hoffer Gittell, J. (2008). Relationships and resilience. *Journal of Applied Behavioral Science, 44,* 25–47.

Holaday, M., & McPhearson, R. (1997). Resilience and severe burns. *Journal of Counseling and Development, 75,* 346–356.

Horne, J., III, & Orr, J. (1998). Assessing behaviors that create resilient organizations. *Employment Relations Today, 24*(4), 29–39.

Huey, S. J., Jr., & Weisz, J. R. (1997). Ego control, ego resiliency, and the five-factor model as predictors of behavioral and emotional problems in clinic-referred children and adolescents. *Journal of Abnormal Psychology, 106,* 404–415.

Hunter, A. J., & Chandler, G. E. (1999). Adolescent resilience. *Image: Journal of Nursing Scholarship, 31,* 243–247.

Johnson, K., Bryant, D., Collins, D., Noe, T., Strader, T., & Berbaum, M. (1998). Preventing and reducing alcohol and other drug use among high-risk youths by increasing family resilience. *Social Work, 43*, 297–308.

Kakabadse, N., & Kakabadse A. (2000). Critical review—outsourcing: A paradigm shift. *Journal of Management Development, 19*, 670–728.

Kirby, L., & Fraser, M. (1997). Risk and resilience in childhood. In M. Fraser (Ed.), *Risk and resilience in childhood* (pp. 10–33). Washington, DC: NASW Press.

Klarreich, S. (1998). Resiliency: The skills needed to move forward in a changing environment. In S. Klarreich (Ed.), *Handbook of organizational health psychology: Programs to make the workplace healthier* (pp. 219–238). Madison, CT: Psychosocial Press.

Kobsa, S. C. (1982). The hardy personality. In G. S. Sauders & J. Suls (Eds.), *Social psychology of health and illness* (pp. 3–32). Hillsdale, NJ: Erlbaum.

Koretz, G. (2001, June 11). Why Americans work so hard. *Business Week*, p. 34.

LaMarch, J. (1997). The resilient worker: Employees who can cope with change. *Hospital Material Management Quarterly, 19*(2), 54–58.

Larson, D., Pattison, E., Blazer, D., Omran, A., & Kaplan, B. (1986). Systematic analysis of research on religious variables in four major psychiatric journals, 1978–1982. *American Journal of Psychiatry, 143*, 329–334.

Lee, J. E. C., Sudom, K. A., & Zamorski, M. A. (2013). Longitudinal analysis of psychological resilience and mental health in Canadian military personnel returning from overseas deployment. *Journal of Occupational Health Psychology, 18*, 327–337.

Lengnick-Hall, C. A., Beck, T. E., & Lengnick-Hall, M. L. (2011). Developing a capacity for organizational resilience through strategic human resource management. *Human Resource Management Review, 21*, 243–255.

Luthans, F. (2002). The need for and meaning of positive organizational behavior. *Journal of Organizational Behavior, 23*, 695–706

Luthans, F., Avey, J. B., Avolio, B. J., Norman, S. M., & Combs, G. J. (2006). Psychological capital development: Toward a micro-intervention. *Journal of Organizational Behavior, 27*, 387–393.

Luthans, F., Avey, J. B., Avolio, B. J., & Peterson, S. (2010). The development and resulting performance impact of positive psychological capital. *Human Resource Development Quarterly, 21*, 41–66.

Luthans, F., Avey, J. B., & Patera, J. L. (2008). Experimental analysis of a web-based training intervention to develop positive psychological capital. *Academy of Management Learning and Education, 7*, 209–221.

Luthans, F., & Avolio, B. (2003). Authentic leadership: A positive development approach. In K. S. Cameron, J. E. Dutton, & R. E. Quinn (Eds.), *Positive organizational scholarship* (pp. 241–258). San Francisco, CA: Berrett-Koehler.

Luthans, F., Avolio, B. J., Avey, J. B., & Norman, S. M. (2007). Positive psychological capital: Measurement and relationship with performance and satisfaction. *Personnel Psychology, 60*, 541–572.

Luthans, F., Luthans, K., & Luthans, B. (2004). Positive psychological capital: Going beyond human and social capital. *Business Horizons*, *47*(1), 45–50.

Luthans, F., Vogelgesang, G. R., & Lester, P. B. (2006). Developing the psychological capital of resiliency. *Human Resource Development Review*, *5*(1), 25–44.

Luthans, F., & Youssef, C. M. (2004). Human, social and now positive psychological capital management: Investing in people for competitive advantage. *Organizational Dynamics*, *33*, 143–160.

Luthans, F., & Youssef, C. M. (2007). Emerging positive organizational behavior. *Journal of Management*, *33*, 321–349.

Maddux, J. E. (2009). Self-efficacy: The power of believing you can. In S. Lopez & C. R. Snyder (Eds.), *Oxford Handbook of positive psychology* (2nd ed., pp. 335–343). New York, NY: Oxford University Press.

Masten, A. S. (2001). Ordinary magic: Resilience process in development. *American Psychologist*, *56*, 227–239.

Masten, A. S., Cutuli, J. J., Herbers, J. E, & Reed, M. G. J. (2009). Resilience in development. In S. J. Lopez & C. R. Snyder (Eds.), *Oxford handbook of positive psychology* (2nd ed., pp. 117–131). New York, NY: Oxford University Press.

McKenny, A. F., Short, J. C., & Payne, T. (2013). Using computer-aided text analysis to elevate constructs: An illustration using psychological capital. *Organizational Research Methods*, *16*, 152–184.

Miller, F. G., Colloca, L., Crouch, R. A., & Kaptchuk, T. J. (Eds.). (2013). *The placebo: A reader*. Baltimore, MD: John Hopkins Press.

Morrison, E. W. (2011). Employee voice behavior: Integration and directions for future research. *Academy of Management Annals*, *5*, 373–412.

Ness, R., & Wintrob, R. (1980). The emotional impact of fundamentalist religious participation. *American Journal of Orthopsychiatry*, *50*, 302–315.

Newman, A., Ucbasaran, D., Zhu, F., & Hirst, G. (2014). Psychological capital: A review and synthesis. *Journal of Organizational Behavior*, *35*, 120–138.

Nguyen, T. D., & Nguyen, T. T. M. (2012). Psychological capital, quality of work life, and quality of life of marketers: Evidence from Viet Nam. *Journal of Macromarketing*, *32*, 87–95.

Paterson, T. A., Luthans, F., & Jeung, W. (2014). Thriving at work: Impact of psychological capital and supervisor support. *Journal of Organizational Behavior*, *35*, 434–446.

Patnaik, R., & Sahoo, P. K. (2010). CEO's legacy to the board: Honesty, resilience or trust? The case of Xerox. *IUP Journal of Corporate Governance*, *9*(1/2), 15–26.

Paul, P. (2005). The power to uplift. *Time*, *165*(3), 46–48.

Peterson, S. J., Luthans, F., Avolio, B. J., Walumbwa, F. O., & Zhang, Z. (2011). Psychological capital and employee performance: A latent growth modeling approach. *Personnel Psychology*, *64*, 427–450.

Powley, E. H., & Powley, W. (2012). Building strength and resilience: How HR leaders enable healing in organizations. *People and Strategy*, *35*(4), 42–47.

Qouta, S., El-Sarraj, A., & Punamaki, R. (2001). Mental flexibility as resiliency factor among children exposed to political violence. *International Journal of Psychology*, *36*(1), 1–7.

Reichard, R. J., & Avolio, B. J. (2005). Where are we? The status of leadership intervention research: A meta-analytic summary. In W. Gardner, B. Avolio, & F. Walumbwa (Eds.), *Authentic leadership theory and practice: Origins, effects and development. Monographs in leadership and management.* (Vol. 3, pp. 203–223). Oxford, UK: Elsevier.

Reivich, K., & Shatte, A. (2002). *The resilience factor: 7 essential skills for overcoming life's inevitable obstacles.* New York, NY: Random House.

Richardson, G. (2002). The metatheory of resilience and resiliency. *Journal of Clinical Psychology, 58*, 307–321.

Robinson, S. L., Kraatz, M. S., & Rousseau, D. M. (1994). Changing obligations and the psychological contract: A longitudinal study. *Academy of Management Journal, 37*, 137–152.

Rudolph, J. W., & Repenning, N. P. (2002). Disaster dynamics: Understanding the role of quantity in organizational collapse. *Administrative Science Quarterly, 47*, 1–30.

Ryff, C., & Singer, B. (2003). Flourishing under fire: Resilience as a prototype of challenged thriving. In C. Keyes & J. Haidt (Eds.), *Flourishing: Positive psychology and the life well-lived* (pp. 15–36). Washington, DC: American Psychological Association.

Sandau-Beckler, P., Devall, E., & de la Rosa, I. (2002). Strengthening family resilience: Prevention and treatment for high-risk substance-affected families. *Journal of Individual Psychology, 58*, 305–327.

Sanders, J. M., & Nee, V. (1996). Immigrant self-employment: The family as social capital and the value of human capital. *American Sociological Review, 61*, 321–349.

Schaubroeck, J. M., Riolli, L. T., Peng, A. C., & Spain, E. S. (2011). Resilience to traumatic exposure among soldiers deployed in combat. *Journal of Occupational Health Psychology, 16*, 18–37.

Seery, M. D., Holman, E., & Silver, R. (2010). Whatever does not kill us: Cumulative lifetime adversity, vulnerability, and resilience. *Journal of Personality and Social Psychology, 99*, 1025–1041.

Seligman, M. (1998). *Learned optimism.* New York, NY: Pocket Books.

Sinclair, R. R., & Britt, T. W. (2013). *Building psychological resilience in military personnel.* Washington, DC: APA.

Smith, C., & Carlson, B. (1997). Stress, coping, and resilience in children and youth. *Social Service Review, 71*, 231–256.

Sonnentag, S., Niessen, C., & Neff, A. (2012). Recovery. In K. S. Cameron & G. M. Spreitzer (Eds.), *Oxford handbook of positive organizational scholarship* (pp. 867–881). New York, NY: Oxford University Press.

Spreitzer, G. M., Sutcliffe, K., Dutton, J. E., Sonenshein, S., & Grant, A. M. (2005). A socially embedded model of thriving at work. *Organization Science, 16*, 537–550.

Stewart, M., Reid, G., & Mangham, C. (1997). Fostering children's resilience. *Journal of Pediatric Nursing, 12*, 21–31.

Sutcliffe, K. M., & Vogus, T. (2003). Organizing for resilience. In K. S. Cameron, J. E. Dutton, & R. E. Quinn (Eds.), *Positive organizational scholarship* (pp. 94–110). San Francisco, CA: Berrett-Koehler.

Tebbi, C., Mallon, J., Richards, M., & Bigler, L. (1987). Religiousity and locus of control of adolescent and cancer patients. *Psychological Reports, 61*, 683–696.

Tedeschi, R., Park, C., & Calhoun, L. (Eds.). (1998). *Posttraumatic growth: Positive changes in the aftermath of crisis.* Mahwah, NJ: Erlbaum.

Teixeira, C. (2001). Community resources and opportunities in ethnic economies: A case study of Portuguese and black entrepreneurs in Toronto. *Urban Studies, 38*, 2055–2078.

Teixeira, E., & Werther, W. B. (2013). Resilience: Continuous renewal of competitive advantages. *Business Horizons, 56*, 333–342.

Välikangas, L., & Romme, A. L. (2012). Building resilience capabilities at "Big Brown Box, Inc." *Strategy and Leadership, 40*, 43–45.

Vaillant, G. E. (1977). *Adaptation to life.* Boston, MA: Little, Brown.

Vaillant, G. E. (2000). The mature defenses. *American Psychologist, 55*, 89–98.

Van Dyne, L., & LePine, J. A. (1998). Helping and voice extra-role behaviors: Evidence of construct and predictive validity. *Academy of Management Journal, 41*, 108–119.

Vickers, M. H., & Kouzmin, A. (2001). Resilience in organizational actors and rearticulating voice. *Public Management Review, 3*(1), 95–119.

Waite, P., & Richardson, G. (2004). Determining the efficacy of resiliency training in the work site. *Journal of Allied Health, 33*, 178–183.

Waterman, R. H., Waterman, J. A., & Collard, B. A. (1994). Toward a career-resilient workforce. *Harvard Business Review, 72*(4), 87–95.

Weick, K. E. (1993). The collapse of sensemaking in organizations: The Mann Gulch disaster. *Administrative Science Quarterly, 38*, 628–652.

Westphal, M., & Bonanno, G. A. (2007). Posttraumatic growth and resilience to trauma: Different sides of the same coin or different coins? *Applied Psychology: An International Review, 56*, 417–427.

Whetten, D., Felin, T., & King, B. (2009). The practice of theory borrowing in organizational studies: Current issues and future directions. *Journal of Management, 35*, 537–563.

Wolin, S., & Wolin, S. (2005). *Project resilience.* Retrieved October 2014, from http://www.projectresilience.com.

Wong, J., & Mason, G. (2001). Reviled, rejected, but resilient: Homeless people in recovery and life skills education. *Georgetown Journal on Poverty Law and Policy, 8*, 475–503.

Worline, M. C., Dutton, J. E., Frost, P. J., Kanov, J., Lilius, J. M., & Maitlis, S. (August, 2002). *Creating fertile soil: The organizing dynamics of resilience.* Paper presented at the annual meeting of the Academy of Management, Denver, CO.

Youssef, C. M., & Luthans, F. (2005a). A positive organizational behavior approach to ethical performance. In R. A. Giacalone, C. Dunn, & C. Jurkiewicz (Eds.), *Positive psychology in business ethics and corporate social responsibility* (pp. 1–22). Greenwich, CT: Information Age.

Youssef, C. M., & Luthans, F. (2005b). Resiliency development of organizations, leaders and employees: Multi-level theory building for sustained performance. In W. Gardner, B. Avolio, & F. Walumbwa (Eds.), *Authentic leadership theory and practice: Origins, effects and development. Monographs in leadership and management.* (Vol. 3, pp. 303–343). Oxford, UK: Elsevier.

Youssef, C. M., & Luthans, F. (2007). Positive organizational behavior in the workplace: The impact of hope, optimism, and resilience. *Journal of Management, 33,* 774–800.

Youssef, C. M., & Luthans, F. (2012). Positive global leadership. *Journal of World Business, 47,* 539–547.

Youssef-Morgan, C. M. (2014). Advancing OB research: An illustration using psychological capital. *Journal of Leadership and Organizational Studies, 21*(2), 130–140.

Youssef-Morgan, C. M., & Luthans, F. (2013). Thinking positive: Leadership across cultures. *Organizational Dynamics, 42,* 198–208.

Zunz, S. (1998). Resiliency and burnout: Protective factors for human service managers. *Administration in Social Work, 22*(3), 39–54.

7

POTENTIAL PSYCAP

CREATIVITY, FLOW, MINDFULNESS, GRATITUDE, AND FORGIVENESS

Opening Video: Mihalyi Csikszentmihalyi on Creativity and Flow

Video link: http://www.youtube.com/watch?v=W9jaOsxjS1E

Video link: http://www.youtube.com/watch?v=HwngIuplE5g

For additional videos you can search using the term 'flow'.

Mihalyi (Mike) Csikszentmihalyi is a professor at Claremont Graduate University. Martin Seligman, generally recognized as the founding father of positive psychology, described Csikszentmihalyi as one of the world's leading researchers on positive psychology and many consider him to be a co-founder of the field. Csikszentmihalyi is most known for his research and writing on creativity and flow.

Questions for reflection and/or discussion:

1. What is creativity? What is innovation? In what ways are they similar *or* different?
2. What causes some people to experience flow, but not others?
3. In what areas of your life do you experience flow most frequently? Explain.
4. What can your organization or your leader do to help you experience flow more often in your job? How about your peers?
5. If you are in a leadership position, what can you do to help your employees experience more flow? What conditions can you create to foster flow?

Opening Video: Ellen Langer: Mindfulness Over Matter

Video link: https://www.youtube.com/watch?v=4XQUJR4uIGM

Harvard psychology professor Ellen Langer is a pioneer of an evidence-based approach to the value of mindfulness. She moves very fast through the concepts and studies of mindfulness and "mindlessness" and cleverly provides many relevant examples to demonstrate the points she is making.

Questions for reflection and/or discussion:

1. Of the many examples Professor Langer provides on mindfulness, which one was most surprising to you? Which research result was most surprising?
2. Drawing from what you learned from Professor Langer's talk, what is the difference between mindfulness and mindlessness?
3. How would you relate mindfulness to the other positive psychological resources covered in this chapter?
4. How would you relate mindfulness to more effective leadership and human resource management?

The positive psychological resources of efficacy, hope, optimism, and resilience, covered in detail in the previous four chapters, have been determined to best meet our PsyCap inclusion criteria laid out in Chapter 2. However, as we indicated, these four were not meant to represent an exhaustive list. The rich emerging body of knowledge on positive psychology (Lopez & Snyder, 2009; also see http://www.positivepsychology.org for a continually updated Web site on this growing literature and related programs and initiatives) and positive organizational scholarship (e.g., Cameron & Spreitzer, 2012; also see http://www.bus.umich.edu/Positive/ for updates) presents a wide range of positively oriented, unique individual, group, and organizational resources, strengths, and virtues. Many of these positive constructs appear highly promising in terms of both their theoretical foundations and potential applicability to the workplace. Some have also been shown to be measurable and developmental—meaning as states we can change them for the better!

In this chapter and the next, we selectively introduce some of these other positive constructs that we propose may have particular relevance and potential for inclusion in PsyCap now and in the future. We provide a concise assessment of each of these positive resources in terms of its "fit" with PsyCap that can help guide future research and practice. Tables in this and the next chapter provide a very brief PsyCap criteria checklist summary of the positive resources covered. Specifically, in this chapter we explore and assess creativity, flow, mindfulness, gratitude, and forgiveness, and in the next chapter emotional intelligence, spirituality, authenticity, and courage are covered. Efficacy, hope, optimism, and resilience are also included in Table 7.1 for benchmark comparison in meeting the PsyCap inclusion criteria of being theory based, measurable, state-like or developmental, and linked to performance and other work-related outcomes. In addition, we also assess each construct conceptually for its fit with PsyCap's two underlying theoretical mechanisms that we use to link and represent the commonality between efficacy, hope, optimism, and resilience. As discussed in Chapter 2, these mechanisms are as follows: (1) an internalized sense of agency, control, and intentionality (Youssef-Morgan & Luthans, 2013) and (2) "positive appraisal of circumstances and probability for success based on motivated effort and perseverance" (Luthans, Avolio, Avey, & Norman, 2007, p. 550). These two specific theoretical criteria provide both support and/or potential boundaries of these potential positive constructs for inclusion in PsyCap.

Our theory-building, research, measurement, and application of PsyCap to human resources and leadership development and performance management so far has mainly focused on the positive states of hope, efficacy, resilience, and optimism (or the HERO within). We feel that this chapter and the next are necessary for keeping PsyCap dynamically evolving, that is, an open system. We recognize that as in the economics domain, there are likely to be additions to psychological capital just as there have been with economic and financial indicators. Today, one cannot consider a country's economic status without considering global economic indicators that didn't exist a number of years ago. Consequently, these chapters are simply meant to recognize the virtually unlimited potential power and impact that positive psychological capital can play in investing and leading today's, and especially the future, workforce. Just as economics and finance are continually searching for new and innovative ways to invest and develop their capital, we feel the same about psychological capital. We hope these chapters not only send a message that PsyCap is dynamic and evolving but also provide a rough map for the continuing journey of PsyCap development. As shown in our brief checklist tables, our proposed psychological resources do not yet precisely meet every one of our established PsyCap criteria, but as the analyses indicate, several of them are already worthy of strong consideration and can serve as a future research agenda and subsequent application.

Similar to the more general positive psychology journey, our aspiration for the future of PsyCap is to have a type of paradigm shift in emphasizing optimal positive human functioning and flourishing in the workplace. In the spirit of this aspirational goal for PsyCap, we seek a multifaceted recognition, understanding

Table 7.1 Assessment of "Fit" With PsyCap for Various High-Potential Positive Constructs

Positive Construct	Theory-Based?	State-Like/ Malleable?	Measurable?	Related to Work Performance?	Related to Other Work Outcomes?	Agentic	Positive Appraisals
Efficacy	✓	✓	✓	✓	✓	✓	✓
Hope	✓	✓	✓	✓	✓	✓	✓
Optimism	✓	✓	✓	✓	✓	✓	✓
Resilience	✓	✓	✓	✓	✓	✓	✓
Creativity	✓	?	✓	?	?	✗	✗
Flow	✓	✓	✓	✓	✓	✓	✓
Mindfulness	✓	✓	✓	?	✓	?	✗
Gratitude	✓	✓	?	?	✓	✓	✓
Forgiveness	✓	✓	✓	?	✓	✓	✓

and appreciation (i.e., as we indicated in Chapter 1, a deeper inquiry) of what constitutes life-span positivity and excellence (see Avolio & Luthans, 2006). We are not as interested in a simple, myopic advocacy perspective of individual positive constructs. Our inquiry into a wide-ranging vista of positive psychological functioning in organizations must consider a higher plane, a metalevel if you wish. Our long-range vision for PsyCap is that it can provide meaning and purpose to more pragmatic patterns coming out of the mainstream organizational behavior literature. These will likely include such constructs as "collective PsyCap" in teams, a "cultural PsyCap" variable, and even "virtual PsyCap," given the way we all interact today and into the future. We now make a systematic inquiry into the best candidates for contributing to this PsyCap vision.

Creativity as Potential PsyCap

Although there are numerous definitions, Simonton (2009) simply defines creativity as the generation of ideas that are (a) original and (b) adaptive. Creativity is often conceptualized and measured along the dimensions of the creative person, the creative process, and the creative product or outcome (Peterson & Seligman, 2004; Simonton, 2009). Although creativity is frequently associated with strikingly revolutionary ideas, it also incorporates the capacity to find novel approaches for day-to-day problem solving, as well as to constructively adapt new ideas and mechanisms so that they positively contribute to how one views others and also oneself in that both can foster greater or lesser creativity (Simonton, 2004).

Traditionally, creativity has been viewed as a dispositional trait that can only be developed at an early age, or even a genetically determined individual difference (Cassandro & Simonton, 2003; Feist, 1998). Thus, the strongest emphasis on its development has been in children (Nickerson, 1999). However, the positive psychology movement has refueled a nature-nurture debate, with genetic and environmental/developmental factors exhibiting complex multiplicative and synergistic interactions in the conceptualization of creativity (Plomin & Daniels, 1987; Simonton, 2009). This debate as we have seen in other fields of psychology and organizational behavior shows that human beings are far more "elastic" than originally thought of by researchers and practitioners. Noted psychologists like Paul Baltes (see Baltes, 2006) have shown that at later points in the life span, depending on how people are nurtured, they may experience even greater creativity and wisdom than at earlier points. Since people spend a lot of time at work during their lifetime, a creative nurturing organizational environment versus one that encourages people to leave their creative brains at the door, may foster in employees greater creativity at all points across the healthy life span.

Particularly relevant for facilitating creativity in the workplace is the impact of intrinsic and extrinsic motivators. Intrinsic factors that have been found to spark creativity in the workplace, or what Zhou and Ren (2012) refer to as the "task context," include job complexity, feedback, goals, creativity expectations, autonomy and discretion, time, and stress. Extrinsic factors stimulating creativity, or what Zhou and Ren (2012) refer to as the "social context," include leadership and supervision, coworker influences, social networks, cultural influences, adequate resources, rewards, and incentives. To stimulate creativity, Amabile and Fisher (2009) suggest organizations and leaders should selectively and synergistically utilize intrinsic and extrinsic motivators to stimulate, affirm, and reward creative behavior.

There are many measures of creativity, with emphases given to the various dimensions of creativity: the creative person, the creative process, and the creative product or outcome (Peterson & Seligman, 2004; Simonton, 2009). For example, the classic Torrance Test of Creative Thinking (TTCT) (Torrance, 1988) is perhaps the most supported instrument available in terms of reliability, validity, and generalizability across contexts and cultures. The TTCT is a process-oriented measure that assesses four creative abilities. These four are considered to be necessary ingredients for the divergent thinking process associated with creativity: fluency, flexibility, originality, and elaboration. On the other hand, where the creative person, rather than the creative process, is the referent for analysis, various personality inventories and projective tests are recommended, including ones that measure the Big Five personality factor called openness to new experiences (Costa & McCrae, 1992; Digman, 1990; Kerr & Gagliardi, 2003). Finally, if the creative product or outcome is the point of emphasis, then various product-specific performance measures and/or outcomes such as meeting customer expectations or customer engagement and loyalty are typically employed.

Does Creativity Meet the PsyCap Criteria?

Based on the creativity literature to date, creativity meets the criteria of being theory based and measurable. However, the criterion of being state-like (open to development) still is a challenge for creativity to become fully part of what we have defined as PsyCap. Research continues to focus on "who" is creative in terms of the intelligence, personality traits, and other relatively stable predictors of creativity (Feist, 1998; Kim, 2008). Although there is a lot of interest in positive psychology in the facilitating task and social mechanisms that can facilitate creativity (Zhou & Ren, 2012) and even the impact of PsyCap (Rego, Sousa, Marques, & Pina e Cunha, 2012; Sweetman, Luthans, Avey, & Luthans, 2011), these positivity mechanisms can be viewed more as moderators and/or mediators rather than as developmental processes (e.g., see Gupta & Singh, 2014).

Well-designed jobs, supportive supervisors and coworkers, a learning goal orientation, and rewards may stimulate creativity in those who are already predisposed toward creativity. For example, a recent study found that in a large Chinese R&D unit, a sample of engineers with varying learning goal orientations seemed to draw from their PsyCap in achieving creativity (Huang & Luthans, 2014). The role of this positive mediator was explained in terms of facilitating confidence in these engineers, allowing them to better endure and cope with setbacks and difficulties, and the positivity overall just made conditions more favorable for fostering their creativity. However, the question that remains unanswered is whether such facilitating positive mechanisms can be used to develop creativity in those who are not endowed with creative talent to begin with.

Since creativity has not yet been fully explored or supported as a state-like resource that is open to development, it follows that it cannot be readily triggered through agentic, intentional thoughts or actions. In other words, if creativity is a trait, then being more or less creative is not open to the conscious choices of the individual. It depends on the individual's dispositions, as well as the contextual factors that facilitate creativity, as discussed in this chapter's opening video. It also follows that creativity does not depend on the individual's appraisals of circumstances and success probabilities (Luthans et al., 2007), which are rarely known at the time that creative ideas and behaviors are elicited. As far as the current literature stands, creativity is still viewed as being a spontaneous outcome of optimal combinations of traits and contextual facilitators, rather than an agentic, calculative capacity.

However, many would have said the same thing about leadership (see Avolio, 2005), and today, it is quite clear that leadership is mostly made, *not* born. We would suggest the same may be true of creativity as it is likely more elastic than traditionally considered based on the life-span research emerging on the brain. Indeed, today most behavioral geneticists would argue that even within a life span we are seeing changes in heritability factors influencing thoughts, emotions, and behavior (see, for example, a study of entrepreneurs, whom many think are born, not made; Zhang et al., 2009).

Finally, with respect to the performance impact criterion, to date, more of the studies treat creativity as an outcome rather than an antecedent to performance or other desirable work-related outcomes. The focus continues to be more on predicting creativity than on its outcomes. Of course, we do not discount the importance of creativity for success at the individual, group, organizational, community, and even country level. Evidence abounds to this notion. However, the complex mechanisms through which creativity as a psychological resource can predict and explain measurable performance and other work-related outcomes remain largely unexplored.

Flow as Potential PsyCap

Coming out of one of the recognized founders of positive psychology is Mihaly Csikszentmihalyi's concept of flow, introduced in this chapter's opening video. Flow is viewed as an optimal experience. It is widely recognized that flow is attained when one has both high skills and is undergoing a significant challenge (Csikszentmihalyi, 1997). Being "in flow" (a sort of euphoric zone) is a feeling that many have experienced, yet few have been able to fully define or comprehend.

Flow involves a different, even deeper perspective than intrinsic motivation. When in flow, accomplishing a task becomes rewarding as an end in itself, rather than a means toward other goals (e.g., pay, promotion, impression management). The individual in flow becomes completely absorbed in the activity (Nakamura & Csikszentmihalyi, 2009). For a person in flow, time is distorted and may even seem to stand still; the person is immersed in a state that is accomplishing something difficult and worthwhile.

Flow as a Positive Appraisal of Circumstances and Success Probabilities

Flow takes place when one's subjectively experienced level of opportunity or challenge in a specific situation is entirely balanced with one's perceived abilities and skills to meet the demands of that situation. When challenges exceed perceived skills, anxiety and diminished self-efficacy preclude engagement, enjoyment, motivation, and, thus, flow. By the same token, when challenges are clearly below one's skill level, boredom and apathy distract attention away from the activity, causing one to lose flow (Csikszentmihalyi, 1975/2000).

Even when challenges and skills are matched, but are at a low level on the challenge and skills continuum, being in flow is unlikely. Flow can only be experienced when the balanced levels of challenge and skill are both at a high level (Csikszentmihalyi, 1997). For example, the mandatory attendance of a monotonic training presentation on the new fire alarm system will not generate feelings of being in flow. Despite the new information disseminated in such a presentation, the ability level required to grasp the information is likely to be kept by the presenter at the lowest level possible, in hopes that even those who lack intelligence or attentiveness will still "get it." Moreover, the level of challenge that passive listening requires does not stretch the capabilities of the participants. Thus, in such a situation, a downward spiral of passiveness and lack of attentiveness precludes flow.

On the contrary, even despite initial resistance, an interactive session or a hands-on drill may lead to more attentiveness and enjoyment, but this is also not flow, as the same messages are communicated. However, a highly skilled athlete or musician faced with an energizing challenge is very likely to enter into flow. Thus, flow is consistent with the conceptualization of PsyCap and shared commonality among its constituent resources as a "positive appraisal of circumstances and probability for success based on motivated effort and perseverance" (Luthans et al., 2007, p. 550).

Flow as State-Like and Agentic

Some studies have attempted to examine the possibility for the presence of dispositions and enduring tendencies for experiencing flow on a more frequent basis, also referred to as an "autotelic personality" (Baumann, 2012). However, the subjective and dynamic nature of flow as "emergent motivation" (Csikszentmihalyi, 1985) seems a more relevant depiction of flow as being more state-like. Specifically, in this view every moment's experience is interacting with the cognitions and emotions of the individual to determine the experienced level of flow through the next moment. This is more consistent with the conceptualization of flow as being "state-like," and thus being open to development. Moreover, since the balance described earlier will vary widely across types of individuals, situations, and challenges, it is hard to imagine that flow would be a trait versus state or state-like. Recent experimental studies have also been successful at manipulating levels of flow through short-term interventions (Keller & Bless, 2008; Moller, Meier, & Wall, 2010).

Characteristics of being in a state of flow include high concentration on the activity, low self-consciousness, a strong sense of agency and control, high self-esteem, and losing track of time. There is even diminished importance of the end goal being pursued in favor of continuing with the activity for the intense enjoyment of the moment (Csikszentmihalyi, 1975; Nakamura & Csikszentmihalyi, 2009). However, there are several exceptions to these criteria. For example, challenging activities that are perceived as "work" or "school" attract more concentration and yield more satisfaction and self-esteem, especially when targeted at the right skill level—stretching one, yet achievable. On the other hand, research has shown that activities that are perceived as "play," "relaxation" (high skill-low challenge such as eating or socializing), or even "serious play" activities that combine work and play, such as extracurricular activities or games, were sometimes more enjoyed, and participants had a greater desire to be pursuing these types of activities (Csikszentmihalyi, 1997; LeFevre, 1988).

Measurement of Flow

Several approaches such as semistructured interviews and questionnaires have been utilized for measuring flow. Some of these measures are specific to particular domains of life. However, the most recognized and supported is perhaps the Experience Sampling Method (Csikszentmihalyi & Larson, 1987). In this unique measurement approach to flow, through a paging device, participants can be prompted at random times to report on their level of flow by completing some brief questions. This method captures the cognitions and emotions of the moment. Despite its demonstrated reliability and validity (Csikszentmihalyi & Larson, 1987), one of the primary criticisms of this method is that when prompted, the participant will have to disengage from the activity to respond to the questions, which in turn may disrupt and reduce experiences of flow. Perhaps in the future, participants can be informed through neural prompting, using a technology like Google Glass, such that it is more precognitive processing providing for less distraction.

More recently, several self-report scales for measuring flow have been developed and validated. Examples include Jackson and Eklund's (2002) Flow State Scale (FSS-2) and Dispositional Flow Scale (DFS-2), as well as short versions of both scales (Jackson & Eklund, 2008). These four scales reflect the relevance and consistency of flow with the conceptualization of the established PsyCap resources as being state-like, but with a trait-like baseline. Another example is Bakker's (2008) Work-Related Flow Scale (WOLF), which is the first recognized flow measure that is specific to the workplace. It measures flow along three dimensions: absorption, work enjoyment, and intrinsic work motivation.

Flow in the Workplace: Relevance and Impact

Several possible explanations of flow, with important workplace implications, can be found in the literature. For example, Csikszentmihalyi (2003) has a book devoted to applying flow to the business world. In one of the chapters, he even has a section called "The Building of Psychological Capital," which he describes as follows: "It is useful to think of enjoyment as the psychological equivalent of building capital, and of pleasure as the equivalent of consumption" (Csikszentmihalyi, 2003, p. 76). So, even though this is one of the very few times the term "psychological capital" has been mentioned outside of a couple of economics articles (found in a Google search), it is used by Csikszentmihalyi in explaining flow, rather than how we are defining it, to conceptualize and apply PsyCap. Nevertheless, the mere fact that he uses the term (and also in a presentation he made at a Positive Psychology Summit) and has a book devoted to flow in the business world suggests the potential flow may have for inclusion in our conception and measurement of PsyCap.

One of the more recent workplace applications of flow and its development took place at Green Cargo, a Swedish, state-owned transportation company. Through training managers to identify workers' strengths, set appropriate goals and challenges with them, and provide timely feedback, workers were able to experience flow in their jobs. As a result, the failing company became profitable for the first time in over a century (March, 2005). Another workplace application was a mixed-methods study at Sandia National Laboratories (SNL), established by the United States Government to research and design national security technology solutions, and run by Lockheed Martin Corporation. This study supported a complex, multidimensional structure of flow among knowledge workers (Quinn, 2005).

Furthermore, there have been some empirical connections made between the positive effects of transformational leadership on group fluency and flexibility (Sosik, Avolio, & Kahai, 1998), and the role of flow and anonymity as mediators between transformational leadership and creativity (Sosik, Kahai, & Avolio, 1999). These particular studies examined how leadership mediated through technology impacted levels of creativity and flow in groups working with group decision support systems.

In addition to the role that flow may play in organizational leadership, it has also been shown to be related to desirable outcomes in software design, computer-mediated communication, medical surgery, and, as noted earlier, has directly been focused on the implications for business activities of all kinds (Csikszentmihalyi, 1997, 2003). Like the other PsyCap states, flow has also been shown to relate to academic, artistic, literary, and sports performance, as well as to physical and psychological health (see Nakamura & Csikszentmihalyi, 2009, for a comprehensive review). As shown in Table 7.1, flow seems to be a good fit for the criteria of PsyCap inclusion, and especially if more research is directly conducted in the workplace, it can potentially be a very promising resource for PsyCap in the future.

Potential Problems That Prevent Flow

Although flow is likely to be facilitated by skill development and opportunities for challenges, there are also some cautions that should be noted in a positive spiral of flow. For example, research indicates that experiencing flow may require a balance between the utilization of energy and its conservation through engaging in pleasant but less demanding activities (Nakamura & Csikszentmihalyi, 2009). The stakes are extremely high in today's competitive work environment, and this may result in pursuing growth and advancement at all costs, including one's well-being. Not only can such a relentless pursuit become physically, mentally, and emotionally draining, and may even lead to a breakdown in performance, effective decision making, and ethical conduct, it can also diminish the positive experiences of flow aspired to in the first place. This is one of the main reasons why we believe that organizational leaders need to recognize the fine line between functional flow and dysfunctional workaholism and blind ambition.

Attention is a salient antecedent for experiencing and sustaining flow. Self-regulation and personal choices of fully allocating one's attentive resources to particular tasks are vital ingredients of the flow state (Csikszentmihalyi & Csikszentmihalyi, 1988). Importantly, the organizational context or culture can facilitate or hinder participants' self-regulation efforts. Although difficult to manage, cognitive distractions tend to be in abundance as organizational leaders and their associates attempt to discern and manage the overabundance and too often an explosion of information they receive every day. Open communication, transparency, and use of relevant filters can help refocus attention and energies, and thus enhance the climate needed for flow to be experienced. At the same time, an emerging generation may be able to handle multiple distractions better than previous generations such that what we consider "in balance" itself may be a moving target for researchers and practitioners.

Physical distractions such as noise and uncomfortable work stations with inadequate lighting, temperature, or ventilation problems are potential inhibitors for experiencing flow. Even more salient, however, are the human dynamics and social distractions such as conflict, power struggles, and lack of trust and transparency that can be very inhibiting and cause attention to languish, drift, or become focused on being more defensive in one's behavior and processing of information. For example, in an environment that is considered to not be psychologically safe (Edmondson, 1999), we would expect that individuals would have a higher level of emotional labor to simply stay in balance. What Edmondson has shown over the last decade with her research is that a psychologically safe climate allows people to explore, be more creative, and to take risks that result in greater innovation. We suspect that a psychologically safe environment is an inducement for flow, whereas emotional distractions such as feelings of guilt, fear, disengagement, or burnout from long hours resulting in inadequate work-life balance can preclude the attainment of flow.

Mindfulness as Potential PsyCap

Although mindfulness has been part of Far Eastern cultural traditions and Buddhism for many centuries, recently there has been increased interest in its relevance and application as part of positive psychology. As seen in the chapter Opening Video, positive psychologist Ellen Langer (2009) defines "mindfulness" (in contrast to "mindlessness") as "a flexible state of mind that is characterized by openness to novelty, sensitivity to context, and engagement with the present moment" (p. 279). It involves developing "the ability to hang on to current objects, to remember them, and not to lose sight of them through distraction, wandering attention, associative thinking, explaining away, or rejection" (Weick & Sutcliffe, 2006, p. 518). In the Western tradition, mindfulness is also viewed from an information processing perspective, where a heightened appreciation of the context leads to learning, refinement of existing categories, and creation of new categories based on present events and experiences, or even a decreased dependence on these coding processes and routines (Langer, 1989; Levinthall & Rerup, 2006; Weick & Sutcliffe, 2006; Vogus, 2012).

Conceptually, mindfulness appears to be similar to flow. For example, both share the common dimensions of high concentration, absorption, and loss of time perception. However, they are distinguished in important ways. For example, flow is associated with detachment or desensitization from contextual experiences, whereas mindfulness is associated with sharpened awareness and processing of those surrounding stimuli (Marianetti & Passmore, 2010). Thus, while both flow and mindfulness share a heightened present moment orientation, flow involves a much narrower attentional breadth (Dane, 2011).

There is substantial support for the benefits of mindfulness in general, and in particular meditation-based mindfulness, which is the most commonly recognized approach for enhancing mindfulness. For example, a meta-analysis of mindfulness-based stress reduction (MBSR) interventions has shown significant physical and psychological health benefits (Grossman, Niemann, Schmidt, & Walach, 2004). Drawing also from neurological evidence, Davidson (2012) has recently discussed how mindfulness can alter brain functions over time, increasing resilience, optimism, compassion, and other positive resources traditionally thought to be "hard-wired."

Does Mindfulness Meet the PsyCap Criteria?

Given the deep roots of mindfulness research and practice, it meets the theory and evidence-based criteria of PsyCap. Furthermore, the state-like nature and developmental potential of mindfulness have been established long before positive psychology, and they have also been supported in contemporary research and practice. Specifically, mindfulness can be developed through a four-step process: (a) knowledge of mindfulness concepts and benefits, (b) purposeful awareness, (c) inclusive and authentic attention, and (d) nonjudgmental acceptance of reality as is, in the present moment (Davidson, 2012; Kabat-Zinn, 1990; Marianetti & Passmore, 2010).

Recently, there has been increased interest in the relevance of mindfulness to the workplace (Glomb, Duffy, Bono, & Yang, 2011; Leroy, Anseel, Dimitrova, & Sels, 2013; Marianetti & Passmore, 2010; Vogus, 2012). For example, Dane and Brummel (2013) found a positive relationship between mindfulness and job performance, and a negative relationship between mindfulness and turnover intentions. Hülsheger, Alberts, Feinholdt, and Lang (2013) found mindfulness to be negatively related to emotional exhaustion and positively related to job satisfaction. This workplace impact complements the already recognized benefits of mindfulness in terms of enhanced physical and mental health, psychological well-being, and social relationships (Brown & Ryan, 2003; Brown, Ryan, & Creswell, 2007). For example, a recent study of separate samples of junior, middle-, and top-level New Zealand managers' level of mindfulness was negatively related to their anxiety and depression and positively related to their psychological capital (Roche, Haar, & Luthans, 2014).

At the organizational level, positive organizational scholars have also used the term "mindful organizing" to describe "a set of social processes that underlie the near-flawless performance of high-reliability organizations" (Vogus, 2012, p. 664). Mindful organizing has been shown to relate to exceptional organizational performance, particularly under conditions of complexity, dynamism, interdependence, and time pressure (see Vogus, 2012, for a comprehensive review).

Taking another perspective, Dane (2011) has proposed that the wide external attentional breadth promoted through mindfulness may actually inhibit performance in static task environments that require more focus. He also proposed that the wide internal attentional breadth and increased attention to intuition promoted through mindfulness may have negative performance effects on novices who lack task expertise, and thus may base their decisions and actions on underdeveloped or biased intuitions. Thus, it is important to account for the various potential moderators in the relationship between mindfulness and work performance. One of the possible explanations of this gap in the literature is that to date the primary emphasis has been on mindfulness as an end in and of itself, as well as its health and well-being benefits, but not necessarily its instrumental value in enhancing work-related climates, processes, and outcomes. Marianetti and Passmore (2010) summarize this notion as follows: "Mindfulness does not have a goal . . .; the purpose is the experience itself" (p. 196).

In terms of measurement, there seems to have been a proliferation of mindfulness measures (see http://www.mindfulexperience.org/measurement for a list of the numerous mindfulness scales and links to studies supporting their validity and reliability). This growth reflects the increased interest in measuring and studying mindfulness across a wide range of populations and contexts (e.g., various age groups, nationalities, and psychological conditions). Although widely recognized mindfulness measures such as Brown and Ryan's (2003) MAAS (Mindful Attention Awareness Scale) is generic enough to be used with workplace samples, validated measures directly developed from and aimed at organizational participants are still needed.

Besides relevant measures, also problematic is that it is too common in the research to use mindfulness interventions, especially meditation training, as a proxy for mindfulness, and then evaluate the outcomes of these interventions without necessarily measuring the participants' levels of mindfulness or assessing its increase over time. Thus, future research should emphasize (a) the use of validated measures of mindfulness, (b) leveraging cross-sectional and longitudinal, as well as experimental, research to further understand and measure meditation and the underlying mechanisms linking it to its many recognized benefits, and (c) examining alternative potential mechanisms and interventions to boost mindfulness and facilitate its outcomes besides meditation. Another potential risk in measuring mindfulness is that engaging in measurement, whether using quantitative or qualitative measures, can in and of itself potentially reduce participants' state of mindfulness (Brown & Ryan, 2004).

There is also some disagreement in the literature as to whether mindfulness meets the theoretic criterion of agentic control and intentional actions of those who practice it. On one hand, mindfulness can be intentionally cultivated by maintaining and redirecting one's attention and focus on the present moment and consciously, but nonjudgmentally, acknowledging and rejecting distractions. This exercise certainly requires intentionality and self-regulation. On the other hand, the resultant state of mindfulness is less subject to the control and scrutiny of the individual, or as Marianetti and Passmore (2010) note: "there is no control over the experience we guide ourselves through" (p. 196) when practicing mindfulness. Thus, the fit of mindfulness with the agentic mechanism requirement of PsyCap is questionable.

Finally, we come to the question of whether mindfulness meets the other theoretic criterion of "positive appraisal of circumstances and probability for success based on motivated effort and perseverance" (Luthans et al., 2007, p. 550). Mindfulness focuses on the present, or the current circumstances, not the future. Its purpose is to slow down and experience the present more fully, to live in the moment, and to see the world as it appears in that moment. It does not attempt to appraise these circumstances positively or negatively, but rather attempts to deliberately resist evaluation and suspend judgment. Thus, mindfulness falls short of meeting the underlying theoretic PsyCap mechanisms.

Gratitude and Forgiveness as Potential PsyCap

Like the other PsyCap resources, gratitude and forgiveness are commonly used in everyday language. For example, gratitude typically means people treating one another with respect and expressing appreciation for one another, and forgiveness means people avoid blaming others and let go of their mistakes (Cameron & Winn, 2012, p. 238). However, also like the others, these two terms are more carefully defined in positive psychology. For example, Emmons (2004, p. 554) defines gratitude as "a sense of thankfulness and joy in response to receiving a gift, whether the gift can be a tangible benefit from a specific other or a moment of peaceful bliss evoked by natural beauty." Furthermore, Watkins, Van Gelder, and Frias (2009) distinguish state gratitude from trait gratitude. State gratitude is an emotion experienced when individuals perceive themselves to be the recipients of something good, and someone else (a human, supernatural, or impersonal benefactor) to be responsible for this benefit. On the other hand, trait gratitude represents the affective disposition to experience gratitude more readily across different contexts. An argument can be made that gratitude complements optimism in that where it may not be possible for an optimistic explanatory style (personal, permanent, and pervasive; see Chapter 5) to internalize a positive event, gratitude may become a substitute for a pessimistic, external appraisal.

Forgiveness, on the other hand, is defined in positive psychology as "the framing of a perceived transgression such that one's attachment to the transgressor, transgression, and sequel of the transgression is transformed from negative to neutral or positive. The source of a transgression, and therefore the object of forgiveness, may be oneself, another person or persons, or a situation that one views as being beyond one's control" (Yamhure Thompson, & Snyder, 2003, p. 302). The meaning and use of forgiveness vary in two major ways. First, forgiveness varies to the extent it incorporates active benevolence, prosocial change, or even love and appreciation toward the source of transgression (versus just passive tolerance, ceasing to blame, or a reduced sense of victimization). Second is the degree to which reconciliation is considered an integral component of forgiveness (Enright & North, 1998; McCullough, Pargament, & Thorensen, 2000; McCullough, Root, Tabak, & Witvliet, 2009).

Although positive psychology tends to treat gratitude and forgiveness as two separate constructs, for our purposes to simply introduce them as potential PsyCap, we include them together. Specifically, we present gratitude and forgiveness as two sides of the same, precious coin. On one side, grateful individuals choose to focus on and appreciate the positives in their lives, including their own and others' strengths, talents, gifts, and prosocial behaviors, as well as favorable events. This gratefulness tends to promote and maintain a positive view of oneself, others, and situational factors and events. On the other side of the coin, forgiveness is a positive approach in dealing with the negatives in one's life, including faults, vulnerabilities, and negative behaviors and outcomes that are perceived in oneself, others, and situational factors and events. However, by forgiving, one is taking a deliberate, positive stance with oneself or others. To forgive means to accept that the future can be more effectively optimized if one does not dwell on the negatives of the past.

We are also now seeing more direct applications of interest focusing on forgiveness in the field of organizational behavior. For example, Fehr and Gelfand (2012) discuss forgiveness as an organizational construct akin to climate. In their work, they examine how organizations and, of course, their leaders create a climate of forgiveness that can positively impact worker well-being, motivation, and performance. For example, they discuss how a climate of forgiveness may impact the justice perceived in an organizational unit, how conflict is addressed more prosocially, and the levels of compassion exhibited by organizational members with each other during difficult challenges.

A combination of gratitude and forgiveness can help shape perceptions and attributions and instill a proactive approach of "positive labeling" and "positive identity" that can enhance one's inventory or "bank" of psychological capital. How? By carrying negative thoughts about another, such as revenge, it draws down the positivity of individuals due to a higher level of emotional labor, and in turn their psychological capital. In laymen's terms, we can argue that revenge consumes the individual in negativity, taking attention away from those things that are positive.

Gratitude can be simply viewed as the extra mile willingly traveled by those with high PsyCap. In the meantime, forgiveness is facilitated and capitalized upon by gratitude as transgressions are positively appraised as opportunities to learn important lessons in life. Then, from the accelerating forgiveness, one's gratitude is intensified toward other, more favorable relationships and situations, and the upward spiral of positivity continues. Forgiveness allows the victim to view the transgressor in a more positive light, resulting in enhancing the possibility for seeing through and being grateful for the positives and the lessons to be learned from that person or event. As noted earlier, these spirals can be fueled by the type of climates created in organizations, which can create a contagion effect of forgiveness and gratitude.

Being able to selectively focus on and be thankful and grateful for what is positive can, in turn, facilitate forgiveness. For example, top management's gratitude for the organization's loyal customers and/or vendors may motivate reciprocation through socially responsible actions to and from all relevant parties (e.g., sales personnel toward customers and vendor sales people toward the organization's supply chain manager). Promoting a culture of gratitude toward valuable employees and customers may, in turn, facilitate forgiveness by employees toward the occasional incidents of employee and customer malice.

An example would be an organization we have worked with that has referred to its customers as "guests" for over 50 years. The intent of the founder was to show his gratitude toward customers by always treating them as guests in his stores. Indeed, he was the first automotive distributor to focus on and offer after-sales service quality in the early 1950s, many years prior to the advent of the service quality movement. And back in 1953, a company doing this called ALJ was and still has its headquarters in Jeddah, Saudi Arabia . . . not Tokyo! Indeed, this company remains the largest independent distributor of Toyota products in the world, and it is a company that Toyota itself learned from in terms of how to positively treat its customers.

Organizational leaders' gratitude toward employees can also be viewed as a form of genuine positive reinforcement with performance impact (e.g., feedback and social recognition; see Peterson & Luthans, 2006; Stajkovic & Luthans, 2003). Leaders' gratitude to employees may result not only in improved performance but also more frequent exhibition of organizational citizenship behaviors and decreased incidences of destructive behaviors such as violence, sabotage, theft, stress, and burnout. Over time, a culture of gratitude can facilitate forgiveness in difficult times (e.g., downsizing and layoffs). This is in line with the positive psychological view of gratitude as a type of moral affect that acts as a "moral barometer" registering received benefits, a "moral motive" to reciprocate, and a "moral reinforcer" for prosocial behaviors (McCullough, Kilpatrick, Emmons, & Larson, 2001).

Do Gratitude and Forgiveness Meet the PsyCap Criteria?

Among the commonalities between gratitude and forgiveness is the similar fit of both constructs with most of our PsyCap inclusion criteria (see Table 7.1). For example, both gratitude and forgiveness have been conceptualized and measured not only as dispositional traits but also developmental states, as is required to be included in PsyCap. Dispositionally, gratitude and forgiveness can be viewed as enduring tendencies, that is, the propensity to experience gratitude in higher-than-usual intensity, frequency, span, and/or density (Emmons, McCullough, & Tsang, 2003; McCullough, Emmons, & Tsang, 2002; Watkins et al., 2009), or the general willingness to forgive (Hebl & Enright, 1993; Yamhure Thompson & Snyder, 2003). These both occur across time and situations.

Despite this support for being dispositional, there is also extensive theory building and empirical research that gratitude and forgiveness can also be state-like and thus open to development. For example, Emmons and Crumpler (2000) were able to develop higher levels of gratitude through asking participants to simply keep weekly journals of things for which they could be thankful. Various other successful interventions have also been implemented to develop gratitude, most of which revolve around encouraging participants to "count their blessings," that is, to think about, write about, and/or express gratitude toward others (Emmons & McCullough, 2003; Seligman, Steen, Park, & Peterson, 2005; Watkins, Woodward, Stone, & Kolts, 2003). Miller (1995) offers a more elaborate approach for developing gratitude through the identification of ungrateful attitudes, substitution of those attitudes with more grateful ones, and then transfer of those more positive attitudes into grateful behaviors. Workplace applications of gratitude development are also beginning to emerge (Emmons, 2003).

There is also evidence that forgiveness can be successfully developed through a four-step process that includes (1) uncovering and self-awareness of underlying cognitions and emotions such as anger and shame; (2) making a decision and commitment to forgive; (3) reframing through acceptance, empathy, and compassion toward the transgressor; and (4) overcoming and finding meaning of the forgiveness experience (Baskin & Enright, 2004). Meta-analytical findings provide support for the strongest forgiveness development interventions being theoretically grounded, individually or group based, process oriented, and longer in duration (Baskin & Enright, 2004; Wade, Worthington, & Meyer, 2005; Worthington, Sandage, & Berry, 2000).

We came across a case example of forgiveness in a program designed to transform juvenile delinquents into productive citizens in Ohio a number of years ago. The program was set up to show the transgressors that when they stole from small store owners, they were significantly impacting the shop's very slim profit margins. Depending on how much they stole, the convicted juveniles were required to work off in the store they robbed the amount taken. Initially the store owners were reluctant to participate in the project; that is, they were not so willing to forgive. However, over time an interesting pattern emerged in both the store owners' and the juveniles' behavior. Many of the shop owners, after the work-off period had expired, actually hired these troubled juveniles permanently.

Applied to current workplace issues, Worthington, Berry, Shivy, and Brownstein (2005) propose forgiveness as necessary and applicable in a downsizing. They suggest that forgiveness can be facilitated through establishing realistic expectations regarding the relative stability of the job, ensuring that the organization acts responsibly and in a transparent manner, and striving to provide help and support for displaced employees. By following recognized guidelines for procedural justice (e.g., Greenberg, 2009), we expect that employees who have been downsized to be more willing to forgive their organizations.

In an earlier chapter, we have briefly given an example about an electronics organization in the Washington, DC, area that went to the extreme on this issue. The CEO indicated that he wanted all workers to be part of the organization's alumni and that when he had to downsize he treated them as alumni of the organization, staying in contact over time to make sure they had secured a new position. Interestingly enough, not only did some of these employees come back to work with the organization when the economy rebounded, but they consistently recommended the company to friends and colleagues as a place to consider for employment. This fits with Fehr and Gelfand's (2012) notion of what might characterize organizational-level forgiveness, as we suspect over time that the founder's forgiveness becomes diffused into the culture and climate.

Reliable and valid measures of state-like forgiveness, as directed toward specific persons, transgressions, or both, are available in the literature (e.g., Mauger et al., 1992; McCullough et al., 1998, 2009; Subkoviak et al., 1995). Unfortunately, such measures for gratitude, on the other hand, are not found. There are valid, reliable, and widely used measures of trait gratitude, such as the Gratitude Questionnaire-6 (GQ-6; McCullough et al., 2002) and the Gratitude Resentment and Appreciation Test (GRAT; Watkins et al., 2003). On the other hand, the common approach to measure state gratitude is by asking participants to rate themselves in the moment on adjectives such as "grateful," "thankful," or "appreciative" (Watkins et al., 2009) or use a one-item general assessment (e.g., Wood, Maltby, Stewart, Linley, & Joseph, 2008).

Moreover, despite the recognized role of gratitude and forgiveness in promoting physical and psychological health, well-being, and freedom of pathological symptoms in the clinical and positive psychology literature (see Emmons, 2004; Emmons & Shelton, 2002; McCullough, 2004; McCullough et al., 2009; and Watkins et al., 2009, for comprehensive reviews), relatively little is still known about the potential impact of gratitude and forgiveness on work performance beyond case studies and anecdotal evidence as cited earlier. Emmons and Mishra (2011) offer a number of mechanisms through which gratitude leads to its desirable outcomes, some of which appear promising for future gratitude research in the context of the workplace. For example, gratitude facilitates coping with stress, reduces toxic emotions resulting from self and social comparisons, reduces materialistic strivings, improves self-esteem, enhances accessibility to positive memories, builds social resources, motivates moral behavior, facilitates goal attainment, and promotes physical health. Each of these can also be seen as an antecedent to success at work.

Although forgiveness has been recognized as having relevance in an organizational context (Aquino, Grover, Goldman, & Folger, 2003; Cameron & Caza, 2002; Fehr & Gelfand, 2012), very little research has been conducted to date. Bright and Exline (2012) have summarized the few studies as mainly falling into two general areas: employee error and creating an organizational culture or climate of forgiveness. With regard to employee errors impacting forgiveness, the process of what happens has been studied (Sutton & Thomas, 2005) and many years ago Bosk (1979) conducted a classic ethnographic study that traced the aftermath and implications of medical errors committed by professional staff. The culture and climate studies also used a qualitative study of forgiveness. For example, in a trucking firm, Bright (2005) found two modes of narrative that promoted forgiveness ("pragmatic" that was needed to support vital relationships and "transcendent" that led to an improved climate and culture). Bright and POS colleagues (Bright, Cameron, & Caza, 2006) have also found in their studies that perceptions of forgiveness climate have had a long-term positive impact on downsized organizations.

Finally, both gratitude and forgiveness are consistent with the PsyCap's agentic mechanism and its positive appraisals. As discussed earlier, the development of both gratitude and forgiveness requires agentic decisions and actions. More specifically, both gratitude and forgiveness are based on intentionally appraising and framing past, present, and future situations in a more positive and appreciative manner. For example, forgiveness can be facilitated through increasing the perceived care worthiness, expected value, and safety of transgressors (McCullough et al., 2009). Similarly, the relationship between trait and state gratitude has been shown to be fully mediated through the benefit recipients' positive appraisals of the benefactor's genuine helpfulness, value, and cost (Wood et al., 2008). Thus, gratitude and forgiveness fit the underlying theoretical mechanisms of PsyCap.

In total, we suggest that both gratitude and forgiveness are highly promising candidates for being included in the future of PsyCap. They seem especially relevant for today's business environment, where questionable ethics and cutthroat competition seem to have too often promoted greed, hatred, and revenge, instead of thankfulness, appreciation, sharing, empathy, and compassion. Future research to fill the void is likely to be met with a lot of gratitude and maybe forgiveness for all concerned, at the individual, group/team, organizational, and especially societal levels. For example, Bright and Exline (2012) have recently conceptualized four levels of forgiveness for future research: intrapersonal, relational, organizational, and collective-group.

Case Study: The Science of Happiness: Gratitude and Forgiveness

Video link: http://youtu.be/oHv6vTKD6lg

Video link: http://youtu.be/8o9_TlZyB_Y

These lighthearted but appealing presentations on the "science" of happiness use real subjects (who did not know what they were going to be doing when they volunteered) to demonstrate the power of gratitude and forgiveness covered in this chapter. If you found these interesting and effective, there are others in this series on You Tube you may want to view.

Questions for reflection and/or discussion:

1. Why do you think it is more effective to deliver the gratitude letter over the phone rather than just by e-mail or regular mail?
2. Who do you think was most positively affected by the gratitude letter—the letter writer or the recipient?
3. Why do you think the "experimenter" had the subjects read their forgiveness piece into a mirror?
4. What lessons will you take away from these two videos? Will you commit to doing these exercises?

References

Amabile, T. M., & Fisher, C. M. (2009). Stimulate creativity by fueling passion. In E. Locke (Ed.), *Handbook of principles of organizational behavior* (2nd ed., pp. 481–497). Oxford, UK: Blackwell.

Aquino, K., Grover, S. L., Goldman, B., & Folger, R. (2003). When push doesn't come to shove: Interpersonal forgiveness in workplace relationships. *Journal of Management Inquiry, 12,* 209–216.

Avolio, B. J. (2005). *Leadership development in balance: Made/Born.* Mahwah, NJ: Erlbaum.

Avolio, B. J., & Luthans, F. (2006). *The high impact leader: Moments matter in accelerating authentic leadership development.* New York, NY: McGraw-Hill.

Bakker, A. B. (2008). The work-related flow inventory: Consturction and initial valuation of the WOLF. *Journal of Vocational Behavior, 72,* 400–414.

Baltes, P. B. (2006). *Lifespan development and the brain.* Cambridge, UK: Cambridge University Press.

Baskin, T., & Enright, R. (2004). Intervention studies on forgiveness: A meta-analysis. *Journal of Counseling and Development, 82,* 79–90.

Baumann, N. (2012). Autotelic personality. In S. Engeser (Ed.), *Advances in flow research* (pp. 165–186). New York, NY: Springer.

Bosk, C. L. (1979). *Forgive and remember: Managing medical failure*. Chicago, IL: University of Chicago Press.

Bright, D. S. (2005). *Forgiveness and change*. Unpublished Ph.D. dissertation, Case Western Reserve University, Cleveland, OH.

Bright, D. S., Cameron, K., & Caza, A. (2006). The amplifying and buffering effects of vistuousness in downsized organizations. *Journal of Business Ethics, 64*, 249–269.

Bright, D. S., & Exline, J. J. (2012). Forgiveness at four levels: Intrapersonal, relational, organizational, and collective-group. In K. Cameron & G. M. Spreitzer (Eds.), *Oxford handbook of positive organizational scholarship* (pp. 244–259). New York, NY: Oxford University Press.

Brown, K. W., & Ryan, R. M. (2003). The benefits of being present: Mindfulness and its role in psychological well-being. *Journal of Personality and Social Psychology, 84*, 822–848.

Brown, K. W., & Ryan, R. M. (2004). Perils and promise in defining and measuring mindfulness: Observations from experience. *Clinical Psychology: Science and Practice, 11*, 242–248.

Brown, K. W., Ryan, R. M., & Creswell, J. D. (2007). Mindfulness: Theoretical foundations and evidence for its salutary effects. *Psychological Inquiry, 18*, 211–237.

Cameron, K., & Caza, A. (2002). Organizational and leadership virtues and the role of forgiveness. *Journal of Leadership and Organizational Studies, 9*, 33–48.

Cameron K., & Spreitzer, G. M. (Eds.). (2012). *Oxford handbook of positive organizational scholarship*. New York, NY: Oxford University Press.

Cameron, K., & Winn, B. (2012). Virtuousness in organizations. In K. Cameron & B. M. Spreitzer (Eds.), *Oxford handbook of positive organizational scholarship* (pp. 231–243). New York, NY: Oxford University Press.

Cassandro, V., & Simonton, K. (2003). Creativity and genius. In C. Keyes & J. Haidt (Eds.), *Flourishing: Positive psychology and the life well-lived* (pp. 163–183). Washington, DC: American Psychological Association.

Costa, P. T., Jr., & McCrae, R. R. (1992). *Revised NEO Personality Inventory (NEO-PI-R) and NEO Five-Factor Inventory (NEO-FFI) manual*. Odessa, FL: Psychological Assessment Resources.

Csikszentmihalyi, M. (1975). *Beyond boredom and anxiety*. San Francisco, CA: Jossey-Bass.

Csikszentmihalyi, M. (1985). Emergent motivation and the evolution of the self. *Advances in Motivation and Achievement, 4*, 93–119.

Csikszentmihalyi, M. (1997). *Finding flow*. New York, NY: Basic.

Csikszentmihalyi, M. (2003). *Good business*. New York, NY: Penguin Books.

Csikszentmihalyi, M., & Csikszentmihalyi, I. (Eds.). (1988). *Optimal experience*. Cambridge, UK: Cambridge University Press.

Csikszentmihalyi, M., & Larson, R. (1987). Validity and reliability of the experience-sampling method. *Journal of Nervous and Mental Disease*, *175*, 526–536.

Dane, E. (2011). Paying attention to mindfulness and its effects on task performance in the workplace. *Journal of Management*, *37*, 997–1018.

Dane, E., & Brummel, B. J. (2013). Examining workplace mindfulness and its relations to job performance and turnover intention. *Human Relations*, *67*, 105–128.

Davidson, R. J. (2012). *The emotional life of your brain*. New York, NY: Hudson.

Digman, J. M. (1990). Personality structure: Emergence of the five-factor model. *Annual Review of Psychology*, *41*, 417–440.

Edmondson, A. (1999). Psychological safety and learning behavior in work teams. *Administrative Science Quarterly*, *44*, 350–383.

Emmons, R. A. (2003). Acts of gratitude in organizations. In K. S. Cameron, J. E. Dutton & R. E. Quinn (Eds.), *Positive organizational scholarship* (pp. 81–93). San Francisco, CA: Berrett-Koehler.

Emmons, R. A. (2004). Gratitude. In C. Peterson & M. Seligman (Eds.), *Character strengths and virtues: A handbook and classification* (pp. 553–568). Oxford, UK: Oxford University Press.

Emmons, R. A., & Crumpler, C. A. (2000). Gratitude as a human strength: Appraising the evidence. *Journal of Social and Clinical Psychology*, *19*, 56–69.

Emmons, R. A., & McCullough, M. E. (2003). Counting blessings versus burdens: An experimental investigation of gratitude and subjective well-being in daily life. *Journal of Personality and Social Psychology*, *84*, 377–389.

Emmons, R., McCullough, M., & Tsang, J. (2003). The assessment of gratitude. In S. Lopez & C. R. Snyder (Eds.), *Positive psychological assessment: A handbook of models and measures* (pp. 327–341). Washington, DC: American Psychological Association.

Emmons, R. A., & Mishra, A. (2011). Why gratitude enhances well-being: What we know, what we need to know. In K. Sheldon, T. Kashdan, & M. Steger (Eds.), *Designing positive psychology: Taking stock and moving forward* (pp. 248–262). New York, NY: Oxford University Press.

Emmons, R. A., & Shelton, C. M. (2002). Gratitude and the science of positive psychology. In C. R. Snyder & S. Lopez (Eds.), *Handbook of positive psychology* (pp. 459–471). Oxford, UK: Oxford University Press.

Enright, R., & North, J. (Eds.). (1998). *Exploring forgiveness*. Madison: University of Wisconsin Press.

Fehr, R., & Gelfand, M. J. (2012). The forgiving organization: A multilevel model of forgiveness at work. *Academy of Management Review*, *37*, 664–688.

Feist, G. (1998). A meta-analysis of personality in scientific and artistic creativity. *Personality and Social Psychology Review*, *2*, 290–309.

Glomb, T. M., Duffy, M. K., Bono, J. E., & Yang, T. (2011). Mindfulness at work. *Research in Personnel and Human Resources Management*, *30*, 115–157.

Greenberg, J. (2009). Promote procedural and interactional justice to enhance individual and organizational outcomes. In E. A. Locke (Ed.), *Handbook of principles of organizational behavior* (pp. 255–271). Chichester, UK: Wiley.

Grossman, P., Niemann, L., Schmidt, S., & Walach, H. (2004). Mindfulness-based stress reduction and health benefits: A meta-analysis. *Journal of Psychosomatic Research, 57*, 35–43.

Gupta, V., & Singh, S. (2014). Psychological capital as a mediator of the relationship between leadership and creative performance behaviors. *International Journal of Human Resource Management, 25*, 1373–1394.

Hebl, J., & Enright, R. (1993). Forgiveness as a psychotherapeutic goal with elderly females. *Psychotherapy, 30*, 658–667.

Hülsheger, U., Alberts, H., Feinholdt, A., & Lang, J. (2013). Benefits of mindfulness at work: The role of mindfulness in emotion regulation, emotional exhaustion, and job satisfaction. *Journal of Applied Psychology, 98*, 310–325.

Huang, L., & Luthans, F. (2014). Toward better understanding of the learning goal orientation—creativity relationship: The role of positive psychological capital. *Applied Psychology: An International Review.* doi:10.111/apps.12028.

Jackson, S. A., & Eklund, R. C. (2002). Assessing flow in physical activity: The Flow State Scale-2 (FSS-2) and Dispositional Flow Scale-2 (DFS-2). *Journal of Sports amd Exercise Psychology, 24*, 133–150.

Jackson, S. A., & Eklund, R. C. (2008). Long and short measures of flow: Examining construct validty of the FSS-2, DFS-2, and new brief counterparts. *Journal of Sports amd Exercise Psychology, 30*, 561–587.

Kabat-Zinn, J. (1990). *Full catastrophe living: How to cope with stress, pain, and illness using mindful meditation.* London, UK: Piatkus.

Keller, J., & Bless, H. (2008). Flow and regulatory compatibility: An experimental approach to the flow model of intrinsic motivation. *Personality and Social Psychology Bulletin, 34*, 196–209.

Kerr, B., & Gagliardi, C. (2003). Measuring creativity in research and practice. In S. Lopez & C. R. Snyder, (Eds.), *Positive psychological assessment: A handbook of models and measures* (pp. 155–169). Washington, DC: American Psychological Association.

Kim, K. H. (2008). Meta-analyses of the relationship of creative achievement to both IQ and divergent thinking test scores. *Journal of Creative Behavior, 42*(2), 106–130.

Langer, E. (1989). *Mindfulness.* Reading, MA: Addison-Wesley.

Langer, E. (2009). Mindfulness versus positive evaluation. In S. Lopez & C. R. Snyder (Eds.), *Oxford handbook of positive psychology* (2nd ed., pp. 279–293). New York, NY: Oxford University Press.

LeFevre, J. (1988). Flow and the quality of experience during work and leisure. In M. Csikszentmihalyi & I. Csikszentmihalyi (Eds.), *Optimal experience* (pp. 307–318). Cambridge, UK: Cambridge University Press.

Leroy, H., Anseel, F., Dimitrova, N. G., & Sels, L. (2013). Mindfulness, an authentic functioning, and work engagement: A growth modeling approach. *Journal of Vocational Behavior, 82,* 238–247.

Levinthall, D. A., & Rerup, C. (2006). Crossing an apparent chasm: Bridging mindful and less mindful perspectives on organizational learning. *Organization Science, 17,* 502–513.

Lopez, S., & Snyder, C. R. (Eds.). (2009). *Oxford handbook of positive psychology* (2nd ed.). New York, NY: Oxford University Press.

Luthans, F., Avolio, B. J., Avey, J. B., & Norman, S. M. (2007). Positive psychological capital: Measurement and relationship with performance and satisfaction. *Personnel Psychology, 60,* 541–572.

March, A. (2005, August). The art of work. *Fast Company,* 77–79.

Marianetti, O., & Passmore, J. (2010). Mindfulness at work: Paying attention to enhance well-being and performance. In A. Linley, S. Harrington, & N. Garcea (Eds.), *Oxford handbook of positive psychology and work* (pp. 189–200). New York, NY: Oxford University Press.

Mauger, P., Perry, J., Freeman, T., Grove, D., McBride, A., et al. (1992). The measurement of forgiveness: Preliminary research. *Journal of Psychology and Christianity, 11,* 170–180.

McCullough, M. (2004). Forgiveness and Mercy. In C. Peterson & M. Seligman (Eds.), *Character strengths and virtues: A handbook and classification* (pp. 445–459). Oxford, UK: Oxford University Press.

McCullough, M., Emmons, R., & Tsang, J. (2002). The grateful disposition: A conceptual and empirical typology. *Journal of Personality and Social Psychology, 82,* 112–127.

McCullough, M., Kilpatrick, S., Emmons, R., & Larson, D. (2001). Gratitude as moral affect. *Psychological Bulletin, 127,* 249–266.

McCullough, M., Pargament, K., & Thorensen, C. (Eds.). (2000). *Forgiveness: Theory, research and practice.* New York, NY: Guilford Press.

McCullough, M., Rachal, K., Sandage, S., Worthington, E., Brown, S., & Hight, T. L. (1998). Interpersonal forgiving in close relationships II: Theoretical elaboration and measurement. *Journal of Personality and Social Psychology, 75,* 1586–1603.

McCullough, M., Root, L. M., Tabak, B. A., & Witvleit, C. (2009). Forgiveness. In S. J. Lopez & C. R. Snyder (Eds.), *Oxford handbook of positive psychology* (2nd ed., pp. 427–435). New York, NY: Oxford University Press.

Miller, T. (1995). *How to want what you have.* New York, NY: Avon.

Moller, A. C., Meier, B. P., & Wall, R. D. (2010). Developing an experimental induction of flow: Effortless action in the lab. In B. Bruya (Ed.), *Effortless attention: A new perspective in the cognitive science of attention and action* (pp. 191–204). Cambridge, MA: MIT Press.

Nakamura, J., & Csikszentmihalyi, M. (2009). Flow theory and research. In S. Lopez & C. R. Snyder (Eds.), *Oxford handbook of positive psychology* (2nd ed., pp. 195–206). New York, NY: Oxford University Press.

Nickerson, R. S. (1999). Enhancing creativity. In R. J. Sternberg (Ed.), *Handbook of creativity* (pp. 392–430). New York, NY: Cambridge University Press.

Peterson, C., & Seligman, M. (2004). *Character strengths and virtues: A handbook and classification*. New York, NY: Oxford University Press.

Peterson, S., & Luthans, F. (2006). The impact of financial and nonfinancial incentives on business unit outcomes over time. *Journal of Applied Psychology, 91,* 156–165.

Plomin, R., & Daniels, D. (1987). Why are children in the same family so different from one another? *Behavioral and Brain Sciences, 10,* 1–16.

Quinn, R. (2005). Flow in knowledge work: High performance experience in the design of national security technology. *Administrative Science Quarterly, 50,* 610–641.

Rego, A., Sousa, F., Marques, C., & Pina e Cunha, M. (2012). Authentic leadership promoting employees' psychological capital and creativity. *Journal of Business Research, 65,* 429–437.

Roche, M., Haar, J., & Luthans, F. (2014). The role of mindfulness and psychological capital on the well-being of organizational leaders. *Journal of Occupational Health Psychology, 19,* 476–489.

Seligman, M. E. P., Steen, T. A., Park, N., & Peterson, C. (2005). Positive psychology progress: Empirical validation of interventions. *American Psychologist, 60,* 410–421.

Simonton, D. (2004). Creativity [originality, ingenuity]. In C. Peterson & M. Seligman (Eds.), *Character strengths and virtues: A handbook and classification* (pp. 109–123). Oxford, UK: Oxford University Press.

Simonton, D. K. (2009). Creativity. In S. J. Lopez & C. R. Snyder (Eds.), *Oxford handbook of positive psychology* (2nd ed., pp. 261–269). New York, NY: Oxford University Press.

Sosik, J. J., Avolio, B. J., & Kahai, S. S. (1998). Inspiring group creativity: Comparing anonymous and identified electronic brainstorming. *Small Group Research, 29,* 3–31.

Sosik, J. J., Kahai, S. S., & Avolio, B. J. (1999). Leadership style, anonymity, and creativity in group decision support systems: The mediating role of optimal flow. *Journal of Creative Behavior, 33,* 227–257.

Stajkovic, A., & Luthans F. (2003) Behavioral management and task performance in organizations: Conceptual background, meta-analysis, and test of alternative models. *Personnel Psychology, 56,* 155–194.

Subkoviak, M., Enright, R., Wu, C., Gassin, E., Freedman, S., Olson, L., . . . Sarinopoulus, I. (1995). Measuring interpersonal forgiveness in late adolescence and middle adulthood. *Journal of Adolescence, 18,* 641–655.

Sutton, G. W., & Thomas, E. K. (2005). Restoring Christian leaders. *American Journal of Pastoral Counseling, 8,* 27–42.

Sweetman, D., Luthans, F., Avey, J. B., & Luthans, B. C. (2011). Relationship between positive psychological capital and creative performance. *Canadian Journal of Administrative Sciences, 28,* 4–13.

Torrance, E. (1988). The nature of creativity as manifest in its testing. In R. Sternberg (Ed.), *The nature of creativity* (pp. 43–75). New York, NY: Cambridge University Press.

Vogus, T. J. (2012). Mindful organizing: Establishing and extending the foundations of highly reliable performance. In K. S. Cameron & G. M. Spreitzer (Eds.), *Oxford handbook of positive organizational scholarship* (pp. 664–676). New York, NY: Oxford University Press.

Wade, N. G., Worthington, E. L., & Meyer, J. E. (2005). But do they work? A meta-analysis of group interventions to promote forgiveness. In E. L. Worthington (Ed.), *Handbook of forgiveness* (pp. 423–439). New York, NY: Routledge.

Watkins, P. C., Van Gelder, M., & Frias, A. (2009). Furthering the science of gratitude. In S. J. Lopez & C. R. Snyder (Eds.), *Oxford handbook of positive psychology* (2nd ed., pp. 437–445). New York, NY: Oxford University Press.

Watkins, P. C., Woodward, K., Stone, T., & Kolts, R. L. (2003). Gratitude and happiness: Development of a measure of gratitude, and relationships with subjective well-being. *Social Behavior and Personality, 31,* 431–451.

Weick, K. E., & Sutcliffe, K. M. (2006). Mindfulness and the quality of organizational attraction. *Organization Science, 17,* 409–421.

Wood, A., Maltby, J., Stewart, R., Linley, P., & Joseph, S. (2008). A social-cognitive model of trait and state levels of gratitude. *Emotion, 8,* 281–290.

Worthington, E. L., Berry, J. W., Shivy, V. A., & Brownstein. E. (2005). Forgiveness and positive psychology in business ethics and corporate social responsibility. In R. A. Giacalone, C. Jurkiewicz, & C. Dunn (Eds.), *Positive psychology in business ethics and corporate social responsibility* (pp. 265–284). Greenwich, CT: Information Age.

Worthington, E., Sandage, S., & Berry, J. (2000). Group interventions to promote forgiveness: What researchers and clinicians ought to know. In M. E. McCullough, K. I. Pargament, & C. E. Thoresen (Eds.), *Forgiveness: Theory, research and practice* (pp. 228–253). New York, NY: Guilford Press.

Yamhure Thompson, L., & Snyder, C. R. (2003). Measuring forgiveness. In S. Lopez & C. R. Snyder (Eds.), *Positive psychological assessment: A handbook of models and measures* (pp. 301–312). Washington, DC: American Psychological Association.

Youssef-Morgan, C. M., & Luthans, F. (2013). Psychological capital theory: Toward a positive holistic model. In A. B. Bakker (Ed.), *Advances in positive organizational psychology* (Vol. 1, pp.145–166). Bingley, UK: Emerald.

Zhang, Z., Zyphur, M., Narayanan, J., Chaturvedi, S., Avolio, B., Lichtenstein, P., & Larsson, G. (2009). The genetic basis of entrepreneurship: Effects of gender and parents. *Organizational Behavior and Human Decision Processes, 110,* 93–107.

Zhou, J., & Ren, R. (2012). Striving for creativity: Building positive contexts in the workplace. In K. S. Cameron & G. M. Spreitzer (Eds.), *Oxford handbook of positive organizational scholarship* (pp. 97–109). New York, NY: Oxford University Press.

8 POTENTIAL PSYCAP

EMOTIONAL INTELLIGENCE, SPIRITUALITY, AUTHENTICITY, AND COURAGE

Opening Video: Daniel Goleman Explains Emotional Intelligence

Video link: http://youtu.be/NeJ3FF1yFyc

About 20 years ago, the psychologist/journalist Daniel Goleman wrote *Emotional Intelligence.* This book became an instant best seller and popularized the work that social scientists such as Howard Gardner had been doing on multiple intelligences and Peter Salovey and John Mayer had been doing with theory and research on social and emotional intelligence. In this video, Goleman is interviewed after publishing his more recent follow-up book on *Working With Emotional Intelligence.*

Questions for reflection and/or discussion:

1. Goleman identifies five skill sets of emotionally intelligent people. Which of these do you think is most important in being an effective employee? Why?
2. Goleman says that unlike IQ, people have a variable profile of their EQ dimensions (i.e., high on some and low on others). Which characteristics of EQ do you feel you are high on, and where might you need improvement?
3. Goleman indicates there are three qualities that organizations are looking for when selecting people and determining who should be placed in leadership positions. What are these three qualities? Discuss the relative importance of each.

As indicated in the introductory comments of the previous chapter, although the positive psychological resources of hope, efficacy, resilience, and optimism best meet the criteria for PsyCap, they were not intended to be the only ones included. Although there are numerous positive resources, we have selected (in no particular order) for further detailed examination those that seem most relevant and have the highest potential for meeting in the near future the PsyCap inclusion criteria (i.e., theory/research based; valid measurement; state-like and open to development; and impact on desired work attitudes, behaviors, and performance). The previous chapter summarized and assessed creativity, flow, mindfulness, gratitude, and forgiveness, and this chapter does the same for emotional intelligence, spirituality, authenticity, and courage. Similar to Table 7.1, we use Table 8.1 to summarize the "fit" of these four positive resources.

Emotional Intelligence as Potential PsyCap

Based on the theory building in social and educational psychology, emotional intelligence (EI) can be defined as the ability to accurately perceive, express, understand, use, and manage emotions in oneself and others (Mayer & Salovey, 1997; Mayer, Salovey, & Caruso, 2000; Salovey, Mayer, Caruso, & Yoo, 2009). In addition to this "ability-based" definition, mixed-model definitions of EI define it as "an array of noncognitive capabilities, competencies, and skills that influence one's ability to succeed in coping with environmental demands and pressures" (Bar-On, 1997, p. 14). Mixed EI models may include intelligence, personality traits, and affect.

One of the most significant developments that triggered the academic attention given to EI was Howard Gardner's (1983) original work on multiple intelligences. He expanded the definition of intelligence beyond cognitive mental abilities (i.e., logical/mathematical and linguistic/verbal dimensions measured in traditional IQ) to include multiple and diverse domains. Gardner's recognized multiple intelligences included not only musical, spatial/visual, bodily/kinesthetic, and intrapersonal domains but also social or interpersonal intelligence.

Initially, Gardner did not specifically include the term "emotional intelligence," and Salovey and Mayer (1990) are usually given credit for the first academic work on EI. However, it was Daniel Goleman's best-selling books (1995, 1998; Goleman, Boyatzis, & McKee, 2002) that catapulted EI into its current highly popular position among management practitioners and consultants. Goleman (1998) identifies the most important dimensions of emotionally intelligent individuals as self-awareness, self-management, self-motivation, empathy, and social skills.

Table 8.1 Assessment of "Fit" With PsyCap for Various High-Potential Positive Constructs

Positive Construct	Theory-Based?	State-Like/ Malleable?	Measurable?	Related to Work Performance?	Related to Other Work Outcomes?	Agentic	Positive Appraisals
Emotional intelligence	?	?	?	?	?	?	x
Spirituality	✓	✓	?	?	✓	?	?
Authenticity	✓	✓	✓	✓	✓	✓	✓
Courage	✓	✓	✓	?	?	✓	✓

Does Emotional Intelligence Measure Up to the PsyCap Criteria?

Of all the resources of PsyCap (both the major four and all the potential ones), emotional intelligence or simply EI (or sometimes called "EQ" as a takeoff from IQ) has undoubtedly received the most attention in the practice of management. EI has almost become conventional wisdom with relatively few tests of validation. By the same token, EI has also received criticism in the academic field of organizational behavior (e.g., see Locke, 2005). Unlike the still largely emerging potential PsyCap capacities presented in the previous chapter and this chapter, applications of EI to the workplace have a considerable presence in the management and organizational behavior literature. For example, Luthans (2002b) initially included EI as part of positive organizational behavior and positive leadership (Luthans, Luthans, Hodgetts, & Luthans, 2001), but he soon dropped it (e.g., see Luthans, 2002a; Luthans, Luthans, & Luthans, 2004; Luthans & Youssef, 2004) because at the time it did not measure up well enough to the PsyCap criteria (especially theoretical foundation, basic research, and valid measurement). Now, over a decade later, although there are certainly remaining problems associated with EI (e.g., see Locke, 2005), we are willing to recognize the progress that has been made in theory building, research, and measurement to reconsider EI as at least a potential contributing factor to PsyCap (e.g., see Ashkanasy & Daus, 2005; Cherniss, 2010; Mayer, Salovey, Caruso, & Cherkasskiy, 2011; O'Boyle, Humphrey, Pollack, Hawver, & Story, 2011; Ybarra, Rees, Kross, & Sanchez-Burks, 2012).

In terms of demonstrated impact in the workplace, Kelley and Caplan (1993) reported early on that star performers at Bell Labs could be predicted by EI better than by cognitive mental abilities. Also, failure of derailed executives studied by the Center for Creative Leadership was also said to be related to deficiencies in their EI, rather than lack of technical capabilities (Gibbs, 1995). In addition, Goleman and colleagues (2002) have attributed applications of EI to effective organizational leadership and work teams. He reports that across organizational sizes, managerial levels, and even national cultures, elements of EI account for about two thirds of the competencies sought by organizations as critical to high performance. The contribution of EI to performance became even more substantial (as high as six out of seven competencies) at higher level professional and managerial positions (Goleman, 1998). However, these early findings from the practitioner-oriented literature were generally extrapolated and provided a rather shaky basis for including EI in PsyCap.

However, more recently, Mayer and Salovey (2004) do provide empirical evidence that relates EI to desirable work outcomes such as superior customer service, as well as less direct outcomes such as effective social functioning, coping styles, and adaptation techniques, and lower incidences of drug and alcohol abuse. Empirical studies show either modest or insignificant relationships between EI and individual and group performance and organizational citizenship behaviors (Day & Carroll, 2004). Meta-analytical findings based on a number of studies support a correlation between EI and performance in the range of .24 to .3 (O'Boyle et al., 2011). However, these meta-analytical findings are also based on prior research, which carries over some of the inherent conceptual and methodological weaknesses of early EI research, which we identified earlier.

Besides business contexts, there have also been a number of noteworthy applications of EI development introduced in education, parenting, politics, and others (e.g., see Salovey, Caruso, & Mayer, 2004; Salovey et al., 2009). However, some empirical findings show the predictive validity of EI in relation to success, satisfaction, well-being, and various "life skills" to be much more limited than originally thought, especially after accounting for personality and cognitive abilities (Bastian, Burns, & Nettelbeck, 2005).

A number of measures also now exist for emotional intelligence, and the most established and supported are Bar-On's (1997) Emotional Quotient Inventory (EQ-i) and the Mayer-Salovey-Caruso Emotional Intelligence Test (MSCEIT) Version 2.0 (Mayer, Salovey, & Caruso, 2001). As discussed earlier, Bar-On primarily defines emotional intelligence in terms of intelligence, affect, and adaptive personality traits, while Mayer, Salovey, and Caruso support the developmental nature of EI as a set of learnable abilities or states (Salovey, Mayer, Caruso, & Lopes, 2003). However, investigations of the convergent, discriminant, and incremental validity of various EI measures show weak convergence (Brackett & Mayer, 2003; Livingstone & Day, 2005), which is indicative of the limited consensus on what EI actually means and how it should be measured. Thus, despite these advances, a more comprehensive theoretical framework, further empirical research, and more valid measurement remain as challenges before EI can be fully integrated into PsyCap.

With respect to PsyCap's agentic perspective, at least the ability-based EI model is somewhat consistent with EI being agentic and intentional (e.g., emotional regulation) (see George, 2000). On the other hand, more recently, Ybarra, Rees, Kross, and Sanchez-Burks (2012) challenged the notion that EI is subject to the control of the individual, because it assumes that emotions are readily recognizable or "readable." It also assumes that emotional recognition and control are deliberate processes, which is not always the case. In many situations, emotional processes have been found to be intuitive, which makes them more consistent with "pure states" than with PsyCap's relatively stable and controllable "state-like" nature. Finally, EI is inconsistent with PsyCap's positive appraisal mechanism. Although EI draws from perceptual and appraisal processes, the emphasis with EI is on the accuracy, rather than the positivity, of the perception, understanding, and use of one's emotions to make sense of things.

We refer those interested in furthering the science of EI to Mayer, Salovey, and Caruso's (2008) review and recommendations, as well as Joseph and Newman's (2010) integrative theoretical framework and meta-analysis. Both references also highlight the weaknesses of mixed EI models as the primary cause of lack of rigor in EI research, and they advise researchers to focus on ability-based models. This type of work bolsters the potential for including EI once it is even better defined, measured, and validated.

Spirituality as Potential PsyCap

The tradition of separation between church and state in the United States, as well as other cultural values such as freedom of religious choice, have led to very little, if any, attention given to topics such as spirituality or religiousness in research or even discussions in organizational behavior and human resources management. However, positive psychology and positive organizational scholarship recognize the role of spirituality (e.g., see Pargament & Mahoney, 2009; Peterson & Seligman, 2004; Sandelands, 2012) and the Academy of Management now has a division on Management, Spirituality, and Religion. There are also dedicated journals (e.g., APA's *Psychology of Religion and Spirituality* is currently on its sixth volume), journal special issues (e.g., *Leadership Quarterly*, October 2005 issue), and a *Handbook of Workplace Spirituality and Organizational Performance* (Giacalone & Jurkiewicz, 2010). In light of these developments, and our own quest for unique positive psychological resources that can potentially contribute to the future of evolving PsyCap, we include at least this beginning discussion of what is meant by spirituality as it applies to the workplace and how it may measure up to the criteria of PsyCap.

More than the other potential positive resources for PsyCap, there is considerable diversity in the conceptualization and research on spirituality and religiousness. For instance, some theorists and researchers treat spirituality and religiousness interchangeably, or at least as conceptually similar, and use the same instruments to measure both constructs. On the other hand, there is empirical research that supports spirituality and religiousness as different constructs, which, although somewhat related, diverge on some of their most salient characteristics (e.g., see Zinnbauer et al., 1997). Yet there has also been concern that the differences between spirituality and religiousness have been overemphasized. Polarizing them as opposite constructs has been critiqued as an inaccurate perspective (Zinnbauer, Pargament, & Scott, 1999).

Hill and colleagues (2000, p. 66) provide a comprehensive definition of spirituality as "the feelings, thoughts, experiences, and behaviors that arise from the search for the sacred. The term 'search' refers to attempts to identify, articulate, maintain, or transform. The term 'sacred' refers to a divine being, divine object, Ultimate Reality, or Divine Truth as perceived by the individual." They then go on to describe the characteristics of religiousness and how to distinguish it from spirituality.

To define religiousness, they add two further dimensions to their definition of spirituality. The first dimension contributing to religiousness is membership into, identification with, and validation and support from a group of people that provides the means and methods for the search for the sacred (e.g., organized religions). This search takes the form of specific rituals, practices, and/or behavioral expectations. The second distinguishing characteristic of religiousness is the potential for nonsacred goals to also be sought in the process. Examples of nonsacred goals include belonging, identity, and others to satisfy extrinsic motives. In other words, religiousness incorporates spirituality, as well as membership and conformance with both intrinsic sacred and extrinsic nonsacred factors (Hill et al., 2000).

More specific to the workplace, Ashmos and Duchon (2000) define workplace spirituality in terms of recognition that (a) employees have an inner (spiritual) life, (b) this inner life nourishes and is nourished by meaningful work, and (c) this process takes place in the context of community. They believe that although employees may express their religious beliefs at work, workplace spirituality integrates both sacred and secular dimensions. Although Milliman, Czaplewski, and Ferguson (2003) drew from Ashmos and Duchon's (2000) conceptualization and measurement of workplace spirituality, they modified it to include only the secular dimensions of meaningful work, sense of community, and alignment with organizational values, to the exclusion of any references to sacred dimensions. Sandelands (2012) takes an opposite extreme, arguing that only transcendent types of spirituality (those based on the idea of a divine, supreme power) can produce a true humanism that is adequate for building a positive business paradigm.

For our purposes of potential PsyCap, we integrate these views on spirituality to include a search for the sacred, as well as a sense of community, meaning and sense making, calling, and intrinsic and extrinsic motivation. Such dimensions seem most relevant to the role spirituality may play in PsyCap. Those with spiritual PsyCap may perceive their jobs as a calling, rather than just the traditional transactional employment contract (Wrzesniewski, 2012). They may still be extrinsically motivated, but more important to them may be their intrinsic motivation to meet or exceed expectations. Put in other terms, those with spiritual PsyCap may exhibit organizational citizenship behaviors that are above and beyond the call of duty, even when they are not directly recognized by the organization's extrinsic reward system (see Organ, 1988, for a discussion of such organizational citizenship).

This view of spirituality relevant to PsyCap is also similar to the effects of transformational over transactional leadership articulated by Bass (1985). Specifically, transformational leaders connect followers through their identification with a higher cause to something more significant and meaningful than a simple transactional exchange. In other words, leaders with spiritual PsyCap may raise their followers' level of identification with the work to be accomplished and in turn their motivation and commitment.

Does Spirituality Measure Up to the PsyCap Criteria?

Spirituality is recently finding its way into the organizational behavior and leadership fields. For example, integral to Fry's (2003, 2005; Fry & Nisiewicz, 2013) spiritual leadership model is membership within an empowered team where one can be understood and appreciated. Moreover, a sense of calling gives meaning and value to spiritual leadership, causing the leader and followers to be intrinsically motivated to make a difference through ethical and socially responsible values, attitudes, and behaviors.

Recently, organizational behavior and leadership scholars who focus on spirituality also make the connection with work-related outcomes. In fact, Dent, Higgins, and Wharff (2005) reviewed 87 scholarly articles written on spirituality and found that most hypothesized relationships between spirituality and organizational performance. Similarly, Reave (2005) reports from her qualitative review of the leadership literature that aspects of spirituality associated with integrity, honesty, and humility have also been found to be related to leadership success on numerous occasions.

Duchon and Plowman (2005) reported a positive relationship between work unit spirituality in hospitals and unit performance, such as patient satisfaction. They speculate that by providing meaning in work connected to the spiritual being of followers, the followers' motivation to perform will be higher than the simple transaction of pay for performance—in other words, they are more intrinsically motivated to perform (Duchon & Plowman, 2005). Similarly, many theories of leadership include constructs such as beliefs and faith, which are part of the models of spirituality being applied to the workplace. Milliman and colleagues (2003) also found workplace spirituality to be significantly related to five work attitudes: organizational commitment, intention to quit, intrinsic work satisfaction, job involvement, and organization-based self-esteem.

Beyond work outcomes, one of the most significantly supported contributions of spirituality is in relation to effective coping with hardships (Pargament, 1997). Other positive outcomes associated with spirituality include enhanced relationships, prosocial (e.g., organizational citizenship) behaviors, physical and psychological well-being, and avoidance of antisocial behaviors such as drug abuse and aggression (see Mattis, 2004, for a comprehensive review). Meta-analytical findings also support a positive relationship between spirituality and quality of life (Sawatzky, Ratner, & Chiu, 2005). In psychotherapy, patients in religious and spiritual treatments showed more improvement than those in secular treatments (Worthington, Hook, Davis, & McDaniel, 2011).

On the other hand, it should also be noted that dimensions of spirituality may deliberately lead to conformance and extrinsic motivation toward nonsacred goals (e.g., Hill et al., 2000). This provides support to negative reactions to organized religions. Moreover, conformance has been associated with dysfunctional group dynamics such as groupthink (Janis, 1982) and rigidity (Barker, 1993), and extrinsic motivation has been debated as a possible diminishing factor for intrinsic motivation (Wiersma, 1992). In other words, spirituality has been associated with both positive and negative outcomes. For example, if spirituality includes extrinsic motivation to nonsacred goals, then this has led to negative reactions such as charges of hypocrisy. To counter such negativity and support the relevance to positive PsyCap, spirituality scholars such as positive psychologist Kenneth Pargament (2002) point out the need to understand and clarify the perceived nature of "the sacred" being searched for, the search process itself, and the underlying motives (i.e., extrinsic vs. intrinsic).

Positive psychology suggests that spirituality in general, and religiousness in particular, is based on some enduring traits acquired through heredity and socialization (e.g., see Mattis, 2004). Yet it is also recognized that the lack of longitudinal and life-span research precludes any conclusive findings. Recent empirical findings also support the state-like nature of spirituality (Davis, Worthington, Hook, & Hill, 2013), which is more consistent with PsyCap.

Fry (2005) provides a multilevel model of the spiritual leadership development process. Specifically, he proposes spirituality can be enhanced through vision, strategies, systems, and goals at the organizational level; empowerment, communication, and power sharing at the team level; and values such as trust, forgiveness, integrity, honesty, courage, and excellence at the individual level. In addition, research on perceptions of sanctification (Mahoney et al., 2005) and desecration (Pargament, Magyar, Benore, & Mahoney, 2005), as well as spiritual conversion (Mahoney & Pargament, 2004) and purification and reframing (Pargament & Mahoney, 2009), supports that spirituality and religiousness may be developmental states. As challenging moments that represent crossroads in one's life are encountered, important perceptions, attributions, and attitudes about life may be altered, as well as one's view of his or her spiritual self (Avolio & Luthans, 2006). Such moments may enhance or diminish the dimensions of spirituality and religiousness.

In line with spirituality and religiousness being both dispositional traits and developmental states, Tsang and McCullough (2003) provide a hierarchical model for conceptualizing and measuring these constructs. They utilize measures that assess operational-level, practical, day-to-day spirituality, while controlling for any potential individual differences. Self-report, single-item measures of religiousness (e.g., how often do you pray/ meditate/ attend religious services?) may be effective in measuring dispositions toward spirituality. However, more elaborate and diversified measures and approaches are necessary to assess the various dimensions of spirituality as a state, such as preliminary ones emerging in the organizational literature (Ashmos & Duchon, 2000; Fry, Vitucci, & Cedello, 2005).

Although there are a number of existing measures of spirituality, they have been found to have limitations. For example, Tsang and McCullough (2003) suggest that researchers should stop developing new spirituality and religiousness instruments until the current scales are revised and integrated to reflect at least four components: disposition (trait), motivation (intrinsic/sacred vs. extrinsic/ nonsacred), coping style (process), and practices (e.g., meditation). Similarly Fry and colleagues' (2005) spiritual leadership and Ashmos and Duchon's (2000) workplace spirituality measures mix behavioral and attribution items, as well as levels of analysis in the same scales, leaving open to question what exactly is being measured with such survey instruments.

Finally, the applicability of PsyCap's agentic and positive appraisal mechanisms largely depends on the form of one's spirituality. While spirituality may induce a sense of control in otherwise uncontrollable situations, there are also problems with adopting "small gods," "false gods," or spiritual pathways that lack breadth and depth. For example, excessive reliance on external or supernatural powers can lead to fatalism and abdicating responsibility. Similarly, spirituality can produce a positive outlook and favorable appraisals of the past, present, and future when one believes in a benevolent, loving, and merciful God. On the other hand, an exclusively positive view of God can be difficult to reconcile with the realities of pain and suffering, which can lead to resentment and cynicism. On the opposite extreme, excessively harsh or punitive beliefs about God can lead to distress (Pargament & Mahoney, 2009). Thus, a balanced perspective seems necessary for a healthy and effective form of spirituality applied to the workplace.

Authenticity as Potential PsyCap

Since the dawning of civilization, authenticity has been of interest to philosophers, politicians, theologians, and now recently positive psychologists (e.g., see Harter, 2002; Seligman, 2002). Being true to one's self is considered in this literature to be the essence of genuine, authentic behavior. Authenticity is viewed as both a terminal value and as instrumental to many other desirable outcomes such as morality, peace, happiness, and contentment. In the destructive aftermath of the recent wave of corporate ethical scandals and downsizing, where society in general and employees in particular have questioned the morality of and have lost trust in their organizational leaders, organizational behavior and leadership scholars and practitioners alike have taken increased interest in authenticity as it applies to both leadership and human resource development (Avolio & Luthans, 2006; Avolio, Gardner, Walumbwa, Luthans, & May, 2004; Cashman, 1998; Gardner, Avolio, Luthans, May, & Walumbwa, 2005; George, 2003).

Sartre (1966) defined authenticity as representing the absence of self-deception, or being true to who you are as an individual. Brumbaugh (1971) defined the authentic individual as someone who displays an ability to make hard choices, as well as being accountable for mistakes made. Authentic individuals recognize their drawbacks, while also continuously striving to achieve their full potential. Kernis (2003) defined authenticity as the "unobstructed operation of one's true, or core, self in one's daily enterprise" (p. 1).

In positive psychology, Harter (2002) defines authenticity as "owning one's own personal experiences, be they thoughts, emotions, needs, wants, preferences, or beliefs . . . that one acts in accord with the true self, expressing oneself in ways that are consistent with inner thoughts and feelings" (p. 232). Others also define authenticity in terms of one's ownership, acceptance, responsibility, and accurate public and private representation of internal states, commitments, feelings, intentions, and behaviors (Sheldon, Davidson, & Pollard, 2004).

Luthans and Avolio (2003) extended the discussions on the authentic individual by building specifically on Harter's definition in their accounts of what constitutes authentic leadership, stating that it is "a process that draws from both positive psychological capacities and a highly developed organizational context, which results in both greater self-awareness and self-regulated positive behaviors on the part of leaders and associates, fostering positive self-development" (p. 243). With this definition, Luthans and Avolio (2003) were clearly going beyond the individual, in that leadership involves others and relationships that are embedded in some context, which these authors recognized as being important to defining authentic leadership as a process.

Substantial conceptual work has been published on what Avolio and colleagues call authentic leadership development (for example, see the June 2005 special issue of *Leadership Quarterly*). Avolio and Luthans (2006) define authentic leadership development, or what they simply call ALD, as "The process that draws upon a leader's life course, psychological capital, moral perspective, and a highly developed supporting organizational climate to produce greater self-awareness and self-regulated positive behaviors, which in turn foster continuous, positive self-development resulting in veritable, sustained performance" (p. 2). Various stages of research on ALD are currently under way ranging from further construct validation with the Authentic Leadership Questionnaire (ALQ), which can be located at http://www.mindgarden.com, or by focusing on leadership development in terms of helping to understand what constitutes real or authentic leadership and its development (e.g., see Avolio, 2010; Gardner, Cogliser, Davis, & Dickens, 2011).

In terms of the authentic leader, Narayana Murthy represents perhaps the prototype of authentic leadership. However, many Americans likely have never heard his name. Yet, if you think about "outsourcing IT to India," Murthy was a leading pioneer in this effort when starting a company called Infosys. There are many examples of this iconic leader's actions and decisions throughout his long career at Infosys that constitute authentic leadership. For example, he and his six cofounders refused to take or give bribes to acquire the technology needed to run their business, which was not standard business practice in India at the time (Barney, 2010). They waited over a year to get their phone, and later a computer was held up because of Murthy's unwillingness to pay the bribe to have it released from customs. Murthy nearly bankrupted his fledging start-up based upon his unwillingness to compromise his ethical and moral standards.

Murthy said in an interview with one of the authors of this book that he wanted to create a company of such high ethical standards that it would be a benchmark for other Indian firms and their leaders to aspire to and emulate. Many of his admirers, including Bill Gates and Warren Buffett, would say that Mr. Murthy has achieved his aspirations of authentic leadership with Infosys, which he founded.

Although PsyCap is already depicted as an important input and outcome of authentic leadership (Avolio & Luthans, 2006; Luthans & Avolio, 2003; Luthans, Norman, & Hughes, 2006) and as a moderator between authentic leadership and performance (Wang, Sui, Luthans, Wang, & Wu, 2014), as a potential PsyCap capacity per se, authenticity is not limited to just the role it may play in leadership. For example, research on self-determination has shown that when leaders facilitate autonomy, provide noncontrolling positive feedback, and acknowledge others' perspectives, this can be conducive to their followers' displays of authenticity (Sheldon et al., 2004). Building authentic followers can result in perceptions of affect toward, and satisfaction with, their work teams and the organization. Such authenticity may manifest itself in terms of increased trust, quality of supervision and the organizational environment, good feelings, and satisfaction with job characteristics (Deci, Connell, & Ryan, 1989). Authenticity has also been found to be associated with self-esteem, positive affect, and hope (Harter, 2002), as well as sustained efforts and an upward spiral of goal attainment (Sheldon et al., 2004).

In addition to the cognitive perspective on authenticity provided by, for example, self-determination theory (Deci et al., 1989), there has been some focus on examining the negative consequences of affective inauthenticity in the context of business ethics and specific areas such as emotional labor (Hochschild, 1979, 1983; Martin, Knopoff, & Beckman, 1998; Morris & Feldman, 1996; Sutton, 1991). At the group or organizational level, authenticity may also enhance trust, which in turn can increase communication, creativity, innovation, and initiative, and ultimately employee performance, commitment, and retention (Colquitt & Salam, 2009). In other words, authenticity has been shown to be associated with positive psychological functioning and desirable performance and attitudinal work outcomes. By the same token, inauthenticity has also been associated with negative outcomes such as unethical behaviors and stress from emotional labor. In other words, authenticity may have convergent and discriminant validity with other PsyCap constructs.

Looking Back to Move Forward on Authentic Leadership

Recent work on applying authenticity to leadership builds on three decades of work examining other positive forms of leadership, such as transformational leadership (Avolio, 2011; Avolio & Walumbwa, 2014; Gardner et al., 2011). This work was motivated by the fact that many leaders may appear to be transformational, in that they behave like such leaders who inspire, intellectually stimulate, show concern for the needs of others, and set ideals for others to aspire to in their leadership. Yet, when the curtain is pulled back and these leaders are exposed, it appears that they are actually pseudo-transformational but quite adept at presenting an image of transformational leadership. This concern was raised as far back as 1988 (Avolio & Gibbons, 1988) in discussions of whether charismatic transformational leaders were also authentic.

Nearly a decade later, the question of whether transformational leadership was genuine or not was raised by Bass and Steidlmeier (1999) in an article where they purposely described genuinely transformational leaders as "authentic" versus those who were labeled "pseudo-transformational" leaders.

Pseudo-transformational leaders behaved like transformational leaders; however, the ethical and moral foundation was absent. According to Burns (1978), who launched the current body of work on transforming leadership, such leadership was defined as morally uplifting, and if absent, they could not be considered transformational.

Additional motivation for introducing authenticity to the leadership literature came from several sources. Several polls of America's leadership conducted by the Kennedy School at Harvard University over the last 10 years have shown declines in the levels of trust US citizens have in their leaders. For example, in 2007, 77% of those polled expressed that there was a crisis of confidence regarding American leaders (Rosenthal, Pittinsky, Purvin, & Montoya, 2007). Some of the lowest trust and confidence ratings were associated with business and government leaders.

Then, before his untimely passing, Ghoshal (2005) summarized the state of business education indicating, "by propagating amoral theories business schools have actively freed their students from any sense of moral responsibility" (p. 76). This damning view of how business schools develop leaders was reinforced by a group of Harvard MBA students and faculty who decided to take an oath committing to being ethical stewards after graduation.

At the same time, in the popular leadership literature, Bill George, former CEO of Medtronic (George, 2003; George & Sims, 2007), was calling for more genuine leadership, which he termed "authentic," defined in very similar ways to the four constructs included in authentic leadership theory. Since his retirement from Medtronic, George came on board at Harvard University's Business School, to develop a course and eventually a program that promoted and developed authentic leadership among Harvard's business students and, of course, future leaders.

In their review of the authenticity literature, Gardner et al. (2011) referenced Henderson and Hoy (1983) as the starting point for the "modern age" of focusing on leader authenticity and described its three components, including (1) one's acceptance of responsibility for one's decisions, actions, mistakes, and performance; (2) the nonmanipulation of others; and (3) the self-confidence or efficacy to take a stand for knowing and doing what is right.

The work of Henderson and Hoy (1983) and later Kernis and Goldman (2006) overlapped, but it did not include all of the four components that are now part of authentic leadership theory and how it is measured (see Walumbwa, Avolio, Gardner, Wernsing, & Peterson, 2008, as well as Chapter 10 for additional discussion of authentic leadership theory). This more recent work has gone beyond the now "traditional" emphasis that Henderson and Hoy and other authors have placed on understanding the "self" or "self-concept/identity" as being at the core of authenticity to include a broader assessment of authentic leadership in terms of the positive constructs that are associated with it as well as a much deeper understanding of how each of the four components of authentic leadership contribute to leaders being viewed as authentic.

Does Authenticity Measure Up to the PsyCap Criteria?

There are multiple measures for assessing authenticity. However, due to the nature of the construct, "faking good" (i.e., social desirability effects) is a potential threat to validity, particularly with existing self-report instruments. Thus, multisource input becomes desirable in measuring authenticity. For example, Henderson and Hoy's (1983) measure is an observation-based instrument that allows followers to assess their leader's authenticity. As noted earlier, Avolio and colleagues have developed and validated the most widely recognized measure of authentic leadership comprised of self-awareness, relational transparency, internalized moral perspective, and balanced processing (Gardner et al., 2011; Walumbwa et al., 2008; Wang et al., 2014).

As with the other potential PsyCap constructs, there could be several pitfalls associated with conceptualizing and measuring authenticity, as well as with its potential outcomes. For example, in the pursuit of extreme authenticity and honesty, some people may lack the social tact of exhibiting empathy while telling the truth. This may cause others to be hurt, get discouraged, feel resentful, or perceptually distort the authentic person's input and feedback. Moreover, as people fill multiple, sometimes conflicting roles, they may adopt several, mutually exclusive selves in various contexts, causing estrangement of one's true self (Harter, 2002).

Each of these pitfalls of authenticity implicitly assumes that people possess one, static true self. We believe that this is not the case. We take the position that people possess multiple selves, some actual, and some possible as noted in the cognitive psychology and leadership literature (Avolio & Luthans, 2006; Lord & Brown, 2004). In order to enhance their authenticity, people do not just need to "discover" a true, actual self that is hidden somewhere. They need to employ their self-awareness, self-regulation, and self-development energies in order to realistically understand the strengths and limitations of their actual selves. They then need to explore and attempt to balance these actual selves with their possible selves, so that they can actualize their full potential (Avolio & Luthans, 2006; Gardner et al., 2005; Luthans & Avolio, 2003).

As one gradually strives toward a desirable, challenging, but attainable possible self (or set of possible selves), the actual self tends to adapt, grow, and develop. Hence, over time, the possible self becomes actualized into one's true self. Authenticity has been developed (Avolio, 2010; Avolio & Luthans, 2006).

This perspective on being able to develop authenticity is particularly relevant to today's challenging work environment. Similar to our discussions on developing the other PsyCap capacities, we offer a developmental perspective that allows organizational members to internally gain control over, and to more authentically act upon, their true, possible selves, rather than becoming complacent and satisfied with a suboptimal, actual self that has been imposed upon them through socialization or cultural barriers (Avolio & Luthans, 2006).

It is also important to note the significant role that others play in authenticity development. Parents, spouses, friends, leaders, mentors, peers, and associates (i.e., significant others) can all contribute to or hinder one's authenticity. Reinforcement of self-expression, support for autonomy and creativity, acceptance of one's own and others' strengths and limitations, and tolerance to unorthodox, out-of-the-box thinking can all contribute to an environment where authenticity can be enhanced, both through internal comprehension and external expression of one's actual, true self (see Harter, 2002). However, others can also contribute to the process of visualizing and shaping one's possible selves through challenging counterproductive or complacent self-views, pushing us outside our comfort zones, and acting as role models with similar applicable life experiences that can guide the authenticity development process (Avolio & Luthans, 2006).

In total, authenticity development is a dynamic process. It involves multiple selves that are discovered, explored, and tested, with multiple social contexts and diversified interpersonal relationships. Authenticity may result in a wide range of capacities (leader, follower, peer, spouse, friend, parent, and so on), all acting as catalysts for changes and effective outcomes.

Authenticity would meet the agentic criteria for PsyCap in that such leaders have to demonstrate that they can suspend judgment as part of the balanced processing component, whereby they can hold opposing points of view that may be in conflict, until they reach a fair decision or conclusion. This type of processing oftentimes occurs when there are competing interests being presented, which would require greater agency on the authentic leader's part to make what is oftentimes a difficult choice or decision.

Authentic leaders also demonstrate transparency even when doing so may put them in a more vulnerable position. We would expect that such displays of transparency would be associated with authentic leaders being viewed by their followers as having a higher level of behavioral integrity, where these leaders are described as being consistent over time in how they share relevant information, even when doing so may compromise their position. This would likely contribute to their followers having greater agency to be transparent with each other and their leader, because they would likely feel safer doing so (Lapidot, Kark, & Shamir, 2007).

In a similar way, we would expect the same to be true for the moral ethical component of authentic leadership. Being able to take an ethical or moral stand on a controversial issue requires a high degree of agency on the part of the leader. Leaders who are seen as authentic exhibit a higher moral perspective and work to create climates and cultures that reflect those perspectives (Hannah, Lester, & Vogelgesang, 2005). Leaders who transmit authentic behaviors would signal to their followers that they should stand up and act in line with their moral values. This occurs where an authentic leader makes clear what is expected of followers in terms of operating at a higher level of moral and ethical conduct (Hannah, Avolio, & Walumbwa, 2011).

In regard to positive appraisals, a core component of authentic leadership involves being a self-aware leader. Authentic leaders demonstrate a high degree of awareness of how others view their leadership, and they understand the limitations of what they can and cannot do, allowing followers room to demonstrate their strengths and capabilities. Through such understanding, authentic leaders are more comfortable with how they transmit leadership, and they would be expected to exhibit higher levels of well-being and positivity as a consequence of such awareness (Ilies, Morgeson, & Nahrgang, 2005). Because they are comfortable "owning" their own personal experiences, including their thoughts, emotions, and desires (Harter, 2002), one would expect them to have a higher positive appraisal of themselves.

As Table 8.1 shows, although mostly associated with leadership so far, such authenticity may have considerable potential for meeting the criteria and contributing to PsyCap development and impact.

Courage as Potential PsyCap

Courage is receiving increasing attention in positive psychology (e.g., see Pury & Lopez, 2009, 2010). Peterson and Seligman (2004) define courage as "emotional strengths that involve the exercise of will to accomplish goals in the faces of opposition, external or internal" (p. 29). Contrary to widely held views, courage should not be equated with fearlessness. In fact, Evans and White (1981) define courage in terms of fear, perceived and objective risk levels. Thus, courage involves fear, as well as a balanced appraisal of the risk and vulnerability levels involved in a particular situation.

Although perceived or actual risk is usually considered a prerequisite for the manifestation of courage, prudent assessment of potential risks and acceptance of the possibility of undesirable consequences also represent integral components of courage (Worline & Steen, 2004). Courage is also not just a virtue that presents itself in extraordinary situations characterized by extremely high risks. It can be exhibited in both ordinary and extraordinary occasions (Lopez, O'Byrne, & Peterson, 2003). The objective of courageous action should also be purposeful, meaningful, and useful, rather than irresponsible (Woodward, 2004), habitual, or devastating to others (Rorty, 1988). Pury, Kowalski, and Spearman (2007) also distinguish general from personal courage, and argue that courage can take on different meanings across individuals and situations.

Does Courage Measure Up to the PsyCap Criteria?

To date, there are limited workplace applications of courage, most of which are rich qualitative accounts of the nature of courage and its expression in the workplace (e.g., see Worline, 2012). For example, Koerner (2014) recently identified three dimensions of courage: (a) a morally worthy goal; (b) a risk, threat, or obstacle; and (c) intentional action. Courage is viewed as the means to minimize the tension that results from incongruities between self and social identities in four distinct situational dimensions: endurance, reaction, opposition, and creation, although opposition is the most commonly recognized antecedent to courageous action. Courageous actions then reconcile identity tensions, leading to a sense of integrity, pride, joy, relief, and confidence. On the other hand, inaction hinders identity reconciliation, leading to shame, regret, and frustration.

Worline's (2010) analysis of over 650 accounts of courage in high-technology organizations also portrays the same individual-collective tension and offers courage as a protective response to threats to collective welfare. Similarly, Quinn and Worline (2008) used the exchanges among the passengers of United Airlines Flight 93, which was hijacked on September 11, 2001, but later crashed into the ground, to show how courageous collective action emerged from personal narratives. They also offered applications to more common social movements and organizations in general.

Despite its intuitive and emotional appeal, courage may not always be welcomed in the workplace. Various constraints may exist in an organizational culture that hinder courageous action or render courageous individuals in a negative light as rule breakers, troublemakers, or norm violators. For example, Worline and Quinn (2003) show that organizational form (market, bureaucracy, clan, or organized anarchy) may enable some values and activities, while constraining others. Courageous, principled action occurs when individuals capitalize upon on their cognitive, affective, and social resources in order to challenge the status quo in support of constrained values that may be in the organization's best interest to explore. For example, the dominant values of organizations in market economies emphasize ambition, competition, efficiency, and initiative. Courage may become necessary in order to promote values that might receive less weight in these organizations, such as loyalty, trust, honesty, integrity, teamwork, and social responsibility (Worline & Quinn, 2003). On the other hand, bureaucracies tend to value accountability, discipline, obedience, and predictability. However, these values may not serve the organization very well in times of turmoil and revolutionary change. Innovators and change agents in such an organizational climate need courage to effectively communicate their ideas and perspectives (Worline & Quinn, 2003).

Whistle-blowing is one of the most frequently cited examples of courageous action in today's organizations. Although controversial, most would agree that whistle-blowing tends to be in the best interest of the organization, at least in the long run. Whistle-blowing can protect the organization's reputation and save considerable financial resources that could otherwise be wasted in litigation costs and damaged reputations/public relations fallout. However, whistle-blowers take substantial risks as they might challenge some of their organizations' established rules and regulations, as well as negatively affect at least short-term profitability and competitiveness. From a personal perspective, risks associated with whistle-blowing may include loss of one's job, retaliation, loss of trust, or social disapproval. Whistle-blowers likely appraise the returns on their risky actions, in terms of justice, greater good, and possibly personal and psychological gains, in order to feel adequate and worthwhile (Miceli & Near, 2005).

In line with these definitions and relevant examples, although courage is viewed as a virtue in positive psychology (Peterson & Seligman, 2004) and thus a highly desirable terminal value, at least in the organizational domain, it may still render both positive and negative outcomes. The courageous organizational participant may reap material, physical, social, and psychological gains, but the potential risks associated with a courageous act may also cause parallel losses. For example, a courageous idea that challenges the status quo may be met with praise and recognition, or it may be rejected. Courageously telling the truth (blowing the whistle) regarding a colleague's wrongdoing may save the organization substantial financial resources and reinforce its ethical values and culture, but it may also weaken interpersonal trust within the work team or reduce the propensity for future open communication. Courage is necessary for entrepreneurs to overcome their fears and take further action, but it may also lead to unrealistic expectations and excessive risk taking (Naughton & Cornwall, 2006).

In one of the few studies with work performance implications, Worline (2003) reported qualitatively gathered courageous stories from the workplace. She found four consistent elements appearing in these stories. The dimensions of courage included individuation, duress, involvement, and constructive opposition. Absent these elements, individuals coding these stories did not view them as representing courage. Individuation was based on viewing the actor as thinking for oneself, being reflective, and acting outside of daily expectations (i.e., standing apart from others). Duress represented the susceptibility to outside forces. Involvement represented having a sense of the organization as a whole and awareness of common direction. Finally, constructive opposition was a felt opposition to one's social group that triggers the person to take individuated action against the flow of what is transpiring in order to reduce duress. Taken together, individuation, duress, and involvement contributed to individuals described in workplace stories of courage as taking constructive opposition. Thus, constructive opposition is viewed as the outcome of the other three factors making up courage. Although conducted in the workplace, this study does not directly test for performance impact.

With respect to measurement, to date very diverse approaches have been utilized for measuring courage. Existing measurement approaches include monitoring of physiological responses associated with courage, qualitative techniques such as structured and unstructured interviews, content analysis, and observation. Adequate self-report survey measures also exist, such as Woodward and Pury's (2007) Courage Scale-23 (WPCS-23), Norton and Weiss's (2009) Courage Measure (CM), and Sekerka, Bagozzi, and Charnigo's (2009) Professional Moral Courage (PMC) survey. Kilmann, O'Hara, and Strauss (2010) have also developed and validated a quantitative Organizational Courage Assessment (OCA) (also see Lopez et al., 2003 for a comprehensive review of courage measures). Overall, the use of multiple measures and the utilization of various methodologies have enhanced the understanding and assessment of courage. Furthermore, there seems to be a high level of agreement emerging in the literature, summarized earlier, on the definition of courage. This general agreement can facilitate the triangulation of the conceptual and empirical study of courage.

Traditionally, courage has been portrayed as a disposition. For example, Shelp (1984) defined courage as "the disposition to voluntarily act, perhaps fearfully, in dangerous circumstance, where the risks are reasonably appraised, in an effort to obtain or preserve some perceived good for oneself or others, recognizing that the desired good may not be realized" (p. 354). There are also inferences of dispositional courage due to its associations with stable traits such as negative affectivity and proactive personality (Miceli & Near, 2005).

However, there are also several approaches that have proposed developing and facilitating courageous action. For example, Worline (2003) describes courage not as a disposition but as a property of social life in which it occurs, or in our terms being more state-like. Courage is seen by Worline as a part of social life produced by moments that matter. Thus, enactment of courage depends on the relationship between individuals and the social life/moments in which they find themselves embedded.

Worline's (2003, p. 99) specific definition of courage is a "form of social life in which individuation is in its constructive opposition to involvement to remedy duress to social life." In other words, courage can change what others view is possible as part of one's social life, whether inside or outside of work in organizations. Most positive psychology conceptualizations of courage support this emergent, context-based nature (Worline, 2012). Pury and Lopez (2009) offer an extensive review that links courage to a number of psychological states and processes, which aligns courage with PsyCap's state-like criterion.

Similar to self-efficacy (see Chapter 3), courage can be enhanced through successful mastery experiences and practice, modeling of brave actions by relevant others, social persuasion and "en-courage-ment" by others, and psychological and physical arousal and wellness. Fostering group cohesion and mutual responsibility may also create a culture where courageous actions are enabled (Worline & Steen, 2004).

Specific developmental attitudes and coping mechanisms have also been found to contribute to the development of courage (Haase, 1987). For example, whistle-blowing, as discussed earlier, can be encouraged through proactively making internal reporting channels available and open, making the organization's stance regarding unethical activity clear, and establishing measures for the protection of whistle-blowers. As whistle-blowing occurs, the organization can react by conducting high-quality investigations of reported violations, promptly correcting wrongdoing, communicating (to the extent possible within privacy limitations) the organization's intolerance to similar offenses, and reinforcing the positive actions taken to deal with the situation (Miceli & Near, 2005). While enhancing courage through building self-efficacy may result in proactive courageous actions despite risk, reducing the risk factors associated with courageous action may at the same time eliminate the need for courage. As generally defined, the presence of risk seems a necessary antecedent for courage.

Finally, with respect to PsyCap's agency and positive appraisal mechanisms, especially when portrayed as an emergent, situational state-like positive resource, courage is agentic, intentional, and controlled by the actor. Shelp (1984) emphasizes the voluntary nature of courage. Worline, Wrzesniewski, and Rafaeli (2002) also highlight freedom of choice as a dimension of courage and highlight agency as a key component of courageous action. Sekerka and colleagues (2009) also incorporate agency as a dimension in the conceptualization and measurement of professional moral courage. Positive appraisals are also integral elements of most of the definitions of courage discussed earlier. Without courage, the dominance of fear and uncertainty may cause risks to be appraised too highly, leading to inaction. Courage also offers accurate cognitive judgments that balance fearlessness and excessive risk taking (Worline et al., 2002).

Although further theory development and research studies of the aforementioned issues raised with regard to courage are necessary, and there is especially a need for better understanding of the role of courage in enhancing work performance, like the other constructs in this chapter, the future looks very promising for courage to be included in PsyCap.

Future Implications and Directions for Research and Practice

In the previous chapter and this one, we have explored several positive resources for potential inclusion in PsyCap. They seem to meet most of the PsyCap inclusion criteria of being positive, theory and researched based, measurable, developmental, and workplace performance related (see Tables 7.1 and 8.1). However, it seems fair to say that the jury is still out on whether they fully meet the PsyCap criteria for inclusion. Nevertheless, assessing how all these other positive resources measure up to the established PsyCap inclusion criteria not only contributes to our better understanding and appreciation of the established HERO components of PsyCap but also enriches our understanding of these other seemingly relevant positive psychological resources and what is needed for them to become fully included in PsyCap.

As noted throughout these two chapters, this overview is not meant to provide a comprehensive list of all potential PsyCap resources, nor is our current assessment of these potential capacities conclusive. Our purpose has been to simply present some directions for continued research and practice that may help expand the domain of PsyCap and keep it dynamic. This can be done through further investigation of the existing and potential PsyCap resources that we present in this book as additional research emerges, as well as through exploring still others using our inclusion criteria as specific guidelines for consistent rigorous assessment and applicability.

Case Study: NSA Whistle-Blower Edward Snowden

Video link: http://www.youtube.com/watch?v=5yB3n9fu-r

This case video features Edward Snowden, known for exposing many allegedly unnecessary privacy violations by the National Security Agency (NSA). Edward Snowden's controversial actions required a lot of courage, and they generated an interesting mix of admiration and opposition.

Questions for reflection and/or discussion:
1. What are the dimensions of courage manifested in Snowden's words and actions?
2. If you were in Snowden's position, would you have acted similarly? How would you have acted differently? Why?

Case Study: What Is It Like Being a Dad?

Video link: http://skitguys.com/videos/item/fatherhood

Many parents will agree that being a parent is one of the most challenging and rewarding jobs in the world. In this video, fatherhood is cleverly portrayed as a combination of most of the positive psychological resources discussed in this book. Specifically, elements of efficacy, hope, optimism, resilience, creativity, flow, mindfulness, gratitude, forgiveness, emotional intelligence, authenticity, spirituality, and courage are all present to varying degrees.

Questions for reflection and/or discussion:
1. Which dimensions of each of the psychological resources discussed in this book do you see in the father character in this video?
2. To what extent is each of these resources as expressed in the video applicable to other roles beyond parenting and family? Consider work and nonwork roles.

References

Ashmos, D. P., & Duchon, D. (2000). Spirituality at work: A conceptualization and measure. *Journal of Management Inquiry, 9,* 134–145.

Ashkanasy, N., & Daus, C. (2005). Rumors of the death of emotional intelligence in organizational behavior are greatly exaggerated. *Journal of Organizational Behavior, 26*, 441–452.

Avolio, B. J. (2011). *Full range leadership development.* Thousand Oaks, CA: Sage.

Avolio, B. J. (2010). Pursuing authentic leadership development. In Nitin Nohria & R. Kurhana (Eds.), *Handbook of leadership theory and practice* (pp. 739–768). Boston, MA: Harvard Business School Publishing.

Avolio, B. J., Gardner, W. L., Walumbwa, F. O., Luthans, F., & May, D. R. (2004). Unlocking the mask: A look at the process by which authentic leaders impact follower attitudes and behaviors. *Leadership Quarterly, 15*, 801–823.

Avolio, B. J., & Gibbons, T. G. (1988). Developing transformational leaders: A life span approach. In J. A. Conger & R. N. Kanungo (Eds.), *Charismatic leadership: The elusive factor in organizational effectiveness* (pp. 276–308). San Francisco, CA: Jossey-Bass.

Avolio, B. J., & Luthans, F. (2006). *The high impact leader: Moments matter in accelerating authentic leadership development.* New York, NY: McGraw-Hill.

Avolio, B. J., & Walumbwa, F. O. (2014). Authentic leadership theory, research and practice: Steps taken and steps that remain. In D. Day (Ed.), *Oxford handbook of leadership and organizations* (pp. 739–768). Oxford, UK: Oxford University Press.

Barney, M. (2010). *Leadership @ Infosys.* New York, NY: Portfolio Penguin.

Bar-On, R. (1997). *BarOn Emotional Quotient Inventory (EQ-i): Technical Manual.* Toronto, ON: Multi-Health Systems.

Barker, J. R. (1993). Tightening the iron cage: Concertive control in self-managing teams. *Administrative Science Quarterly, 38*, 408–437.

Bass, B. M. (1985). *Leadership and performance beyond expectations.* New York, NY: Free Press.

Bass, B. M., & Steidlmeier, P. (1999). Ethics, character, and authentic transformational leadership. *Leadership Quarterly, 10*, 181–218.

Bastian, V. A., Burns, N. R., & Nettelbeck, T. (2005). Emotional intelligence predicts life skills, but not as well as personality and cognitive abilities. *Personality and Individual Differences, 39*, 1135–1145.

Brackett, M. A., & Mayer, J. D. (2003). Convergent, discriminant, and incremental validity of competing measures of emotional intelligence. *Personality and Social Psychology Bulletin, 29*, 1147–1158.

Brumbaugh, R. B. (1971). Authenticity and theories of administrative behavior. *Administrative Science Quarterly, 16*, 108–112.

Burns, J. M. (1978). *Leadership.* New York, NY: Harper & Row.

Cashman, K. (1998). *Leadership from the inside out: Becoming a leader for life.* Provo, UT: Executive Excellence.

Cherniss, C. (2010). Emotional intelligence: New insights and further clarifications. *Industrial and Organizational Psychology, 3*, 183–191.

Colquitt, J. A., & Salam, S. (2009). Foster trust through ability, benevolence, and integrity. In E. Locke (Ed.), *Handbook of principles of organizational behavior*, (2nd ed., pp. 389–404). Oxford, UK: Blackwell.

Davis, D. E., Worthington, E. L., Hook, J. N., & Hill, P. C. (2013). Research on religion/spirituality and forgiveness: A meta-analytic review. *Psychology of Religion and Spirituality, 5*, 233–241.

Day, A. L., & Carroll, S. A. (2004). Using an ability-based measure of emotional intelligence to predict individual performance, group performance, and group citizenship behaviours. *Personality and Individual Differences, 36*, 1443–1458.

Deci, E. L., Connell, J. P., & Ryan, R. M. (1989). Self-determination in a work organization. *Journal of Applied Psychology, 74*, 580–590.

Dent, E. B., Higgins, M. E., & Wharff, D. M. (2005). Spirituality and leadership: An empirical review of definitions, distinctions, and embedded assumptions. *Leadership Quarterly, 16*, 625–654.

Duchon, D., & Plowman, D. A. (2005). Nurturing the spirit at work: Impact on work unit peformance. *Leadership Quarterly, 16*, 807–834.

Evans, P. D., & White, D. G. (1981). Towards an empirical definition of courage. *Behavioral Research and Therapy, 19*, 419–424.

Fry, L. W. (2003). Toward a theory of spiritual leadership. *Leadership Quarterly, 14*, 693–727.

Fry, L. W. (2005). Toward a theory of ethical and spiritual well-being, and corporate social responsibility through spiritual leadership. In R. A. Giacalone, C. Jurkiewicz, & C. Dunn (Eds.), *Positive psychology in business ethics and corporate social responsibility* (pp. 47–83). Greenwich, CT: Information Age.

Fry, L. W., & Nisiewicz, M. S. (2013). *Maximizing the triple bottom line through spiritual leadership*. Redwood City, CA: Stanford University Press.

Fry, L. W., Vitucci, S., & Cedillo, M. (2005). Spiritual leadership and army transformation: Theory, measurement, and establishing a baseline. *Leadership Quarterly, 16*, 835–862.

Gardner, H. (1983). *Frames of the mind: The theory of multiple intelligences*. New York, NY: Basic Books.

Gardner, W. L., Avolio, B. J., Luthans, F., May, D. R., & Walumbwa, F. O. (2005). "Can you see the real me?" A self-based model of authentic leader and follower development. *Leadership Quarterly, 16*, 343–372.

Gardner, W. L., Cogliser, C. C., Davis, K. M., & Dickens, M. P. (2011). Authentic leadership: A review of the literature and research agenda. *Leadership Quarterly, 22*, 1120–1145.

George, J. M. (2000). Emotions and leadership: The role of emotional intelligence. *Human Relations, 53*, 1027–1055.

George, W. (2003). *Authentic leadership: Rediscovering the secrets to creating lasting value*. San Francisco, CA: Jossey-Bass.

George, W., & Sims, P. (2007). *True north: Discover your authentic leadership.* San Francisco, CA: Jossey-Bass.

Ghoshal, S. (2005). Bad management theories are destroying good management practices. *Academy of Management Learning and Education, 4,* 75–91.

Giacalone, R. A., & Jurkiewicz, C. L. (2010). *Handbook of workplace spirituality and organizational performance.* Armonk, NY: M.E. Sharpe.

Gibbs, N. (1995, October 2). The EQ factor. *Time,* 60–67.

Goleman, D. (1995). *Emotional intelligence.* New York, NY: Bantam Books.

Goleman, D. (1998). *Working with emotional intelligence.* New York, NY: Bantam Books.

Goleman, D., Boyatzis, R., & McKee, A. (2002). *Primal leadership: Realizing the power of emotional intelligence.* Boston, MA: Harvard Business School.

Haase, J. (1987). Components of courage in chronically ill adolescents: A phenomenological study. *Advances in Nursing Science, 9*(2), 64–80.

Hannah, S. T., Avolio, B. J., & Walumbwa, F. O. (2011). Relationships between authentic leadership, moral courage, ethical and pro-social behaviors. *Business Ethics Quarterly, 21,* 555–578.

Hannah, S. T., Lester, P. B., & Vogelgesang, G. R. (2005). Moral leadership: Explicating the moral component of authentic leadership. In W. B. Gardner, B. J. Avolio, & F. O. Walumbwa (Eds.), *Authentic leadership theory and practice: Origins, effects, and development. Monographs in leadership and management* (Vol. 3, pp. 43–82). Oxford, UK: Elsevier/JAI Press.

Harter, S. (2002). Authenticity. In C. R. Snyder & S. Lopez (Eds.), *Handbook of positive psychology* (pp. 382–394). Oxford, UK: Oxford University Press.

Henderson, J., & Hoy, W. (1983). Leader authenticity: The development and test of an operational measure. *Educational and Psychological Research, 3,* 63–75.

Hill, P., Pargament, K., Hood, R., Jr., McCullough, M., Swyers, J., Larson, D., & Zinnbauer, B. (2000). Conceptualizing religion and spirituality: Points of commonality, points of departure. *Journal for the Theory of Social Behaviour, 30,* 51–77.

Hochschild, A. (1979). Emotion work, feeling rules, and social structure. *American Journal of Sociology, 85,* 551–575.

Hochschild, A. (1983). *The managed heart: Commercialization of human feeling.* Berkeley: University of California Press.

Ilies, R., Morgeson, F. P., & Nahrgang, J. D. (2005). Authentic leadership and eudaemonic well-being: Understanding leader-follower outcomes. *Leadership Quarterly, 16,* 373–394.

Janis, I. (1982). *Groupthink* (2nd ed.). Boston, MA: Houghton Mifflin.

Joseph, D. L., & Newman, D. A. (2010). Emotional intelligence: An integrative meta-analysis and cascading model. *Journal of Applied Psychology, 95,* 54–78.

Kelley, R., & Caplan, J. (1993). How Bell Labs creates star performers. *Harvard Business Review, 71*(4), 128–139.

Kernis, M. H. (2003). Toward a conceptualization of optimal self-esteem. *Psychological Inquiry, 14,* 1–26.

Kernis, M. H., & Goldman, B. M. (2006). A multicomponent conceptualization of authenticity: Theory and research. In M. P. Zanna (Ed.), *Advances in experimental social psychology* (pp. 284–357). San Diego, CA: Elsevier.

Kilmann, R. H., O'Hara, L. A., & Strauss, J. P. (2010). Developing and validating a quantitative measure of organizational courage. *Journal of Business Psychology, 25,* 15–23.

Koerner, M. M. (2014). Courage as identity work: Accounts of workplace courage. *Academy of Management Journal, 27,* 63–93.

Lapidot, Y., Kark, R., & Shamir, B. (2007). The impact of situational vulnerability on the development and erosion of followers' trust in their leader. *Leadership Quarterly, 18,* 16–34.

Livingstone, H., & Day, A. L. (2005). Comparing the construct and criterion-related validity of ability-based and mixed-model measures of emotional intelligence. *Educational and Psychological Measurement, 65,* 851–873.

Locke, E. A. (2005). Why emotional intelligence is an invalid concept. *Journal of Organizational Behavior, 26,* 425–431.

Lopez, S., O'Byrne, K., & Peterson, S. (2003). Profiling courage. In S. Lopez & C. R. Snyder (Eds.), *Positive psychological assessment: A handbook of models and measures* (pp. 185–197). Washington, DC: American Psychological Association.

Lord, R. G., & Brown, D. J. (2004). *Leadership processes and follower self identity.* Mahwah, NJ: Erlbaum.

Luthans, F. (2002a). The need for and meaning of positive organizational behavior. *Journal of Organizational Behavior, 23,* 695–706.

Luthans, F. (2002b). Positive organizational behavior: Developing and managing psychological strengths. *Academy of Management Executive, 16,* 57–72.

Luthans, F., & Avolio, B. (2003). Authentic leadership: A positive development approach. In K. S. Cameron, J. E. Dutton, & R. E. Quinn (Eds.), *Positive organizational scholarship* (pp. 241–258). San Francisco, CA: Berrett-Koehler.

Luthans, F., Luthans, K., Hodgetts, R., & Luthans, B. C. (2001). Positive Approach to Leadership (PAL): Implications for today's organizations. *Journal of Leadership Studies, 8*(2), 3–20.

Luthans, F., Luthans, K. W., & Luthans, B. C. (2004). Positive psychological capital: Going beyond human and social capital. *Business Horizons, 47,* 45–50.

Luthans, F., Norman, S. M., & Hughes, L. (2006). Authentic leadership. In R. Burke & C. Cooper (Eds.), *Inspiring leaders* (pp. 84–104). London, UK: Routledge, Taylor & Francis.

Luthans, F., & Youssef, C. M. (2004). Human, social and now positive psychological capital management: Investing in people for competitive advantage. *Organizational Dynamics, 33,* 143–160.

Mahoney, A., & Pargament, K. (2004). Sacred changes: Spiritual conversion and transformation. *Journal of Clinical Psychology, 60,* 481–492.

Mahoney, A., Pargament, K., Cole, B., Jewell, T., Magyar, G., Tarakeshwar, N., . . . Phillips, R. (2005). A higher purpose: The sanctification of strivings in a community sample. *International Journal for the Psychology of Religion, 15,* 239–262.

Martin, J., Knopoff, K., & Beckman, C. (1998). An alternative to bureaucratic impersonality and emotional labor: Bounded emotionality at the Body Shop. *Administrative Science Quarterly, 43,* 429–469.

Mattis, J. (2004). Spirituality [religiousness, faith, purpose]. In C. Peterson & M. Seligman (Eds.), *Character strengths and virtues: A handbook and classification* (pp. 599–622). Oxford, UK: Oxford University Press.

Mayer, J., & Salovey, P. (1997). What is emotional intelligence? In P. Salovey & D. Sluyter (Eds.), *Emotional development and emotional intelligence: Educational implications* (pp. 3–34). New York, NY: Basic Books.

Mayer, J., & Salovey, P. (2004). Social intelligence [emotional intelligence, personal intelligence]. In C. Peterson & M. Seligman (Eds.), *Character strengths and virtues: A handbook and classification* (pp. 337–353). Oxford, UK: Oxford University Press.

Mayer, J., Salovey, P., & Caruso, D. (2000). Models of emotional intelligence. In R. Sternberg (Ed.), *Handbook of intelligence* (pp. 396–420). Cambridge, UK: University of Cambridge.

Mayer, J., Salovey, P., & Caruso, D. (2001). *The Mayer-Salovey-Caruso Emotional Intelligence Test (MSCEIT).* Toronto, ON: Multi-Health Systems.

Mayer, J. D., Salovey, P., & Caruso, D. R. (2008). Emotional intelligence: New ability or eclectic mix of traits? *American Psychologist, 63,* 503–517.

Mayer, J. D., Salovey, P., Caruso, D., & Cherkasskiy, L. (2011). What is emotional intelligence and why does it matter? In R. J. Sternberg & J. Kaufman (Eds.), *The handbook of intelligence* (3rd ed., pp. 528–549). New York, NY: Cambridge University Press.

Miceli, M., & Near, J. (2005). Whistle-blowing and positive psychology. In R. A. Giacalone, C. Jurkiewicz, & C. Dunn (Eds.), *Positive psychology in business ethics and corporate social responsibility* (pp.85–102). Greenwich, CT: Information Age.

Milliman, J., Czaplewski, A. J., & Ferguson, J. (2003). Workplace spirituality and employee work attitudes: An exploratory empirical assessment. *Journal of Organizational Change Management, 16,* 426–447.

Morris, J. A. & Feldman, D. C. (1996). The dimensions, antecedents, and consequences of emotional labor. *Academy of Management Review, 21,* 986–1010.

Naughton, M. J., & Cornwall, J. R. (2006). The virtue of courage in entrepreneurship: Engaging the catholic social tradition and the life-cycle of the business. *Business Ethics Quarterly, 16,* 69–93.

Norton, P. J., & Weiss, B. J. (2009). The role of courage on behavioral approach in a fear-eliciting situation: A proof-of-concept pilot study. *Journal of Anxiety Disorders, 23,* 212–217.

O'Boyle, E. H., Humphrey, R. H., Pollack, J. M., Hawver, T. H., & Story, P. A. (2011). The relation between emotional intelligence and job performance: A meta-analysis. *Journal of Organizational Behavior, 35,* 788–818.

Organ, D. (1988). *Organizational citizenship behavior: The good soldier syndrome.* Lexington, MA: Lexington.

Pargament, K. (1997). *The psychology of religion and coping: Theory, research, and practice.* New York, NY: Guilford Press.

Pargament, K. (2002). The bitter and the sweet: An evaluation of the costs and benefits of religiousness. *Psychological Inquiry, 13,* 168–181.

Pargament, K., Magyar, G., Benore, E., & Mahoney, A. (2005). Sacrilege: A study of sacred loss and desecration and their implications for health and well-being in a community sample. *Journal for the Scientific Study of Religion, 44,* 59–78.

Pargament, K., & Mahoney, A. (2009). Spirituality: The search for the sacred. In S. Lopez & C. R. Snyder (Eds.), *Handbook of positive psychology* (2nd ed., pp. 611–619). New York, NY: Oxford University Press.

Peterson, C., & Seligman, M. (2004). *Character strengths and virtues: A handbook and classification.* New York, NY: Oxford University Press.

Pury, C. L. S., Kowalski, R. M., & Spearman, J. (2007). Distinctions between general and personal courage. *Journal of Positive Psychology, 2,* 99–114.

Pury, C. L. S., & Lopez, S. J. (2009). Courage. In S. J. Lopez & C. R. Snyder (Eds.), *Oxford handbook of positive psychology* (2nd ed., pp. 375–382). New York, NY: Oxford University Press.

Pury, C. L. S., & Lopez, S. J. (Eds.) (2010). *The psychology of courage: Modern research on an ancient virtue.* Washington, DC: American Psychological Asssociation.

Quinn, R., & Worline, M. C. (2008). Enabling courageous collective action: Conversations from United Airlines Flight 93. *Organization Science, 19,* 497–516.

Reave, L. (2005). Spiritual values and practices related to leadership effectiveness. *Leadership Quarterly, 16,* 655–688.

Rorty, A. O. (1988). *Mind in action: Essays in the philosophy of mind.* Boston, MA: Beacon Press.

Rosenthal, S. A., Pittinsky, T. L., Purvin, D. M., & Montoya, R. M. (2007). *National Leadership Index 2007: A national study of confidence in leadership.* Center for Public Leadership, John F. Kennedy School of Government, Harvard University, Cambridge, MA.

Sartre, J. P. (1966). *The age of reason.* New York, NY: Knopf.

Salovey, P., Caruso, D., & Mayer, J. (2004). Emotional intelligence in practice. In P. A. Linley & S. Joseph (Eds.), *Positive psychology in practice* (pp. 447–463). Hoboken, NJ: Wiley.

Salovey, P., & Mayer, J. (1990). Emotional intelligence. *Imagination, Cognition, and Personality, 9*, 185–211.

Salovey, P., Mayer, J., Caruso, D., & Lopes, P. (2003). Measuring emotional intelligence as a set of abilities with the Mayer-Salovey-Caruso Emotional Intelligence Test. In S. Lopez & C. R. Snyder (Eds.), *Positive psychological assessment: A handbook of models and measures* (pp. 251–265). Washington, DC: American Psychological Association.

Salovey, P., Mayer, J., Caruso, D., & Yoo, S. H. (2009). The positive psychology of emotional intelligence. In S. Lopez & C. R. Snyder (Eds.), *Oxford handbook of positive psychology* (2nd ed., pp. 237–248). New York, NY: Oxford University Press.

Sandelands, L. E. (2012). In God we trust: A comparison of spiritualities at work. In K. S. Cameron & G. M. Spreitzer (Eds.), *Oxford handbook of positive organizational scholarship* (pp. 1001–1013). New York, NY: Oxford University Press.

Sawatzky, R., Ratner, P. A., & Chiu, L. (2005). A meta-analysis of the relationship between spirituality and quality of life. *Social Indicators Research, 72*, 153–188.

Seligman, M. E. P. (2002). *Authentic happiness.* New York, NY: Free Press.

Sekerka, L. E., Bagozzi, R. P., & Charnigo, R. (2009) Facing ethical challenges in the workplace: Conceptualizing and measuring professional moral courage. *Journal of Business Ethics, 89*, 565–579.

Sheldon, K., Davidson, L., & Pollard, E. (2004). Integrity [authenticity, honesty]. In C. Peterson & M. Seligman (Eds.), *Character strengths and virtues: A handbook and classification* (pp. 249–271). Oxford, UK: Oxford University Press.

Shelp, E. (1984). Courage: A neglected virtue in the patient-physician relationship. *Social Science and Medicine, 18*, 351–360.

Sutton, R. I. (1991). Maintaining norms about expressed emotions: The case of bill collectors. *Administrative Science Quarterly, 36*, 245–268.

Tsang, J., & McCullough, M. (2003). Measuring religious constructs: A hierarchical approach to construct organization and scale selection. In S. Lopez & C. R. Snyder (Eds.), *Positive psychological assessment: A handbook of models and measures* (pp. 345–360). Washington, DC: American Psychological Association.

Walumbwa, F. O., Avolio, B. J., Gardner, W. L., Wernsing, T. S., & Peterson, S. J. (2008). Authentic leadership: Development and validation of a theory-based measure. *Journal of Management, 34*, 89–126.

Wang, H., Sui, Y., Luthans, F., Wang, D., & Wu, Y. (2014). Impact of authentic leadership on performance: Role of followers' positive psychological capital and relational processes. *Journal of Organizational Behavior, 35*, 5–21.

Wiersma, U. P. (1992). The effects of extrinsic rewards in intrinsic motivation: A meta-analysis. *Journal of Occupational and Organizational Psychology, 65*, 101–114.

Woodward, C. R. (2004). Hardiness and the concept of courage. *Consulting Psychology Journal, 56*, 173–185.

Woodward, C. R., & Pury, C. L. S. (2007). The construct of courage: Categorization and measurement. *Consulting Psychology Journal: Practice and Research*, 59, 135–147.

Worline, M. C. (2003). *Dancing the cliff edge: The place of courage in social life.* Unpublished Ph.D. dissertation, University of Michigan, Ann Arbor.

Worline, M. C. (2010). Understanding the role of courage in social life. In C. Pury & S. Lopez (Eds.), *The psychology of courage: Modern research on an ancient virtue* (pp. 209–226). Washington, DC: American Psychological Association.

Worline, M. C. (2012). Courage in organizations: An integrative review of the "difficult virtue." In K. S. Cameron & G. M. Spreitzer (Eds.), *Oxford handbook of positive organizational scholarship* (pp. 304–315). New York, NY: Oxford University Press.

Worline, M., & Quinn, R. (2003). Courageous principled action. In K. S. Cameron, J. E. Dutton, & R. E. Quinn (Eds.), *Positive organizational scholarship* (pp. 138–157). San Francisco, CA: Berrett-Koehler.

Worline, M., & Steen, T. (2004). Bravery [Valor]. In C. Peterson & M. Seligman (Eds.), *Character strengths and virtues: A handbook and classification* (pp. 213–228). Oxford, UK: Oxford University Press.

Worline, M., Wrzesniewski, A., & Rafaeli, A. (2002). Courage and work: Breaking routines to improve performance. In R. G. Lord, R. J. Klimoski, & R. Kanfer (Eds.), *Emotions in the workplace: Understanding the structure and role of emotions in organizational behavior* (pp. 295–330). San Francisco, CA: Jossey-Bass.

Worthington, E. L., Hook, J. N., Davis, D. E., & McDaniel, M. A. (2011). Religion and spirituality. *Journal of Clinical Psychology*, 67, 204–214.

Wrzesniewski, A. (2012). Callings. In K. S. Cameron & G. M. Spreitzer (Eds.), *Oxford handbook of positive organizational scholarship* (pp. 45–55). New York, NY: Oxford University Press.

Ybarra, O., Rees, L., Kross, E., & Sanchez-Burks, J. (2012). Social context and the psychology of emotional intelligence. In K. S. Cameron & G. M. Spreitzer (Eds.), *Oxford handbook of positive organizational scholarship* (pp. 201–214). New York, NY: Oxford University Press.

Zinnbauer, B., Pargament, K., Cole, B., Rye, M., Butter, E., Belavich, T., . . . Kadar, J. (1997). Religion and spirituality: Unfuzzying the fuzzy. *Journal for the Scientific Study of Religion*, 36, 549–564.

Zinnbauer, B., Pargament, K., & Scott, A. (1999). The emerging meanings of religiousness and spirituality: Problems and prospects. *Journal of Personality*, 67, 889–919.

9 MEASUREMENT AND DEVELOPMENT OF PSYCAP

ASSESSING THE RETURN ON INVESTMENT

Opening Videos: Wayne Cascio, John Boudreau, and Richard Beaty on Strategic Human Resources

Video link: http://www.youtube.com/watch?v=VmAGhC-yUUQ

Video link: http://www.youtube.com/watch?v=j3rZSIqZ0pM

Video link: http://www.youtube.com/watch?v=YnyPWy64li4#t=349

Wayne Cascio, John Boudreau, and Richard Beaty are all widely recognized scholar-practitioners in the area of strategic human resources and experts on quantifying the value added and return on investment in human resources.

Questions for reflection and/or discussion:

1. Based on these three videos, what are the key factors to building competitive advantage based on human resources?
2. How is strategic human resources similar to/ different from the strategic use of any other type of organizational resource?
3. Applying what you have learned so far about PsyCap, how can it be used to build competitive advantage?
4. What information would your organization need to gather in order to quantify the value added and return on investment in PsyCap?

Capturing the strategic value added and competitive advantage that can be achieved through emphasis on human resource selection, placement, and development has become one of the most important priorities for human resource researchers and practitioners. With global competition heating up, the demand for increased accountability, changing workforce demographics, and tightening budgets, the challenge of assessing the investments in and dollar return from human resources is now more pertinent than ever (e.g., Becker, Huselid, & Beaty, 2009; Boudreau & Jesuthasan, 2011; Campbell, Coff, & Kryscynski, 2012; Cascio & Boudreau, 2011; Combs, Liu, Hall, & Ketchen, 2006; Crook, Todd, Combs, Woehr, & Ketchen, 2011; Flumer & Ployhart, 2014; Wright, Coff, & Moliterno, 2014). However, despite this spotlighted attention, debates regarding the reliability, validity, and utility of various approaches for quantifying the return on investment and value of human resources and their development are far from resolved (Latham & Whyte, 1994; Skarlicki, Latham, & Whyte, 1996; Whyte & Latham, 1997). Yet the "bottom line" for our proposed PsyCap as presented in this book is that it must be validly measured, can be developed, and have demonstrated performance impact. The investment in the PsyCap development of organizational participants must be able to show dollars and cents return on that investment.

In this chapter, we discuss in detail our state-of-the-art validated measures of PsyCap within and beyond the workplace. You have been introduced to some of these assessments in Chapters 1 and 2. The 24-item Psychological Capital Questionnaire (PCQ-24; Luthans, Avolio, Avey, & Norman, 2007; Luthans, Youssef, & Avolio, 2007) and its 12-item short-version (PCQ-12; Avey, Avolio, & Luthans, 2011) are both available at www.mindgarden.com, where permission to use them can at present be obtained free of charge for researchers, and at a modest cost for other forms of use in consulting, training, and development. Instructions for the PCQ and some sample items representing each of the four dimensions of PsyCap are shown in Figure 9.1. Another recent measure that we discuss here is the Implicit Psychological Capital Questionnaire (I-PCQ; Harms & Luthans, 2012). This I-PCQ is presented and explained in its entirety in the Harms and Luthans (2012) *Journal of Organizational Behavior* article and discussed next. This I-PCQ questionnaire is shown in Figure 9.2 can be used by simply citing the source.

In this chapter, we also describe our micro-intervention model that we have successfully used to develop PsyCap over the years (Luthans, Avey, Avolio, Norman, & Combs, 2006; Luthans, Avey, Avolio, & Peterson, 2010; Luthans, Avey, & Patera, 2008; Luthans, Luthans, & Avey, 2014). The PsyCap measures and micro-intervention for development are based on the preceding Chapters 3–6 on efficacy, hope, optimism, and resilience. Finally, we propose

FIGURE 9.1 PCQ sample items. *Instructions:* These statements describe how you may think about yourself *right now.* Use the following scale to indicate your level of agreement or disagreement with each statement.

	Strongly Disagree	Disagree	Somewhat Disagree	Somewhat Agree	Agree	Strongly Agree				
	1	**2**	**3**	**4**	**5**	**6**				

1.	I feel confident analyzing a long-term problem to find a solution.	1	2	3	4	5	6
7.	If I should find myself in a jam at work, I could think of many ways to get out of it.	1	2	3	4	5	6
13.	When I have a setback at work, I have trouble recovering from it, moving on. (R)	1	2	3	4	5	6
19.	When things are uncertain for me at work, I usually expect the best.	1	2	3	4	5	6

FIGURE 9.2 The Implicit Psychological Capital Questionnaire (I-PCQ). In the following you will see a series of three statements. Your task is to invent stories about people you choose in order to answer these statements. Try to imagine what is going on. Think about what happened before, who the characters are, what they are thinking and feeling, what will happen next, and how will the story end. You don't need to write the story down; just think about it until it is clear in your mind. Then respond to the items after each of the three statements using your own thoughts about what the character is thinking and feeling. Plan to spend around 2–4 minutes per story. There are no right or wrong stories. Imagine whatever kind of story you like.

SOMEONE TALKS TO HIS/HER SUPERVISOR

Remember your task is to invent a story about someone in this statement. Again, you don't need to write the story down; just think about it until it is clear in your mind. Then respond to the following items using your own thoughts about what the character is thinking and feeling. Rate the degree to which the character in your story thinks or feels using the following scale:

	The opposite is very true of this character	The opposite is somewhat true of this character	The opposite is slightly true of this character	Irrelevant thought/feeling for this character	Slightly true of this character	Somewhat true of this character	Very true of this character
1. Feeling smart or intelligent	O	O	O	O	O	O	O
2. Believing that he/she can accomplish his/her goal	O	O	O	O	O	O	O
3. Expecting good things to happen in the future	O	O	O	O	O	O	O
4. Feeling satisfied with his/her life	O	O	O	O	O	O	O
5. Being concerned about being seen as important	O	O	O	O	O	O	O
6. Feeling accepted by others	O	O	O	O	O	O	O
7. Believing that he/she can bounce back from any setbacks that have occurred	O	O	O	O	O	O	O
8. Feeling confident and self-assured in his/her ability	O	O	O	O	O	O	O

Note: To those using the Harms & Luthans I-PCQ: Repeat the above exact survey items and response scale format for two additional pages with these statements at the top: "Someone Has a New Job" and "Someone Makes a Mistake at Work." Remember that the 7-point scale ranges from –3 on the left anchor to 0 in the middle to +3 on the right anchor. The I-PCQ score is calculated from items 2 (hope), 3 (optimism), 7 (resiliency), and 8 (efficacy) from all three statements. The other four items are intended to be filler items.

Source: Adapted from Harms, P., & Luthans, F. (2012). Measuring implicit psychological constructs in organizational behavior: An example using psychological capital. Journal of Organizational Behavior, 33, 589–594.

a simple, practical, but theoretically sound approach for assessing the return on investment in PsyCap development. For the assessment of the return on investment, we draw from the extensive body of knowledge on utility analysis used in human resource management (Cascio & Boudreau, 2011). We provide some specific examples and propose alternative approaches to help minimize some of the potential pitfalls of such analysis.

Characteristics of PsyCap Measures

Various instruments for measuring efficacy, hope, optimism, resilience, and other potential positive psychological constructs have been designed, researched, and validated. Attention to these measures has greatly accelerated with the emergence of the field of positive psychology (e.g., for a comprehensive summary of the various measures, see Lopez & Snyder, 2003). The following provides a brief overview of the characteristics of the widely recognized published measures with demonstrated reliability and validity that we drew from in developing our PsyCap measures.

Scales Utilized

Multiple types of theory-based scales have been employed in measuring positive psychological strengths and resources. For example, Bandura (1997) provides considerable theory and research that efficacy should be measured in terms of magnitude and strength. The magnitude dimension of efficacy is the level of task difficulty in which a person expects to be able to perform. It is measured by respondents' yes/no answer to a question of whether or not they can perform a specific task at a certain level, with the level being gradually increased. The strength dimension of efficacy is the degree of certainty that a person possesses about the ability to perform at each level of difficulty, measured by the respondent's reported percentage of confidence or what Bandura refers to as efficacy at each level (Bandura, 1997, 2012; Locke, Frederick, Lee, & Bobko, 1984; Stajkovic & Luthans, 1998a, 1998b).

To date, however, there is research supporting Likert-type continuous scales as being comparable to scales using the magnitude-strength approach in measuring efficacy. These Likert scales have been found to yield similar factor structures, reliability, and validity as the traditional magnitude-strength efficacy measures (Maurer & Pierce, 1998). For example, Parker's (1998) efficacy instrument, which we draw from for measuring this dimension of PsyCap in the PCQ, utilizes a Likert scale relevant to the workplace and is the form we use in all three PsyCap questionnaires (PCQ-24, PCQ-12, and I-PCQ).

Length of Questionnaire

One of the primary criticisms of many reliable and valid positive psychological measures is the large number of items they incorporate (Lopez & Snyder, 2003). For example, Seligman (1998) has a 48-item measure of optimism, while the Scheier and Carver (1985) instrument, from which we adapt some of the items to measure this component of PsyCap in the PCQs, uses a total of only 12 items to measure optimism. Coupled with the necessity of measuring several predictors, outcomes, and control variables, most often administered in a single survey, the integration of a large number of long scales may cause such long survey measures to reduce voluntary response rates and the reliability of each measure. Moreover, science ideally tries to search for the most parsimonious representation or solution, and in this case it is to measure our selected PsyCap constructs with the least number of items necessary for achieving adequate levels of reliability and validity, but no less. That is why we offer both a preferred 24-item scale, but to help reduce lengthy surveys, also a 12-item PCQ to gather data in PsyCap research. Shorter versions of scales may not necessarily be as reliable because the more times you measure something, the higher the likelihood you may not cover its full domain. Yet, once you know a lot about a construct, you can rely on shorter scales by considering them to be "representative" of the domain to which you are applying those measures.

Wording and Context

The existing positive psychological measures in general have been developed and validated either very generically or in a broad spectrum of specific contexts. Most of these measures come out of clinical usage and are not directly applicable to the workplace (Lopez & Snyder, 2003). The exceptions are Parker's (1998) work role breadth self-efficacy scale and Snyder (2000), who provides a domain-specific hope scale which includes the workplace as one of six domains. On the other hand, most of the resilience scales in the literature are primarily oriented toward assessing children and youth, because, as we discussed in Chapter 6, for many years interest in this psychological resource has been almost solely aimed at clinical, at-risk youth in the developmental psychology literature (e.g., Masten, 2001; Masten, Cutuli, Herbers, & Reed, 2009). Thus, although there is a broad and deep literature to support the questionnaires we have drawn from to measure PsyCap, most of the evidence has not been accumulated in the workplace with working adults and thus needed to have the wording adapted. Yet, since our first book, there have literally been thousands of studies using these measures, so today, there is a much broader and deeper base of research in these areas focusing on work settings.

For this reason, the current three PsyCap measures are all specifically worded for the work context. The PCQ-12 has also been successfully used in a growing number of published research studies (e.g., Avey, Avolio, & Luthans, 2011; Baron, Franklin, & Hmieleski, 2014; Huang & Luthans, 2014; Norman, Avolio, & Luthans, 2010) and adapted to measure Relationships PsyCap and Health PsyCap (see Luthans, Youssef, Sweetman, & Harms, 2013). The PCQ-24 has also been successfully adapted to other domains such as job search (e.g., Chen & Lim, 2012), the marketing field (Friend, Johnson, Luthans, & Sohi, to date unpublished), education (Luthans, Luthans, & Avey, 2014; Luthans, Luthans, & Jensen, 2012), and for cross-cultural application (Dollwet & Reichard, 2013). However, the wording is typically adapted to the specific domain. This adaptation helps overcome a common problem in psychological research when measures are extrapolated to a different situation that may be either too narrow or too broad compared to what was intended (Bandura, 2012). Other researchers have also adopted a similar approach in designing context-specific or conceptually different PsyCap measures from the PCQ (e.g., Abbas, Raja, Darr, & Bouckenooghe, 2013; Gupta & Singh, 2014; Vogelgesang, Clapp-Smith, & Osland, 2014; Wernsing, 2014).

The I-PCQ (Harms & Luthans, 2012) wording can also be readily adapted to different situations. The positive, neutral, and negative stimulating trigger phrases (as opposed to the ink blots or TAT pictures used in the classic projective personality tests) can be tailored to the particular context in which it is used (e.g., healthcare, education, business, military). Additionally, this scale has the advantage of mitigating social desirability or lying, since its implicit nature makes it harder and less enticing for respondents to try to guess its purpose or fake their answers (Krasikova, Harms, & Luthans, 2012). The basic idea is that respondents assess the extent to which statements that tap into the definitions of efficacy, hope, optimism, and resilience represent "someone" (not themselves) in a story that the respondents make up in their heads. Then the positive, negative, and neutral situations triggered by the word phrases yield the respondents' PsyCap score. The use of such implicit scales commonly used in personality assessment is now gaining attention in the organizational behavior field as well (De Houwer, Teige-Mocigemba, Spruyt, & Moors, 2009).

Theoretical Framework Supporting PsyCap Measurement

Besides the domain issue, there are also other considerations from a theoretical perspective that could affect PsyCap measurement. First, most of the traditional scales that have been used to measure positive strengths and resources were originally designed to measure the opposite end of the continuum (i.e., negative psychological pathologies). The bipolarity versus independence of positive and seemingly opposite negative psychological capacities has received increased emphasis in positive psychological research (e.g., see Kubzansky, Kubzansky, & Maselko, 2004, and Peterson & Chang, 2002, for a comprehensive review of this issue in relation to optimism and pessimism; Schaufeli & Bakker, 2004, for the relationship between burnout and engagement; Dunlop & Lee, 2004, and Sackett, Berry, Wiemann, & Laczo, 2006, for organizational citizenship behaviors and counterproductive work behaviors; Cacioppo & Berntson, 1994, and Pittinsky, Rosenthal, & Montoya, 2011, for positive and negative attitudes and evaluative processes; and Watson, Clark, & Tellegen, 1988, for positive and negative affect). For this reason, the measures we specifically draw from for PsyCap (i.e., the PCQ) generally assume independent positivity, meaning as a separate and distinct construct.

Second, one of the most salient PsyCap inclusion criteria is that the psychological resources should be state-like and thus developmental, rather than just being stable, relatively fixed dispositional traits. The positive psychological measures that make up the PCQ generally indicate a clear distinction regarding this developmental criterion. For example, Parker's (1998) measure that we drew from in building our PsyCap questionnaire assesses the state of efficacy. By contrast, in Judge and Bono's (2001) core self-evaluation model, the trait of generalized efficacy is what is being measured. Similarly, Snyder (2000) provides two different scales, a state hope scale (Snyder et al., 1996), which we drew from in constructing our PsyCap measure, and a different dispositional hope scale. For our PCQ subscales of optimism (Scheier & Carver, 1985) and resilience (Wagnild & Young 1993), we systematically adapted the language from these recognized published scales to make them as state-like and work related as possible.

In most positive psychology measures, this distinction between stable dispositions and situational states is not clear. We recognize that a psychometrically sound (i.e., reliable) scale needs to show a certain level of stability over time. However, PsyCap presents a challenge because its state-like variability is an integral theoretical mechanism of the core construct, rather than an artifact of measurement error. Striking a balance between stability and sensitivity to change and development is of key importance to understanding and assessing PsyCap and was recognized in constructing our PCQ measures.

Wright (2007) provides a useful guideline for state-like psychological resources such as PsyCap as being relatively stable over a 6-month period. On the other hand, traits and trait-like characteristics such as personality tend to show high correlations over longer stretches of time (Conley, 1984). In validating the PCQ-24, to determine the relative degree of stability over time for emotions and personality and core self-evaluation traits, we calculated test-retest reliabilities.

After disattenuating for internal reliability, we found PsyCap was indeed "state-like." That is, on the one hand, it was relatively more stable than the emotional states, but on the other hand, relatively less stable than the personality and self-evaluation traits (Luthans et al., 2007). In other words, we empirically demonstrated that PsyCap does meet the "state-like" criterion, and its position on the state-trait continuum shown in Figure 2.1 in Chapter 2.

Finally, especially within positive psychology, many of the constructs are conceptualized and measured as outcomes in and of themselves (for example, see our discussions in Chapters 7 and 8 on other potential PsyCap constructs). Although it is desirable to have confident, hopeful, optimistic, resilient, creative, and mindful organizational leaders and employees in and of themselves (the major goal of positive psychology), of more value to positive organizational behavior (see Chapter 2) is the potential impact these may have on employee performance and desired attitudinal outcomes. Therefore, we conceive our PsyCap constructs more often as inputs or antecedents. Although PsyCap research may show these positive resources and the core construct itself may also be outcomes say of authentic leadership (Avolio & Luthans, 2006), or even as moderators/mediators of desired outcomes (Gooty, Gavin, Johnson, Frazier, & Snow, 2009; Huang & Luthans, 2014; Liu, 2013; Luthans, Norman, Avolio, & Avey, 2008; Wang, Sui, Luthans, Wang, & Wu, 2014), we generally portray PsyCap as an antecedent to performance outcomes, as an investment in human resources.

PsyCap should be of high interest to organizational leaders and decision makers who allocate scarce resources (financial resources, as well as time and energy) to develop their people's high-potential strengths and psychological resources. To the degree we can show how investing in PsyCap provides a high return on development and in turn performance, the more likely organizational leaders will begin to include PsyCap in their "standard" metrics for gauging organizational performance. One of the advantages of doing so is that unlike most economic indicators, which are lagging measures of performance, PsyCap is a leading indicator or predictor of performance as we and our colleagues have repeatedly demonstrated in both lab and field research.

Measuring PsyCap in the Workplace

In developing our PCQ measures, we drew from recognized, published definitions and measures of efficacy (Parker, 1998), hope (Snyder et al., 1996), optimism (Scheier & Carver, 1985), and resilience (Wagnild & Young, 1993). Each of these four standard scales is of varying number of items and points on Likert scales, and degrees of being state-like and relevant to the workplace. In constructing the PCQ-24, based on content and face validity, six items were systematically selected by an expert panel from each of the four standard measures, the wording was adapted as needed for the workplace and to be state-like, and responses were put into a 6-point Likert scale.

The PCQ-12 items were extracted from the PCQ-24, with three items for efficacy, four items for hope (two for agency and two for pathways), three items for resilience, and two items for optimism. These 12 items were selected by Avey et al. (2011) by following and meeting the psychometric criteria provided by Stanton and colleagues (2002). Unlike the PCQ self-report measures, as discussed earlier, the I-PCQ developed items utilizing the definitions of efficacy, hope, optimism, and resilience and then adding some filler items. As shown in Figure 9.2, it asks respondents to assess the extent to which each definition resembles "someone" (not themselves) in positive (e.g., "Someone has a new job"), negative ("Someone makes a mistake at work"), and neutral ("Someone talks to his/her supervisor") situations. Beyond the variation in the total number of items and the number of items measuring each psychological resource, the three PsyCap measures also vary in the number of reverse-scored items (three in PCQ-24, none in PCQ-12 and I-PCQ) and the number of fillers (none in PCQ-24 and PCQ-12, and four in I-PCQ).

Although the standard scales that we drew from in constructing the two PCQ measures have considerable psychometric support, we also conducted extensive analyses on all three PsyCap measures, including both exploratory and confirmatory factor analyses and reliabilities across diverse samples, which provided psychometric support for these measures (see Avey, Avolio et al., 2011; Harms & Luthans, 2012; Krasikova et al., 2012; Luthans, Avolio et al., 2007; Luthans et al., 2013; Wernsing, 2014). Obviously, there are a number of limitations with any questionnaire measure, and PsyCap measures are no exception. However, our studies so far support the validity and reliability of these measures in numerous organizations throughout the world, translated into many different languages (see Avey, Reichard, Luthans, & Mhatre, 2011, for a meta-analysis; Newman, Ucbasaran, Zhu, & Hirst, 2014, for a recent literature review; Dawkins, Martin, Scott, & Sanderson, 2013, for a psychometric review and critical analysis; and Wernsing, 2014, for a test of PsyCap's measurement invariance across 12 national cultures).

Empirically Relating PsyCap Measures to Work-Related Outcomes

As indicated in the opening two chapters, since PsyCap emerged at the turn of the century, there has been considerable interest in it, and empirical research has grown exponentially. Studies have empirically analyzed the relationship of the individual confidence/efficacy, hope, optimism, and resilience positive resources, and the overall core construct of PsyCap, with a wide range of work-related outcomes. For example, the Avey and colleagues (2011) meta-analysis, including 51 independent samples (N = 12,567 subjects), covered in the introductory part of the book, indicated significant positive relationships between PsyCap and desirable employee attitudes (job satisfaction, organizational commitment, and well-being), desirable employee behaviors (organizational citizenship behaviors), and a variety of performance measures (self-reported, supervisory evaluations, and objective). The same meta-analysis also showed significant negative relationships between PsyCap and undesirable employee attitudes (cynicism, turnover intentions, job stress, and anxiety) and undesirable employee behaviors (counterproductive work behaviors).

As also previously indicated, the more recent Newman and colleagues (2014) literature review identified other PsyCap studies that have further refined the impact of PsyCap on organizationally relevant constructs. For example, PsyCap has been shown to have a moderating effect on the relationship between authentic leadership and performance (Wang, Sui, Luthans, Wang, & Wu, 2014) and a mediated effect on entrepreneurs' well-being (Baron et al., 2014). Overall, empirical findings to date indicate that the percentage of the variation in the outcomes explained by the PsyCap predictor ranges from about 10% to 25%.

On the surface, and as portrayed in conventional wisdom, the four "HERO within" components of PsyCap appear interchangeable and to have considerable overlap. However, as was pointed out in Chapter 2, empirical research in positive psychology has clearly demonstrated that these four resources have convergent, but importantly also discriminant, validities (e.g., see Alarcon, Bowling, Khazon, 2013; Bryant & Cvengros, 2004; Carifio & Rhodes, 2002; Magaletta & Oliver, 1999). In other words, even though empirically there are some similarities between the four (i.e., convergent validity), empirically there are also differences between them (discriminant validity).

Importantly, when the four are combined into the composite of PsyCap as a second-order core construct, through confirmatory factor analysis its multidimensional structure (Law, Wong, & Mobley, 1998) has been consistently demonstrated (e.g., Avey Reichard, et al., 2011; Chen & Lim, 2012; Luthans, Avolio et al., 2007; and for a comprehensive review, see Dawkins et al., 2013). In addition, PsyCap has empirically shown higher correlations with outcomes than any of the individual four resources by themselves (e.g., see Huang & Luthans, 2014; Luthans, Avolio et al., 2007). Finally, research has shown the additive value of PsyCap in predicting desired work attitudes and behaviors beyond demographics and established self-evaluation and personality traits and person-organization (and job) fit (Avey, Luthans, & Youssef, 2010).

As we indicated in Chapter 2, PsyCap does appear to have a synergistic effect; that is, the whole (PsyCap) is greater than the sum of its parts (i.e., confidence, hope, optimism, and resilience). As explained in an example by Avey, Avolio, and Luthans (2011, p. 283): "while the hopeful person sets goals, the efficacious person also ensures setting and accepting challenging goals with an optimistic expectation of success. This in turn contributes to the individual's motivated, increased effort. Moreover, if one is planning multiple pathways (i.e., hope) to resiliently bounce back from setbacks and continues pursuing success by choosing alternate routes when necessary, this may in turn enable continued optimistic expectations." In other words, one resource interacts with and feeds off the other(s) to yield effort and behavior greater than the sum of the parts. As noted in Chapter 2, we are currently empirically exploring various combinations of the 4 components of PsyCap through a person-centered (as opposed to variable-centered) latent profile analysis (LPA, see Meyer, Stanley, & Vandenberg, 2013) to determine if certain profiles hold across diverse samples and differentially effect outcomes (see to date unpublished work by Bouckenooghe, DeClercq, Raja, & Luthans). Furthermore, under the variable-centered approach as potential macro-level, contextual confounds such as industry, organization size, business unit size, and managerial span of control, as well as employee-level demographic variables such as age, gender, ethnic background, education, and tenure, are controlled for, more variability could be accounted for, yielding even higher explained variation (e.g., see Avey, Reichard, et al., 2011; Luthans, Avolio et al., 2007; Youssef & Luthans, 2007).

These results have been supported among numerous samples, such as engineers and technicians in a very large aerospace firm; executives in a logistics firm; financial advisors; nurses in a hospital; bank employees; soldiers and police officers; employees in an insurance services company; workers in a manufacturing company; fast food managers; retail clothing employees; entrepreneurs and small business owners; information technology engineers; federal, state, and local government employees; and many others. Similar results were obtained across cultures, among samples such as global managers stationed around the world with a *Fortune*-100 multinational firm; Indian knowledge workers; Chinese software engineers and factory workers; Vietnamese sales employees; Egyptian factory workers and pharmaceutical, petroleum, and telecommunication employees; white-collar employees from Italy; top-, middle- and lower level organizational leaders and entrepreneurs from New Zealand; Portuguese shop clerks; and the list goes on. The number of permissions granted on a regular basis for studies utilizing our PsyCap measures across the world, and the subsequent numbers of published academic journal articles and empirical papers presented at academic conferences, is very encouraging and indicative of a steady track record supporting the reliability and predictive validity of these instruments. However, we also agree with the recent comprehensive review and critical analysis of PsyCap conducted by Dawkins et al. (2013), which calls for further conceptual development and future in-depth research on the psychometric properties of PsyCap as critical to continuing to grow this domain of research and practice. Also, these results provide further evidence to support the use of PsyCap in determining the value of human resources, as one very intangible asset that matters to organizational performance.

Although the results vary somewhat, for the purpose of illustrations and examples in the remainder of this chapter, it is clear that a statistically significant amount of variation in outcomes is explained by PsyCap (e.g., see Avey, Reichard et al., 2011). For practical purposes, we follow the recommendation that researchers and organizational decision makers be encouraged to utilize the methods and statistical analysis that best fit their conceptual frameworks, data, assumptions, and needs (see Goldstein, 1986; Sackett & Mullen, 1993).

Developing PsyCap in the Workplace

In previous chapters, we have presented several approaches and specific guidelines for developing each of the PsyCap resources. For example, in Chapter 3, efficacy was said to be developed through mastery experiences, modeling and vicarious learning, social persuasion, and physiological and psychological arousal. In Chapter 4, hope was said to be developed through goal setting, participation, and contingency planning for alternative pathways to attain goals. Then in Chapter 5, optimism was said to be developed through leniency for the past, appreciation for the present, and opportunity seeking for the future. Finally, in Chapter 6 resiliency was said to be developed through asset-focused strategies, risk-focused strategies, and process-focused strategies to influence the interpretation and utilization of assets and risks. Several developmental approaches were also presented in Chapters 7 and 8 for the other potential positive psychological resources to help illustrate meeting the criteria for inclusion into PsyCap.

Since our development of reliable and valid measures of PsyCap and their demonstrated relationship to workplace outcomes, we have also turned our research attention to the development of PsyCap through micro-intervention studies. These short, highly focused interventions use pretest-posttest (using PCQ measures) control group experimental designs. These micro-interventions consist of 2- to 3-hour (the length depends on the size of the group and how many exercises and video clip examples are used) workshops generally following the PsyCap Intervention (PCI) model shown in Figure 9.3. The participants'

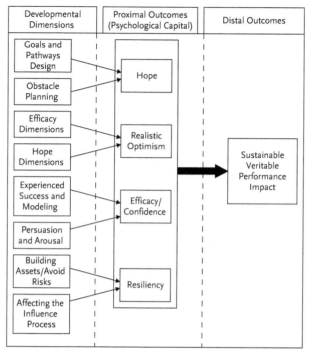

FIGURE 9.3 Psychological capital intervention (PCI). The PCI is intended to affect each state as well as the overall level of PsyCap for performance impact.

Source: Adapted from Luthans, F., Avey, J. B., Avolio, B. J., Norman, S. M., & Combs, G. J. (2006). Psychological capital development: Toward a micro-intervention. *Journal of Organizational Behavior, 27,* 387–393.

PsyCap in these very short, micro-intervention studies increased on average about 2%. Importantly, this statistically significant increase in PsyCap development has occurred in the experimental groups undergoing the PCI session, but not in the randomly assigned control groups undergoing a commonly used group dynamics exercise (e.g., "Desert Survival") under the same conditions with equivalent participants.

The initial micro-intervention studies under highly controlled conditions (e.g., the random assignment to experimental and control groups) were conducted with emerging adults (management students). These subjects are considered an important age group for development research in and of themselves (Arnett, 2000). Importantly, however, the same positive results (about 2% increase in measured PsyCap) have also been found in 2- to 3-hour micro-intervention studies with a broad array of managers and employees from a number of different types of jobs and organizations, in online as well as face-to-face training settings (Luthans et al., 2006, 2008, 2010).

Based on this emerging empirical evidence, for the purpose of illustrations and examples in this chapter, we use 2% as the average potential increase in PsyCap through using our PCI 2- to 3-hour micro-intervention workshops. Although higher percentages have been reported in the literature on various human resource interventions in the workplace (e.g., see Hunter & Schmidt, 1983, for a review), we prefer to use this relatively conservative estimate based on our research to illustrate the potential gains that may result from developing PsyCap through short, highly focused micro-interventions in the workplace.

Assessing the Return on PsyCap Investment

Although in recent years there has been increased demand for and attempted implementation of quantifying the impact of human resource investments, the approaches vary widely in terms of content, depth, breadth, and complexity. We encourage review of this utility analysis literature for background information and technical depth (e.g., see Brogden & Taylor, 1950; Cascio & Boudreau, 2011; Cascio & Ramos, 1986; Cronbach & Gleser, 1965; Hunter & Schmidt, 1983; Hunter, Schmidt, & Judiesch, 1990; Schmidt, Hunter, McKenzie, & Muldrow, 1979). We also acknowledge critiques of utility analysis that provide several warning signs, both regarding its conceptual validity and statistical reliability, as well as in terms of its practicality and credibility in applications to human resource management practice (e.g., Latham & Whyte, 1994; Whyte & Latham, 1997).

In this assessment, we chose to present a relatively simple, practical, but methodologically sound approach to assessing the potential return on PsyCap investment. The approach we use here is conceptually similar to that used in traditional utility analysis. However, research has found that the complexity of traditional utility analysis may actually challenge the credibility of its results as perceived by managers, possibly even reversing its intended impact (Latham & Whyte, 1994).

In reaction to the criticism that you can "lie with statistics" or find any result you want, decision makers have sometimes reduced their support of otherwise promising human resource management investments when presented with very positive findings from complex utility analyses (Latham & Whyte, 1994; Whyte & Latham, 1997). As a result of this type of backlash, utility analysis has been recently elaborated by human resource management scholars (Cascio & Boudreau, 2011) and simplified by management consultants and practitioners (e.g., Kravetz, 2004). We will next apply utility analysis to PsyCap and its development, and we end the chapter by recognizing the potential limitations and pitfalls.

We present several hypothetical examples for calculating the financial impact that PsyCap could potentially have in some of today's largest and most prominent global firms, as well as in more typical medium and small firms. These examples offer alternative approaches based on objectives and data availability. Based on our meta-analytical research findings (Avey, Reichard, et al., 2011), we use .3 as a conservative estimate of the correlation coefficient between PsyCap and performance, and 2% as the increase in PsyCap that can be obtained in a short developmental micro-intervention (i.e., our PCI approach briefly outlined in Fig. 9.3).

Example 1: The Impact PsyCap May Have on Very Large Global Firms

To determine performance impact, objective data are very difficult to obtain (Dess & Robinson, 1984). However, in order to illustrate the financial impact that PsyCap may potentially have in the world's largest firms, we can use the publicly available sales revenue and profits of the top global companies on the *Forbes* list. Recent financial data on the top 10 are presented in Table 9.1. As shown, the sales revenue results for these top-10 companies range from $103 to $467 billion, with a mean of $207 billion and a standard deviation of $139 billion. Their profits range from $14 to $45 billion, with a mean of $25 billion and a standard deviation of $11 billion.

One widely recognized way to estimate the average financial impact that PsyCap may potentially have in these top-10 huge global firms is to use the following utility analysis equation (Cascio & Boudreau, 2011; Hunter & Schmidt, 1983; Skarlicki, Latham, & Whyte, 1996):

$$U = NTr_{xy}SD_y$$

where

U = the dollar value of the performance that may be explained by PsyCap
N = the number of companies or units being assessed
T = the average duration of PsyCap's effect on performance
r_{xy} = the correlation coefficient between PsyCap and performance
SD_y = the standard deviation of outcomes

Assuming that we are examining an average company out of the 10 companies in Table 9.1 ($N = 1$), and focusing on the contribution PsyCap may have over the period of a single year ($T = 1$), the potential financial impact PsyCap may have is calculated as follows:

$$U_{sales} = 1 \times 1 \times 0.3 \times 139 = \$42 \text{ billion}$$
$$U_{profits} = 1 \times 1 \times 0.3 \times 11 = \$3 \text{ billion}$$

In other words, as a gross example for illustrative purposes, the average of these top-10 global companies may potentially have roughly $42 billion of its sales revenue and $3 billion of its profits explained by PsyCap.

Table 9.1 Example 1: Sales Revenues and Profits of the Top 10 of the *Forbes* Global 2000 Companies

Forbes Global 2000 Rank	Company Name	Country	Industry	Sales ($ billion)	Profits ($ billion)
1	ICBC	China	Banking	134.8	37.8
2	China Construction Bank	China	Banking	113.1	30.6
3	JP Morgan Chase	United States	Banking	108.2	21.3
4	General Electric	United States	Conglomerate	147.4	13.6
5	ExxonMobil	United States	Oil and gas	420.7	44.9
6	HSBC	United Kingdom	Banking	104.9	14.3
7	Royal Dutch Shell	Netherlands	Oil and gas	467.2	26.6
8	Agricultural Bank of China	China	Banking	103	23
9	Berkshire Hathaway	United States	Conglomerate	162.5	14.8
9	PetroChina	China	Oil and gas	308.9	18.3
Mean				207.1	24.5
Standard deviation				139.2	10.6

By increasing the levels of PsyCap through a developmental intervention, there should be financial impact on these firms. Specifically, the following modified utility analysis formula can be used to estimate the impact that PsyCap development of micro- interventions may potentially have on the financial outcomes of the average of these very large firms:

$$\Delta U = NTr_{xy}SD_y(\Delta PsyCap)$$

where:

ΔU = the increase in the dollar value of outcomes due to PsyCap development

$\Delta PsyCap$ = the percentage increase resulting from a PsyCap developmental intervention

Again, using our initial PsyCap intervention research findings of 2% from short 2- to 3-hour micro-interventions as the estimate of $\Delta PsyCap$ in the calculations for the example:

$$\Delta U_{sales} = 1 \times 1 \times 0.3 \times 139 \times 0.02 = \$834 \text{ million increase}$$

$$\Delta U_{profits} = 1 \times 1 \times 0.3 \times 11 \times 0.02 = \$66 \text{ million increase}$$

This can be roughly interpreted as regardless of what the existing level of PsyCap is in these 10 very large global companies, they have the potential for increasing their sales revenues by $834 million and their profits by double-digit millions on an annual basis through PsyCap development micro-interventions.

Just as a 2% increase in market share of these global firms would result in a huge impact in their financial revenues, this analysis indicates that a similar 2% increase in PsyCap may also have a significant impact. In order to accurately assess net gains, and return on PsyCap investment or what we have called return on development or ROD (Avolio & Luthans, 2006), intervention costs (e.g., the hourly costs of the participants away from their jobs and facilitator/training overhead costs) would have to be subtracted from the above figures. However, especially when compared to the rate of return on traditional economic capital, the ROD on PsyCap investment may be, relatively speaking, much greater (Youssef & Luthans, 2007).

Example 2: The Impact PsyCap May Have on Medium-Sized Firms

To provide a more complete picture, it is important to report the utility of PsyCap not only for the largest of today's organizations but also in high-potential medium-sized and small companies. Table 9.2 reports recent 12 months sales data for the top-10 companies on *Forbes* most recent list of Mid-Cap Stocks. A mid-cap is defined in these data as a company with a market capitalization around $2–$10 billion.

As shown in Table 9.2, sales revenues of these 10 midsized companies range from $257 million to $2 billion, with a mean of $778 million and a standard deviation of $633 million. To estimate the average utility of PsyCap in these 10 firms selected, we use the following equation, again assuming only the average single company (N = 1), a 1-year period (T = 1), and our.3 correlation between PsyCap and performance and 2% as our PsyCap micro-intervention development increase:

$$U_{sales} = NTr_{xy}SD_y = 1 \times 1 \times 0.3 \times 633 = \$190 \text{ million}$$

$$\Delta U_{sales} = NTr_{xy}SD_y(\Delta PsyCap) = 1 \times 1 \times 0.3 \times 633 \times 0.02 = \$4 \text{ million}$$

In other words, this illustration indicates that for the average of these 10 midsized companies, PsyCap may explain $190 million of their revenue. However, even if these companies had commendable human resource management practices and their employees had a high level of PsyCap, the average of these

Table 9.2 Example 2: Sales Revenues of the Top 10 of *Forbes* 100 Mid-Cap Stocks

Forbes 100 Best Mid-Caps	Company Name	Industry	Sales ($ million)
1	Myriad Genetics	Healthcare	327
2	Deckers Outdoor	Apparel/footwear	738
3	InterDigital	Technology	259
4	Netflix	Retail	1,503
5	Allegiant Travel	Transportation	529
6	Quality Systems	Technology	257
7	Strayer Education	Business services	452
8	Aeropostale	Retail	2,033
9	Amedisys	Healthcare	1,381
10	Capella Education	Business services	298
Mean			777.7
Standard deviation			633.2

midsized firms may still have the potential for increasing their sales revenues by about $4 million through short PsyCap development interventions.

Example 3: The Impact PsyCap May Have on Small Firms

Using a similar utility analysis approach that was used for the large and medium firms, a recent *Forbes* 200 Best Small Companies list was drawn from to provide the data in Table 9.3 As shown in Table 9.3, sales revenues of these 10 smaller companies range from $143 to $866 million, with a mean of $497 million and a standard deviation of $250 million. Using the same assumptions as the other two examples, the utility of PsyCap for the average of these 10 companies over a 1-year period can be calculated as follows:

$$U_{sales} = NTr_{xy}SD_y = 1 \times 1 \times 0.3 \times 250 = \$75 \text{ million}$$

$$\Delta U_{sales} = NTr_{xy}SD_y(\Delta PsyCap) = 1 \times 1 \times 0.3 \times 250 \times 0.02 = \$1.5 \text{ million}$$

In other words, for the average of these 10 smaller companies, PsyCap can potentially explain about $75 million of their sales revenue, and this amount may be increased by $1.5 million through PsyCap development micro-interventions.

Example 4: When Performance Data Are Irrelevant or Unavailable

Even in the absence of objective performance measures, an estimate of the utility of PsyCap return on investment and development can still be made. For example, Kravetz (2004) suggests that "the cost of keeping an employee on the payroll" is a conservative estimate of the dollar value of that employee's productivity. The reasoning is very simple—unless employees are at least contributing what they are costing, the organization would not keep them on the payroll. This employee cost includes not only salary but also government-mandated and additional benefits, plus a share of overhead costs such as facilities space, technological processes, equipment, and other indirect expenses. Kravetz (2004) estimates these additional costs usually range from 75% to 250% of an employee's salary. He suggests that for utility analysis purposes, the total cost of keeping an employee on the payroll (and thus the contribution made) should be set at about twice the employee's direct salary. These estimates are also in line with other utility analysis references (e.g., Cascio & Boudreau, 2011).

Table 9.3 Example 3: Sales Revenues of the Top 10 of *Forbes* Best Small Companies

Forbes Best Small Companies	Company Name	State	Industry	Sales ($ million)
1	Questcor Pharmaceuticals	CA	Pharmaceuticals	621
2	Grand Canyon Education	AZ	Business and personal services	558
3	Proto Labs	MN	Software and programming	143
4	InvenSense	CA	Semiconductors	225
5	Sturm, Ruger	CT	Recreational products	595
6	EPAM Systems	PA	Computer services	493
7	Cirrus Logic	TX	Semiconductors	866
8	US Silica Holdings	MD	Construction materials	487
9	FleetCor Technologies	GA	Business and personal services	804
10	Annie's	CA	Food processing	175
Mean				496.7
Standard deviation				249.9

Applying this rule of thumb, we can then estimate the utility of PsyCap contribution and the value of its development using the following slightly adapted formulas:

$$U_{productivity} = NTr_{xy}(2S)$$

$$\Delta U_{productivity} = NTr_{xy}(2S)(\Delta PsyCap)$$

where:

$U_{productivity}$ = the dollar value of employee productivity (contribution) that can be explained by PsyCap in this case

$\Delta U_{productivity}$ = the increase in the dollar value of productivity (contribution) due to increased PsyCap through its development

N = the number of employees

T = the average tenure

S = the average salary

For example, say an organization employs 500 employees, who, on average, earn an annual salary of $50,000 and stay with the organization for 5 years. With these conservative assumptions, then using Kravetz's (2004) rule of thumb for estimating productivity or contribution (i.e., twice the average salary) and the .3 relationship between PsyCap and performance based upon our initial research, the utility of PsyCap can be calculated as follows:

$$U_{productivity} = 500 \times 5 \times 0.3 \times 2 \times 50,000 = \$75 \text{ million}$$

Furthermore, again using the 2% increase in PsyCap based on our short development interventions, the change in productivity (contribution) in this example can be calculated as follows:

$$\Delta U_{productivity} = 500 \times 5 \times 0.3 \times 2 \times 50,000 \times 0.02 = \$1.5 \text{ million}$$

It should be noted that these results are very similar to those using traditional utility analysis for small companies (see Example 3). We expect over time, organizations that effectively employ evidence-based practices in general (e.g., see Latham, 2009), and PsyCap investment, development, and management, in particular, can potentially experience considerable growth and value. Specifically, we would propose that the return on investment in PsyCap would be much higher than has been obtained from traditional economic capital, and yet like traditional capital, we can expend compounding interest.

To provide research support for this assertion, we can draw from actual data of 74 engineering managers ($100,900 average annual salary) in a high-tech manufacturing firm who went through our 2.5-hour psychological capital intervention (see the PCI model in Fig. 9.3). These study participants had a .33 correlation between their PsyCap and performance. They also had a 1.5% increase in PsyCap as a result of the micro-intervention development session. We then calculated a 270% return on development (ROD) (see Luthans et al., 2006). This return on PsyCap development is based on $73,919 of increased contribution using the utility analysis formula over just a 1-year period (74 × 1 × 0.33 × 2 × $100,900 × 0.015), minus the high 2.5 hourly wage rate ($50/hour) of these managers (multiplied by 2 for the additional benefits/indirect costs), and the estimated facilitator/training overhead costs ($1,500) for conducting the micro-intervention (PCI). This total cost of $20,000 for the PCI ([74 × 2.5 × $50/hour × 2] + 1,500) is used to derive the 270% ROD ([73,919 − 20,000]/20,000). This result from a real example using actual data, of course, is much higher than traditional economic and financial capital has typically been able to return.

This return on investment in PsyCap from this sample of engineering managers can be seen to be even more dramatic if we were able to have the same effect from our PsyCap development intervention on all the employees of this very large high-tech firm. It has about 170,000 employees who average $62,500 in wages and salaries. Using the same utility analysis and assuming the same results obtained in our study of the sample of engineering managers from this very large firm yields over $100 million in contribution, with an ROD of well over 200%, depending on the size of the training groups.

By using the Kravetz (2004) rule of thumb (i.e., two times salary to measure contribution), the higher up the salary scale a group of managers or employees rank, the more likely that developing this group's PsyCap will have substantial results and contribution to the organization's performance. Furthermore, developing these highly paid employees will not only leverage their contribution and performance but may also have a cascading, trickle-down effect on their associates' PsyCap (e.g., see Story, Youssef, Luthans, Barbuto, & Bovaird, 2013, for an empirical demonstration of this PsyCap contagion effect). Such an effect will have a positive impact on employee attitudes, behaviors, and performance throughout the organization (Avolio & Luthans, 2006; Luthans & Avolio, 2003).

Using an extreme example to make a point, a 2% increase in the PsyCap of John Hammergren, CEO of McKesson medical supply company and the highest paid CEO a few years ago (total compensation was $131.2 million), by himself, may have the potential of increasing McKesson's annual performance by close to $1 million. With this extreme example, we do not intend to imply that this leader by himself will have such a dramatic impact on performance from a small increase in his PsyCap. Instead, we are simply suggesting that the higher up the individual is in any organization, the greater the potential cumulative impact (through others in terms of the cascading or social contagion effect) that an increase in PsyCap will have (see Avolio & Luthans, 2006; Luthans & Avolio, 2003; Story et al., 2013).

Potential Limitations and Pitfalls

Although the earlier analysis of PsyCap measurement, relationship with performance, and return on development is quite promising to date, there are also several potential limitations and pitfalls that need to be recognized. We classify these potential limitations and pitfalls into three categories: those that can impede the reliable and valid measurement of PsyCap, those that can threaten the accuracy of performance assessment and impact, and those that can occur in estimating and calculating the return on PsyCap investment.

Pitfalls in Measuring PsyCap

Earlier in this chapter, we presented some of the potential internal, external, and overall construct validity challenges that the measurement of PsyCap may present. Being true to the PsyCap criteria of focusing on positive (rather than negative), workplace-specific (rather than generic or other contexts), and developmental states (rather than relatively fixed, dispositional traits) that are related to performance (rather than being outcomes in and of themselves), our validated PsyCap measures directly address such concerns. For example, Podsakoff, MacKenzie, Lee, and Podsakoff (2003) summarize several potential biases in using surveys for measuring any psychological variables, including PsyCap. These biases include consistency, social desirability, leniency, acquiescence, transient mood states, and item ambiguity. Despite their positivity, the most commonly used PsyCap subscales have not been found to be significantly influenced by such biases (e.g., for hope measurement, see Snyder, 2002). However, we recommend controlling for potential biases such as social desirability when measuring PsyCap. Short instruments to do this are now available, such as Reynolds's (1982) short version of the classic Marlowe-Crowne Social Desirability Scale (Crowne & Marlowe, 1960), which has been supported by research to be even more valid and reliable than the original long version (Loo & Thorpe, 2000). Furthermore, as mentioned earlier, the I-PCQ was purposely developed to help combat social desirability.

Other ways in which our PsyCap measures take into consideration and limit some of the potential biases are the inclusion of reverse-scored items, multiple administrations of the scale at different points in time, using randomly assigned control groups for intervention studies, and the use of well-developed and tested items that are adapted from established, standardized measures from positive psychology. Nonetheless, potential threats still exist. For example, Podsakoff and colleagues (2003) suggest that the use of a common scale format and fixed anchors may increase common method biases. However, we have not found significant differences between the factor structures yielded by the scales of our PCQ instruments and those from the literature for measuring the various PsyCap resources.

Moreover, shorter scales can cause more consistency due to answers to previous items continuing to be present in the respondent's short-term memory. This can be further increased by the lack of intermixing of items that measure the various PsyCap capacities. Intermixing of items and varying the scales and anchors are possible. On the other hand, there are tradeoffs, particularly in organizational behavior research, where lengthy instruments have been found to significantly reduce response rates.

Clearly any survey measure such as our three PCQ instruments will have limitations. For the future development and refinement of measuring PsyCap, we propose to move toward a triangulation strategy. Specifically, one can use questionnaire surveys (the PCQ measures), observation, and interviews to triangulate around what an individual's PsyCap score ends up being based on multiple sources (e.g., see Berson & Avolio, 2004 for an example of how to use triangulation to estimate leadership behavior). At this stage of development of PsyCap, we also recommend the use of qualitative methods to gain better insight and depth of understanding (e.g., see Creswell, 2013). In the future, within the same PsyCap study, we recommend and are beginning to use (e.g., Fagan, 2014) the increasingly popular mixed-methods approach, which involves collecting, analyzing, and mixing both quantitative and qualitative data in a systematic study design (see Creswell & Plano-Clark, 2011).

New technology is emerging where cameras can capture people's facial expressions and measure, at least minimally, their levels of positivity, if not more specific components of PsyCap. Imagine a world where organizations sample throughout the day nonverbal expressions to gauge the level of PsyCap in their workforce. That world already exists in terms of the technology being available to make such futuristic assessments.

Only through the use of such multimethods can we eventually reduce to a minimum the bias inherent in sole use of surveys that may artificially increase (or decrease) PsyCap scores.

Pitfalls in Measuring Performance

One of the continuing issues facing organizational behavior research is the collection of objective performance data. Performance measures too often tend to be nonexistent, very subjective, outdated, infrequent, inadequate, or not voluntarily made available. When objective performance measures are not directly available, using multiple measures may be able to compensate, even if some of these supplemental/substitute measures are subjective (Dess & Robinson, 1984). Moreover, Chakravarthy (1986) shows that even when present, traditional performance measures are often insufficient, and he highlights the utility of incorporating satisfaction measures, which have been consistently shown to be related to performance (see the meta-analysis of Judge, Thorensen, Bono, & Patton, 2001). Harter, Schmidt, and Hayes (2002, 2003) also support the use of composite measures of performance, including productivity and profitability, as well as turnover and customer satisfaction.

In our research, we have found integrating various measures of performance (e.g., objective quality and quantity data, financial and sales data, supervisor's evaluation, self-reported assessment, and merit-based salary information), as well as administering validated measures of attitudinal outcomes (e.g., job satisfaction, intentions to quit, organizational commitment) to provide a more complete picture of performance (Avey, Luthans, & Youssef, 2010; Avey, Reichard, et al., 2011; Luthans, Avolio et al., 2007; Youssef & Luthans, 2007). To avoid common source biases, outcome assessments can be obtained from a different source (e.g., organizational data or the respondent's manager) or from the respondents themselves but at a different point in time, in a different location, or through a different medium. Anonymity should be ensured, which can present a hurdle in relating each respondent's predictor to outcome data. However, various procedural and statistical approaches have been found to be effective in such situations (Podsakoff et al., 2003).

It is important to remember that supervisory performance appraisals of individuals may appear objective but still be based on subjective premises. The most objective measures of performance are those based on actual hard data (e.g., productivity numbers or sales made). Obviously, other issues such as shared input, technology, and even luck may enter into these objective data as well. Moreover, supervisory ratings that are commonly utilized in performance appraisals are usually influenced by a number of variables such as the rated employee's organizational citizenship behaviors (Schmidt, 2009), as well as a multitude of perceptual and attributional biases that may influence the supervisor's rating. However, even with these potential problems, such outside ratings are still considered preferable to self-ratings.

Another significant, but generally overlooked, issue regarding the measurement of performance is getting the right range and dimensions of performance. For example, we would suggest that the PsyCap measure is more likely to predict a broader range of performance criteria given the nature of the constructs that comprise this scale. Specifically, constructs such as efficacy, hope, optimism, and resilience are likely to predict in the upper ranges of human performance by their very nature, especially measures that tap into durability and sustainability. Thus, if the performance measure captures "typical" performance ranges in organizations, then the PsyCap measure may very well underpredict because the top end of the performance range is not available, or what would be called a criterion deficiency. We propose the need to examine performance not only under ordinary but also extraordinary conditions before we can settle on the metarelationship of PsyCap to performance.

An example from the transformational leadership literature illustrates this point about the need to examine performance ranges. Lim and Ployhart (2004) reported that the validity of the transformational leadership scale went from .30 to .60 when predicting typical versus extraordinary performance. Because the transformational leadership scale was designed to predict performance beyond expectations, it is not surprising that it predicts extraordinary performance much better than just typical performance. We believe the same problem with how organizations measure performance may exist for the studies that have been completed to date focusing on PsyCap. Future research needs to test this proposition of better prediction of high levels of performance.

Pitfalls in Measuring the Return on PsyCap Investment

Besides the possible measurement problems associated with PsyCap and performance, the work of Podsakoff and colleagues (2003) can also contribute to addressing the potential pitfalls in conducting utility analysis when assessing the return on PsyCap development interventions in terms of the impact on performance and attitudinal outcomes. One primary concern would be common method biases may result in small or nonexistent relationships that are found and exaggerated, but strong, true relationships are not uncovered or are diminished.

Most of our research results on PsyCap were obtained through studies in which common method biases were minimized, both procedurally and statistically. However, Cote and Buckley's (1987) extensive, multidisciplinary analysis suggests that even if there were some common method biases, our results that PsyCap accounts for on average about 10% (performance) to 20% (attitudes) of the variance may actually have a higher true variance. However, as discussed earlier, strong PsyCap measurement instruments, diversified outcome measures and sources, and controlling for potential confounds, are factors that have contributed to the reliability and validity of our studies to date.

More specifically in relation to the utility calculations, one of the most frequently cited difficulties is the estimation of SD_y, the standard deviation of the outcome of interest. Our calculations in the examples outlined earlier are no exception. Besides the limitations of outcome data scarcity and relevance, various assumptions such as randomness and normality may not necessarily apply across situations. Indeed, companies would prefer a skewed distribution of performance, which means that the performance distribution is shifted upward. Having a normal distribution reflecting one's performance would not be advantageous for a high-performing organization.

Our illustrative cases of utility analysis did not utilize random samples of companies. However, researchers and practitioners can ensure that these assumptions are met by utilizing company-specific, longitudinal data. Such data can either constitute a random sample of outcomes that one has the opportunity to collect from a larger sample of data that accrues, or, ideally, a complete data set of outcomes that accrue over time for each of the organizations being studied (i.e., the y-population). Such future research can facilitate the use of more realistic estimates of SD_y, particularly in intervention research, where such data are infrequently reported (Hunter & Schmidt, 1983).

Moreover, PsyCap is by definition a malleable state. This state-like criterion implies its potential for development and thus variability not only across respondents but also within respondents over time, meaning intraindividual change. Although PsyCap variability and developmental potential are conceptually and practically desirable, they represent challenges to our currently available methodologies. We have utilized randomly assigned control groups in our intervention research designs as a way to manage such challenges. Our longitudinal research has also supported similar conclusions (Avey, Luthans, Smith, & Palmer, 2010; Peterson, Luthans, Avolio, Walumbwa, & Zhang, 2011). We feel such design steps must be taken to scientifically evaluate the impact of PsyCap and its development over time.

Finally, an important challenge in assessing the impact of PsyCap is choosing the appropriate level of analysis for the outcomes being assessed. Statistically, individual-level outcomes are the simplest to relate to PsyCap, since it is also measured at the individual level. However, such outcomes are not always available, and they may not necessarily be of the highest priority or significance to organizations, which increasingly rely upon the integration of work across units to perform. For instance, a large healthcare organization is promoting team-to-team integration to provide seamless care across its healthcare system. The organizational leaders have learned that the handoffs between parts of the organization can make a tremendous difference in the quality of care and safety.

With increasing trends toward examining how organizations work across boundaries, the utilization of important group- and organizational-level outcomes, such as the sales and profits figures used in the utility analysis examples earlier, may be of highest interest to organizations. For example, Harter and colleagues (2002) and Peterson and Luthans (2003) utilized business-level outcomes to assess the impact of employee engagement and leader hope, usually examined at the individual level versus linking them to organizational-level outcomes. However, aggregation may not always be statistically possible or justifiable, particularly because one oftentimes finds high within-group variability in psychological measures such as PsyCap. These high levels of variability do not justify aggregation in that the mean would not be representative of the group's variance on a particular measure.

Various approaches have now been proposed for elevating PsyCap to higher levels of analysis (e.g., see McKenny, Short, & Payne, 2013; Newman et al., 2014), and empirical research is emerging in this area (e.g., Clapp-Smith, Vogelgesang, & Avey, 2009; Haar, Roche, & Luthans, 2014; Mathe-Soulek, Scott-Halsell, Kim, & Krawczyk, 2014; Memili, Welsh, & Kaciak, 2014; Memili, Welsh, & Luthans, 2013; Peterson & Zhang, 2011). This research is based on the premise that PsyCap at the individual level is isomorphic with the group level, which we would suggest is a valid assumption. This means that the meaning of PsyCap for individuals and the group or organizational level is essentially the same. Changing the referent on PsyCap measures from the individual to a group level would provide for an interesting avenue for future research to explore group- or organizational-level PsyCap.

In conclusion, in order to meet the criteria, and differentiate from almost all human resource management approaches through the years, PsyCap must show performance impact. In this chapter, we have attempted to demonstrate such PsyCap impact on performance and ROD, as well as how it can be done as validly as possible in the future.

Case Study: Investing in People at Google

Video link: http://www.youtube.com/watch?v=aOZhbOhEunY

Video link: http://www.youtube.com/watch?v=9No-FiEInLA

Google has been at the top of *Fortune*'s 100 Best Companies to Work For list since 2012. These two videos show some of the many reasons why employees love working for Google, and how Google invests in their development, growth, and commitment.

Questions for reflection and/or discussion:

1. Which dimensions of each of the HERO resources do you see in Google employees?
2. How does Google nurture its employees' psychological resources?
3. Which components of the Google culture can be applied to your present (or past) workplace, or to a broad range of organizations? Which components are probably just unique to Google?
4. Overall, does the culture in your present (or past) workplace promote or hinder PsyCap development? Explain.

References

Abbas, M., Raja, U., Darr, W., & Bouckenooghe, D. (2013). Combined effects of perceived politics and psychological capital on job satisfaction, turnover intentions, and performance. *Journal of Management*, doi:10.1177/0149206313495411.

Alarcon, G. M., Bowling, N. A., & Khazon, S. (2013). Great expectations: A meta-analytic examination of optimism and hope. *Personality and Individual Differences, 54,* 821–827.

Arnett, J. J. (2000). Emerging adulthood: A theory of development from the late teens through the twenties. *American Psychologist, 55,* 469–480.

Avey, J. B., Avolio, B. J., & Luthans, F. (2011). Experimentally analyzing the impact of leader positivity on follower positivity and performance. *Leadership Quarterly, 22,* 282–294.

Avey, J. B., Luthans, F., Smith, R. M., & Palmer, N. F. (2010). Impact of positive psychological capital on employee well-being over time. *Journal of Occupational Health Psychology, 15,* 17–28.

Avey, J. B., Luthans, F., & Youssef, C. M. (2010). The additive value of positive psychological capital in predicting work attitudes and behaviors. *Journal of Management, 36,* 430–452.

Avey, J. B., Reichard, R. J., Luthans, F., & Mhatre, K. H. (2011). Meta-analysis of the impact of positive psychological capital on employee attitudes, behaviors, and performance. *Human Resource Development Quarterly, 22*, 127–152.

Avolio, B., & Luthans, F. (2006). *The high impact leader.* New York, NY: McGraw-Hill.

Bandura, A. (1997). *Self-efficacy: The exercise of control.* New York, NY: Freeman.

Bandura, A. (2012). On the functional properties of perceived self-efficacy revisited. *Journal of Management, 38*, 9–44.

Baron, R. A., Franklin, R. J., & Hmieleski, K. M. (2014). Why entrepreneurs often experience low, not high levels of stress: The joint effects of selection and psychological capital. *Journal of Management*, doi:10.1177/0149206313495411.

Becker, B. E., Huselid, M. A., & Beaty, R. W. (2009). *The differentiated workforce: Transforming talent into strategic impact.* Boston, MA: Harvard.

Berson, Y., & Avolio, B. J. (2004). Linking transformational and strategic leadership: Examining the leadership system of a high-technology organization in a turbulent environment. *Leadership Quarterly, 15*, 625–646.

Boudreau, J. W., & Jesuthasan, R. (2011). *Transformative HR: How great companies use evidence-based change.* New York, NY: Wiley.

Brogden, H. E., & Taylor, E. K. (1950). The dollar criterion: Applying the cost accounting concept to criterion construction. *Personnel Psychology, 3*, 133–154.

Bryant, F. B., & Cvengros, J. A. (2004). Distinguishing between hope and optimism. *Journal of Social and Clinical Psychology, 11*, 273–302.

Cacioppo, J. T., & Berntson, G. G. (1994). Relationship between attitudes and evaluative space: A critical review, with emphasis on the separability of positive and negative substrates. *Psychological Bulletin, 115*, 401–423.

Campbell, B. J., Coff, R., & Kryscynski, D. (2012). Rethinking sustained competitive advantage from human capital. *Academy of Management Review, 37*, 376–395.

Carifio, J., & Rhodes, I. (2002). Construct validities and the empirical relationships between optimism, hope, self-efficacy, and locus of control. *Work, 19*, 125–136.

Cascio, W. F., & Boudreau, J. W. (2011). *Investing in people: Financial impact of human resource initiatives* (2nd ed.). Upper Saddle River, NJ: Pearson.

Cascio, W. F., & Ramos, R. A. (1986). Development and application of a new method for assessing job performance and behavioral/economic terms. *Journal of Applied Psychology, 71*, 20–28.

Chakravarthy, B. S. (1986). Measuring strategic performance. *Strategic Management Journal, 7*, 437–458.

Chen, D. J. Q., & Lim, V. K. G. (2012). Strength in adversity: The influence of psychological capital on job search. *Journal of Organizational Behavior, 33*, 811–839.

Clapp-Smith, R., Vogelgesang, G. R., & Avey, J. B. (2009). Authentic leadership and positive psychological capital: The mediating role of trust at the group level of analysis. *Journal of Leadership and Organizational Studies, 15*, 227–240.

Combs, J. G., Liu, Y., Hall, A., & Ketchen, D. (2006). How much do high-performance work practices matter? A meta-analysis of their effects on organizational performance. *Personnel Psychology, 59,* 501–528.

Conley, J. J. (1984). The hierarchy of consistency: A review and model of longitudinal findings on adult individual differences in intelligence, personality, and self-opinion. *Personality and Individual Differences, 5,* 11–25.

Cote, J., & Buckley, R. (1987). Estimating trait, method, and error variance: Generalizing across 70 construct validation studies. *Journal of Marketing Research, 24,* 315–318.

Creswell, J. W. (2013). *Qualitative inquiry and research design: Choosing among five approaches* (5th ed.). Thousand Oaks, CA: Sage.

Creswell, J. W., & Plano-Clark, V. L. (2011). *Designing and conducting mixed methods research* (2nd ed.). Thousand Oaks, CA: Sage.

Cronbach, L. J., & Gleser, G. C. (1965). *Psychological tests and personnel decisions* (2nd ed.). Urbana: University of Illinois Press.

Crook, T. R., Todd, S. Y., Combs, J. G., Woehr, D. J., & Ketchen, D. J. (2011). Does human capital matter? A meta-analysis of the relationship between human capital and firm performance. *Journal of Applied Psychology, 96,* 443–456.

Crowne, D. P., & Marlowe, D. (1960). A new scale of social desirability independent of psychopathology. *Journal of Counseling Psychology, 24,* 349–354.

Dawkins, S., Martin, A., Scott, J., & Sanderson, K. (2013). Building on the positive: A psychometric review and critical analysis of the construct of psychological capital. *Journal of Occupational and Organizational Psychology, 86,* 348–370.

De Houwer, J., Teige-Mocigemba, S., Spruyt, A., & Moors, A. (2009). Implicit measures: A normative analysis and review. *Psychological Bulletin, 135,* 347–368.

Dess, G. G., & Robinson, R. B., Jr. (1984). Measuring organizational performance in the absence of objective measures: The case of the privately held firm and conglomerate business unit. *Strategic Management Journal, 5,* 265–273.

Dollwet, M., & Reichard, R. (2013). Assessing cross-cultural skills: Validation of a new measure of cross-cultural psychological capital. *International Journal of Human Resource Management.* doi.org/10.1080/09585192.2013.845239.

Dunlop, P. D., & Lee, K. (2004). Workplace deviance, organizational citizenship behavior, and business unit performance: The bad apples do spoil the whole barrel. *Journal of Organizational Behavior, 25,* 67–80.

Flumer, I. S., & Ployhart, R. E. (2014). "Our most important asset": A multidiciplinary/ multilevel review of human capital valuation for research and practice. *Journal of Management, 40,* 161–192.

Fagan, H. (2014). *PsyCap and the impact on the development of intercultural sensitivity of healthcare educators: A mixed methods study.* Unpublished Ph.D. dissertation, University of Nebraska, Lincoln.

Goldstein, I. L. (1986). *Training in organizations: Needs, assessment, development, and evaluation.* Monterey, CA: Brookes/Cole.

Gooty, J., Gavin, M., Johnson, P., Frazier, L., & Snow, D. (2009) In the eyes of the beholder: Transformational leadership, positive psychological capital and performance. *Journal of Leadership and Organization Studies, 15,* 353–357.

Gupta, V., & Singh, S. (2014). Psychological capital as a mediator of the relationship between leadership and creative performance behaviors. *International Journal of Human Resource Management, 25,* 1373–1394.

Haar, J., Roche, M., & Luthans, F. (August 1–5, 2014). *Do leaders' psychological capital and engagement influence follower teams or vice-versa.* Paper presented at Academy of Management Conference, Philadelphia, PA.

Harms, P., & Luthans, F. (2012). Measuring implicit psychological constructs in organizational behavior: An example using psychological capital. *Journal of Organizational Behavior, 33,* 589–594.

Harter, J., Schmidt, F., & Hayes, T. (2002). Business-unit-level relationship between employee satisfaction, employee engagement, and business outcomes: A meta-analysis. *Journal of Applied Psychology, 87,* 268–279.

Harter, J., Schmidt, F., & Hayes, T. (2003). Well-being in the workplace and its relationship to business outcomes: A review of the Gallup studies. In C. Keyes & J. Haidt (Eds.), *Flourishing: Positive psychology and the life well-lived* (pp. 205–224). Washington, DC: American Psychological Association.

Huang, L., & Luthans, F. (2014). Toward better understanding of the learning goal orientation-creativity relationship: The role of positive psychological capital. *Applied Psychology: An International Review,* doi:10.1111/apps.12028.

Hunter, J. E., & Schmidt, F. L. (1983). Quantifying the effects of psychological interventions on employee job performance and work-force productivity. *American Psychologist, 38,* 473–478.

Hunter, J. E., Schmidt, F. L., & Judiesch, M. K. (1990). Individual differences in output variability as a function of job complexity. *Journal of Applied Psychology, 75,* 28–42.

Judge, T. A., & Bono, J. E. (2001). Relationship of core self-evaluations traits—self-esteem, generalized self-efficacy, locus of control, and emotional stability—with job satisfaction and job performance: A meta-analysis. *Journal of Applied Psychology, 86,* 80–92.

Judge, T. A., Thorensen, C. J., Bono, J. E. & Patton, G. K. (2001). The job satisfaction-job performance relationship: A qualitative and quantitative review. *Psychological Bulletin, 127,* 376–407.

Krasikova, D. V., Harms, P. D., & Luthans, F. (April, 2012). *Telling stories: Validating an implicit measure of psychological capital.* Paper presented at 27th Meeting of Society for Industrial and Organizational Psychology, San Diego, CA.

Kravetz, D. (2004). *Measuring human capital: Converting workplace behavior into dollars.* Mesa, AZ: KAP.

Kubzansky, L. D., Kubzansky, P. E., & Maselko, J. (2004). Optimism and pessimism in the context of health: Bipolar opposites or separate constructs? *Personality and Social Psychology Bulletin, 30,* 943–956.

Latham, G. P. (2009). *Becoming the evidence-based manager: Making the science of management work for you.* Boston, MA: SHRM/Davies-Black.

Latham, G. P., & Whyte, G. (1994). The futility of utility analysis. *Personnel Psychology, 47,* 31–46.

Law, K. S., Wong, C., & Mobley, W. H. (1998). Toward a taxonomy of multidimensional constructs. *Academy of Management Review, 23,* 741–755.

Lim, B. C., & Ployhart, R.E. (2004). Transformational leadership: Relations to the five-factor model and team performance in typical and maximum contexts. *Journal of Applied Psychology, 89,* 610–621.

Liu, Y. (2013). Moderating effect of positive psychological capital in Taiwan's life insurance industry. *Social Behavior and Personality, 41,* 109–112.

Locke, E., Frederick, E., Lee, C., & Bobko, P. (1984). Effects of self-efficacy, goals and task strategies on task performance. *Journal of Applied Psychology, 69,* 241–251.

Loo, R., & Thorpe, K. (2000). Confirmatory factor analyses of the full and short versions of the Marlowe-Crowne social desirability scale. *Journal of Social Psychology, 140,* 628–635.

Lopez, S., & Snyder, C. R. (Eds.). (2003). *Positive psychological assessment: A handbook of models and measures.* Washington, DC: American Psychological Association.

Luthans, F., Yousef, C. M., & Avolio, B, J. (2007). *Psychological capital: Developing the human competitive edge.* Oxford: Oxford Press.

Luthans, B. C., Luthans, K. W., & Avey, J. B. (2014). Building the leaders of tomorrow: The development of academic psychological capital. *Journal of Leadership and Organizational Studies, 21,* 191–200.

Luthans, B. C., Luthans, K. W., & Jensen, S. (2012). The impact of business school students' psychological capital on academic performance. *Journal of Education for Business, 87,* 253–259.

Luthans, F., Avey, J. B., Avolio, B. J., Norman, S. M., & Combs, G. J. (2006). Psychological capital development: Toward a micro-intervention. *Journal of Organizational Behavior, 27,* 387–393.

Luthans, F., Avey, J. B., Avolio, B. J., & Peterson, S. (2010). The development and resulting performance impact of positive psychological capital. *Human Resource Development Quarterly, 21,* 41–66.

Luthans, F., Avey, J. B., & Patera, J. L. (2008). Experimental analysis of a web-based training intervention to develop positive psychological capital. *Academy of Management Learning and Education, 7,* 209–221.

Luthans, F., & Avolio, B. (2003). Authentic leadership: A positive development approach. In K. S. Cameron, J. E. Dutton, & R. E. Quinn (Eds.), *Positive organizational scholarship* (pp. 241–258). San Francisco, CA: Berrett-Koehler.

Luthans, F., Avolio, B. J., Avey, J. B., & Norman, S. M. (2007). Positive psychological capital: Measurement and relationship with performance and satisfaction. *Personnel Psychology, 60,* 541–572.

Luthans, F., Norman, S. M., Avolio, B. J., & Avey, J. B. (2008). The mediating role of psychological capital in the supportive organizational climate-employee performance relationship. *Journal of Organizational Behavior, 29,* 219–238.

Luthans, F., Youssef, C. M., & Avolio, B. J. (2007). *Psychological capital: Developing the human competitive edge.* New York, NY: Oxford University Press, Appendix, 237–238.

Luthans, F., Youssef, C. M., Sweetman, D., & Harms, P. (2013). Meeting the leadership challenge of employee well-being through relationship PsyCap and health PsyCap. *Journal of Leadership and Organizational Studies, 20,* 114–129.

Magaletta, P. R., & Oliver, J. M. (1999). The hope construct, will and ways: Their relations with efficacy, optimism, and general well-being. *Journal of Clinical Psychology, 55,* 539–551.

Maurer, T. J., & Pierce, H. R. (1998). A comparison of Likert scale and traditional measures of self-efficacy. *Journal of Applied Psychology, 83,* 324–329.

Masten, A. S. (2001). Ordinary magic: Resilience process in development. *American Psychologist, 56,* 227–239.

Masten, A. S., Cutuli, J. J., Herbers, J. E, & Reed, M. G. J. (2009). Resilience in development. In S. J. Lopez & C. R. Snyder (Eds.), *Oxford handbook of positive psychology* (2nd ed., pp. 117–131). New York, NY: Oxford University Press.

Mathe-Soulek, K., Scott-Halsell, S., Kim, S., & Krawczyk, M. (2014). Psychological capital in the quick service restaurant industry: A study of unit level performance. *Journal of Hospitality and Tourism Research,* doi:10.1177/10963348014550923.

McKenny, A. F., Short, J. C., & Payne, T. (2013). Using computer-aided text analysis to elevate constructs: An illustration using psychological capital. *Organizational Research Methods, 16,* 152–184.

Memili, E., Welsh, D. H. B., & Kaciak, E. (2014). Organizational psychological capital of family franchise firms through the lens of the leader-member exchange theory. *Journal of Leadership and Organization Studies, 21,* 200–209.

Memili, E., Welsh, D. H. B., & Luthans, F. (2013). Going beyond research on goal setting: A proposed role for organizational psychological capital of family firms. *Entrepreneurhsip Theory and Practice, 37,* 1289–1296.

Meyer, J. P., Stanley, L. J., & Vandenberg, R. J. (2013). A person-centered approach to the study of commitment. *Human Resource Management Review, 23,* 190–202.

Newman, A., Ucbasaran, D., Zhu, F., & Hirst, G. (2014). Psychological capital: A review and synthesis. *Journal of Organizational Behavior, 35,* S120–S138.

Norman, S. M., Avolio, B. J., & Luthans, F. (2010). The impact of positivity and transparency on trust in leaders and their perceived effectiveness. *Leadership Quarterly, 21,* 350–364.

Parker, S. (1998). Enhancing role breadth self-efficacy: The roles of job enrichment and other organizational interventions. *Journal of Applied Psychology, 6,* 835–852.

Peterson, C., & Chang, E. (2002). Optimism and flourishing. In C. Keyes & J. Haidt (Eds.), *Flourishing: Positive psychology and the life well-lived* (pp. 55–79). Washington, DC: American Psychological Association.

Peterson, S., & Luthans, F. (2003). The positive impact of development of hopeful leaders. *Leadership and Organizational Development Journal, 24,* 26–31.

Peterson, S. J., Luthans, F., Avolio, B. J., Walumbwa, F. O., & Zhang, Z. (2011). Psychological capital and employee performance: A latent growth modeling approach. *Personnel Psychology, 64,* 427–450.

Peterson, S. J., & Zhang, Z. (2011). Examining the relationships between top management team psychological characteristics, transformational leadership, and business unit performance. In M. A. Carpenter (Ed.), *Handbook of top management research* (pp. 127–149). New York, NY: Edward Elgar.

Pittinsky, T. L., Rosenthal, S., & Montoya, R. M. (2011). Liking is not the opposite of disliking: The functional separability of positive and negative attitudes toward minority groups. *Cultural Diversity and Ethnic Minority Psychology, 17,* 134–143.

Podsakoff, P., MacKenzie, S., Lee, J., & Podsakoff, N. (2003). Common method biases in behavioral research: A critical review of the literature and recommended remedies. *Journal of Applied Psychology, 88,* 879–903.

Reynolds, W. (1982). Development of reliable and valid short forms of the Marlowe-Crowne social desirability scale. *Journal of Clinical Psychology, 38,* 119–125.

Sackett, P. R., Berry, C. M., Wiemann, S. A., & Laczo, R. M. (2006). Citizenship and counterproductive behavior: Clarifying relations between the two domains. *Human Performance, 19,* 441–464.

Sackett, P. R., & Mullen, E. J. (1993). Beyond formal experimental design: Towards an expanded view of the training evaluation process. *Personnel Psychology, 46,* 613–627.

Schaufeli, W. B., & Bakker, A. B. (2004). Job demands, job resources, and their relationship with burnout and engagement: A multi-sample study. *Journal of Organizational Behavior, 25,* 293–315.

Scheier, M., & Carver, C. (1985). Optimism, coping, and health: Assessment and implications of generalized outcome expectancies. *Health Psychology, 4,* 219–247.

Schmidt, F. (2009). Select on intelligence. In E. Locke (Ed.), *Handbook of principles of organizational behavior* (2nd ed., pp. 3–17). West Sussex, UK: Wiley.

Schmidt, F. L., Hunter, J. E., McKenzie, R. C., & Muldrow, T. W. (1979). Impact of valid selection procedures on work-force productivity. *Journal of Applied Psychology, 64,* 609–626.

Seligman, M. E. P. (1998). *Learned optimism.* New York, NY: Pocket Books.

Skarlicki, D. P., Latham, G. P., & Whyte, G. (1996). Utility analysis: Its evolution and tenuous role in human resource management decision making. *Revue Canadienne des Sciences de l'Administration, 13*(1), 13–21.

Snyder, C. R. (2000). *Handbook of hope.* San Diego, CA: Academic Press.

Snyder, C. R. (2002). Hope theory: Rainbows in the mind. *Psychological Inquiry, 13,* 249–275.

Snyder, C. R., Sympson, S. C., Ybasco, F. C., Borders, T. F., Babyak, M. A., & Higgins, R. L. (1996). Development and validation of the state hope scale. *Journal of Personality and Social Psychology, 70,* 321–335.

Stajkovic, A. D., & Luthans, F. (1998a). Self-efficacy and work-related performance: A meta-analysis. *Psychological Bulletin, 124,* 240–261.

Stajkovic, A. D., & Luthans, F. (1998b). Social cognitive theory and self-efficacy: Going beyond traditional motivational and behavioral approaches. *Organizational Dynamics, 26,* 62–74.

Stanton, J. M., Sinar, E. F., Balzar, W. K., & Smith, P. C. (2002). Issues and strategies for reducing the length of self-report scales. *Personnel Psychology, 55,* 167–194.

Story, J. S., Youssef, C. M., Luthans, F., Barbuto, J. E., & Bovaird, J. (2013). Contagion effect of global leaders' positive psychological capital on followers: Does distance and quality of relationship matter? *International Journal of Human Resource Management, 24,* 2534–2553.

Vogelgesang, G., Clapp-Smith, R., & Osland, J. (2014). The relationship between positive psychological capital and global mindset in the context of global leadership. *Journal of Leadership and Organization Studies, 21,* 165–178.

Wagnild, G., & Young, H. (1993). Development and psychometric evaluation of the resiliency scale. *Journal of Nursing Measurement, 1*(2), 165–178.

Wang, H., Sui, Y., Luthans, F., Wang, D., & Wu, Y. (2014). Impact of authentic leadership on performance: Role of followers' positive psychological capital and relational processes. *Journal of Organizational Behavior, 35,* 5–21.

Watson, D., Clark, L. A., & Tellegen, A. (1988). Development and validation of brief measures of positive and negative affect: The PANAS scales. *Journal of Personality and Social Psychology, 54,* 1063–1070.

Wernsing, T. (2014). Psychological capital: A test of measurement invariance across 12 national cultures. *Journal of Leadership and Organization Studies, 21,* 179–190.

Whyte, G., & Latham, G. (1997). The futility of utility analysis revisited: When even an expert fails. *Personnel Psychology, 50,* 601–610.

Wright, P. M., Coff, R., & Moliterno, T. P. (2014). Strategic human capital: Crossing the great divide. *Journal of Management, 40,* 353–370.

Wright, T. A. (2007). A look at two methodological challenges for scholars interested in positive organizational behavior. In D. Nelson & C. L. Cooper (Eds.), *Positive organizational behavior: Accentuating the positive at work* (pp. 177–190). Thousand Oaks, CA: Sage.

Youssef, C. M., & Luthans, F. (2007). Positive organizational behavior in the workplace: The impact of hope, optimism, and resilience. *Journal of Management, 33,* 774–800.

10 THE PSYCAP JOURNEY

NOW AND INTO THE FUTURE

Opening Video: Fred Luthans on Summary of PsyCap

Video link: https://www.youtube.com/watch?v=R5Lx89Qmz
YI&feature=youtu.be

(If this link does not work for you simply search You Tube for
Fred Luthans, Happiness Lincoln Summit).

In this final chapter video, in an informal presentation for a
"Happiness Lincoln" event, Professor Luthans provides a brief
(30-minute) overview of the background, components, research
and application of PsyCap.

Questions for reflection and/or discussion:

1. In your own words, where does PsyCap come from? What
   are the roots and criteria of inclusion for the PsyCap
   components?
2. How does PsyCap fit in (or not) with other recognized forms
   of capital?
3. In brief, what are the HERO components of PsyCap? What,
   if any, other positive psychological resources would you recommend for inclusion in PsyCap? Why, or why not?
4. To you, what is the most impressive research findings and
   applications?

Since publishing our first book on PsyCap several years ago, it has
been very encouraging to see that scholars and practitioners in
numerous fields and various countries around the world are showing

considerable interest in PsyCap. As mentioned at the beginning of this book, PsyCap has gone beyond private-sector, for-profit organizations. It has been applied to military personnel, pilots, police officers, mental health and social work professionals, educators, golfers and coaches and athletes in most sports, nurses and other healthcare personnel, public-sector workers, and volunteers. Besides employees and leaders in all types of organizations, it has also been applied to schoolchildren, adolescents, at-risk youth, college students, the unemployed, and the elderly. The evidence indicates that nearly everyone can benefit from a healthy dose of positivity, not only at work but also in various life domains. This presents researchers and evidence-based practitioners across disciplines with tremendous opportunities. However, there are always the risks and challenges of oversimplifying a construct's nomological network or of overgeneralizing a construct without taking into consideration the contextual factors that shape its value, utility, and influence on the desired outcomes. The purpose of this concluding chapter is to offer those interested in expanding the science and practice of PsyCap with a summary of where we stand now and a roadmap for the journey into the future.

Proposed Conceptual Models

Several comprehensive conceptual models have been proposed for PsyCap. The first of these models appeared in the *Oxford Handbook of Positive Psychology and Work* and is shown in Figure 10.1. The purpose of this model was to offer a "big picture" approach to PsyCap and to address several challenges in PsyCap research and positive psychology in general, namely: (1) a balance between positive and negative constructs, (2) a wide range of traits and states, (3) multiple levels of analysis, and (4) multiple outcomes (Youssef & Luthans, 2010).

More specifically, to better understand positivity, it cannot be isolated from a balanced understanding of negativity and negative constructs. As explained throughout this book, negative constructs such as hopelessness and helplessness may not necessarily represent the polar opposite end of the same continuum as the positive constructs we discuss in this book. Instead, negativity should be treated as an independent set of constructs and mechanisms that influence, shape, balance, but sometimes overwhelm the development of positivity (Cameron, 2008; also see Chapter 1 for a detailed treatment of this issue).

Furthermore, understanding, developing, and investing in PsyCap occurs within the boundaries of individual-level traits and trait-like characteristics (the nature-nurture debate), which need to be recognized. The trait-state continuum (see Fig. 2.1 and associated discussion in Chapter 2) has been a common theme throughout this book, and it has been emphasized in relation to each of the

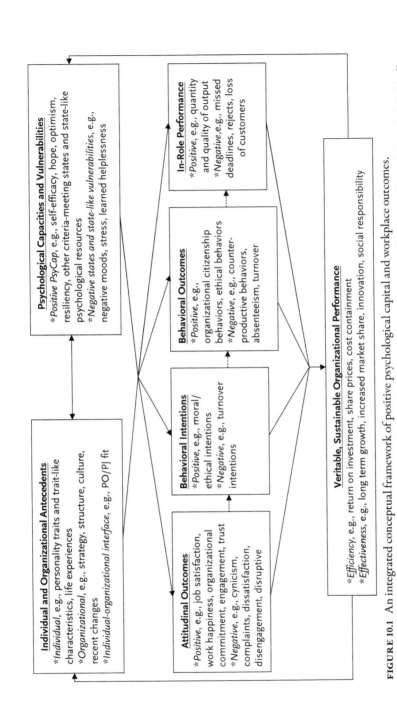

FIGURE 10.1 An integrated conceptual framework of positive psychological capital and workplace outcomes.

Source: Adapted from Youssef, C.M., & Luthans, F. (2010). An integrated model of psychological capital in the workplace. In P.A. Lindley, S. Harrington, & N. Garcea (Eds.), *Oxford handbook of positive psychology and work*. (pp. 277–288). Oxford, UK: Oxford.

current and potential psychological resources that constitute PsyCap. Although baseline traits and trait-like characteristics may be viewed by many as limitations, recent advances in neurological research show that even such relatively stable characteristics can become more malleable under the right conditions (Davidson, 2012; Pluess & Belsky, 2013).

Additionally, although PsyCap is primarily an individual-level construct, its understanding and application require a multilevel approach, especially in terms of its antecedents and outcomes. Various contextual factors can certainly influence one's level of PsyCap. Later in this chapter, we also discuss how group and organizational factors can moderate the relationship between PsyCap and various outcomes, and that PsyCap itself can be elevated to higher levels of analysis (e.g., see McKenny, Short, & Payne, 2013). Importantly, the outcomes of PsyCap development in the near future are expected to materialize not only at the individual level but also at the group, organizational, and community/societal levels.

Finally, although the PsyCap inclusion criteria emphasize a tangible performance impact, it should not be viewed as a purely utilitarian paradigm. A quantifiable return on investment is necessary for organizational decision makers to justify their resource allocation decisions and priorities to various stakeholders, especially in today's competitive environment and slim margins. However, it is not intended to be at the expense of other important outcomes. We believe that the financial impact of PsyCap can only be realized through triggering a veritable cycle of positive attitudes, intentions, and behaviors, as shown in the middle section of Figure 10.1 (Youssef & Luthans, 2010). Some of the mechanisms linking PsyCap to its various outcomes are discussed later in this chapter.

In other words, PsyCap is not simply another behavioral reinforcement approach based on just rewards and recognition. Instead, as we propose in a second conceptual framework, presented in the *Oxford Handbook of Happiness*, PsyCap can trigger an upward spiral that engages cognitive, affective, conative, and social mechanisms, leading to exceptional performance and other desirable outcomes (Youssef & Luthans, 2013). Cognitively, PsyCap shapes how we interpret situations. Specifically, PsyCap yields "positive appraisal of circumstances and probability for success" (Luthans, Avolio, Avey, & Norman, 2007, p. 550), which boosts effort, motivation, and perseverance. Affectively, PsyCap induces a wide range of positive states, which can promote the broadening of thought-action repertoires and building of physical, psychological, and social resources (Fredrickson, 2009). Conatively, PsyCap enhances agentic thinking and efficacious goal pursuit, leading to more purposeful and intentional actions and a sense of control (Bandura, 2001, 2008, 2012). Socially, PsyCap, and positivity in general, increases mutual attraction, which facilitates relationships, networks, and connections (Dutton & Ragins, 2006).

A third model has been proposed in *Advances in Positive Organizational Psychology* and is shown in Figure 10.2 (Youssef-Morgan & Luthans, 2013). This model builds on the previous two models, particularly the agency, malleability, and social mechanisms underlying PsyCap. In addition, this model goes beyond the work context, to address the potential benefits of PsyCap in the domains of health and relationships. Importantly, the relationships across life domains are proposed to be reciprocal, which means that each domain causally influences and is causally influenced by the others over time. These dynamic work-life enrichment interfaces (Demerouti, 2012; Greenhaus & Powell, 2006; McNall, Niclin, & Masuda, 2010) and positive, self-reinforcing spirals in general (Fredrickson, 2003; Luthans, Youssef, & Rawski, 2011; Salanova, Bakker, & Llorens, 2006; Walter & Bruch, 2008) are receiving considerable interest and support.

Authentic Leadership

Besides the comprehensive PsyCap theoretical models is the closely related parallel development that has taken place in authentic leadership. PsyCap

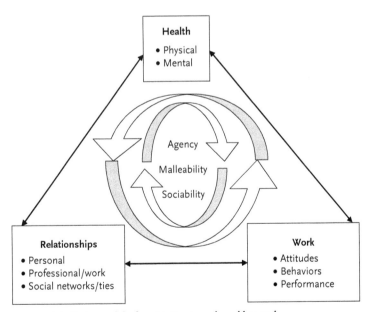

FIGURE 10.2 A holistic model of positivity at work and beyond.
Source: Youssef-Morgan, C. M., & Luthans, F. (2013). Psychological capital theory: Toward a positive holistic model. In A. Bakker (Ed.), *Advances in positive organizational psychology* (pp. 145–166). Bingley, UK: Emerald. Used with permission of the publisher.

played an important role in the original conceptualizations of authentic leadership (Avolio & Luthans, 2006; Luthans & Avolio, 2003) and was briefly introduced in Chapter 8 when discussing authenticity as a potential component of PsyCap. In the past decade, there have been hundreds of studies examining authentic leadership in contexts ranging from combat leadership to classroom leadership. During this period of time, considerable effort has been put into demonstrating that authentic leadership can be differentiated from other positive leadership constructs such as transformational, ethical, and spiritual leadership, and of course also PsyCap per se (e.g., see Gardner, Cogliser, Davis, & Dickens, 2011).

This research has clearly shown that authentic leadership adds to the positive leadership literature in three distinct ways. First, like PsyCap, authentic leadership represents a higher order construct. This underscores the importance of examining the component constructs associated with authentic leadership in combination when developing such leadership, as well as predicting psychological and/or performance outcomes. Second, authentic leadership augments other positive leadership constructs such as humility, and other styles in predicting performance outcomes. It provides an additional "leadership base" to account for the total variance that positive leadership will account for in any individual- or group-level performance outcomes. Third, the emergence of the theoretical and empirical work on authentic leadership has supported the justification for examining these components of leadership as the basis from which other positive forms of leadership—and we would now add followership—emerge and develop, such as transformational leadership.

Today, building on the work of Avolio and Gardner (2005), as well as a number of other papers reviewed by Gardner et al. (2011) that emerged in the literature at that time and subsequently, the leadership literature has settled on four core components or constructs comprising authentic leadership. These constructs include leader self-awareness, balanced processing, transparency, and moral/ethics. A substantial body of evidence supporting this four-component model of authentic leadership has been confirmed in a broad range of samples around the globe and in a variety of organizational contexts (e.g., see Avolio, 2011; Caza, Bagozzi, Woolley, Levy, & Caza, 2010; Moriano, Molero, & Mangin, 2011). Moreover, authentic leadership has also been applied to the group or team level and has demonstrated similar results.

Hannah, Walumbwa, and Fry (2011) examined the cross-level effects of authentic leadership showing how a team leader's level of authenticity predicted the mean levels of authenticity exhibited in teams led by those leaders. They showed that team members transfer the leader's authenticity into their own interactions within the team. More self-aware team members, who also were more transparent, balanced, and ethical, interacted with each other, enhancing the team's aggregate authentic leadership. The higher team mean levels of authenticity and greater consistency in displaying such behaviors within the team were also evident in higher performing teams.

Walumbwa, Hartnell, Aryee, and Christensen (2011) examined creativity in work groups measuring authentic leadership, communication climate, and the level of sharing of knowledge exhibited in work groups. Ratings of authentic leadership were positively related to work group creativity. This relationship was also mediated by the communication climate and knowledge sharing that was evidenced in these work groups. These authors also reported that authentic leadership accounted for 14% of variance in the group's level of creativity above and beyond the leaders being rated transformational. This finding shows that authentic leadership augmented transformational leadership in predicting this outcome.

Additional research continues to produce important relationships between authentic leadership and outcomes. Giallonardo, Wong, and Iwasiw (2010) reported that authentic leadership was positively related to the job satisfaction of nurses, which was partially mediated by the nurses' level of work engagement. Wong, Laschnger, and Cummings (2010) reported that ratings of authentic leadership were positively related to employee voice behavior and perceived quality of care, again among nurses. Authentic leadership has also been shown to be positively related to trust in leadership (Clapp-Smith, Vogelgesang, & Avey, 2009), organizational commitment (Jensen & Luthans, 2006), follower citizenship behavior, voice and work engagement (Giallonardo et al., 2010), follower job performance (Wang, Sui, Luthans, Wang & Wu, 2014; Wong & Cummings, 2009), psychological well-being (Toor, Ofori, & Arain, 2007), and firm performance (Hmieleski, Cole, & Baron, 2012).

Overall, research accumulated over the last decade has clearly substantiated most of the foundational predictions of the early models/theories of authentic leadership (Avolio & Gardner, 2005). What remains is to extend this foundational work on the constructs comprising authentic leadership into the domain of authentic leadership development. Indeed, the original developmental model associated with authentic leadership development involving PsyCap (Luthans & Avolio, 2003) remains largely untested and is likely the next frontier in research on authentic leadership. Most important, in this model shown in Figure 10.3 we initially conceived of the integration of PsyCap constructs and positive forms of leadership, and the next 10 years of theory and research need to focus on how this can best happen for optimal positive impact on performance.

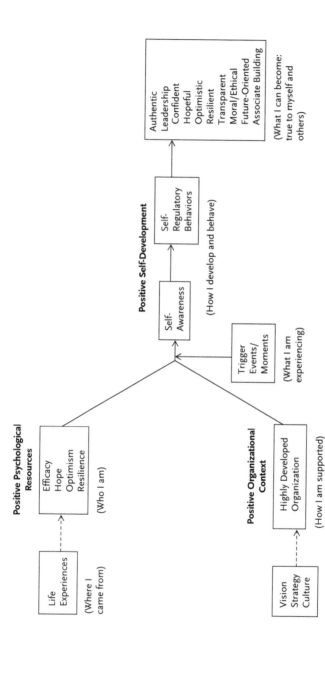

FIGURE 10.3 Authentic leadership development model.

Source: Adapted from Luthans, F., & Avolio, B. J. (2003). Authentic leadership development. In K. S. Cameron, J. E. Dutton, & R. E. Quinn (Eds.), *Positive organizational scholarship* (pp. 241–258). San Francisco, CA: Berrett-Koehler.

Support and Gaps in the PsyCap Conceptual Models

Using the PsyCap conceptual models as a foundation (see Figs. 10.1 & 10.2), we now briefly summarize the findings to date supporting many components of these models and highlight some important gaps and emerging areas for additional research. Many of these findings have been discussed in more detail in previous chapters, but our goal here is to just offer a concise snapshot so we know where we are now and where we need to go. Importantly, we highlight and summarize the underlying theoretical mechanisms linking PsyCap to its antecedents, mediators, moderators, and outcomes in order to guide future theory building and empirical research toward more viable and explanatory models, and to inform effective evidence-based practice. We will briefly summarize the support to date along the common themes of PsyCap outcomes, antecedents, mediators, and moderators.

PsyCap Outcomes

The vast majority of empirical PsyCap studies support its relationship with a wide range of desirable work outcomes. For example, the previously referenced Avey, Reichard, Luthans, and Mhatre's (2011) meta-analysis of 51 PsyCap studies up to that time supported significant positive relationships between employees' PsyCap and positive job attitudes (satisfaction, organizational commitment, psychological well-being), behaviors (organizational citizenship behaviors), and performance (self-ratings, supervisory ratings, and objective measures). There were also significant negative relationships between PsyCap and negative job attitudes (cynicism, turnover intentions, stress, anxiety) and behaviors (deviance). These findings have been replicated across a wide range of jobs, populations, and cultures and have been further supported by the previously cited Newman and colleagues' (2014) recent comprehensive PsyCap review.

Furthermore, longitudinal studies support PsyCap as a predictor of performance (Peterson, Luthans, Avolio, Walumbwa, & Zhang, 2011) and well-being (Avey, Luthans, Smith, & Palmer, 2010; Roche, Haar & Luthans, 2014). Recent findings also support PsyCap as a predictor of thriving and self-development (Patterson, Luthans, & Jeung, 2014). Beyond the workplace, PsyCap also predicts satisfaction with health and relationships, as well as objective outcomes in those domains of life such as time spent with family and friends, body mass index, and cholesterol levels (Luthans, Youssef, Sweetman, & Harms, 2013).

While it is encouraging that PsyCap can predict all of these important outcomes, the advancement of scientific research and evidence-based practice also requires the ability to explain the underlying theoretical mechanisms for the relationships between PsyCap and its outcomes. This is where we see many published articles—and in our roles as peer reviewers and editors, many rejected submissions—fall short. Thus, to guide high-quality future research, we provide the reader with a summary of theoretical mechanisms that can explain relationships between PsyCap and each of its empirically supported outcomes, as well as some exemplary references that effectively build out these important theoretical arguments. This summary is presented in Table 10.1. Many of these mechanisms have also been discussed in detail in previous chapters. It is our hope that future research and practice utilize this summary to expand the role of PsyCap beyond prediction, toward explanation, understanding of cause-and-effect relationships, and, most important, promotion of positive change and competitive advantage through leveraging psychological capital development.

The Case of Well-Being

We can use the relationship between PsyCap and well-being as a case in point to derive and explain the underlying mechanisms for this relationship. Although often used interchangeably with happiness, well-being is generally recognized as a broader construct that encompasses one's perceptions and feelings of emotional well-being (positive and negative affect, life satisfaction, and happiness), psychological well-being (self-acceptance, personal growth, purpose in life, environmental mastery, autonomy, and positive relations with others), and social well-being (social acceptance, actualization, contribution, coherence, and integration) (for comprehensive reviews, see Diener, Suh, Lucas, & Smith, 1999; Keyes & Magyar-Moe, 2003). In addition, of course, well-being is also associated with the widely recognized dimensions of physical and mental well-being (freedom from diagnosable physical and mental illnesses).

Well-being is desirable in and of itself, as well as due to its relationship with many important outcomes, both at and beyond the workplace. For example, the happy-productive worker hypothesis has been extensively studied and supported by considerable research over the years (e.g., see Wright & Cropanzano, 2004). The quantifiable cost savings associated with employee well-being are also becoming well documented and shown to be substantial (Cascio & Boudreau, 2011). Also, research by Judge and colleagues supports that life satisfaction and well-being are causal antecedents of job satisfaction (Judge & Watanabe, 1993), which in turn is strongly related to work performance (Judge, Thoresen, Bono, & Patton, 2001). Moreover, happiness and life satisfaction have been shown to be related to physical and psychological health (Ryff & Singer, 2003), personal striving, coping with stress (Diener & Fujita, 1995; Emmons, 1992; Folkman, 1997; Fordyce, 1988), and satisfaction with important life domains (Diener, 2000; Diener et al., 1999). Meta-analytical findings by Lyubomirsky, King, and Diener (2005) also

Table 10.1 PsyCap Outcomes and Underlying Theoretical Mechanisms

Outcome	Mechanisms	Exemplary References
Performance	Efficacy: Agency, self-determination, goal selection, perseverance	Luthans, Avolio et al., 2007
	Hope: Goal setting, contingency planning	
	Optimism: Positive appraisals, optimistic explanatory style	
	Resilience: Bouncing back and beyond	
Satisfaction	Positive appraisals	Luthans et al. (2013)
Commitment	Need fulfillment	Avey, Reichard et al. (2011)
Happiness/well-being	Positive appraisals, satisfaction with important life domains, memory retention	Luthans et al. (2013)
		Youssef & Luthans (2013); Bakker & Oerlemans (2012)
	Mitigating negative processes and negativity bias	Avey, Luthans, Smith et al. (2010); Youssef & Luthans (2013)
	Resource theories; broaden-and-build	Sheldon et al. (2013)
	Variety	Diener et al. (2009)
	Goal pursuit and progress	Luthans et al. (2013)
Health	Agency	Youssef-Morgan & Luthans (2013)
	Agency, malleability, sociability	Davidson (2012)
	Brain function	
Relationships	Social resources, emotional contagion	Luthans et al. (2013)
	Agency, malleability, sociability	Youssef-Morgan & Luthans (2013)
Thriving/self-development	Agentic work behaviors	Paterson et al. (2014)
Citizenship (OCB)	Broaden-and-build	Avey, Luthans, & Youssef (2010)
Deviance (CWB)	Resilience and coping	Avey, Luthans, & Youssef (2010)
Cynicism	Positive emotions, negative emotions, agency	Avey, Luthans, & Youssef (2010)
Stress/anxiety	Attraction-selection-attrition	Baron et al. (2014)
	Positive appraisals, coping, cognitive resources	Avey et al. (2009)
Intentions to quit/turnover	Positive expectancies, resilient adaptation, and bouncing back	Avey, Luthans, & Youssef (2010)

link happiness and well-being with success in numerous areas of life, drawing from cross-sectional, longitudinal, and experimental evidence to support a causal direction from happiness and well-being to success, rather than the other way around.

As shown in Table 10.1, several theoretical mechanisms can be used to conceptually link PsyCap to well-being. First, well-being is shaped by one's cognitive and affective appraisals of life in general and of specific events and circumstances (Bakker & Oerlemans, 2012; Diener, Oishi, & Lucas, 2009). As discussed throughout this book, PsyCap provides a viable mechanism for positive appraisals to be formed for past, present, and future events, based on positive explanatory styles of the past, motivated effort and perseverance in the present, and positive expectancies and intentional goal pursuit for the future. Second, related to these positive appraisals, PsyCap can help mitigate the negative appraisals associated with our prevalent negativity bias (Baumeister, Bratslavsky, Finkenauer, & Vohs, 2001; also see Chapter 1 for a detailed discussion). In the workplace, PsyCap can promote positive forms of well-being and help manage common problems associated with unrealistic goals and ambitions such as workaholism and burnout (Bakker & Oerlemans, 2012).

Third, an integral component of well-being is satisfaction with important life domains (Diener, 2000; Diener et al., 1999). PsyCap has been shown to predict satisfaction with important life domains such as work, relationships, and health (Luthans et al., 2013). Fourth, Diener and colleagues (2000) also demonstrated that well-being as an overall appraisal of satisfaction with life goes beyond the sum of domain-specific satisfaction appraisals. Well-being is also shaped by retained memories of various life events, which have been demonstrated to be both quantitatively and qualitatively different from real-time experiences (Kahneman, 2011; Kim-Prieto, Diener, Tamir, Scollon, & Diener, 2005). Positivity (i.e., PsyCap) can facilitate the attention, interpretation, and memory retention processes necessary for a lasting impact on well-being (Diener & Biswas-Diener, 2008; Lyubomirsky, 2001).

Fifth, based on resource theories, PsyCap can be considered a psychological resource. Cognitive evaluations of availability of resources are often used as indicators of global assessments of wellness (Wright & Hobfoll, 2004). Thus, a perceived reservoir of psychological resources (PsyCap) can facilitate well-being appraisals (Avey, Luthans, Smith et al., 2010). Drawing from the broaden-and-build theory (Fredrickson, 2003), positivity and PsyCap can help build this reservoir of psychological resources, leading to higher well-being. Finally, hedonic adaptation can be detrimental to well-being. Sheldon, Boehm, and Lyubomirsky (2013) propose variety as a key mechanism for preventing hedonic adaptation and sustaining well-being. Similarly, actively pursuing and making progress on important goals can help sustain well-being (Diener et al., 2009). Agentic goal pursuit is an integral component of PsyCap, and it can provide the necessary variety to boost well-being.

In the same way that we derived these six theoretical mechanisms that link PsyCap to well-being, Table 10.1 can be used to build compelling theoretical arguments for the relationship between PsyCap and a number of other important outcomes. We strongly encourage PsyCap scholars and evidence-based practitioners to build on these and other theoretical mechanisms, not just rely on deterministic models and data mining, to support the relationships and generate the desired outcomes and changes they aspire to see.

PsyCap Antecedents

Besides outcomes, conceptualizing PsyCap also requires an understanding of its antecedents, or what typically occupies what our close colleague James Avey (2014) calls the "left side" group of variables of most theoretical models. As emphasized throughout this book, PsyCap is a developmental, state-like psychological resource, with a trait-like baseline. Thus, various traits and trait-like characteristics are likely to influence PsyCap and its developmental potential. Furthermore, PsyCap may be influenced by various contextual factors. Avey (2014) investigated three general categories of PsyCap antecedents: demographics (e.g., age, gender, and tenure), individual differences (e.g., self-esteem and proactive personality), and contextual factors (e.g., leadership and job design). He found the strongest support for individual differences, followed by leadership (e.g., authentic, ethical, and abusive supervision), then job characteristics (e.g., task complexity), and finally age. Although in this Avey study gender and tenure were not supported as antecedents of PsyCap, in another study Combs, Milosevic, Jeung, and Griffith (2012) did find a positive relationship between the strength of participants' ethnic identity and their PsyCap. Similarly, in an experimental study by Avey, Avolio, and Luthans (2011), the contextual factors of leader positivity (PsyCap) and problem complexity were supported as antecedents to follower PsyCap. Luthans, Norman, Avolio, and Avey (2008) also found a supportive organizational climate to predict PsyCap and Liu (2013) found those who perceived higher levels of supervisor support had higher levels of PsyCap.

PsyCap studies typically include demographics, individual differences, and contextual factors as control variables. For example, Avey, Luthans, and Youssef (2010) controlled for age, gender, tenure, annual salary, job level, level of education, two of the Big Five personality traits (extroversion and conscientiousness), core self-evaluations, person-organization fit, and person-job fit. PsyCap explained additional variance in most of the outcomes (organizational citizenship behaviors, cynicism, intentions to quit, and counterproductive workplace behaviors) beyond these demographic, individual difference, and contextual variables. Similarly, Luthans, Avolio, Avey, and Norman (2007) accounted for age, education, the Big

Five personality traits, and core self-evaluations. They found only extroversion, conscientiousness, and core self-evaluations to be related to PsyCap and its outcomes.

However, controlling for demographics, individual differences, and contextual factors is not the same as including them as antecedents within an integrated conceptual framework. Control variables are typically treated as "usual suspects" to be ruled out. Although control variables should also have a strong conceptual basis (Aguinis & Vandenberg, 2014), delineating a particular variable as an antecedent to PsyCap indicates that this variable has not had a systematic relationship with the outcomes and thus accounts for some variance in those outcomes but also systematically relates to, predicts, and explains PsyCap. Thus, the underlying mechanisms through which demographics, individual differences, and contextual factors influence (or fail to influence) PsyCap become integral components of the conceptual framework. For example, generalized efficacy, a component of core self-evaluations, is likely to be an antecedent to the more state-like and domain-specific self-efficacy component of PsyCap, because generalized efficacy establishes the trait foundation and baseline that can facilitate or hinder the intentional development of self-efficacy.

Importantly, conceptualizing various PsyCap antecedents and the mechanisms that causally link them to PsyCap also places PsyCap as a mediator between these antecedents and various PsyCap outcomes. For example, authentic leadership is supported as an antecedent of PsyCap (Avey, 2014). This implies that the relationship between authentic leadership and followers' attitudes, behaviors, and performance is at least partially mediated by PsyCap, and that PsyCap helps explain this relationship. Thus, it is necessary to build the theoretical foundations for PsyCap as a mediating mechanism between its antecedents and its outcomes by answering questions such as: How do authentic leaders build their followers' efficacy, hope, optimism, and resilience? How do they enrich their followers' sense of agency, motivation, appraisals of past and present circumstances, and perceived chances of success in the future? Boundary conditions are also important to consider, such as whether there comes a point at which followers' PsyCap becomes a leadership substitute or neutralizer, and if so, when and under what conditions. It is possible that in some situations there may be nonlinear relationships, and such possibilities should be adequately theorized and empirically examined. This also brings to the surface the importance of investigating various PsyCap mediators and moderators, which we discuss next.

PsyCap Mediators and Moderators

Unlike PsyCap antecedents and outcomes, the study of PsyCap mediators and moderators is still emerging. For example, Avey, Wernsing, and Luthans (2008) found that positive emotions mediated the relationship between PsyCap and employee attitudes and behaviors relevant to organizational change. Drawing from cognitive mediation theory and affective events theory, they proposed that the cognitive appraisals promoted by PsyCap are likely to precede emotional reactions to change. As discussed in Chapter 2, as a state-like resource, PsyCap may influence the more proximal and transient "pure" states such as positive emotions, which in turn can influence attitudes and behaviors. Similarly, some more proximal outcomes may mediate the relationship between PsyCap and more distal outcomes. For example, stress has been shown to mediate the relationship between PsyCap and well-being in entrepreneurs (Baron, Franklin, & Hmieleski, 2014) and soldiers (Schaubroeck, Riolli, Peng, & Spain, 2011). Also, in demonstrating the contagion effect global leaders' PsyCap have on their followers' PsyCap, Story and colleagues (2013) found the quality of the leader–follower relationship (i.e., LMX) mediated this contagion impact.

At the group level of analysis, Clapp-Smith, Vogelgesang, and Avey (2009) also found trust in management to mediate the relationship between PsyCap and financial performance (sales growth). They explain this relationship as follows: "The communal principles of group trust in management create an organizing force, changing the common goal (sales) from the individual's achievement to a team success" (p. 232). In other words, individual-level PsyCap may promote striving toward and achieving individual goals, but at the group level, it is also conducive to trust in management, which promotes the pursuit of team goals and success.

We should also note that at some stage it becomes more valuable and informative to operationalize some of the theoretical mechanisms linking PsyCap to its outcomes into measurable variables that can then be tested as mediators. For example, as shown in Table 10.1 and Figure 10.2, agency is often theorized as an important mechanism through which the outcomes of PsyCap are realized. However, to test this notion empirically, Paterson, Luthans, and Jeung (2014) proposed and measured task focus and heedful relating as an operationalization of agentic work behaviors and tested them as mediators in the relationship between PsyCap and thriving. Task focus was supported as a mediator, while heedful relating was only supported as an outcome of PsyCap but not a mediator between PsyCap and thriving. These findings shed additional light on what may or may not constitute agency when applied as a mediating mechanism.

Moving on to potential moderators, the meta-analysis by Avey and colleagues (2011) showed that the relationship between PsyCap and its outcomes is stronger in studies conducted in the United States compared to other countries, and in samples from the service sector compared to other sectors. Furthermore, in the study by Avey and colleagues (2008) cited earlier, where positive emotions mediated the relationship between PsyCap and attitudinal and behavioral outcomes related to organizational change, mindfulness (heightened awareness) was found to moderate the relationship between PsyCap and positive emotions, such that the benefits of PsyCap in enhancing positive emotions were shown to be more pronounced at higher levels of mindfulness. In another study, Norman and colleagues (2010) found that participants' identity with their organization moderated the relationship between their PsyCap and their organizational citizenship, as well as their deviant behaviors. In other words, the more they identified with their organization, the stronger the positive relationship with their organizational citizenship behaviors and negative relationship with their deviant behaviors.

At the group level of analysis, transformational leadership was found to moderate the relationship between top management teams' psychological capital and unit performance such that the relationship is significant and positive at high levels of transformational leadership but not significant at low levels (Peterson & Zhang, 2011). This finding implies that the presence of transformational leadership may be necessary for the benefits of team-level positivity to materialize in terms of unit performance. Besides leadership, the dynamic nature of an industry was found to moderate the relationship between the PsyCap of entrepreneurs and new venture performance, with the more dynamic the environment, the stronger the relationship (Hmieleski & Carr, 2008).

We should note that many of PsyCap's antecedents, or variables often included in PsyCap models as control variables, should also be seriously considered conceptually and tested empirically as potential moderators in the relationship between PsyCap and its antecedents, outcomes, or both. For example, Baron and colleagues (2014) found that age moderated the stress-reducing benefits of PsyCap in entrepreneurs such that older entrepreneurs experienced a stronger negative relationship between PsyCap and stress. Thus, conceptualizing age only as an antecedent, or including it as a control variable, does not necessarily reflect the full contribution of this demographic variable within a holistic PsyCap theoretical framework.

Similarly, trait-like individual differences have been generally supported as antecedents to various states and state-like resources, which in turn mediate the relationship between trait-like individual differences and various outcomes (Chen, Gully, Whiteman, & Kilcullen, 2000). However, at the intra-individual level, Ilies and colleagues (2006) found trait-like individual differences to moderate the relationship between states and outcomes within individuals over time. Specifically, although there was a relationship between momentary positive affect and organizational citizenship behaviors, employees with higher agreeableness levels engaged in more consistent organizational citizenship behavior patterns over time. In other words, their behaviors were less dependent on their more momentary positive affect than their less agreeable counterparts.

These findings indicate that the benefits of PsyCap may go beyond its direct and mediated effects. Interactions with other individual and contextual factors can explain additional, unique variance in performance and other desirable outcomes, which need to be accounted for in order to gain a better understanding of the full range of benefits that PsyCap can contribute. These results also point to some of the boundary conditions that can render higher or lower PsyCap benefits, which necessitate careful consideration of a broader range of moderators. This is particularly important when PsyCap is applied across levels of analysis, as we discuss next.

PsyCap Across Levels of Analysis

As noted earlier in this book, PsyCap has been applied at the group (Clapp-Smith et al., 2009; Haar, Roche, & Luthans, 2014; Peterson & Zhang, 2011) and organizational (McKenny, Short & Payne, 2013; Mathe-Soulek, Scott-Halsell, Kim, & Krawczyk, 2014; Memili, Welsh, & Luthans, 2014) levels of analysis. There are also implications for PsyCap development from positivity initiatives at the community (e.g., see Positivity Matters-Lincoln, NE Web site) and even country levels (e.g., see Bandura's work on building efficacy in African countries through television programming). We also emphasize, in order to build a strong evidence-based management theory and practice for the study and application of PsyCap, it is important to build a compelling conceptual case and integrated theoretical framework, rather than just rely on empirical, data-driven support, to expand the boundaries of PsyCap.

It is possible to elevate PsyCap beyond the individual level of analysis, not only because empirical studies to date show promising results in that direction but also because of its "conceptual isomorphism" and "functional isomorphism" across levels of analysis. Conceptual isomorphism refers to whether the operationalization and nomological network of the construct varies across levels of analysis. Functional isomorphism refers to whether the higher level construct predicts the same outcomes as its lower level counterpart. McKenny and colleagues (2013) make the case that PsyCap reflects both conceptual and functional isomorphism when elevated to higher levels of analysis.

For example, Bandura (1997, p. 477) has defined collective efficacy as "a group's shared belief in its conjoint capabilities to organize and execute the courses of action required to produce given levels of attainments." This definition is clearly conceptually isomorphic with individual-level efficacy (see Chapter 3). Furthermore, meta-analyses at the group level also support the relationship between collective efficacy and performance (Gully, Incalcaterra, Joshi, & Beaubien, 2002; Stajkovic, Lee, & Nyberg, 2009), which supports its functional isomorphism. Similarly, the positive organizational scholarship literature provides substantial conceptual support, and in some cases emerging empirical support, for the conceptual and functional isomorphism of hope, resilience, and many other individual psychological resources at the organizational level. This type of "theory borrowing" is integral for the advancement of organizational research (Whetten, Felin, & King, 2009).

Kozlowski and Klein's (2000) multilevel theory development framework emphasizes that the potential for the elevation to a higher level of analysis depends on answers to the essential *what, how, when, where,* and *why* (or sometimes more importantly *why not*) questions in relation to that construct. Applied to PsyCap, the "what" and "where" emergence of PsyCap across levels of analysis are justified by the conceptual and functional isomorphism. In the same way that individuals exhibit efficacy, hope, optimism, and resilience, groups, organizations, and other collectives also exhibit these characteristics and can benefit from them through enhanced performance. On the other hand, the "when" and "why" questions require an in-depth study of potential mediation and moderation mechanisms, because they may vary across levels of analysis. Thus, answering the "how" question requires going beyond the simple aggregation models most commonly used in organizational research.

Chan (1998) offers five alternative models for elevating constructs to higher levels of analysis. To date, only three of these models have been applied to PsyCap: (a) additive models, where higher level constructs are operationalized as the summation or average of the lower level construct; (b) direct consensus models, in which higher level constructs are operationalized in terms of within-group agreement regarding the lower level construct; and (c) referent shift models, which replace the lower level referent with the higher level referent in operationalizing the higher level construct prior to assessing within-group agreement. The other two models are (d) dispersion models, in which variability, not within-group agreement, is the focal construct and operationalization of the higher level construct, and (e) process models, which emphasize dynamic or episodic change processes and the mechanisms through which these processes transfer across levels of analysis.

Dispersion and process models are promising in PsyCap research because they emphasize the heterogeneity and dynamism of PsyCap, which may not necessarily be captured by the other three models. Kozlowski and Klein (2000) propose a wide range of dispersion models, such as "patterned emergence," "minimum/maximum emergence," and others. Applying patterned emergence to PsyCap, a group may exhibit a unique collective PsyCap profile, which may predict group- and individual-level outcomes beyond simple aggregation. Similarly, in minimum/maximum emergence, the group's PsyCap may be best reflected by its weakest or strongest link, respectively. For example, contagion theories would imply that a few highly positive individuals may pull the rest of the team's positivity level. Similarly, a critical mass of very negative individuals can be toxic to the rest of the group. Unfortunately, these models are more challenging to operationalize and apply in empirical research.

Finally, although the individual level of analysis is a natural starting point for psychological resources such as PsyCap, Kozlowski, Chao, Grand, Braun, and Kuljanin (2013) emphasize that the multilevel modeling of a construct should take into consideration (a) bottom-up emergence mechanisms and (b) top-down contextual influence processes. Bottom-up emergence mechanisms start at lower levels of analysis and elevate the construct to a higher level. This has been the direction that PsyCap research has progressed to date, although the micro-foundations literature (e.g., Barney & Felin, 2013; Devinney, 2013) supports the intra-individual level as a more appropriate starting point. On the other hand, in top-down mechanisms, lower level constructs and phenomena are shaped, facilitated, and constrained by higher level contextual factors. Both directions are necessary for a richer, fuller understanding of how PsyCap operates, how it can be developed, and how it can be leveraged for optimal functioning at various levels.

Future Implications and Directions for PsyCap Research and Practice

As we conclude the book, we offer a few final observations and advice for those who are interested in integrating PsyCap within their future research agenda or for the more effective practice of human resource management and development.

- Unlike most cases of innovation, where early adopters must assume a high level of risk and tolerate possible dismal or negative returns (at least in the short term), we have shown that PsyCap as presented in this book offers a unique potential for a low-risk and low-cost, very high return on investment.
- Our hope is that this book will stimulate further research and application that will refine our understanding of PsyCap and the efficacy of its development processes. Moreover, in light of the recent criticisms of quantitative research in general, and utility analysis in particular, we encourage the use of classic research designs, but we do not wish to simply dismiss insignificant or unexpected empirical findings as "errors" without further investigation. For example, meta-analytic findings have enhanced our understanding of potential moderators for PsyCap–outcomes relationships (Avey, Reichard et al., 2011).

- A wider range of quantitative and qualitative methods and triangulation of results can provide further support and help expand PsyCap research. For example, hierarchical linear modeling can facilitate the elevation of PsyCap to higher levels of analysis, and latent growth modeling can enhance our understanding of its dynamic trajectories over time. Looking into growing PsyCap in teams and larger collectives such as organizations will also engage a significant part of the future research agenda.

- Many other potential psychological resources such as those suggested in Chapters 7 and 8 should be empirically examined for their convergence with PsyCap, thus expanding and enriching the construct.

- One of the big challenges as we look downstream is connecting the growth in work on PsyCap to the authentic leadership development (ALD) process. We expect that ALD will drive PsyCap growth and vice versa. Demonstrating how each can contribute to the other's growth over time will become an important research agenda item.

- We have only begun to scratch the surface on how PsyCap develops in other cultures as well as the nature of its impact on performance. We envision a great deal more work being done cross-culturally in applying PsyCap to different cultural contexts.

- Finally, in line with the "big picture" perspective that we encouraged you to maintain at the beginning of this book and again in this chapter, we emphasize that even as more PsyCap theory building and research emerges, it is important to maintain a broad, cross-disciplinary perspective in the study of human behavior in general, and PsyCap in particular. Various synergies are likely to exist as research across life domains is integrated. Much can be learned from transferring knowledge not only from positive psychology, positive organizational scholarship, and positive organizational behavior but also from education, clinical psychology, sports, healthcare, and other social settings in the workplace, and vice versa. A broader perspective can also facilitate the integration of cross-cultural dimensions, the understanding of which is vital for competitiveness *and* positive collaboration in today's global environment. Whereas the first book initiated the PsyCap journey, we hope you agree this book has moved PsyCap ahead and this chapter has pointed it in the right direction on this never-ending journey.

References

Aguinis, H., & Vandenberg, R. J. (2014). An ounce of prevention is worth a pound of cure: Improving research quality before data collection. *Annual Review of Organizational Psychology and Organizational Behavior, 1,* 569–595.

Avey, J. B. (2014). The left side of psychological capital: New evidence on the antecedents of PsyCap. *Journal of Leadership and Organizational Studies, 21,* 141–149.

Avey, J. B., Avolio, B. J., & Luthans, F. (2011). Experimentally analyzing the impact of leader positivity on follower positivity and performance. *Leadership Quarterly, 22,* 282–294.

Avey, J. B., Luthans, F., & Jensen, S. (2009). Psychological capital: A positive resource for combating stress and turnover. *Human Resource Management, 48,* 677–693.

Avey, J. B., Luthans, F., Smith, R. M., & Palmer, N. F. (2010). Impact of positive psychological capital on employee well-being over time. *Journal of Occupational Health Psychology, 15,* 17–28.

Avey, J. B., Luthans, F., & Youssef, C. M. (2010). The additive value of positive psychological capital in predicting work attitudes and behaviors. *Journal of Management, 36,* 430–452.

Avey, J. B., Reichard, R. J., Luthans, F., & Mhatre, K. H. (2011). Meta-analysis of the impact of positive psychological capital on employee attitudes, behaviors, and performance. *Human Resource Development Quarterly, 22,* 127–152.

Avey, J. B., Wernsing, T. S., & Luthans, F. (2008). Can positive employees help positive organizational change? *Journal of Applied Behavioral Science, 44,* 48–70.

Avolio, B. J. (2011). *Full range leadership development.* Thousand Oaks, CA: Sage.

Avolio, B.J. & Luthans, F. (2006). *The high impact leader: Moments matter in accelerating authentic leadership development.* New York, NY: Mc-Graw-Hill.

Avolio, B. J., & Gardner, W. L. (2005). Authentic leadership development: Getting to the root of positive forms of leadership. *Leadership Quarterly, 16,* 315–338.

Bakker, A. B., & Oerlemans, W. G. M. (2012). Subjective well-being in organizations. In K. Cameron & G. M. Spreitzer (Eds.), *Oxford handbook of positive organizational scholarship* (pp. 178–189). New York, NY: Oxford University Press.

Bandura, A. (1997). *Self-efficacy: The exercise of control.* New York, NY: Freeman.

Bandura, A. (2001). Social cognitive theory: An agentic perspective. *Annual Review of Psychology, 52,* 1–26.

Bandura, A. (2008). An agentic perspective on positive psychology. In S. J. Lopez (Ed.), *Positive psychology: Exploring the best in people* (pp. 167–196). Westport, CT: Greenwood.

Bandura, A. (2012). On the functional properties of perceived self-efficacy revisited. *Journal of Management, 38,* 9–44.

Baron, R. A., Franklin, R. J., & Hmieleski, K. M. (2014). Why entrepreneurs often experience low, not high levels of stress: The joint effects of selection and psychological capital. *Journal of Management.* doi:10.1177/0149206313495411.

Barney, J., & Felin, T. (2013). What are microfoundations? *Academy of Management Perspectives, 27,* 138–155.

Baumeister, R. F., Bratslavsky, E., Finkenauer, C., & Vohs, K. D. (2001). Bad is stronger than good. *Review of General Psychology, 5,* 323–370.

Cameron, K. S. (2008). Paradox in positive organizational change. *Journal of Applied Behavioral Science, 44*, 7–24.

Cascio, W. F., & Boudreau, J. W. (2011). *Investing in people: Financial impact of human resource initiatives* (2nd ed.). Upper Saddle River, NJ: Pearson Education.

Caza, A., Bagozzi, R. P., Woolley, L., Levy, L., & Caza, B. B. (2010). Psychological capital and authentic leadership: Measurement structure, gender comparison, and cultural extension. *Asia Pacific Journal of Business Administration, 2*, 53–70.

Chan, D. (1998). Functional relations among constructs in the same content domain at different levels of analysis: A typology of composition models. *Journal of Applied Psychology, 83*, 234–246.

Chen, G., Gully, S. M., Whiteman, J. A., & Kilcullen, R. N. (2000). Examination of relationships among trait-like individual differences, state-like individual differences, and learning performance. *Journal of Applied Psychology, 85*, 835–847.

Clapp-Smith, R., Vogelgesang, G. R., & Avey, J. B. (2009). Authentic leadership and positive psychological capital: The mediating role of trust at the group level of analysis. *Organizational Studies, 15*, 227–240.

Combs, G. M., Milosevic, I., Jeung, W., & Griffith, J. (2012). Ethnic identity and job attribute preferences: The role of collectivism and psychological capital. *Journal of Leadership and Organizational Studies, 19*, 5–16.

Davidson, R. (2012). *The emotional life of your brain.* New York, NY: Hudson/Penguin.

Demerouti, E. (2012). The spillover and crossover of resources among partners: The role of work–self and family–self facilitation. *Journal of Occupational Health Psychology, 17*, 184–195.

Devinney, T. M. (2013). Is microfoundational thinking critical to management thought and practice? *Academy of Management Perspectives, 27*, 81–84.

Diener, E. (2000). Subjective well-being: The science of happiness and a proposal for a national index. *American Psychologist, 55*, 34–43.

Diener, E., & Biswas-Diener, R. (2008). *Happiness: Unlocking the mysteries of psychological wealth.* Malden, MA: Blackwell.

Diener, E., & Fujita, F. (1995). Resource, personal striving, and subjective well-being: A monothetic and idiographic approach. *Journal of Personality and Social Psychology, 68*, 926–935.

Diener, E., Napa-Scollon, C. K., Oishi, S., Dzokoto, V., & Suh, E. M. (2000). Positivity and the construction of life satisfaction judgments: Global happiness is not the sum of its parts. *Journal of Happiness Studies, 1*, 159–176.

Diener, E., Oishi, S., & Lucas, R. E. (2009). Subjective well-being: The science of happiness and life satisafation. In S. Lopez & C. R. Snyder (Eds.), *Oxford handbook of positive psychology* (2nd ed., pp.187–194). New York, NY: Oxford University Press.

Diener, E., Suh, E. M., Lucas, R. E., & Smith, H. L. (1999). Subjective well-being: Three decades of progress. *Psychological Bulletin, 125*, 276–302.

Dutton, J. E., & Ragins, B. R. (Eds.). (2006). *Exploring positive relationships at work: Building a theoretical and research foundation.* London, UK: Psychology Press.

Emmons, R. A. (1992). Abstract versus concrete goals: Personal striving level, physical illness, and psychological well-being. *Journal of Personality and Social Psychology*, *62*, 292–300.

Folkman, S. (1997). Positive psychological states and coping with severe stress. *Social Science and Medicine*, *45*, 1207–1221.

Fordyce, M. W. (1988). A review of research on the happiness measures: A sixty second index of happiness and health. *Social Indicators Research*, *20*, 355–381.

Fredrickson, B. L. (2003). Positive emotions and upward spirals in organizations. In K. S. Cameron, J. E. Dutton, & R. E. Quinn (Eds.), *Positive organizational scholarship* (pp. 63–175). San Francisco, CA: Berrett-Koehler.

Fredrickson, B. L. (2009). *Positivity*. New York, NY: Crown/ Random House.

Gardner, W. L., Cogliser, C. C., Davis, K. M., & Dickens, M. P. (2011). Authentic leadership: A review of the literature and research agenda. *Leadership Quarterly*, *22*, 1120–1145.

Giallonardo, L. M., Wong, C. A., & Iwasiw, C. L. (2010). Authentic leadership of preceptors: Predictor of new graduate nurses' work engagement and job satisfaction. *Journal of Nursing Management*, *18*, 993–1003.

Greenhaus, J. H., & Powell, G. N. (2006). When work and families are allies: A theory of work-family enrichment. *Academy of Management Review*, *31*, 72–92.

Gully, S. M., Incalcaterra, K. A., Joshi, A., & Beaubien, J. M. (2002). A meta-analysis of team-efficacy, potency, and performance: Interdependence and level of analysis as moderators of observed relationships. *Journal of Applied Psychology*, *87*, 819–832.

Haar, J. M., Roche, M. A., & Luthans, F. (August 1–5, 2014). *Do leaders' psychological capital and engagement influence follower teams or vice-versa?* Paper presented at Academy of Management Conference, Philadelphia, PA.

Hannah, S. T., Walumbwa, F. O., & Fry, J. (2011). Leadership in action teams: Team leader and members' authenticity, authenticity strength, and performance outcomes. *Personnel Psychology*, *64*, 771–801.

Hmieleski, K. M., & Carr, J. C. (2008). The relationship between entrepreneur psychological capital and new venture performance. *Frontiers of Entrepreneurship Research*. Babson Park, MA: Babson College.

Hmieleski, K. M., Cole, M. S., & Baron, R. A. (2012). Shared authentic leadership and new venture performance. *Journal of Management*, *38*, 1476–1499.

Ilies, R., Scott, B. A., & Judge, T. A. (2006). The interactive effects of personal traits and experienced states on intraindividual patterns of citizenship behavior. *Academy of Management Journal*, *49*, 561–575.

Jensen, S. M., & Luthans, F. (2006). Entrepreneurs as authentic leaders: Impact on employees' attitudes. *Leadership and Organization Development Journal*, *27*, 646–666.

Judge, T. A., Thoresen, C. J., Bono, J. E., & Patton, G. K. (2001). The job satisfaction-job performance relationship: A qualitative and quantitative review. *Psychological Bulletin*, *127*, 376–407.

Judge, T. A., & Watanabe, S. (1993). Another look at the job-satisfaction-life satisfaction relationship. *Journal of Applied Psychology, 78,* 939–948.

Kahneman, D. (2011). *Thinking fast and slow.* New York, NY: Farrar, Straus and Giroux.

Keyes, C., & Magyar-Moe, J. (2003). The measurement and utility of adult subjective well-being. In S. Lopez & C. R. Snyder (Eds.), *Positive psychological assessment: A handbook of models and measures* (pp. 411–425). Washington, DC: American Psychological Association.

Kim-Prieto, C., Diener, E., Tamir, M., Scollon, C. N., & Diener, M. (2005). Integrating the diverse definitions of happiness: A time-sequential framework of subjective well-being. *Journal of Happiness Studies, 6,* 261–300.

Kozlowski, S. W. J., Chao, G. T., Grand, J. A., Braun, M. T., & Kuljanin, G. (2013). Advancing multilevel research design: Capturing the dynamics of emergence. *Organizational Research Methods, 16,* 581–615.

Kozlowski, S. W. J., & Klein, K. J. (2000). A multilevel approach to theory and research in organizations: Contextual, temporal, and emergent processes. In K. J. Klein & S. W. J. Kozlowski (Eds.), *Multilevel theory, research and methods in organizations: Foundations, extensions, and new directions* (pp. 3–90). San Francisco, CA: Jossey-Bass.

Liu, Y. (2013). Moderating effect of positive psychological capital in Taiwan's life insurance industry. *Social Behavior and Personality, 41,* 109–112.

Luthans, F., & Avolio, B. J. (2003). Authentic leadership development. In K. S. Cameron, J. E. Dutton, & R. E. Quinn (Eds.), *Positive organizational scholarship* (pp. 241–258). San Francisco. CA: Berrett-Koehler.

Luthans, F., Avolio, B. J., Avey, J. B., & Norman, S. M. (2007). Psychological capital: Measurement and relationship with performance and satisfaction. *Personnel Psychology, 60,* 541–572.

Luthans, F., Norman, S. M., Avolio, B. J., & Avey, J. B. (2008). The mediating role of psychological capital in the supportive organizational climate-employee performance relationship. *Journal of Organizational Behavior, 29,* 219–238.

Luthans, F., Youssef, C. M., & Rawski, S. L. (2011). A tale of two paradigms: The impact of psychological capital and reinforcing feedback on problem solving and innovation. *Journal of Organizational Behavior Management, 31,* 333–350.

Luthans, F., Youssef, C. M., Sweetman, D., & Harms, P. (2013). Meeting the leadership challenge of employee well-being through relationship PsyCap and health PsyCap. *Journal of Leadership and Organizational Studies, 20,* 114–129.

Lyubomirsky, S. (2001). Why are some people happier than others? The role of cognitive and motivational processes in well-being. *American Psychologist, 56,* 239–249.

Lyubomirsky, S., King, L., & Diener, E. (2005). The benefits of frequent positive affect: Does happiness lead to success? *Psychological Bulletin, 131,* 803–855.

Mathe-Soulek, K., Scott-Halsell, S., Kim, S., & Krawczyk, M. (2014). Psychological capital in the quick service restaurant industry: A study of unit level performance. *Journal of Hospitality and Tourism Research,* doi: 10.1177/10963348014550923.

McKenny, A. F., Short, J. C., & Payne, T. (2013). Using computer-aided text analysis to elevate constructs: An illustration using psychological capital. *Organizational Research Methods, 16*, 152–184.

McNall, L. A., Nicklin, J. M., & Masuda, A. D. (2010). A meta-analytic review of the consequences associated with work–family enrichment. *Journal of Business and Psychology, 25*, 381–396.

Memili, E., Welsh, D., & Luthans, F. (2014). Going beyond research on goal setting: A proposed role for organizational psychological capital of family firms. *Entrepreneurhsip Theory and Practice, 37*, 1289–1296.

Moriano, J. A., Molero, F., & Mangin, J. P. L. (2011). Authentic leadership: Concept and validation of the ALQ in Spain. *Psicothema, 23*, 336–341.

Newman, A., Ucbasaran, D., Zhu, F., & Hirst, G. (2014). Psychological capital: A review and synthesis. *Journal of Organizational Behavior, 35*, S120–S138.

Norman, S. M., Avey, J. B., Nimnicht, J. L., & Graber-Pigeon, N. P. (2010). The interactive effects of psychological capital and organizational identity on employee citizenship and deviance behaviors. *Journal of Leadership and Organizational Studies, 17*, 380–391.

Paterson, T. A., Luthans, F., & Jeung, W. (2014). Thriving at work: Impact of psychological capital and supervisor support. *Journal of Organizational Behavior, 35*, 434–446.

Peterson, S. J., Luthans, F., Avolio, B. J., Walumbwa, F. O., & Zhang, Z. (2011). Psychological capital and employee performance: A latent growth modeling approach. *Personnel Psychology, 64*, 427–450.

Peterson, S. J., & Zhang, Z. (2011). Examining the relationships between top management team psychological characteristics, transformational leadership, and business unit performance. In M. A. Carpenter (Ed.), *Handbook of top management research* (pp. 127–149). New York, NY: Edward Elgar.

Pluess, M., & Belsky, J. (2013). Vantage sensitivity: Individual differences in response to positive experiences. *Psychological Bulletin, 139*, 901–916.

Roche, M., Haar, J., & Luthans, F. (2014). The role of mindfulness and psychological capital on the well-being of leaders. *Journal of Occupational Health Psychology*. in press.

Ryff, C. D., & Singer, B. (2003). The role of emotion on pathways to positive health. In R. J. Davidson, K. R., Scherer, & H. H. Goldsmith (Eds.), *Handbook of affective sciences*. New York, NY: Oxford University Press.

Salanova, M., Bakker, A. B., & Llorens, S. (2006). Flow at work: Evidence for an upward spiral of personal and organizational resources. *Journal of Happiness Studies, 7*, 1–22.

Schaubroeck, J., Riolli, L., Peng, A. C., & Spain, E. (2011). Positive psychological traits, appraisal and well-being among soldiers deployed in combat: Individual resilience to different levels of traumatic exposure. *Journal of Occupational Health Psychology, 16*, 18–37.

Sheldon, K. M., Boehm, J., & Lyubomirsky, S. (2013). Variety is the spice of happiness: The hedonic adaptation prevention model. In S. A. David, I. Boniwell, &

A. C. Ayers (Eds.), *Oxford handbook of happiness* (pp. 901–914). New York, NY: Oxford University Press.

Stajkovic, A. D., Lee, D., & Nyberg, A. (2009). Collective efficacy, group potency, and group performance: Meta-analysis of their relationships, and test of a mediation model. *Journal of Applied Psychology, 94,* 814–828.

Toor, S-R., Ofori, G., & Arain, F. M. (2007). Authentic leadership style and its implications in project management. *Business Review, 2,* 31–55.

Walter, F., & Bruch, H. (2008). The positive group affect spiral: A dynamic model of the emergence of positive affective similarity in work groups. *Journal of Organizational Behavior, 29,* 239–261.

Walumbwa, F. O., Hartnell, A. L., Aryee, S., & Christensen, C. A. (August, 2011). *Fostering creativity in work groups: Authentic leadership, communication climate, and knowledge sharing.* Paper presented at the Academy of Management Annual Meetings, San Antonio, TX.

Wang, H., Sui, Y., Luthans, F., Wang, D., & Wu, Y. (2014). Impact of authentic leadership on performance: Role of followers positive psychological capital and relational processes. *Journal of Organizational Behavior, 35,* 5–21.

Whetten, D., Felin, T., & King, B. (2009). The practice of theory borrowing in organization studies. *Journal of Management, 35,* 537–563.

Wong, C. A., & Cummings, G. G. (2009). The influence of authentic leadership behaviors on trust and work outcomes of health care staff. *Journal of Leadership Studies, 3,* 6–23.

Wong, C. A., Laschnger, H. K. S., & Cummings, G. G. (2010). Authentic leadership and nurses' voice behavior and perceptions of care quality. *Journal of Nursing Management, 18,* 889–900.

Wright, T. A., & Cropanzano, R. (2004). The role of psychological well-being in job performance: A fresh look at an age-old quest. *Organizational Dynamics, 33,* 338–351.

Wright, T. A., & Hobfoll, S. E. (2004). Commitment, psychological well-being and job performance: An examination of conservation of resources (COR) theory and job burnout. *Journal of Business and Management, 9,* 389–406.

Youssef, C. M., & Luthans, F. (2010). An integrated model of psychological capital in the workplace. In A. Linley, S. Harrington, & N. Garcea (Eds.), *Oxford handbook of positive psychology and work* (pp. 277–288). New York, NY: Oxford University Press.

Youssef, C. M., & Luthans, F. (2013). Developing psychological capital in organizations: Cognitive, affective, conative, and social contributions of happiness. In S. A. David, I. Boniwell, & A. C. Ayers (Eds.), *Oxford handbook of happiness* (pp. 751–766). New York, NY: Oxford University Press.

Youssef-Morgan, C. M., & Luthans, F. (2013). Psychological capital theory: Toward a positive holistic model. In A. Bakker (Ed.), *Advances in positive organizational psychology* (pp. 145–166). Bingley, UK: Emerald.

INDEX